BATMA

PRIVATE CASEB

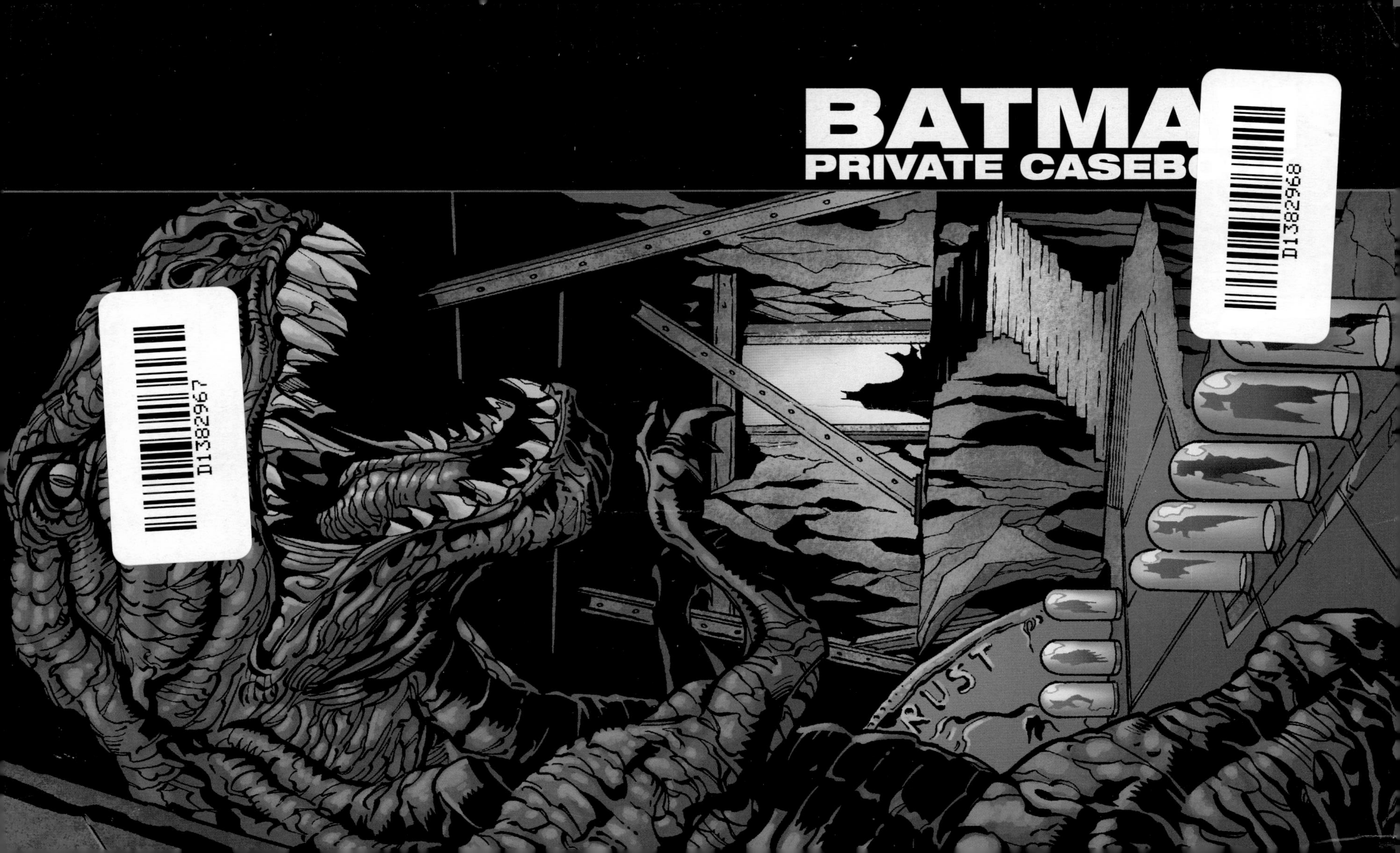
RUST

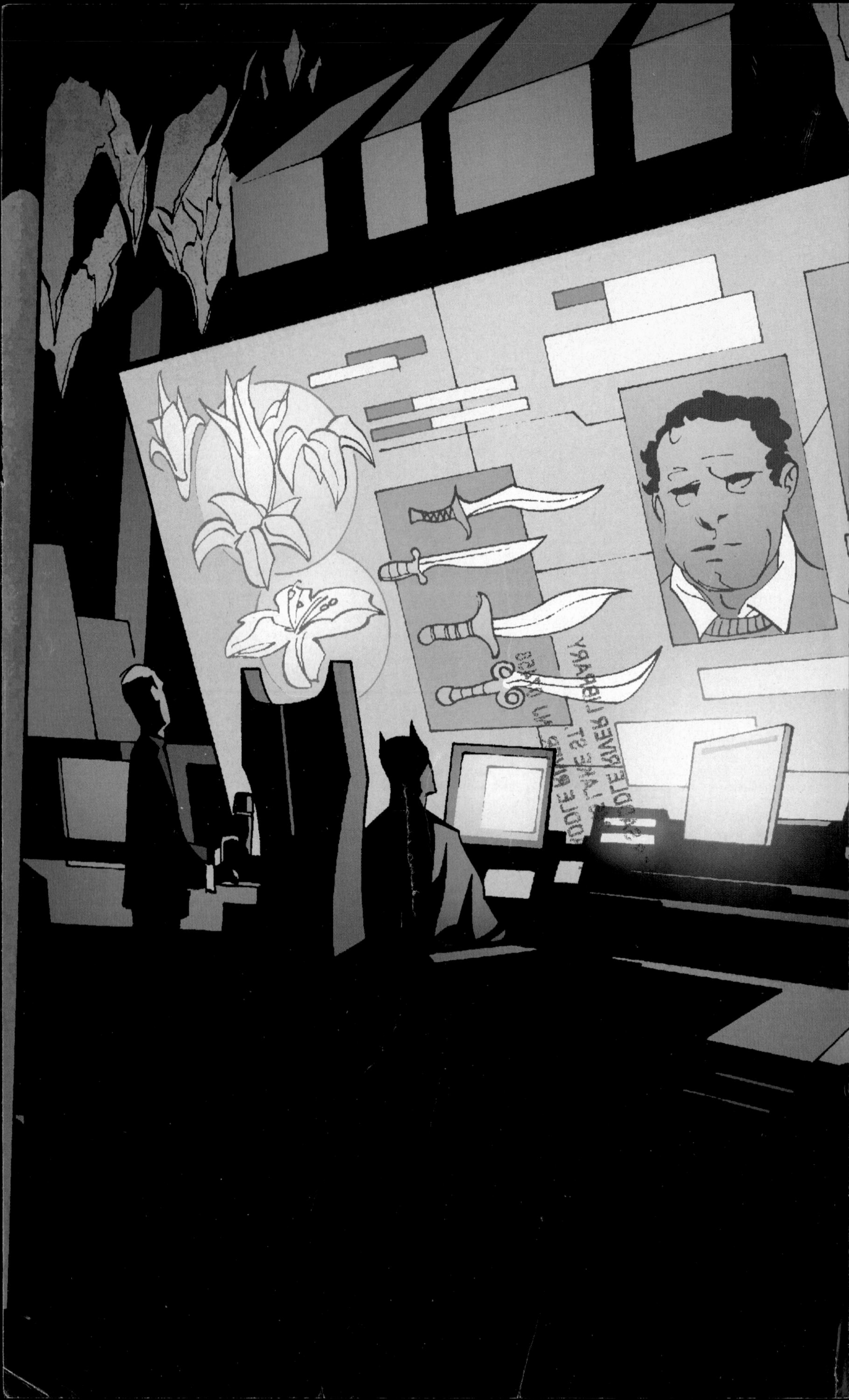

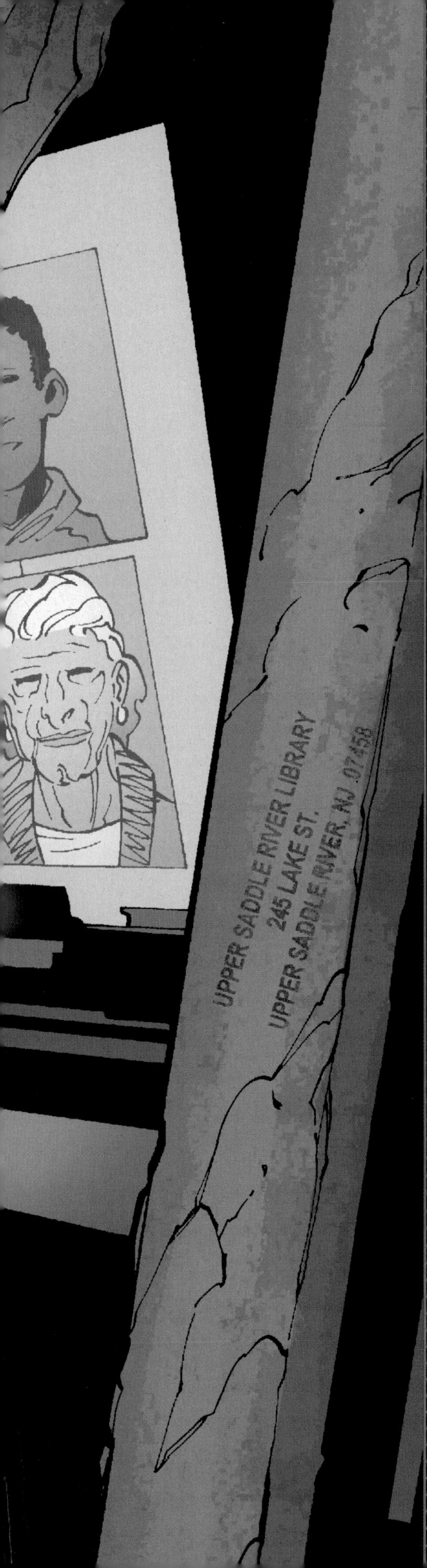

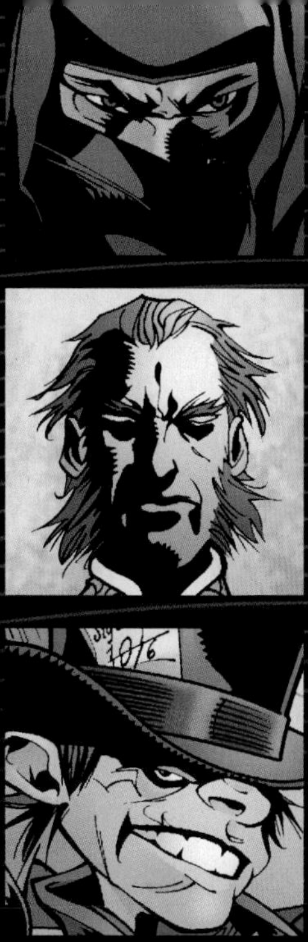

BATMAN
PRIVATE CASEBOOK

Paul Dini with Peter Milligan Writers

Dustin Nguyen Penciller

Derek Fridolfs Inker

John Kalisz Colorist

Randy Gentile Sal Cipriano
Steve Wands John J. Hill Letterers

Dustin Nguyen Original Series Covers

Batman created by Bob Kane

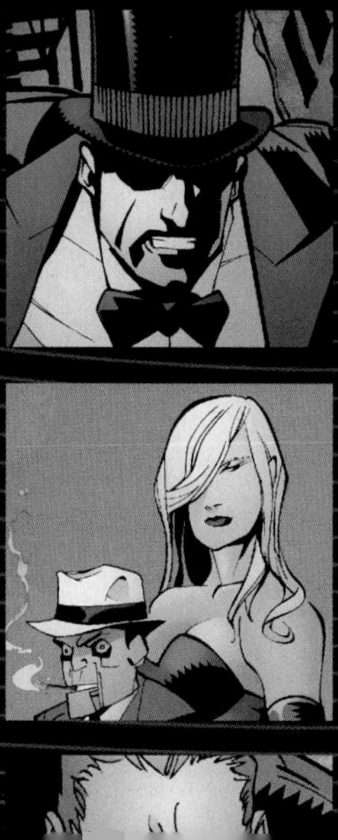

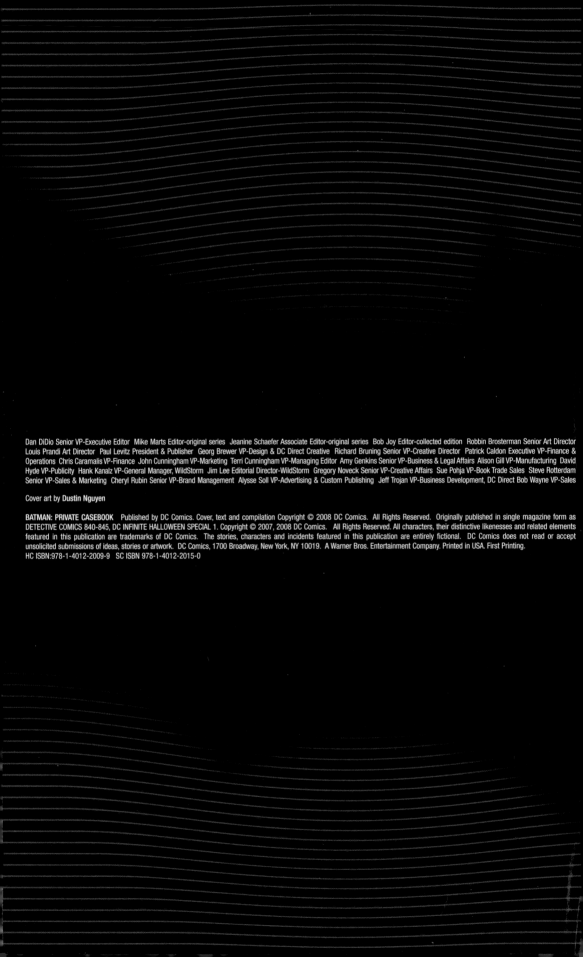

Dan DiDio Senior VP-Executive Editor   Mike Marts Editor-original series   Jeanine Schaefer Associate Editor-original series   Bob Joy Editor-collected edition   Robbin Brosterman Senior Art Director
Louis Prandi Art Director   Paul Levitz President & Publisher   Georg Brewer VP-Design & DC Direct Creative   Richard Bruning Senior VP-Creative Director   Patrick Caldon Executive VP-Finance &
Operations   Chris Caramalis VP-Finance   John Cunningham VP-Marketing   Terri Cunningham VP-Managing Editor   Amy Genkins Senior VP-Business & Legal Affairs   Alison Gill VP-Manufacturing   David
Hyde VP-Publicity   Hank Kanalz VP-General Manager, WildStorm   Jim Lee Editorial Director-WildStorm   Gregory Noveck Senior VP-Creative Affairs   Sue Pohja VP-Book Trade Sales   Steve Rotterdam
Senior VP-Sales & Marketing   Cheryl Rubin Senior VP-Brand Management   Alysse Soll VP-Advertising & Custom Publishing   Jeff Trojan VP-Business Development, DC Direct   Bob Wayne VP-Sales

Cover art by **Dustin Nguyen**

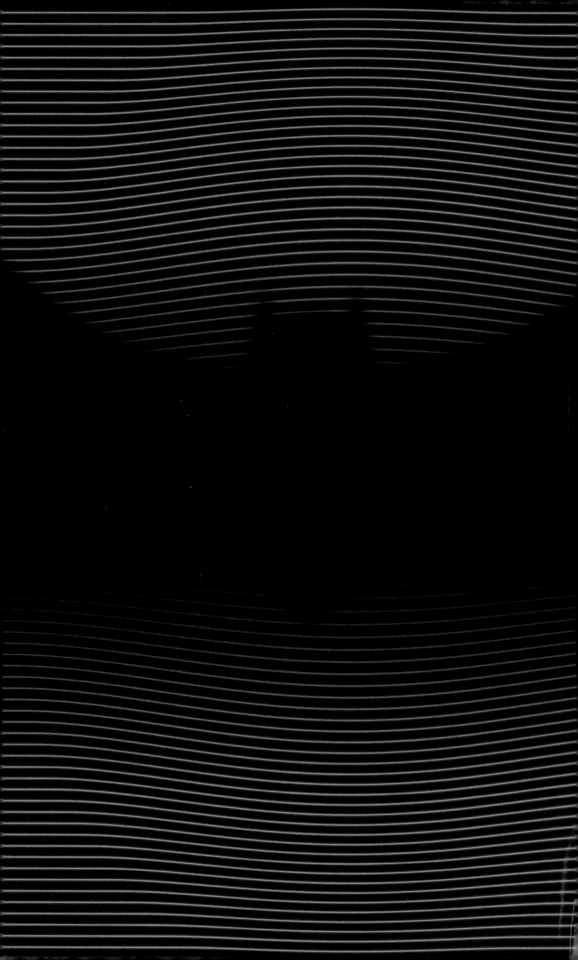

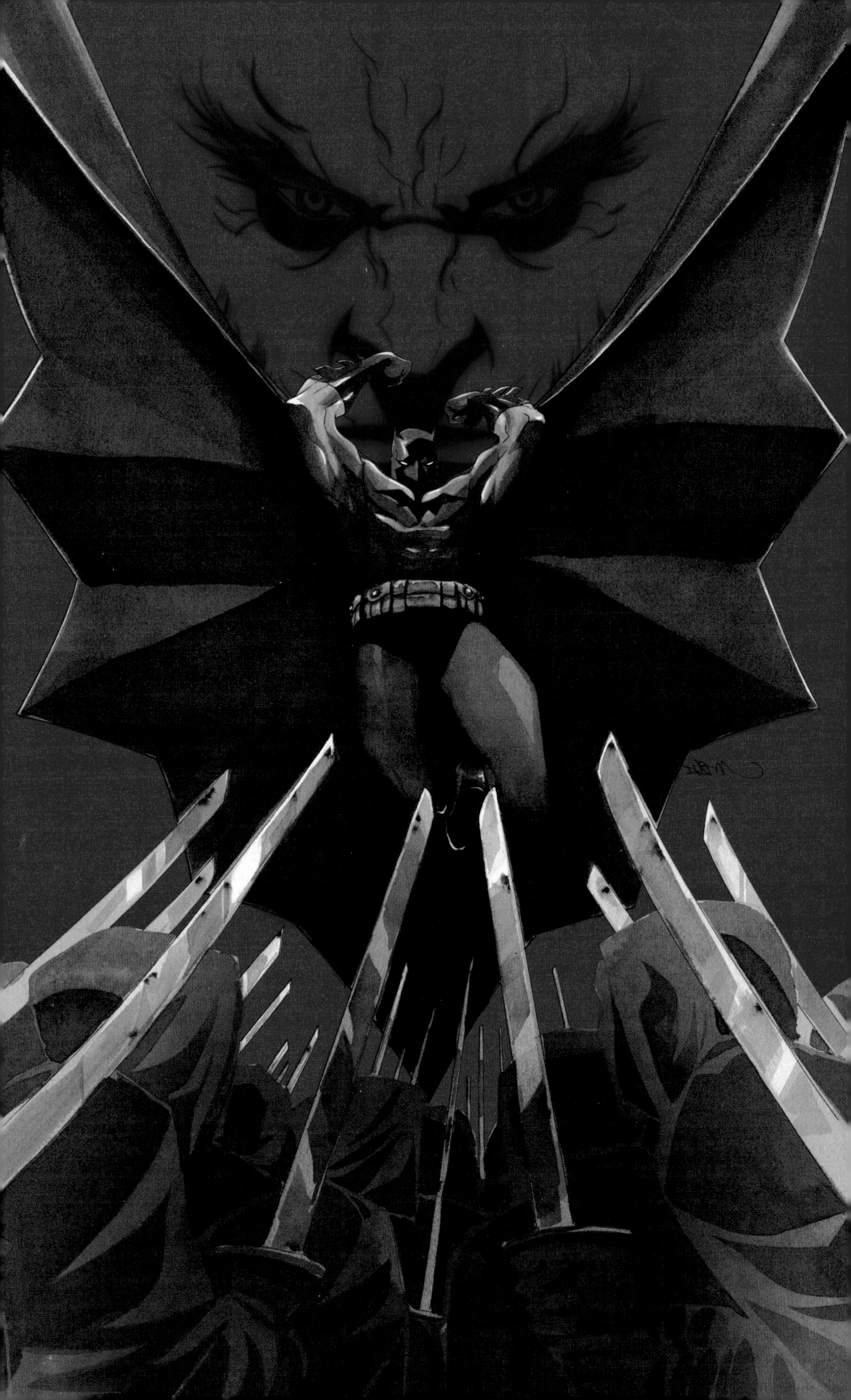

The Resurrection of Ra's al Ghul
- Epilogue

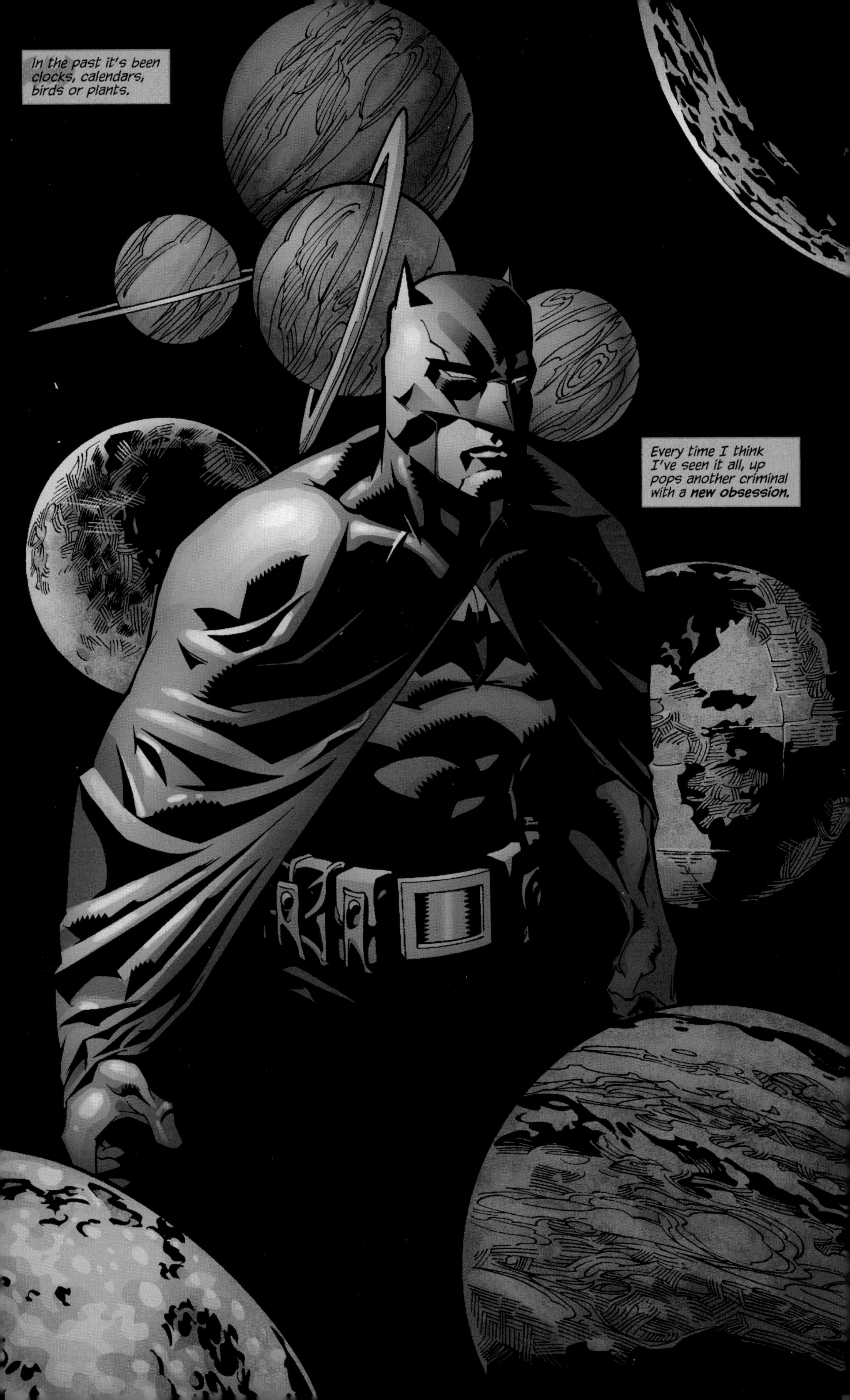
In the past it's been clocks, calendars, birds or plants.
Every time I think I've seen it all, up pops another criminal with a **new obsession.**

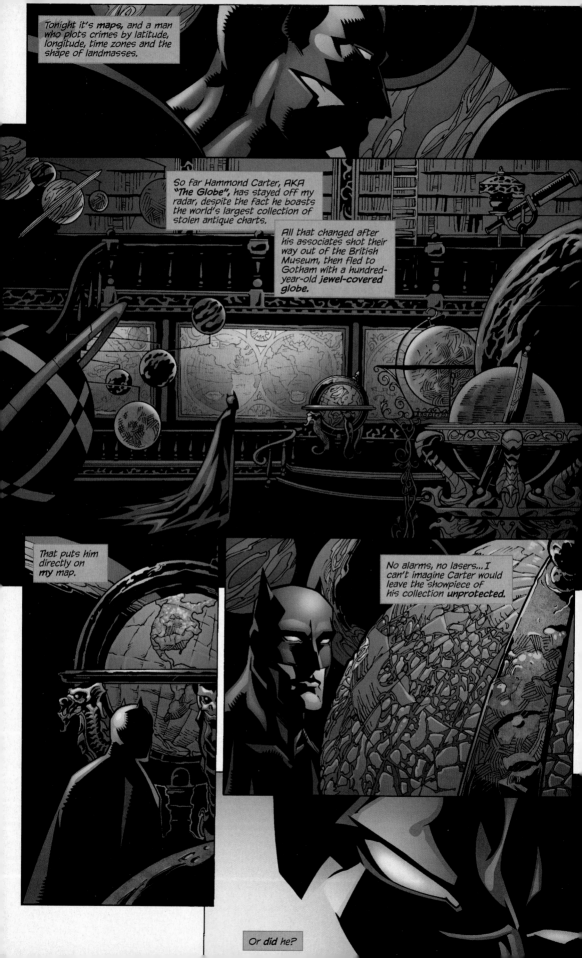

Tonight it's **maps**, and a man who plots crimes by latitude, longitude, time zones and the shape of landmasses.

So far Hammond Carter, AKA **"The Globe"**, has stayed off my radar, despite the fact he boasts the world's largest collection of stolen antique charts.

All that changed after his associates shot their way out of the British Museum, then fled to Gotham with a hundred-year-old **jewel-covered globe.**

That puts him directly on **my map.**

No alarms, no lasers...I can't imagine Carter would leave the showpiece of his collection **unprotected.**

Or **did** he?

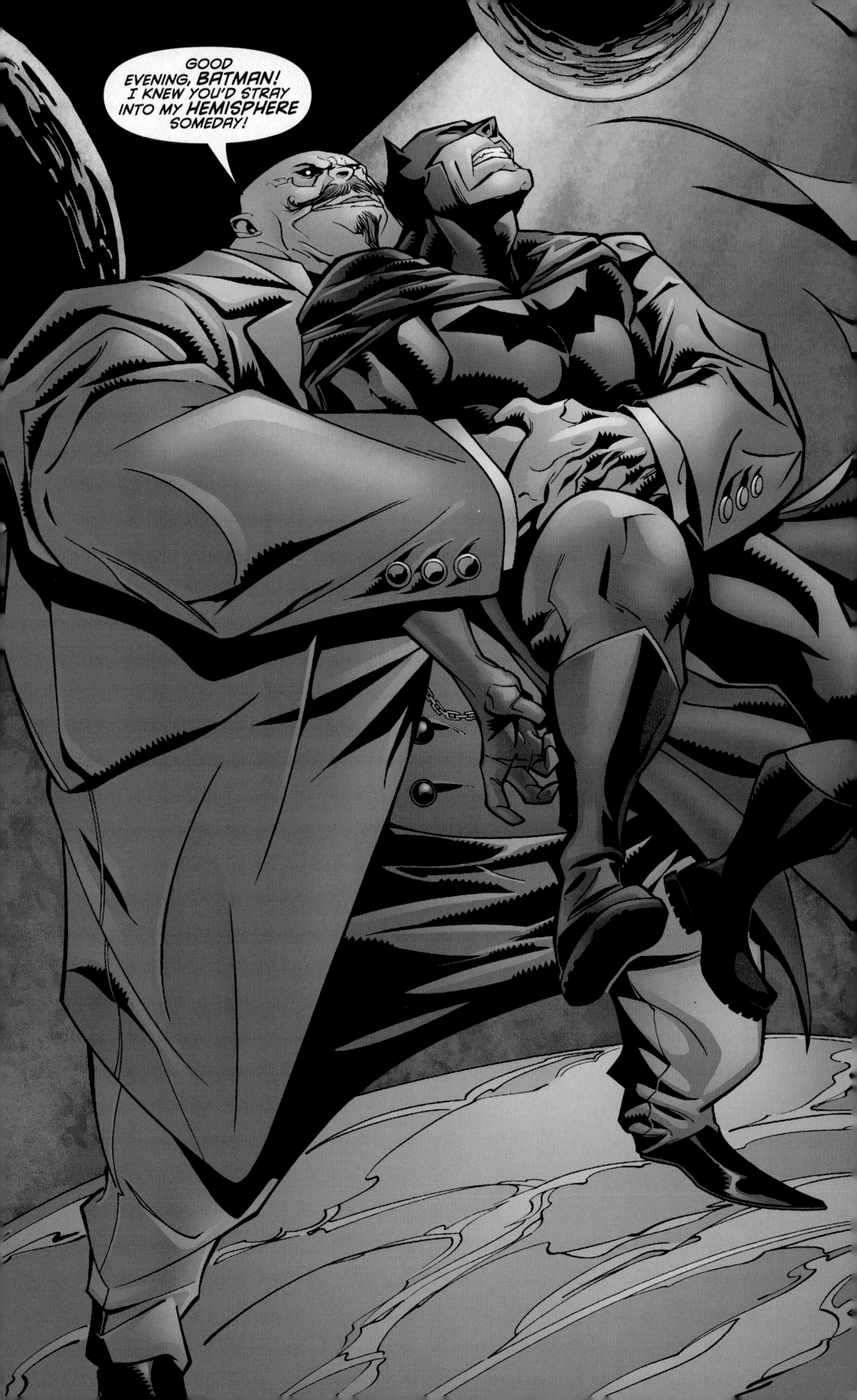
GOOD EVENING, BATMAN! I KNEW YOU'D STRAY INTO MY HEMISPHERE SOMEDAY!

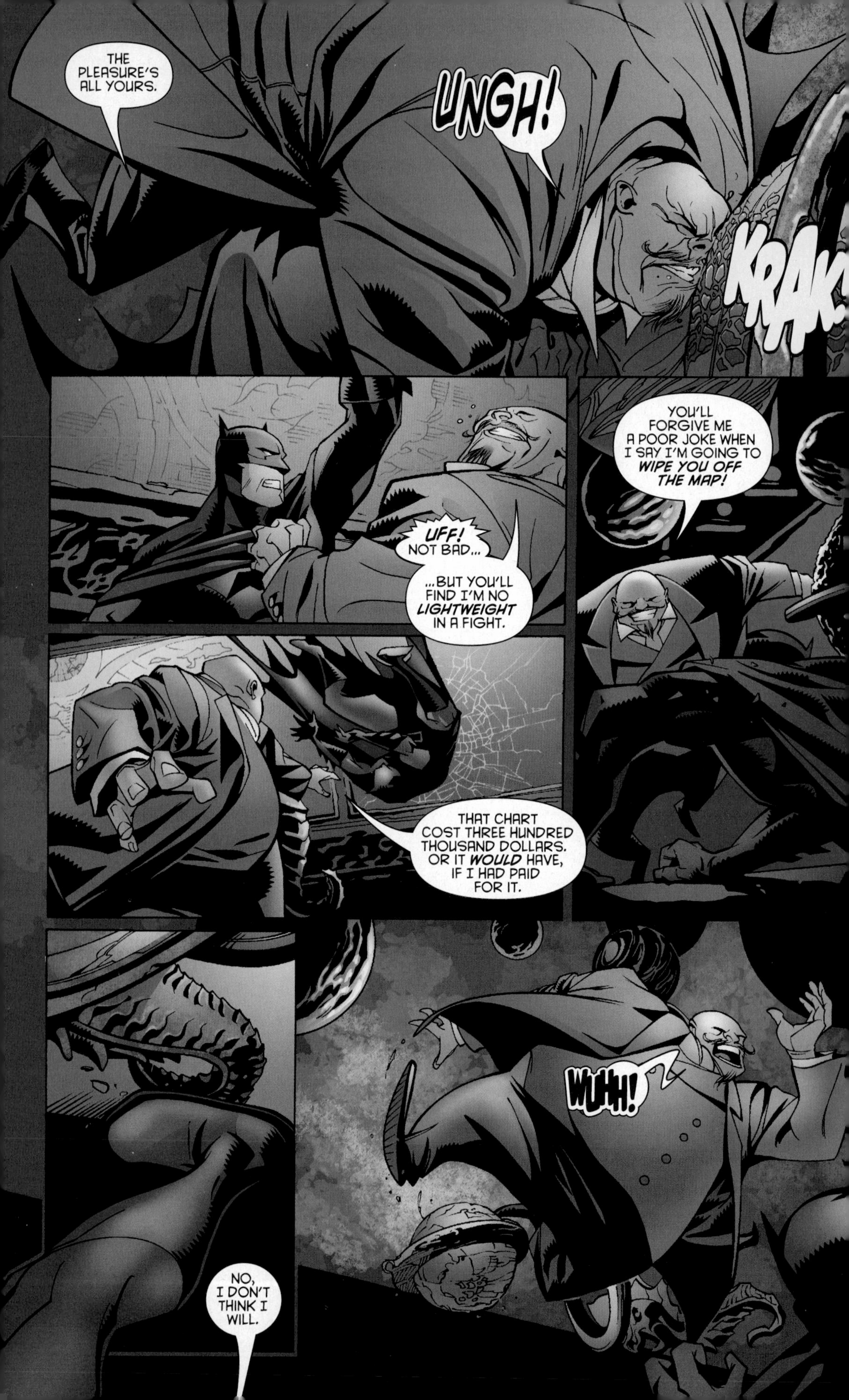
THE PLEASURE'S ALL YOURS.
UNGH!
KRAK!
UFF! NOT BAD...
...BUT YOU'LL FIND I'M NO LIGHTWEIGHT IN A FIGHT.
YOU'LL FORGIVE ME A POOR JOKE WHEN I SAY I'M GOING TO WIPE YOU OFF THE MAP!
THAT CHART COST THREE HUNDRED THOUSAND DOLLARS. OR IT WOULD HAVE, IF I HAD PAID FOR IT.
NO, I DON'T THINK I WILL.
WUHH!

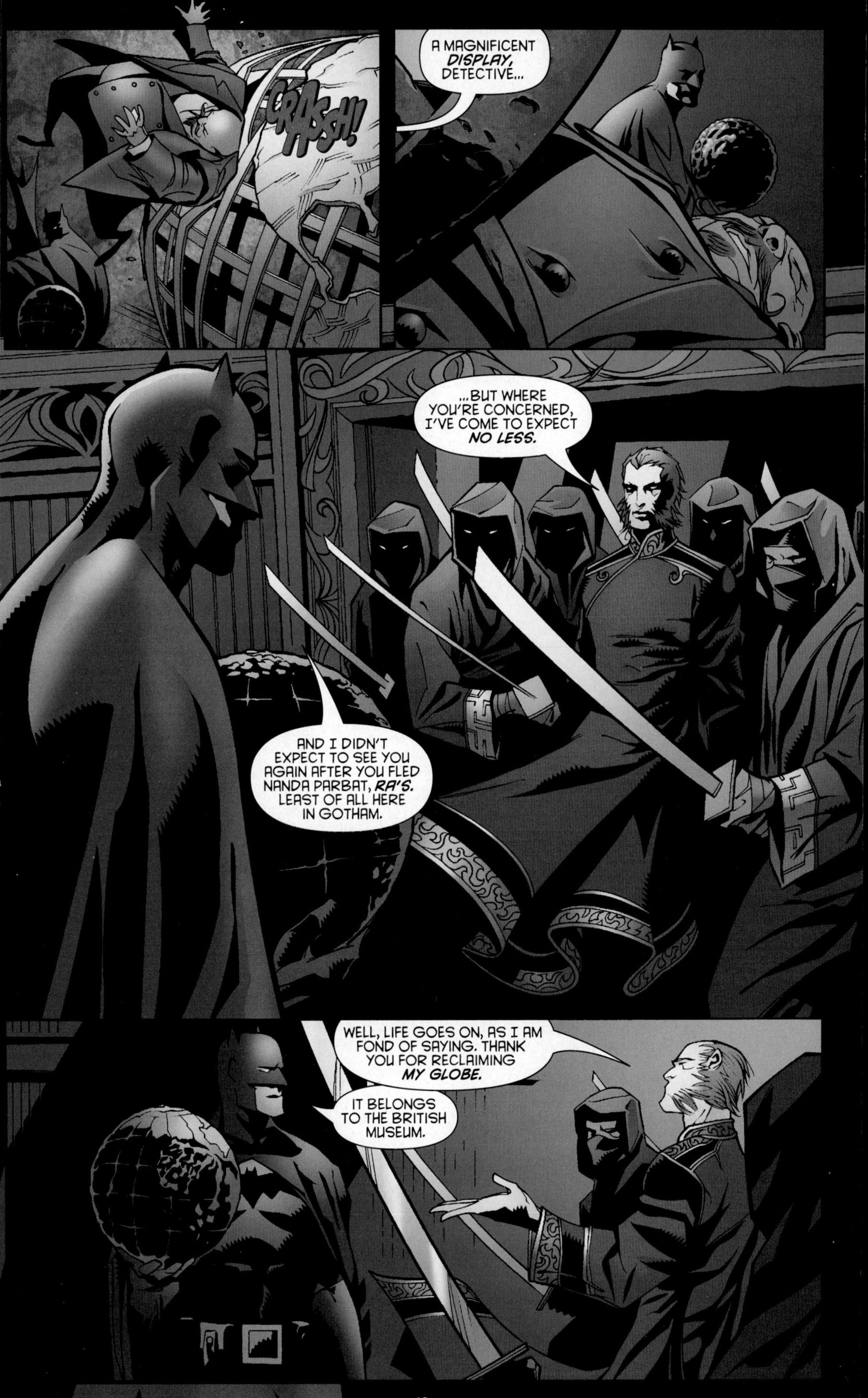
CRASSH!
A MAGNIFICENT DISPLAY, DETECTIVE...
...BUT WHERE YOU'RE CONCERNED, I'VE COME TO EXPECT NO LESS.
AND I DIDN'T EXPECT TO SEE YOU AGAIN AFTER YOU FLED NANDA PARBAT, RA'S. LEAST OF ALL HERE IN GOTHAM.
WELL, LIFE GOES ON, AS I AM FOND OF SAYING. THANK YOU FOR RECLAIMING MY GLOBE.
IT BELONGS TO THE BRITISH MUSEUM.

ACTUALLY, *NO.* I WAS THE ONE WHO LEAKED ITS PROBABLE WHEREABOUTS THROUGH THE GOTHAM UNDERWORLD, KNOWING YOU WOULD NOT PASS UP AN OPPORTUNITY TO APPREHEND CARTER.

HERE IS MY *RECEIPT* SIGNED BY PETER CARL FABERGÉ FOR ITS CREATION IN ST. PETERSBURG, 1901.

GIVEN MY OFTEN-MOBILE LIFESTYLE, THE JEWELED GLOBE, LIKE SO MANY OF MY TREASURES, HAD BECOME *MISPLACED* OVER THE YEARS.

I'D LIKE IT BACK, PLEASE.

FINE.

DISAPPOINTING.

HAD YOUR NATURAL INQUISITIVENESS WON OVER YOUR DESIRE TO INTIMIDATE ME LIKE A *CRIMINAL,* YOU WOULD NOT HAVE TREATED THE GLOBE LIKE A *COMMON TRINKET.*

HAD YOU BUT *THOUGHT* FIRST, YOU WOULD HAVE SUSPECTED THIS ORB HAS A VALUE *FAR* BEYOND ITS JEWELLED SURFACE.

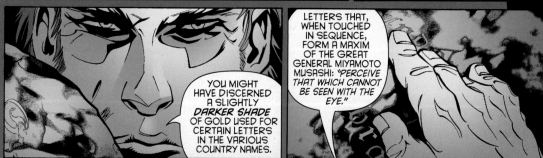

YOU MIGHT HAVE DISCERNED A SLIGHTLY *DARKER SHADE* OF GOLD USED FOR CERTAIN LETTERS IN THE VARIOUS COUNTRY NAMES.

LETTERS THAT, WHEN TOUCHED IN SEQUENCE, FORM A MAXIM OF THE GREAT GENERAL MIYAMOTO MUSASHI: *"PERCEIVE THAT WHICH CANNOT BE SEEN WITH THE EYE."*

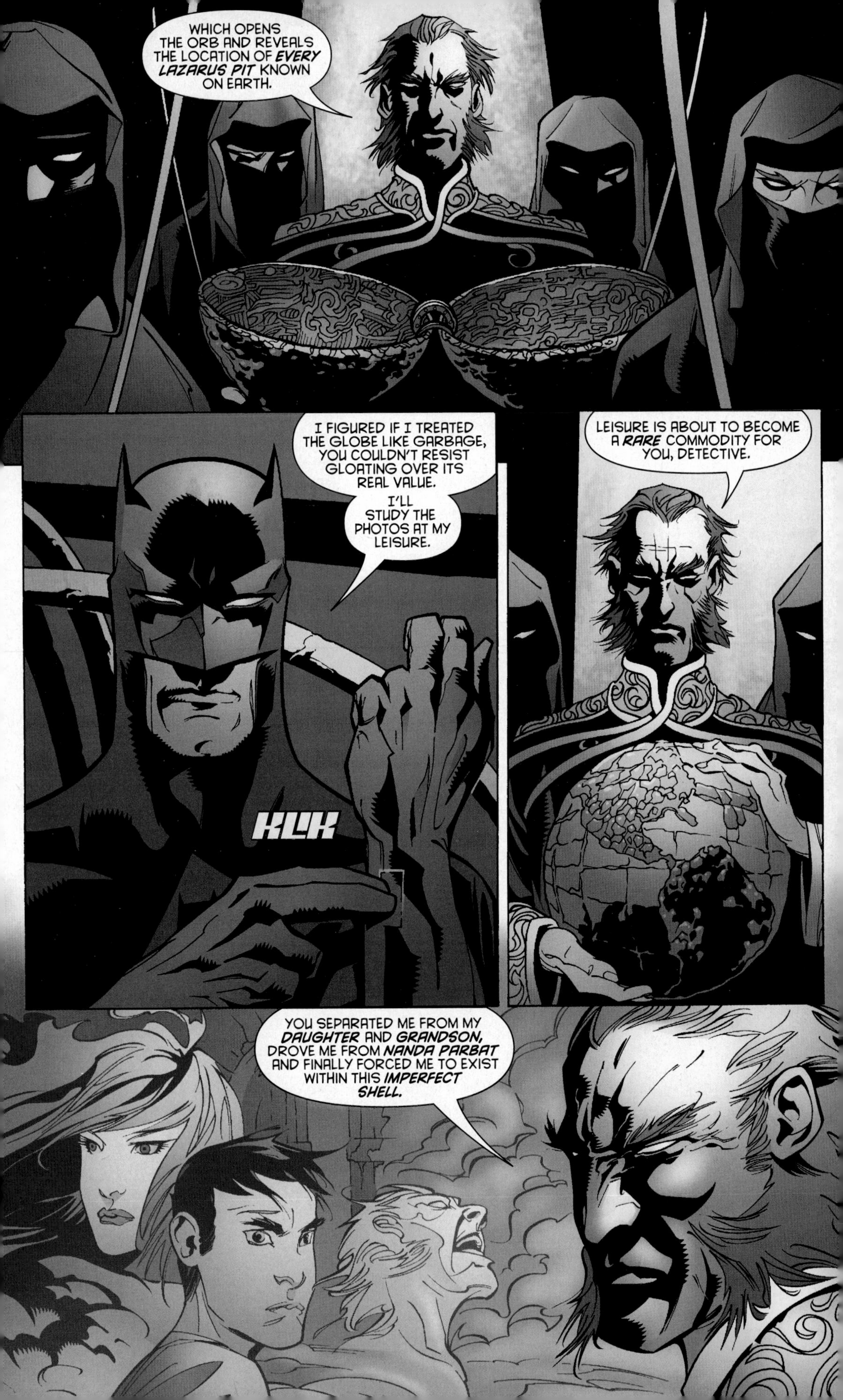
WHICH OPENS THE ORB AND REVEALS THE LOCATION OF *EVERY LAZARUS PIT* KNOWN ON EARTH.
I FIGURED IF I TREATED THE GLOBE LIKE GARBAGE, YOU COULDN'T RESIST GLOATING OVER ITS REAL VALUE.
I'LL STUDY THE PHOTOS AT MY LEISURE.
KLIK
LEISURE IS ABOUT TO BECOME A *RARE* COMMODITY FOR YOU, DETECTIVE.
YOU SEPARATED ME FROM MY *DAUGHTER* AND *GRANDSON*, DROVE ME FROM *NANDA PARBAT* AND FINALLY FORCED ME TO EXIST WITHIN THIS *IMPERFECT SHELL.*

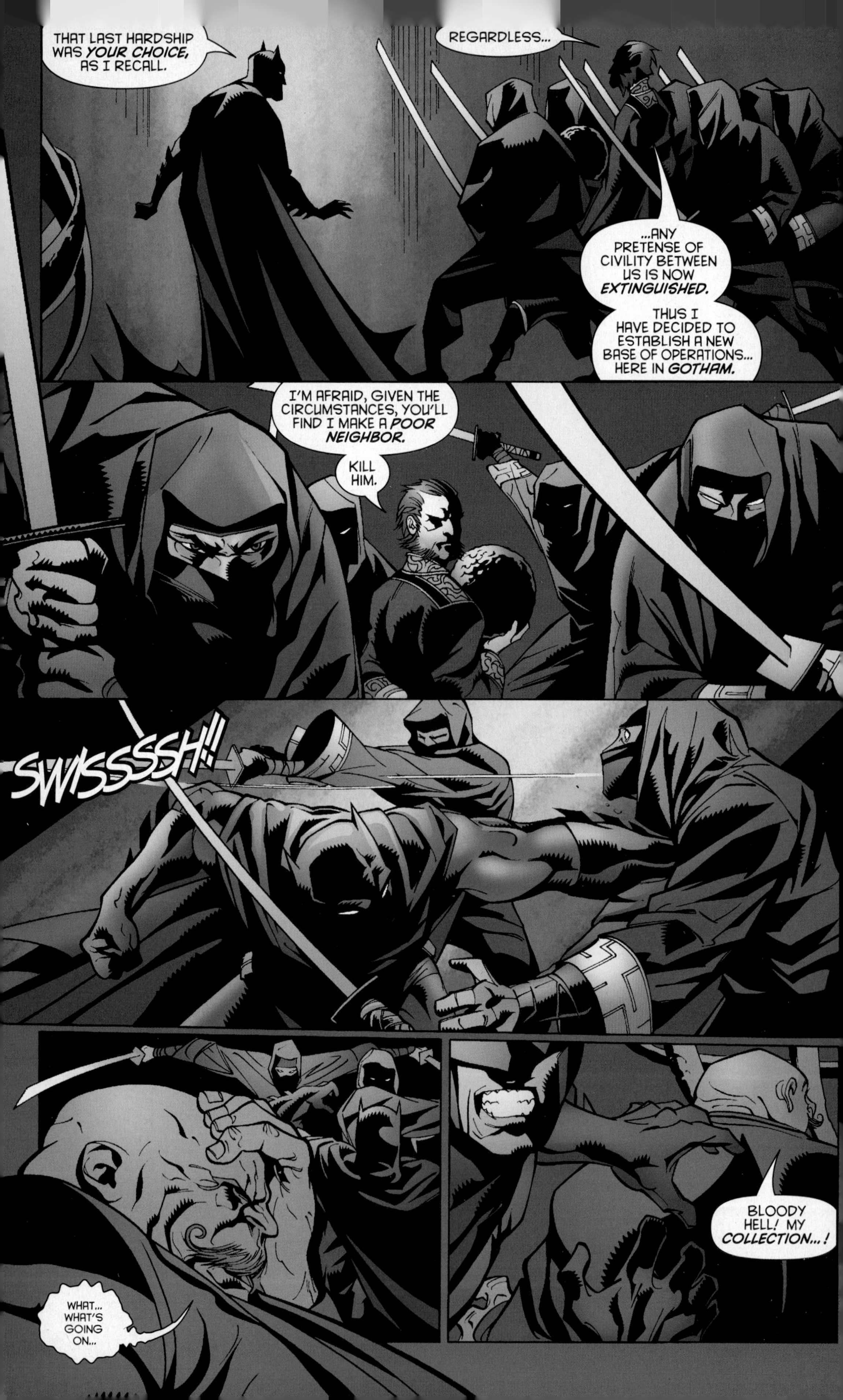
THAT LAST HARDSHIP WAS *YOUR CHOICE,* AS I RECALL.
REGARDLESS...
...ANY PRETENSE OF CIVILITY BETWEEN US IS NOW *EXTINGUISHED.*
THUS I HAVE DECIDED TO ESTABLISH A NEW BASE OF OPERATIONS... HERE IN *GOTHAM.*
I'M AFRAID, GIVEN THE CIRCUMSTANCES, YOU'LL FIND I MAKE A *POOR NEIGHBOR.*
KILL HIM.
SWISSSSH!!
WHAT... WHAT'S GOING ON...
BLOODY HELL! MY *COLLECTION...!*

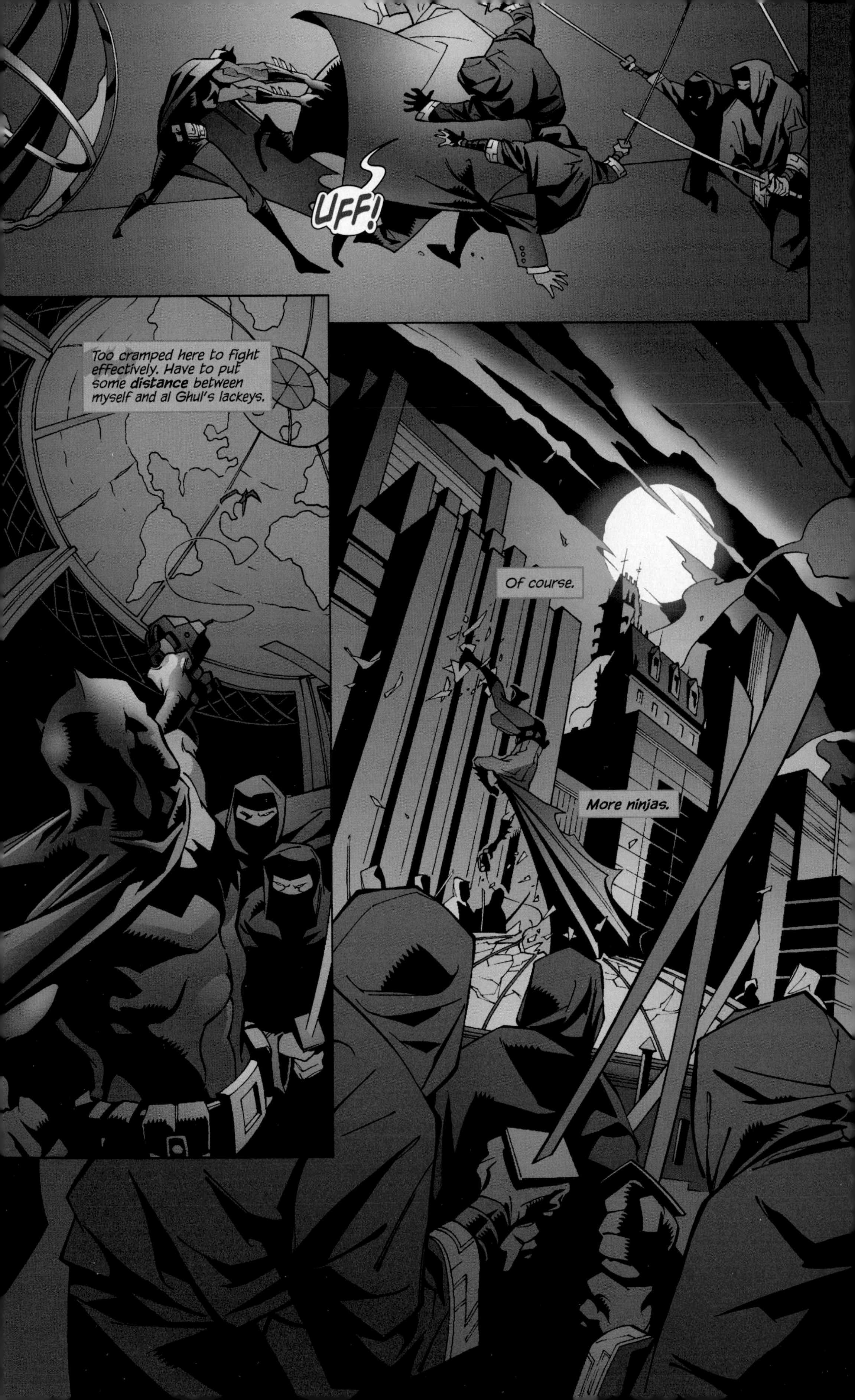
UFF!
Too cramped here to fight effectively. Have to put some distance between myself and al Ghul's lackeys.
Of course.
More ninjas.

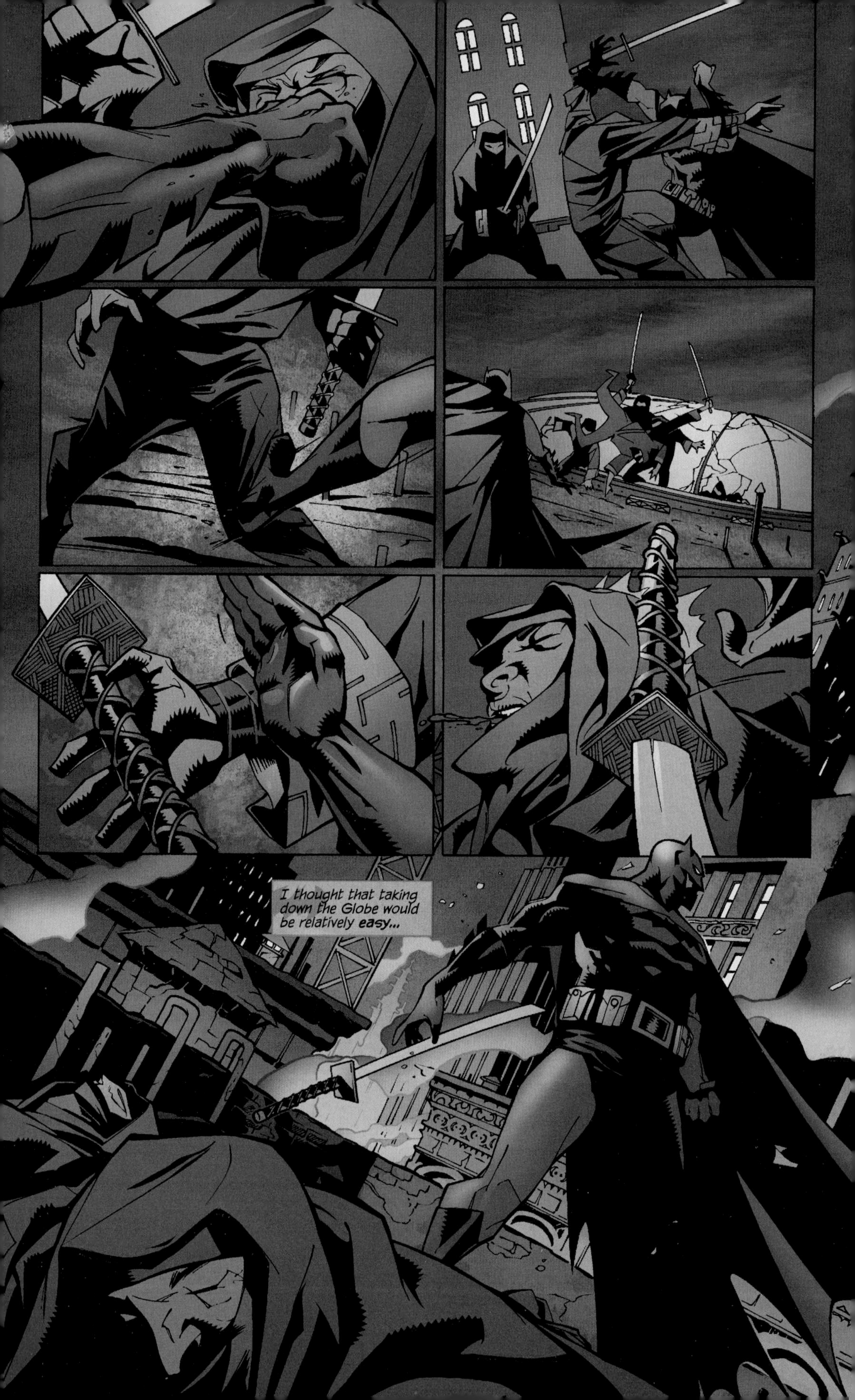
I thought that taking down the Globe would be relatively easy...

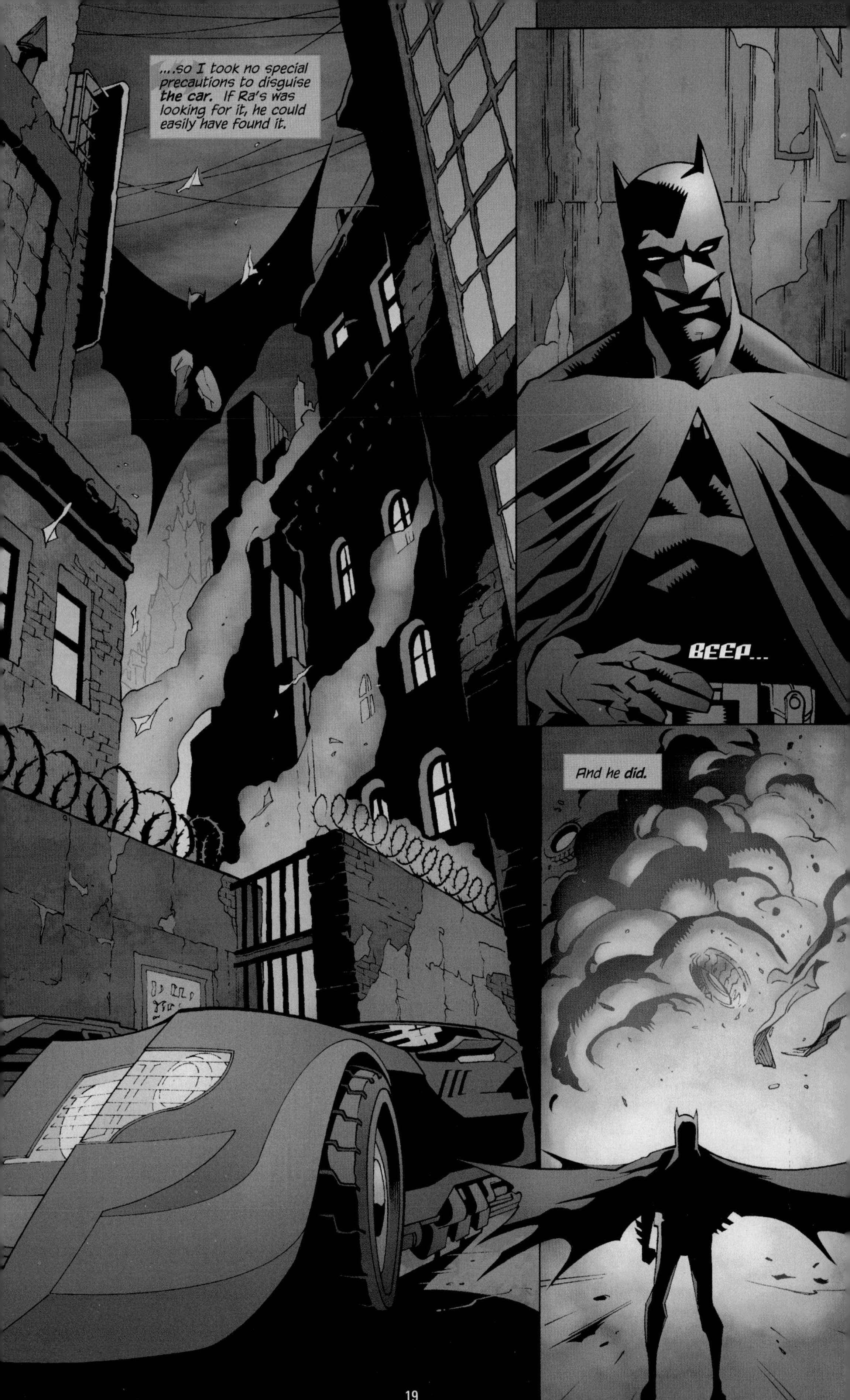

....so I took no special precautions to disguise **the car.** If Ra's was looking for it, he could easily have found it.
BEEP...
And he **did.**

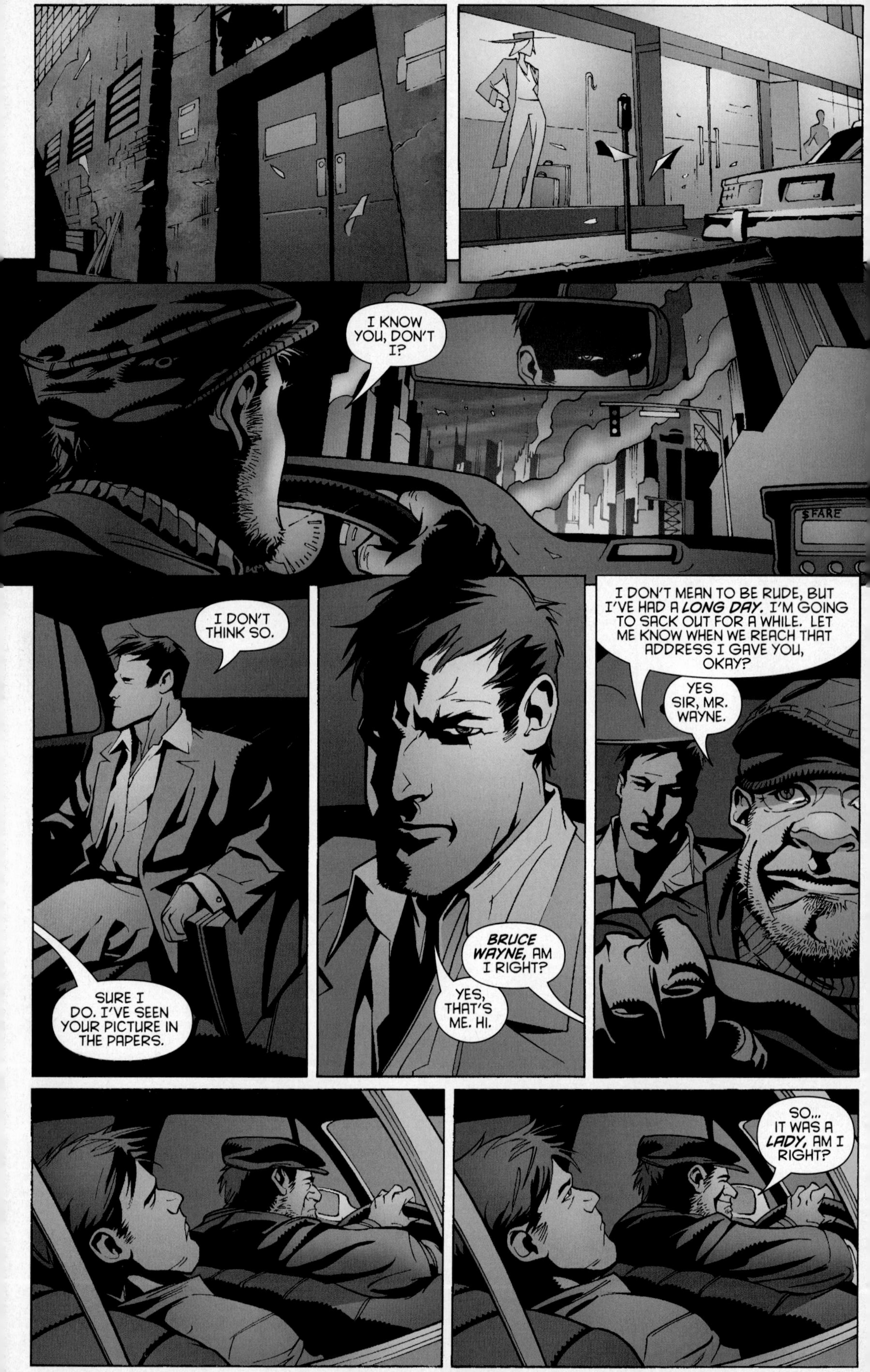

I KNOW YOU, DON'T I?
$FARE
I DON'T THINK SO.
SURE I DO. I'VE SEEN YOUR PICTURE IN THE PAPERS.
BRUCE WAYNE, AM I RIGHT?
YES, THAT'S ME. HI.
I DON'T MEAN TO BE RUDE, BUT I'VE HAD A LONG DAY. I'M GOING TO SACK OUT FOR A WHILE. LET ME KNOW WHEN WE REACH THAT ADDRESS I GAVE YOU, OKAY?
YES SIR, MR. WAYNE.
SO... IT WAS A LADY, AM I RIGHT?

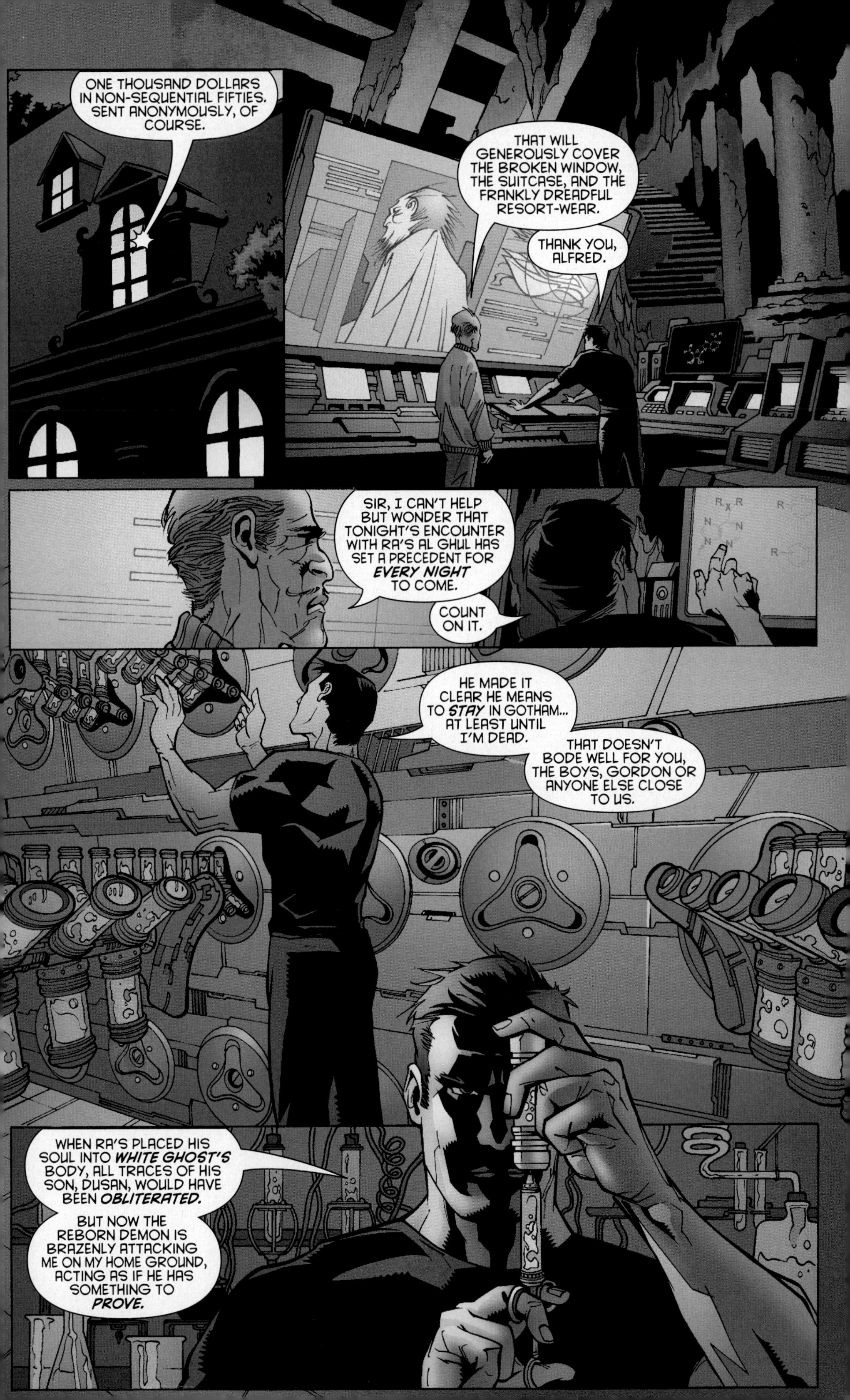
ONE THOUSAND DOLLARS IN NON-SEQUENTIAL FIFTIES. SENT ANONYMOUSLY, OF COURSE.
THAT WILL GENEROUSLY COVER THE BROKEN WINDOW, THE SUITCASE, AND THE FRANKLY DREADFUL RESORT-WEAR.
THANK YOU, ALFRED.
SIR, I CAN'T HELP BUT WONDER THAT TONIGHT'S ENCOUNTER WITH RA'S AL GHUL HAS SET A PRECEDENT FOR EVERY NIGHT TO COME.
COUNT ON IT.
HE MADE IT CLEAR HE MEANS TO STAY IN GOTHAM... AT LEAST UNTIL I'M DEAD.
THAT DOESN'T BODE WELL FOR YOU, THE BOYS, GORDON OR ANYONE ELSE CLOSE TO US.
WHEN RA'S PLACED HIS SOUL INTO WHITE GHOST'S BODY, ALL TRACES OF HIS SON, DUSAN, WOULD HAVE BEEN OBLITERATED.
BUT NOW THE REBORN DEMON IS BRAZENLY ATTACKING ME ON MY HOME GROUND, ACTING AS IF HE HAS SOMETHING TO PROVE.

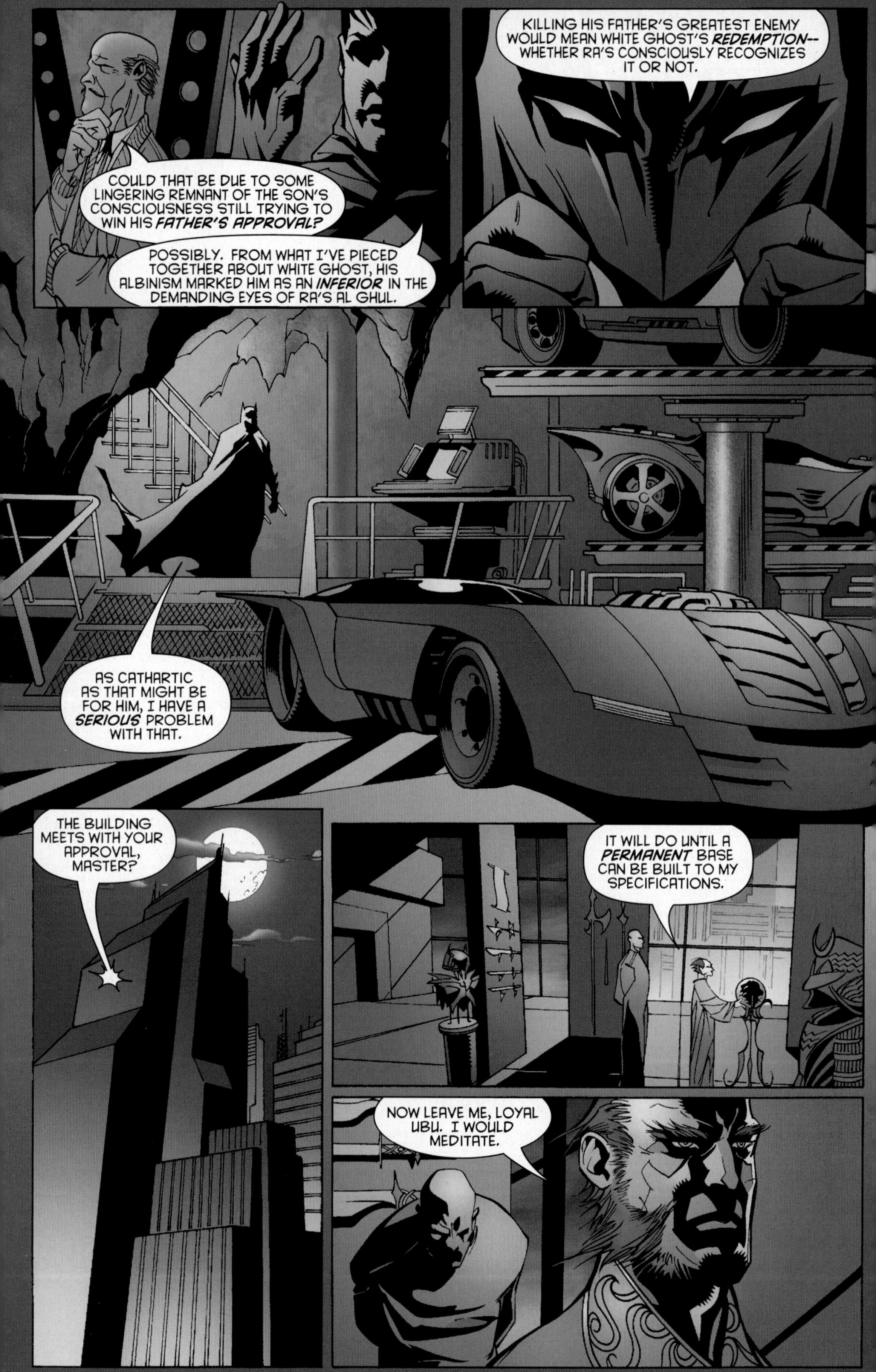
COULD THAT BE DUE TO SOME LINGERING REMNANT OF THE SON'S CONSCIOUSNESS STILL TRYING TO WIN HIS FATHER'S APPROVAL?
POSSIBLY. FROM WHAT I'VE PIECED TOGETHER ABOUT WHITE GHOST, HIS ALBINISM MARKED HIM AS AN INFERIOR IN THE DEMANDING EYES OF RA'S AL GHUL.
KILLING HIS FATHER'S GREATEST ENEMY WOULD MEAN WHITE GHOST'S REDEMPTION-- WHETHER RA'S CONSCIOUSLY RECOGNIZES IT OR NOT.
AS CATHARTIC AS THAT MIGHT BE FOR HIM, I HAVE A SERIOUS PROBLEM WITH THAT.
THE BUILDING MEETS WITH YOUR APPROVAL, MASTER?
IT WILL DO UNTIL A PERMANENT BASE CAN BE BUILT TO MY SPECIFICATIONS.
NOW LEAVE ME, LOYAL UBU. I WOULD MEDITATE.

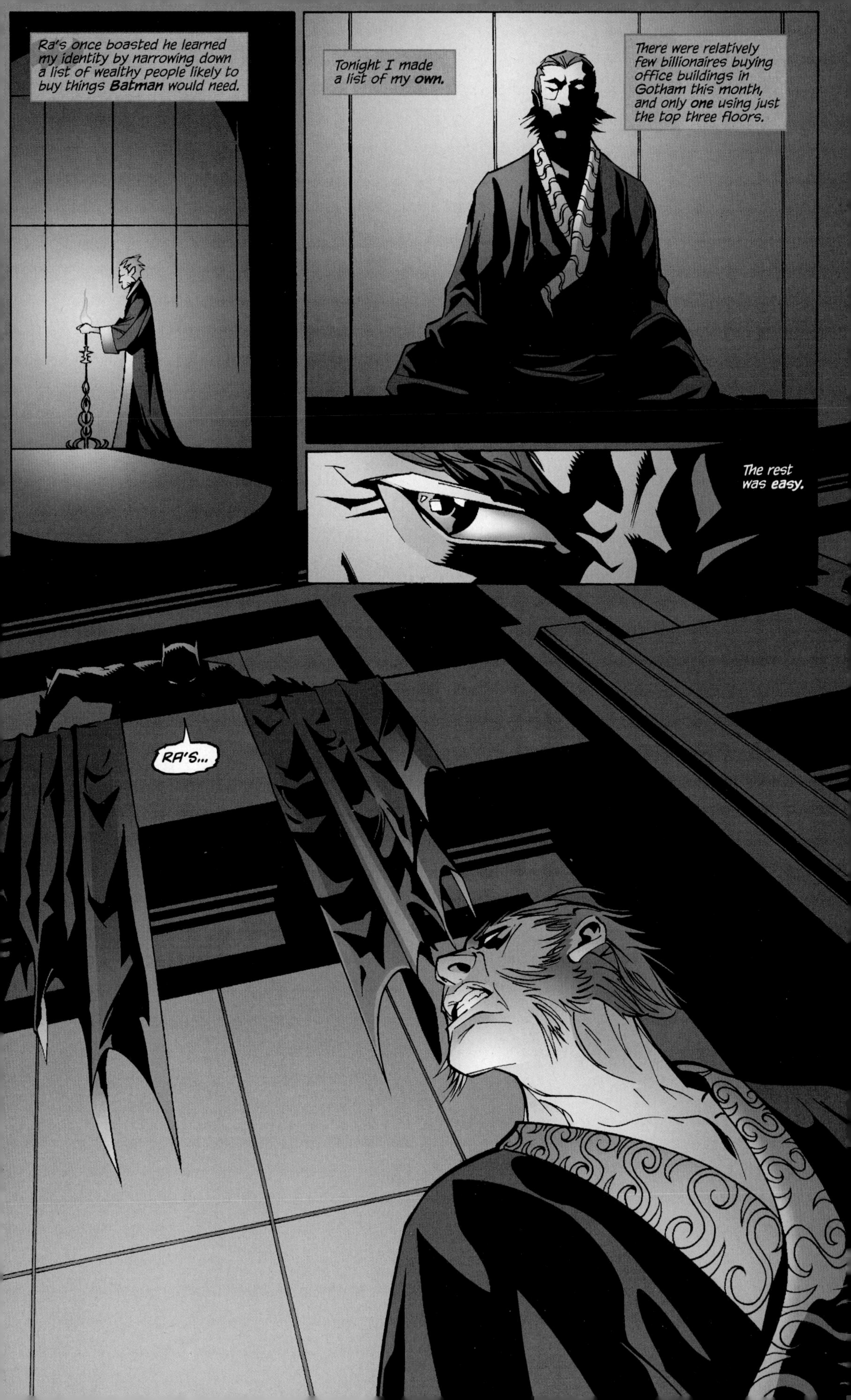
Ra's once boasted he learned my identity by narrowing down a list of wealthy people likely to buy things **Batman** would need.
Tonight I made a list of my **own.**
There were relatively few billionaires buying office buildings in Gotham this month, and only **one** using just the top three floors.
The rest was **easy.**
RA'S...

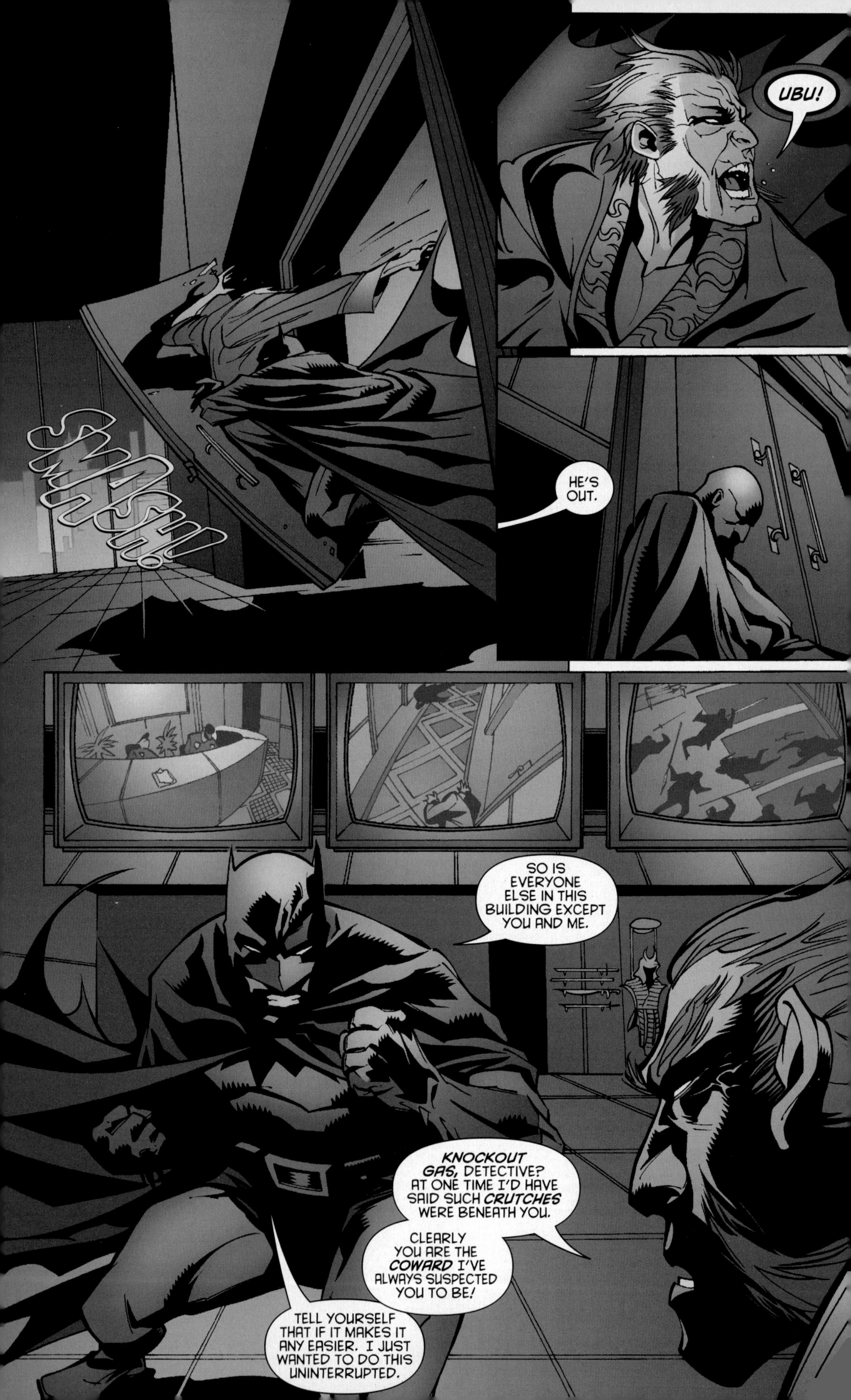

SMASH!
UBU!
HE'S OUT.
SO IS EVERYONE ELSE IN THIS BUILDING EXCEPT YOU AND ME.
KNOCKOUT GAS, DETECTIVE? AT ONE TIME I'D HAVE SAID SUCH CRUTCHES WERE BENEATH YOU.
CLEARLY YOU ARE THE COWARD I'VE ALWAYS SUSPECTED YOU TO BE!
TELL YOURSELF THAT IF IT MAKES IT ANY EASIER. I JUST WANTED TO DO THIS UNINTERRUPTED.

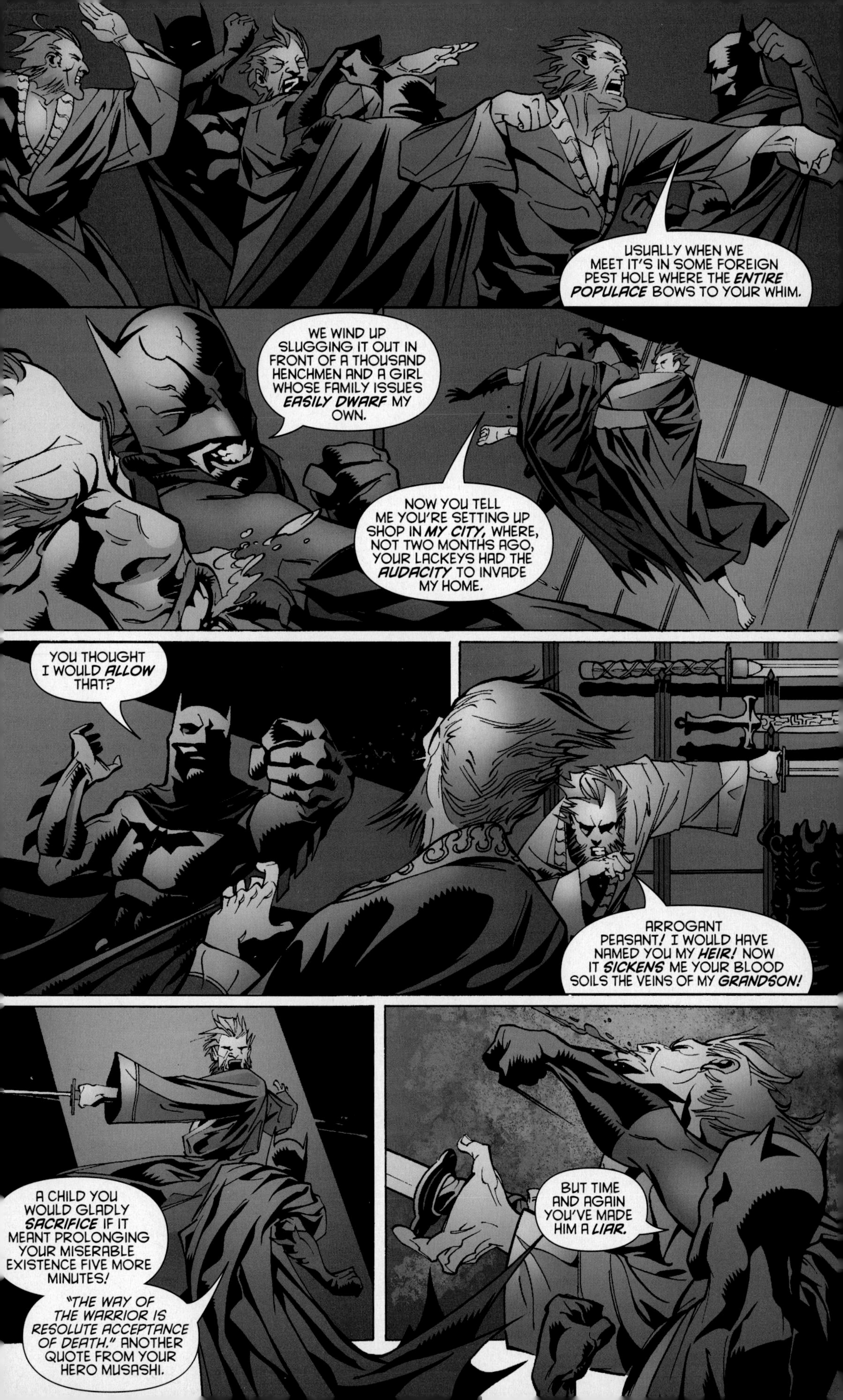
USUALLY WHEN WE MEET IT'S IN SOME FOREIGN PEST HOLE WHERE THE ENTIRE POPULACE BOWS TO YOUR WHIM.
WE WIND UP SLUGGING IT OUT IN FRONT OF A THOUSAND HENCHMEN AND A GIRL WHOSE FAMILY ISSUES EASILY DWARF MY OWN.
NOW YOU TELL ME YOU'RE SETTING UP SHOP IN MY CITY, WHERE, NOT TWO MONTHS AGO, YOUR LACKEYS HAD THE AUDACITY TO INVADE MY HOME.
YOU THOUGHT I WOULD ALLOW THAT?
ARROGANT PEASANT! I WOULD HAVE NAMED YOU MY HEIR! NOW IT SICKENS ME YOUR BLOOD SOILS THE VEINS OF MY GRANDSON!
A CHILD YOU WOULD GLADLY SACRIFICE IF IT MEANT PROLONGING YOUR MISERABLE EXISTENCE FIVE MORE MINUTES!
"THE WAY OF THE WARRIOR IS RESOLUTE ACCEPTANCE OF DEATH." ANOTHER QUOTE FROM YOUR HERO MUSASHI.
BUT TIME AND AGAIN YOU'VE MADE HIM A LIAR.

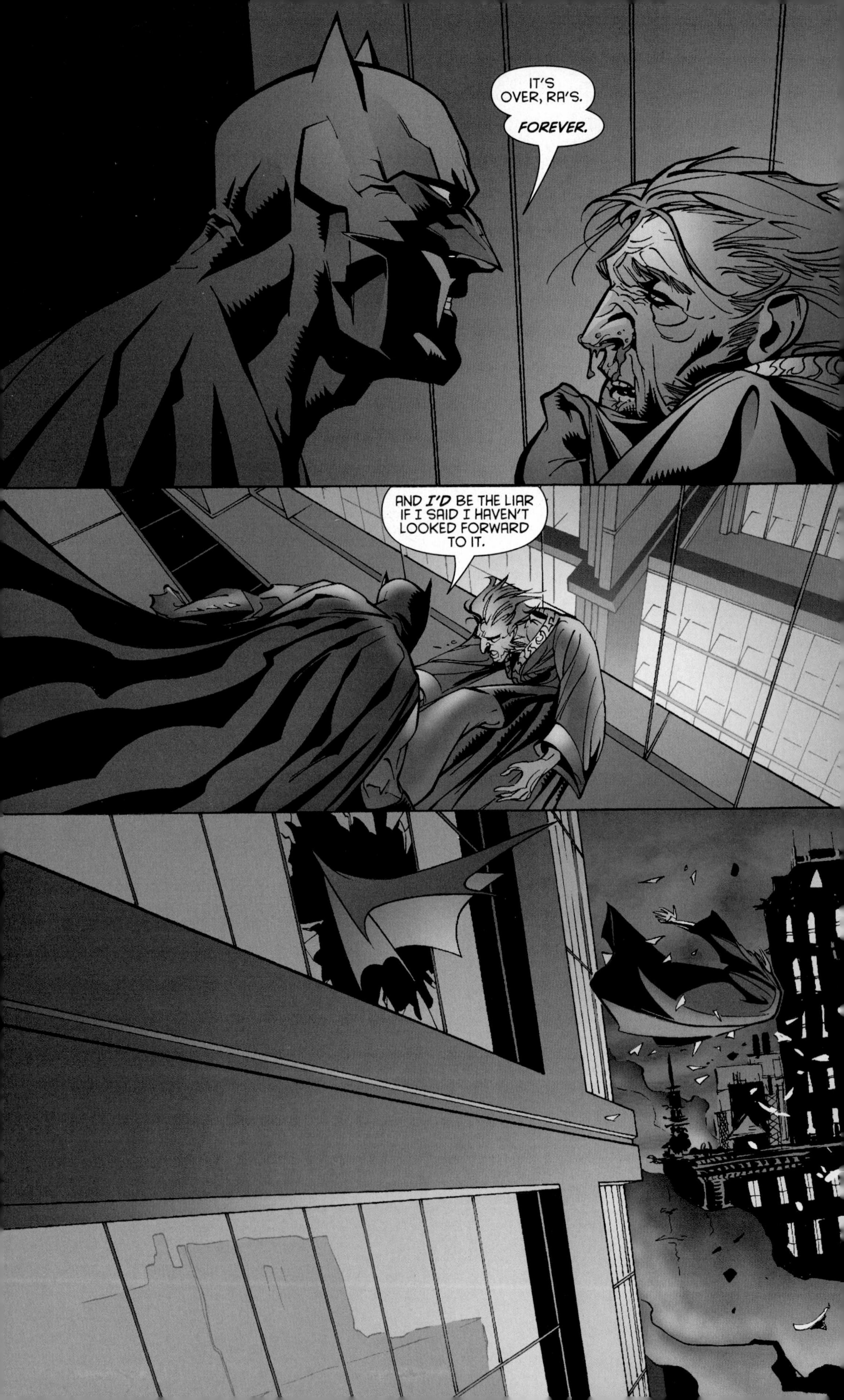
IT'S OVER, RA'S.
FOREVER.
AND *I'D* BE THE LIAR IF I SAID I HAVEN'T LOOKED FORWARD TO IT.

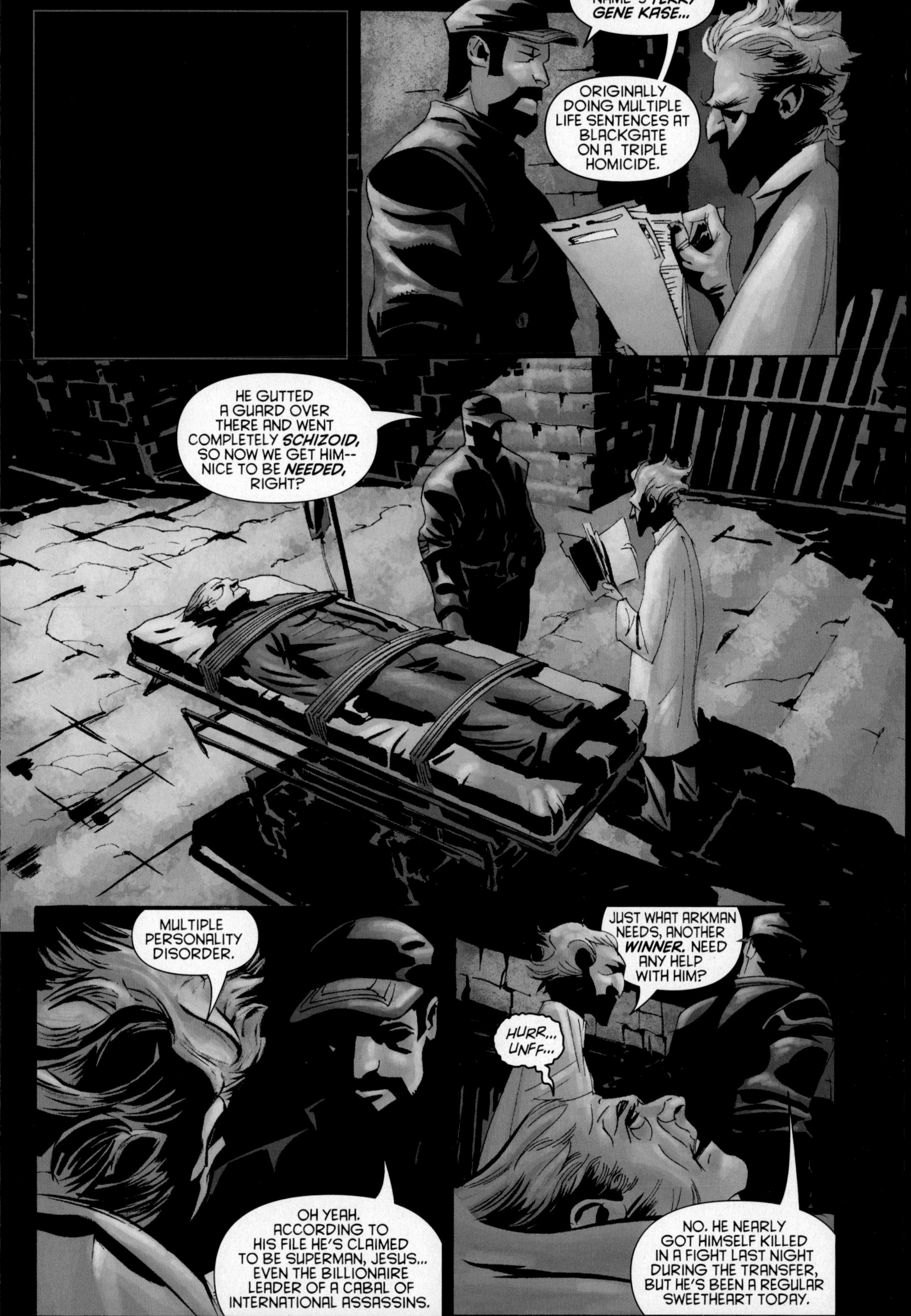
...GOT HIS FILE RIGHT HERE. NAME'S *TERRY GENE KASE*...
ORIGINALLY DOING MULTIPLE LIFE SENTENCES AT BLACKGATE ON A TRIPLE HOMICIDE.
HE GUTTED A GUARD OVER THERE AND WENT COMPLETELY *SCHIZOID*, SO NOW WE GET HIM--NICE TO BE *NEEDED*, RIGHT?
MULTIPLE PERSONALITY DISORDER.
OH YEAH. ACCORDING TO HIS FILE HE'S CLAIMED TO BE SUPERMAN, JESUS... EVEN THE BILLIONAIRE LEADER OF A CABAL OF INTERNATIONAL ASSASSINS.
JUST WHAT ARKMAN NEEDS, ANOTHER *WINNER*. NEED ANY HELP WITH HIM?
HURR... UNFF...
NO. HE NEARLY GOT HIMSELF KILLED IN A FIGHT LAST NIGHT DURING THE TRANSFER, BUT HE'S BEEN A REGULAR SWEETHEART TODAY.

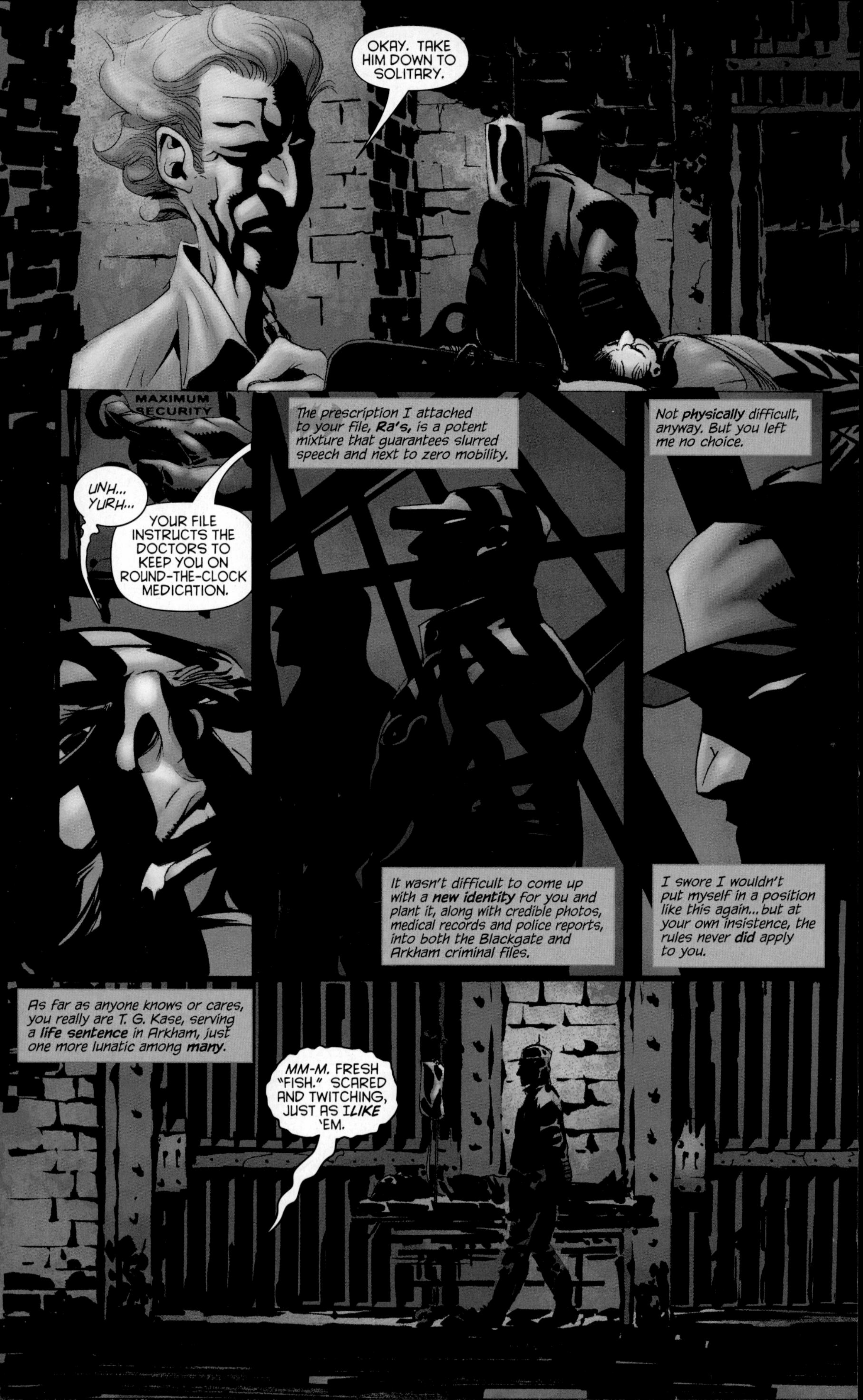
OKAY. TAKE HIM DOWN TO SOLITARY.
MAXIMUM SECURITY
UNH... YURH...
YOUR FILE INSTRUCTS THE DOCTORS TO KEEP YOU ON ROUND-THE-CLOCK MEDICATION.
The prescription I attached to your file, Ra's, is a potent mixture that guarantees slurred speech and next to zero mobility.
It wasn't difficult to come up with a new identity for you and plant it, along with credible photos, medical records and police reports, into both the Blackgate and Arkham criminal files.
Not physically difficult, anyway. But you left me no choice.
I swore I wouldn't put myself in a position like this again... but at your own insistence, the rules never did apply to you.
As far as anyone knows or cares, you really are T. G. Kase, serving a life sentence in Arkham, just one more lunatic among many.
MM-M. FRESH "FISH." SCARED AND TWITCHING, JUST AS I LIKE 'EM.

BETTER WATCH YOURSELF, SHARK. THIS GUY'S A *MANIAC*.
DON'T WORRY, SCREW. I'LL BREAK HIM IN.
AHR.. NNUH...
THAT SOUNDED LIKE A PLEA, OR POSSIBLY A THREAT.
I know your people will look for you. Maybe you'll get lucky and they'll spring you tomorrow.
EITHER WAY, IT'S TIME FOR ANOTHER DOSE.
Maybe you'll rot here for decades.

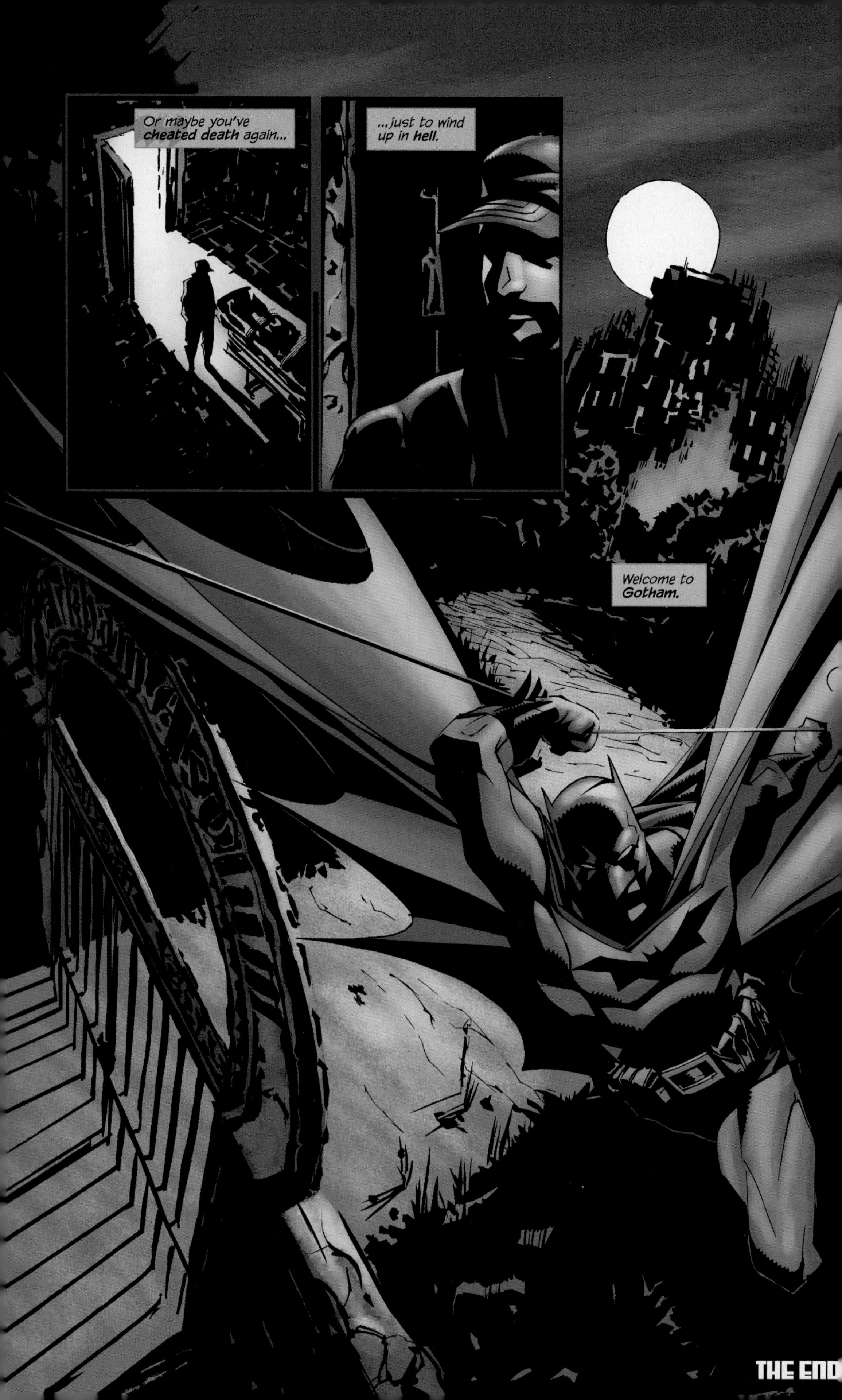

Or maybe you've cheated death again...
...just to wind up in hell.
Welcome to Gotham.
THE END

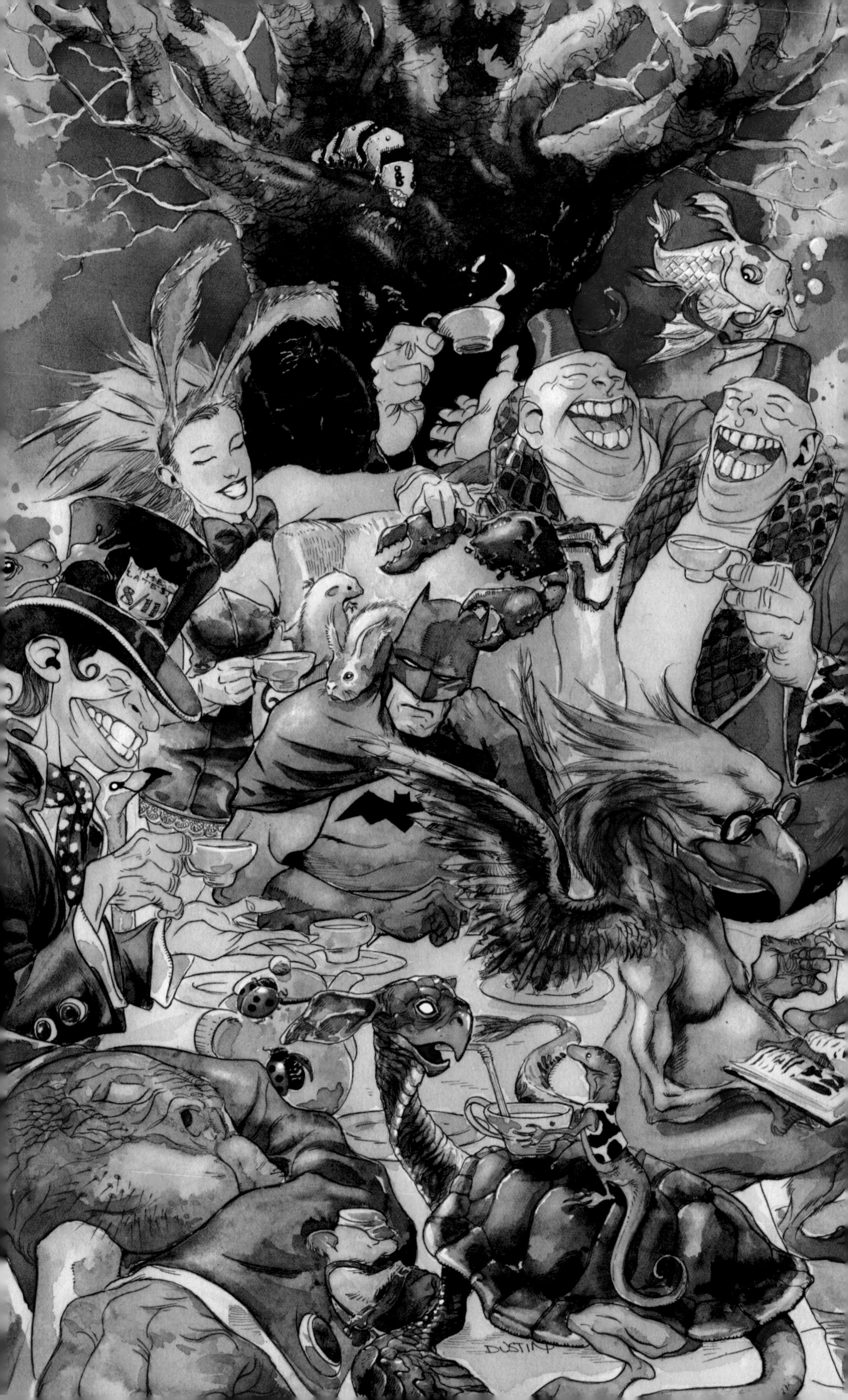
LATEST
8/11
DUSTIN

The Wonderland Gang!

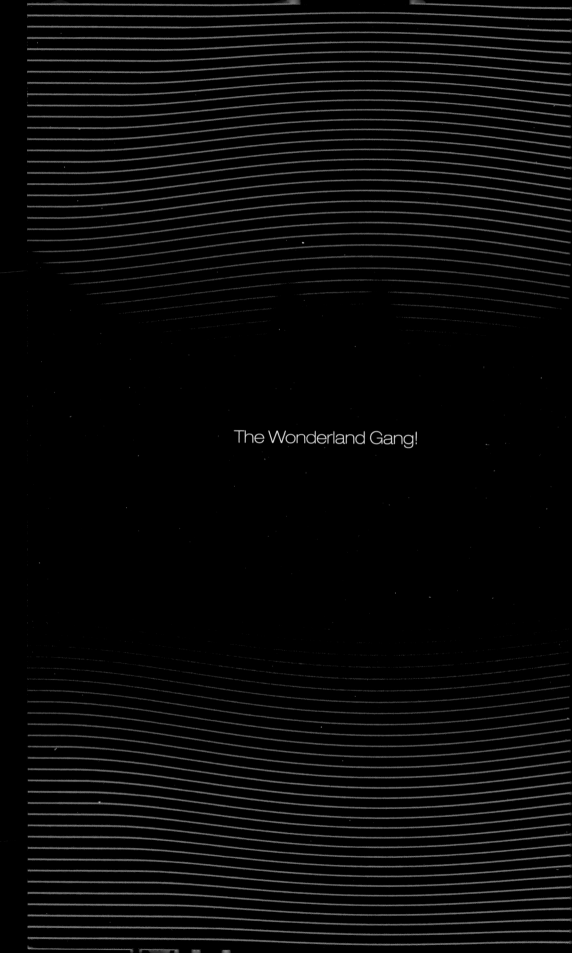

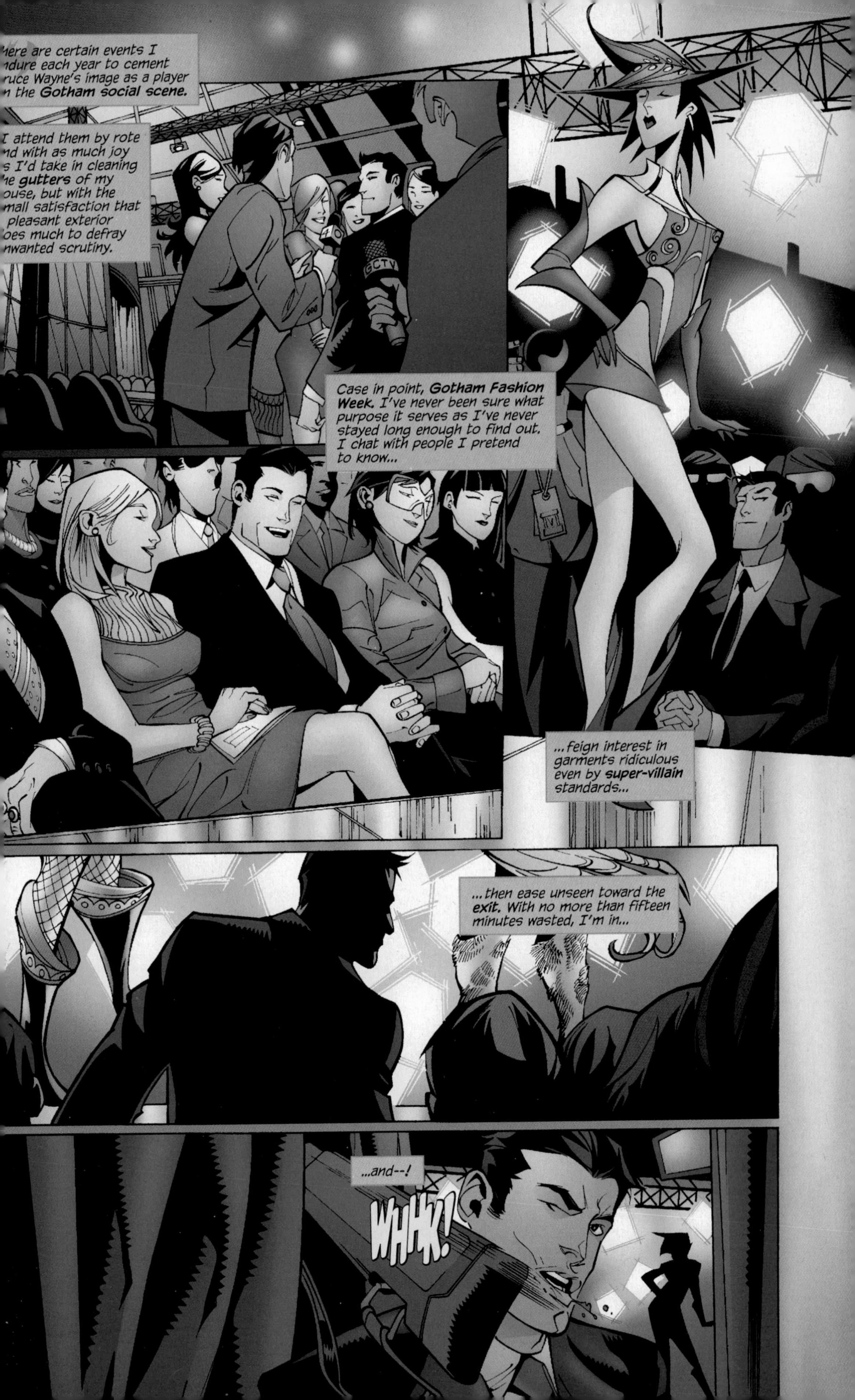
here are certain events I
ndure each year to cement
ruce Wayne's image as a player
n the Gotham social scene.
I attend them by rote
nd with as much joy
s I'd take in cleaning
he gutters of my
ouse, but with the
mall satisfaction that
pleasant exterior
oes much to defray
nwanted scrutiny.
GCTV
Case in point, Gotham Fashion Week. I've never been sure what purpose it serves as I've never stayed long enough to find out. I chat with people I pretend to know...
...feign interest in garments ridiculous even by super-villain standards...
...then ease unseen toward the exit. With no more than fifteen minutes wasted, I'm in...
...and--!
WHHK!

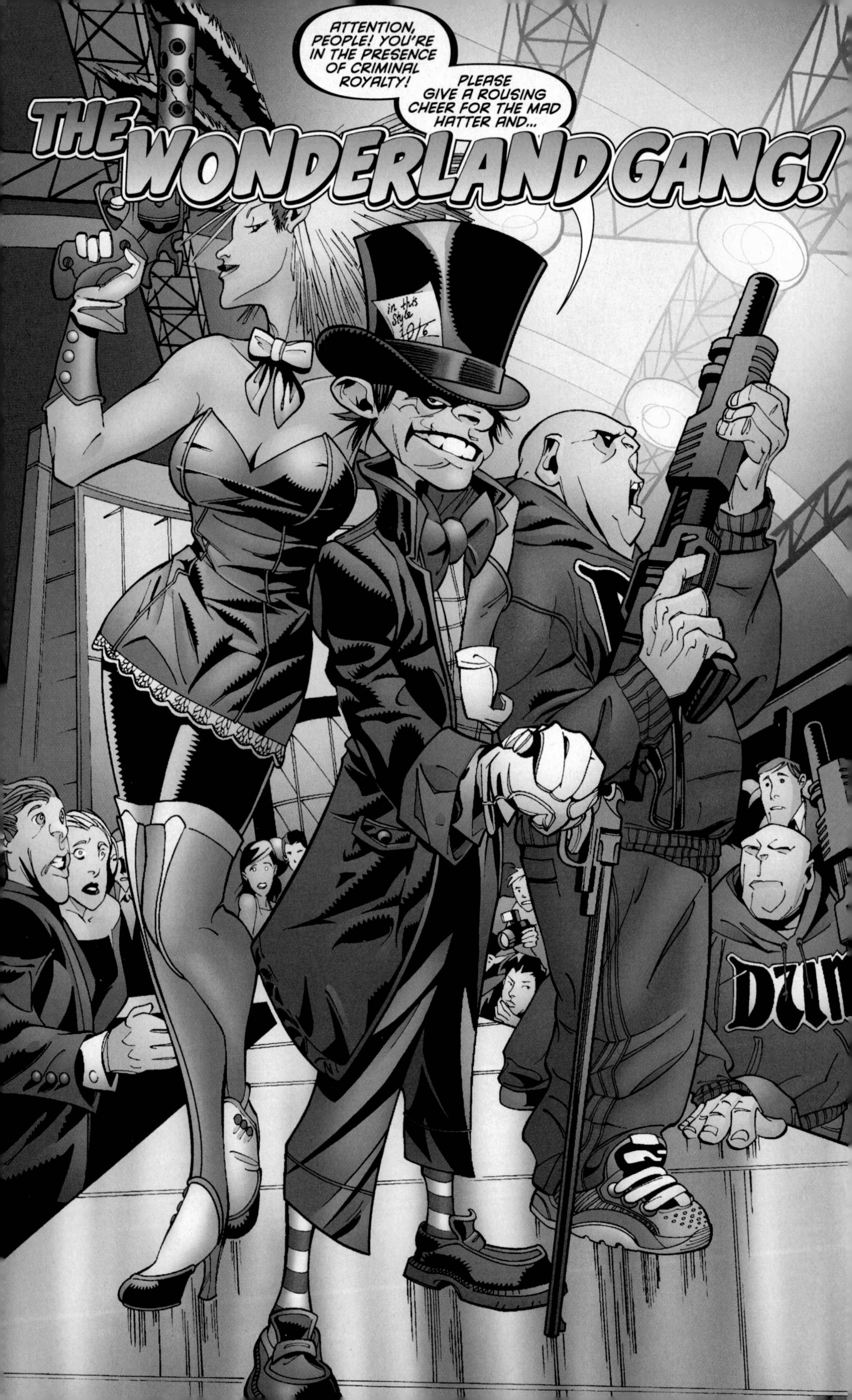
ATTENTION, PEOPLE! YOU'RE IN THE PRESENCE OF CRIMINAL ROYALTY!
PLEASE GIVE A ROUSING CHEER FOR THE MAD HATTER AND...
THE WONDERLAND GANG!
in this Style 10/6

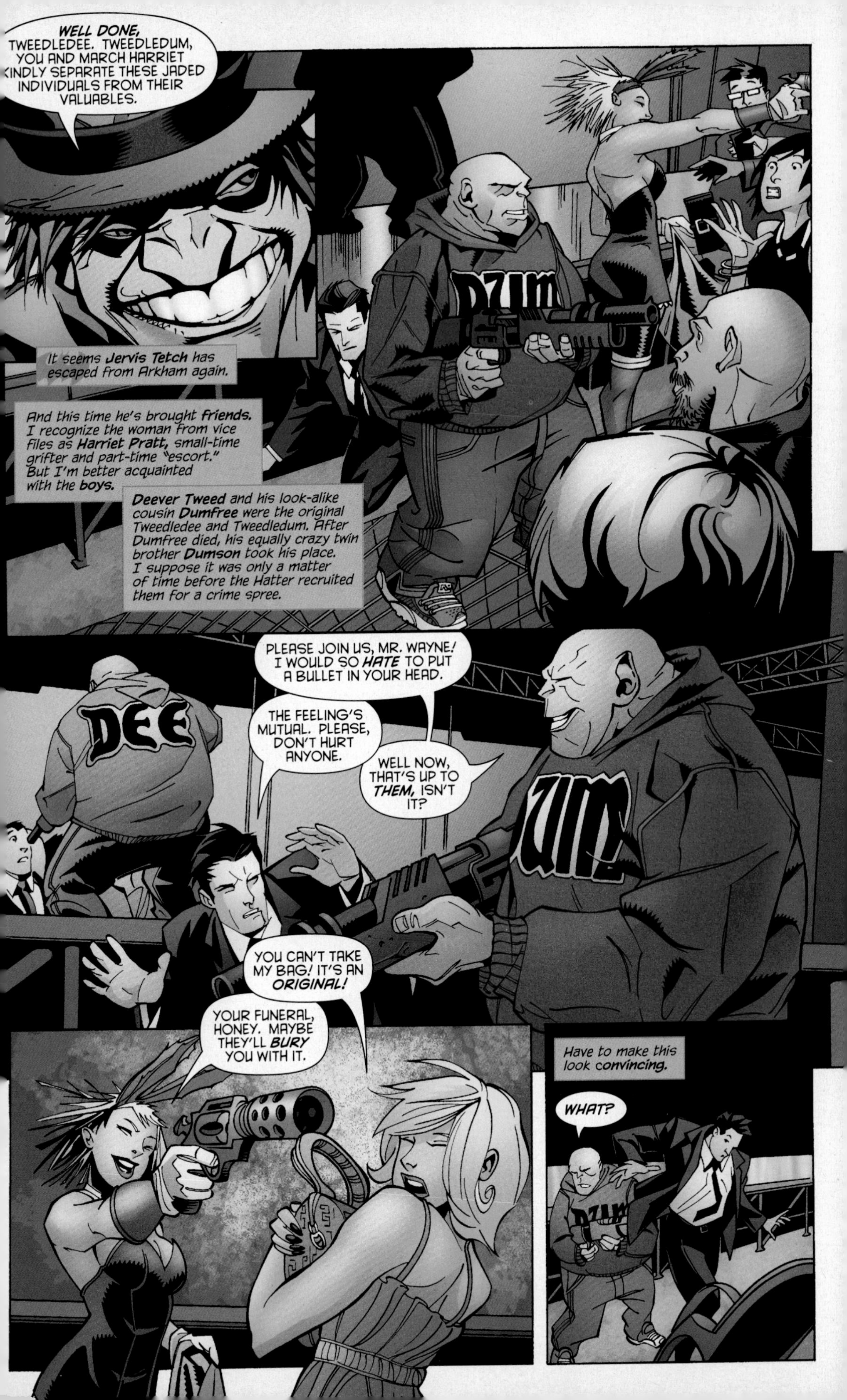

WELL DONE, TWEEDLEDEE. TWEEDLEDUM, YOU AND MARCH HARRIET KINDLY SEPARATE THESE JADED INDIVIDUALS FROM THEIR VALUABLES.
DUM
It seems Jervis Tetch has escaped from Arkham again.
And this time he's brought friends. I recognize the woman from vice files as Harriet Pratt, small-time grifter and part-time "escort." But I'm better acquainted with the boys.
Deever Tweed and his look-alike cousin Dumfree were the original Tweedledee and Tweedledum. After Dumfree died, his equally crazy twin brother Dumson took his place. I suppose it was only a matter of time before the Hatter recruited them for a crime spree.
DEE
PLEASE JOIN US, MR. WAYNE! I WOULD SO HATE TO PUT A BULLET IN YOUR HEAD.
THE FEELING'S MUTUAL. PLEASE, DON'T HURT ANYONE.
WELL NOW, THAT'S UP TO THEM, ISN'T IT?
DUM
YOU CAN'T TAKE MY BAG! IT'S AN ORIGINAL!
YOUR FUNERAL, HONEY. MAYBE THEY'LL BURY YOU WITH IT.
Have to make this look convincing.
WHAT?

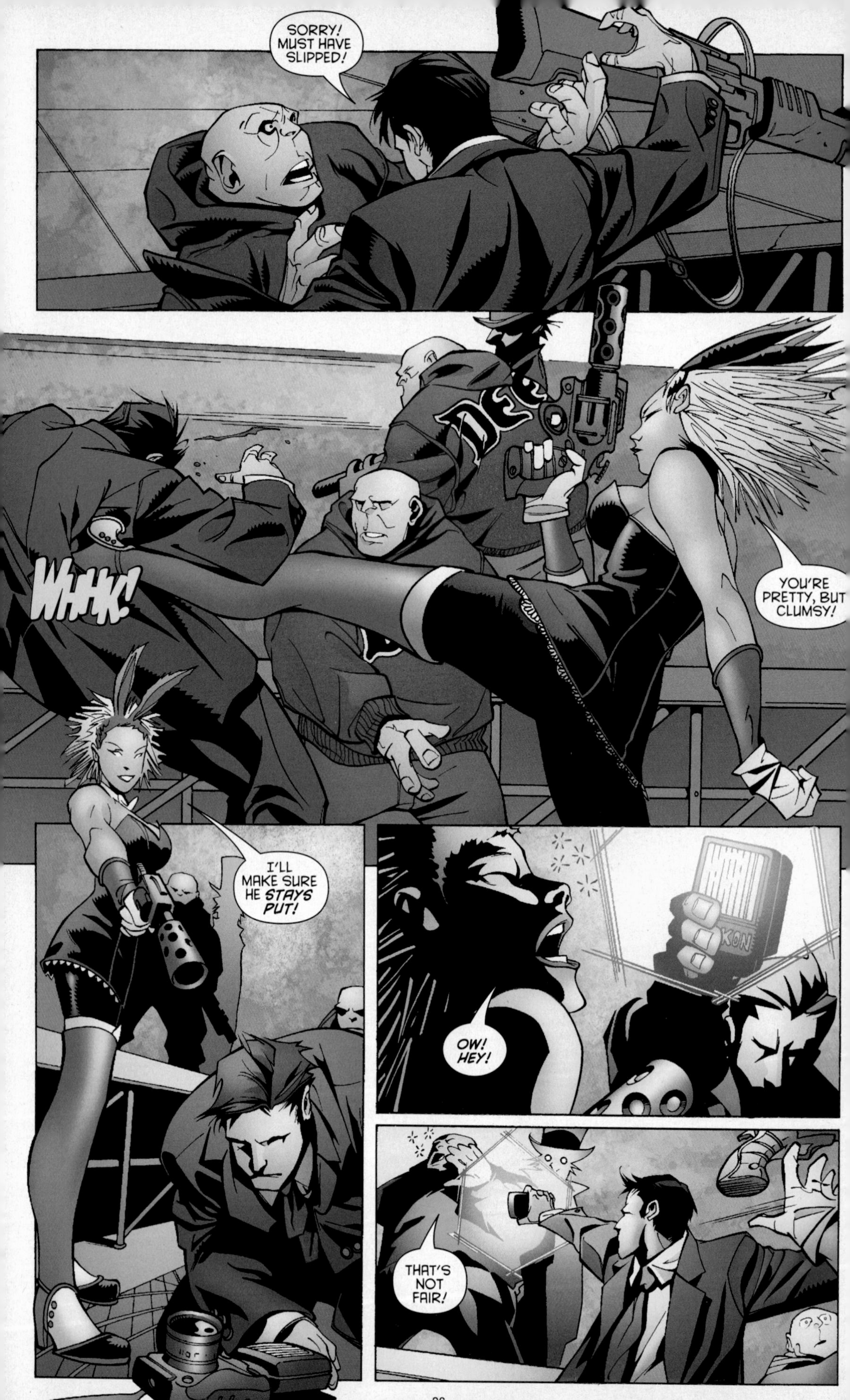
SORRY! MUST HAVE SLIPPED!
WHHK!
YOU'RE PRETTY, BUT CLUMSY!
I'LL MAKE SURE HE STAYS PUT!
OW! HEY!
THAT'S NOT FAIR!

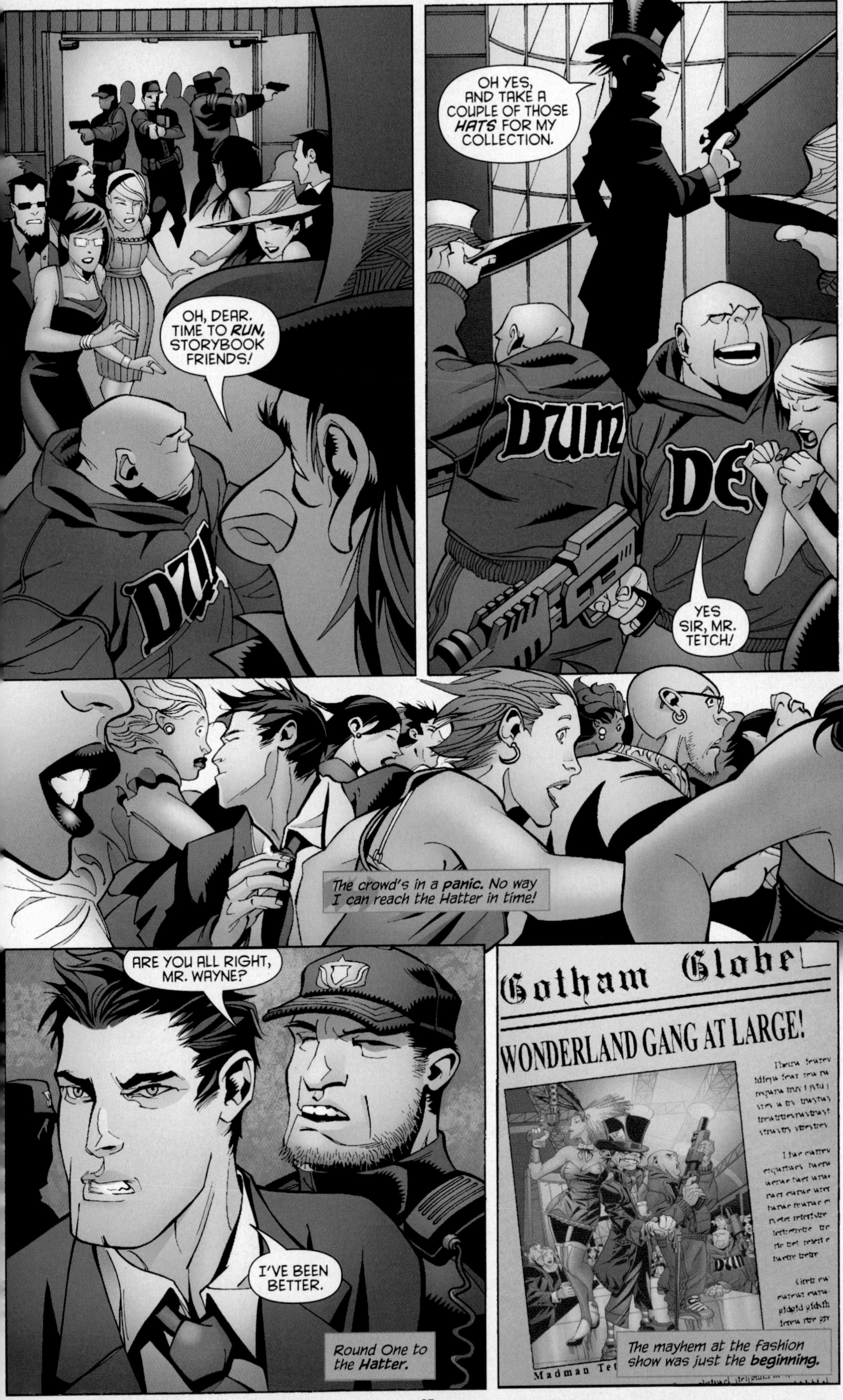

OH, DEAR. TIME TO *RUN*, STORYBOOK FRIENDS!
OH YES, AND TAKE A COUPLE OF THOSE *HATS* FOR MY COLLECTION.
YES SIR, MR. TETCH!
The crowd's in a **panic.** No way I can reach the Hatter in time!
ARE YOU ALL RIGHT, MR. WAYNE?
I'VE BEEN BETTER.
Round One to the **Hatter.**
Gotham Globe
WONDERLAND GANG AT LARGE!
The mayhem at the fashion show was just the **beginning.**

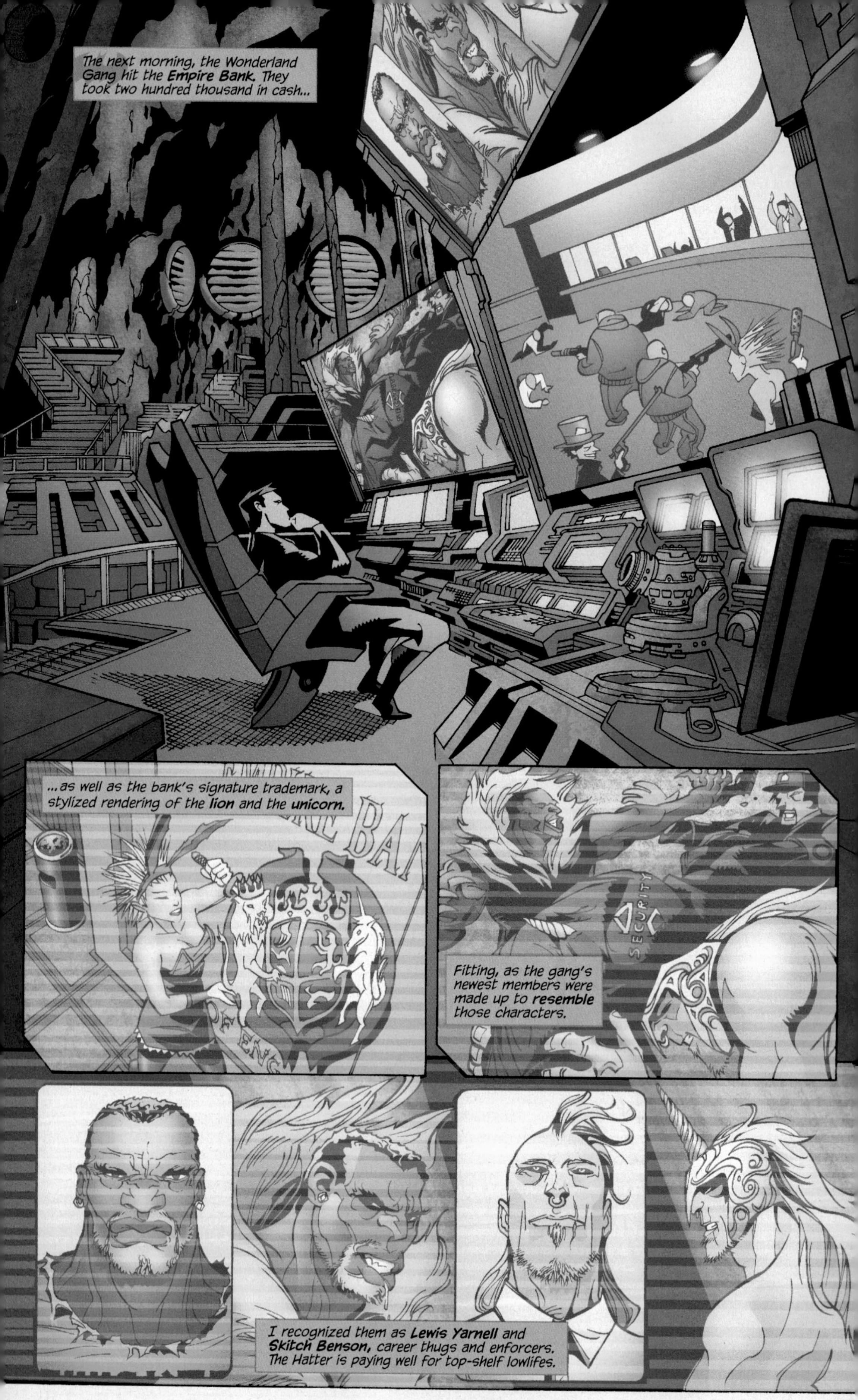
The next morning, the Wonderland Gang hit the Empire Bank. They took two hundred thousand in cash...
...as well as the bank's signature trademark, a stylized rendering of the lion and the unicorn.
SECURITY
Fitting, as the gang's newest members were made up to resemble those characters.
I recognized them as Lewis Yarnell and Skitch Benson, career thugs and enforcers. The Hatter is paying well for top-shelf lowlifes.

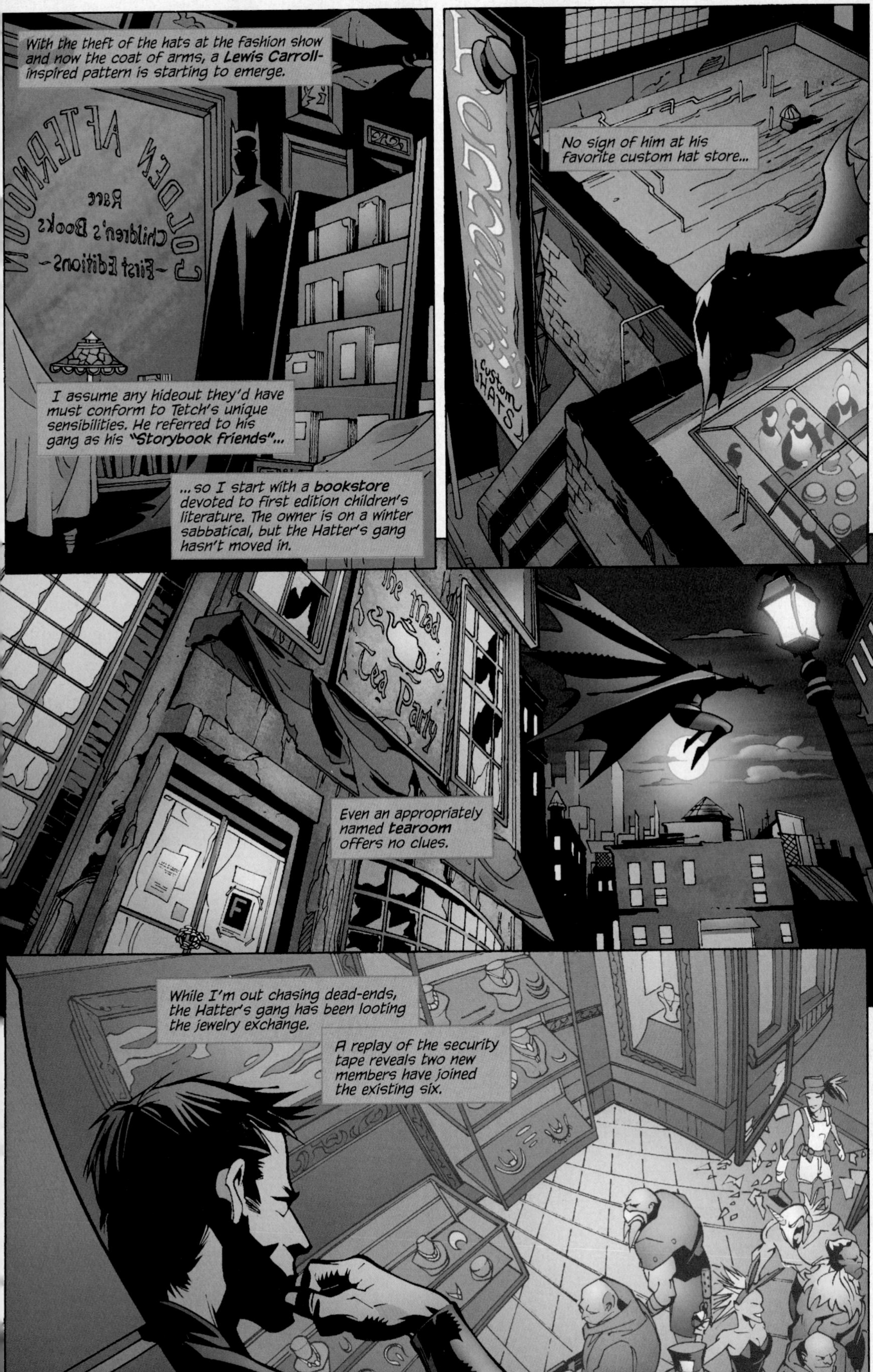

With the theft of the hats at the fashion show and now the coat of arms, a Lewis Carroll-inspired pattern is starting to emerge.
GOLDEN AFTERNOON
Rare
Children's Books
~First Editions~
I assume any hideout they'd have must conform to Tetch's unique sensibilities. He referred to his gang as his "Storybook friends"...
...so I start with a bookstore devoted to first edition children's literature. The owner is on a winter sabbatical, but the Hatter's gang hasn't moved in.
No sign of him at his favorite custom hat store...
Custom HATS
The Mad Tea Party
Even an appropriately named tearoom offers no clues.
While I'm out chasing dead-ends, the Hatter's gang has been looting the jewelry exchange.
A replay of the security tape reveals two new members have joined the existing six.

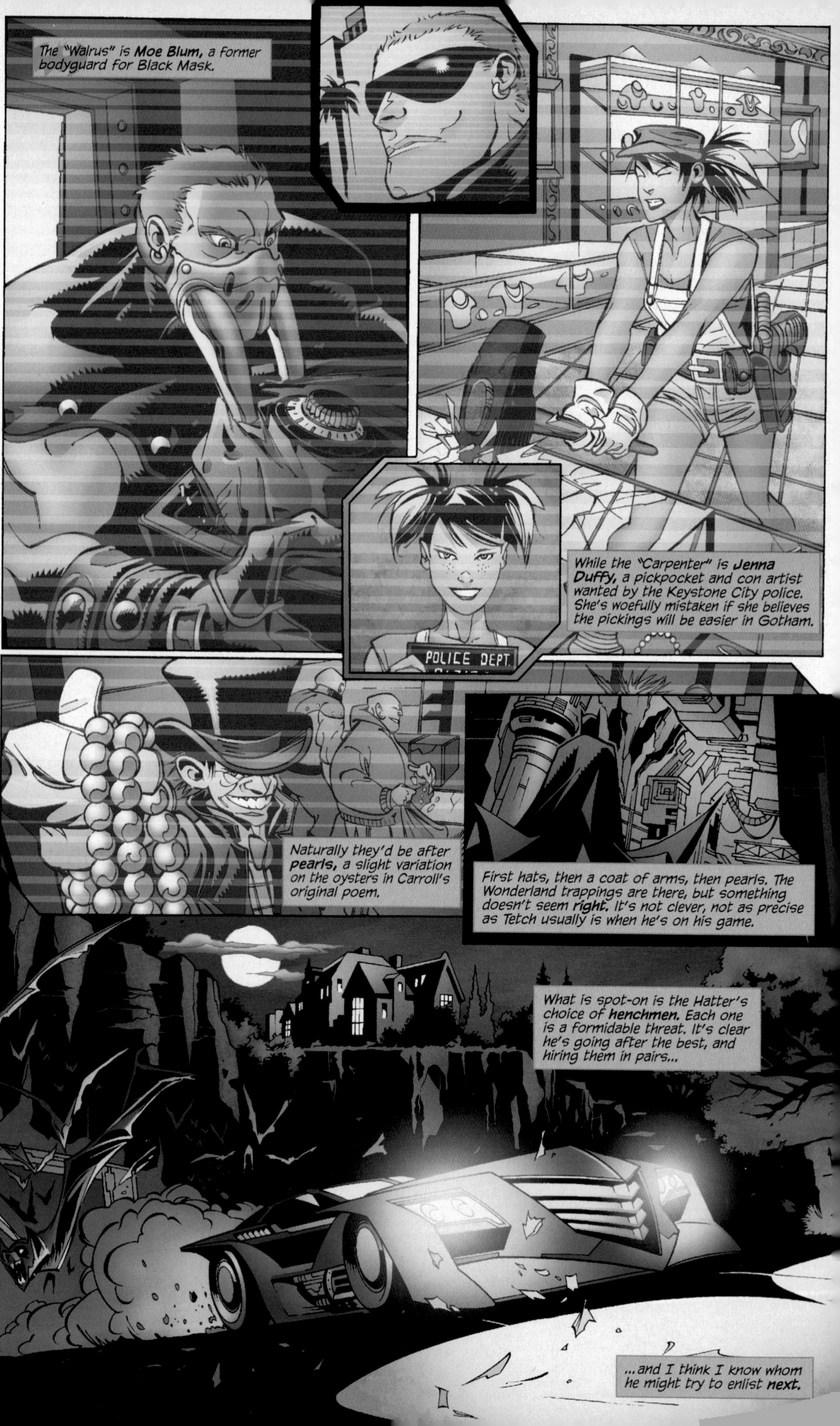
The "Walrus" is Moe Blum, a former bodyguard for Black Mask.
POLICE DEPT.
While the "Carpenter" is Jenna Duffy, a pickpocket and con artist wanted by the Keystone City police. She's woefully mistaken if she believes the pickings will be easier in Gotham.
Naturally they'd be after pearls, a slight variation on the oysters in Carroll's original poem.
First hats, then a coat of arms, then pearls. The Wonderland trappings are there, but something doesn't seem right. It's not clever, not as precise as Tetch usually is when he's on his game.
What is spot-on is the Hatter's choice of henchmen. Each one is a formidable threat. It's clear he's going after the best, and hiring them in pairs...
...and I think I know whom he might try to enlist next.

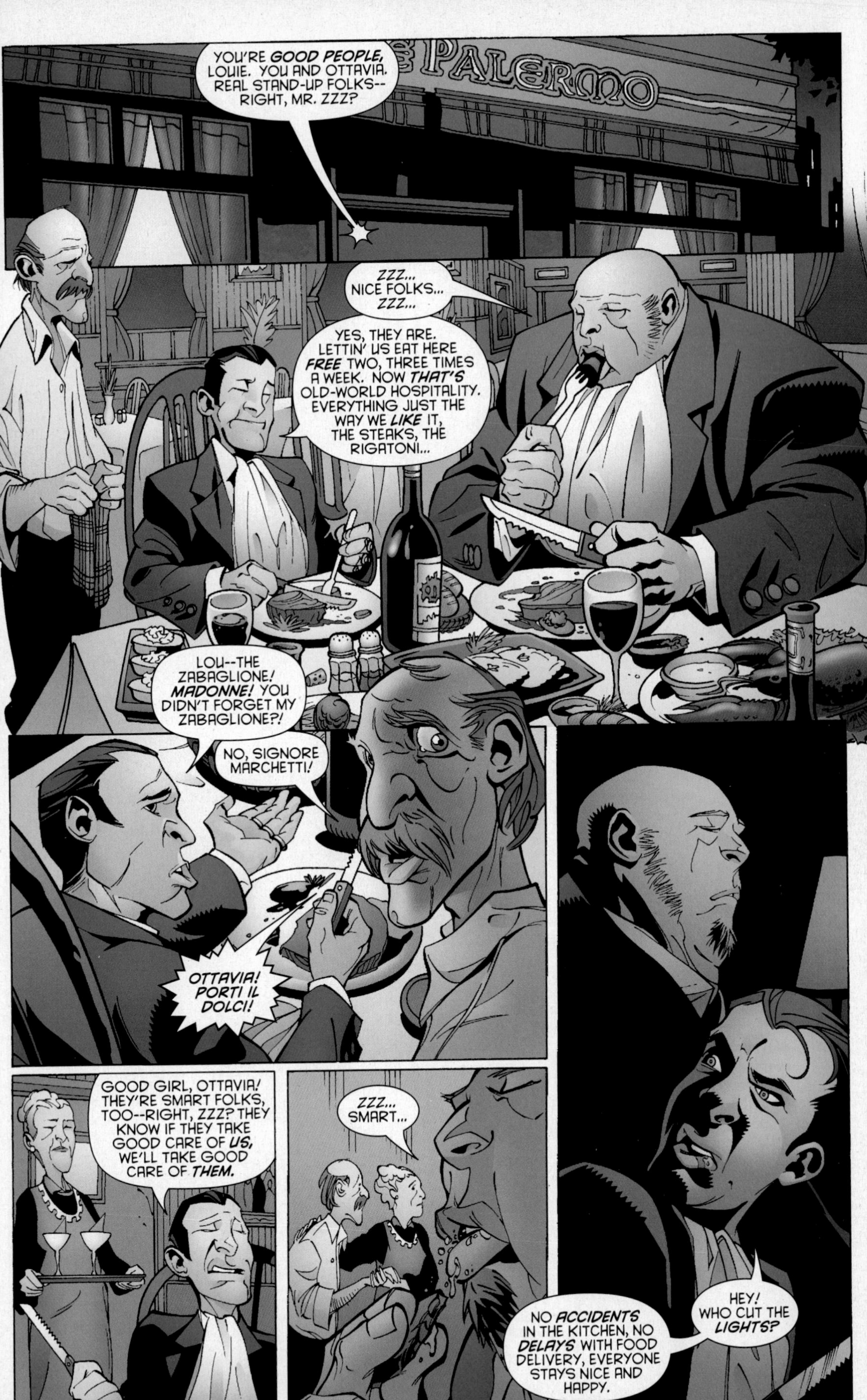
YOU'RE GOOD PEOPLE, LOUIE. YOU AND OTTAVIA. REAL STAND-UP FOLKS-- RIGHT, MR. ZZZ?
PALERMO
ZZZ... NICE FOLKS... ZZZ...
YES, THEY ARE. LETTIN' US EAT HERE FREE TWO, THREE TIMES A WEEK. NOW THAT'S OLD-WORLD HOSPITALITY. EVERYTHING JUST THE WAY WE LIKE IT, THE STEAKS, THE RIGATONI...
LOU--THE ZABAGLIONE! MADONNE! YOU DIDN'T FORGET MY ZABAGLIONE?!
NO, SIGNORE MARCHETTI!
OTTAVIA! PORTI IL DOLCI!
GOOD GIRL, OTTAVIA! THEY'RE SMART FOLKS, TOO--RIGHT, ZZZ? THEY KNOW IF THEY TAKE GOOD CARE OF US, WE'LL TAKE GOOD CARE OF THEM.
ZZZ... SMART...
NO ACCIDENTS IN THE KITCHEN, NO DELAYS WITH FOOD DELIVERY, EVERYONE STAYS NICE AND HAPPY.
HEY! WHO CUT THE LIGHTS?

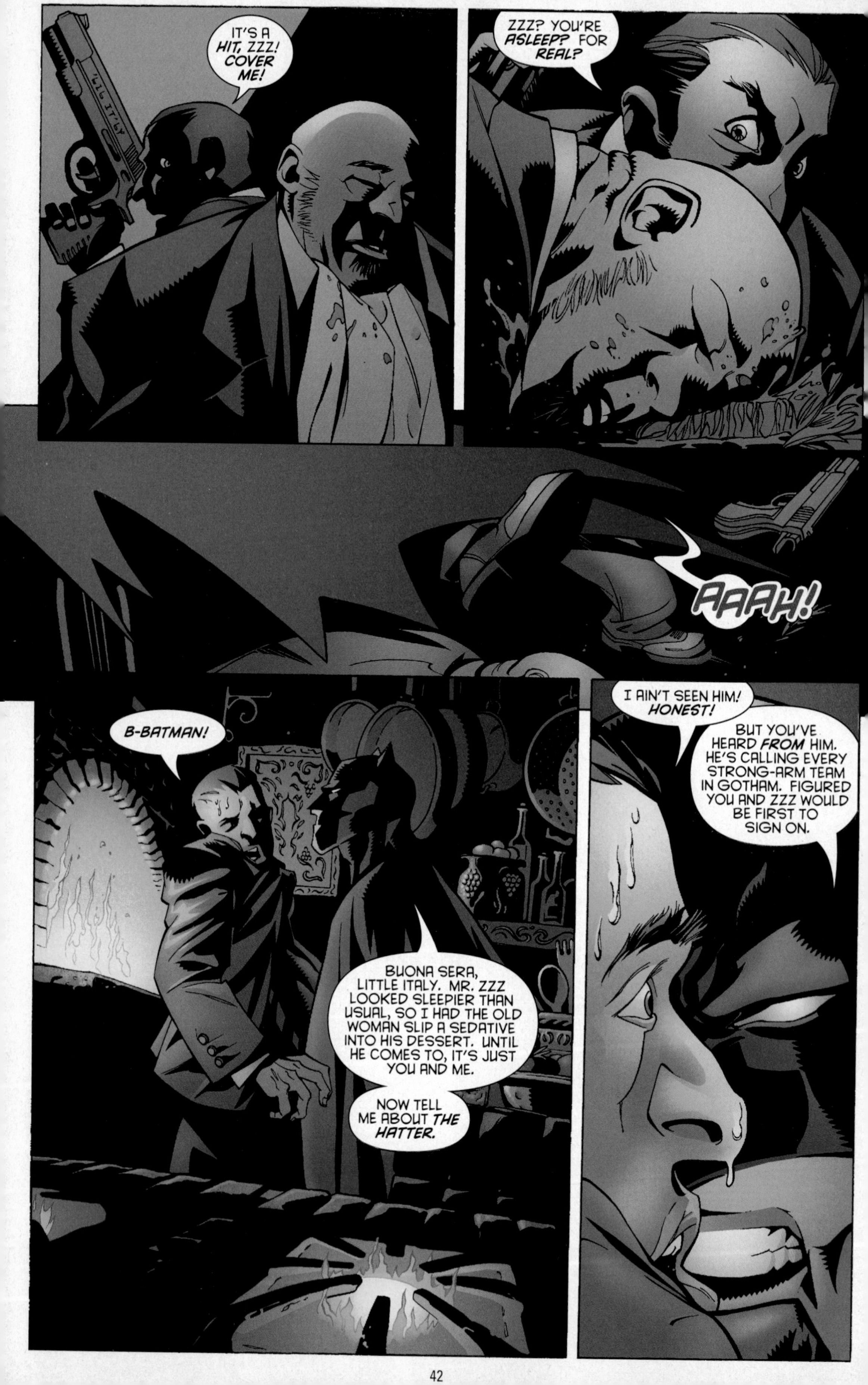
IT'S A HIT, ZZZ! COVER ME!
ZZZ? YOU'RE ASLEEP? FOR REAL?
AAAH!
B-BATMAN!
BUONA SERA, LITTLE ITALY. MR. ZZZ LOOKED SLEEPIER THAN USUAL, SO I HAD THE OLD WOMAN SLIP A SEDATIVE INTO HIS DESSERT. UNTIL HE COMES TO, IT'S JUST YOU AND ME.
NOW TELL ME ABOUT THE HATTER.
I AIN'T SEEN HIM! HONEST!
BUT YOU'VE HEARD FROM HIM. HE'S CALLING EVERY STRONG-ARM TEAM IN GOTHAM. FIGURED YOU AND ZZZ WOULD BE FIRST TO SIGN ON.

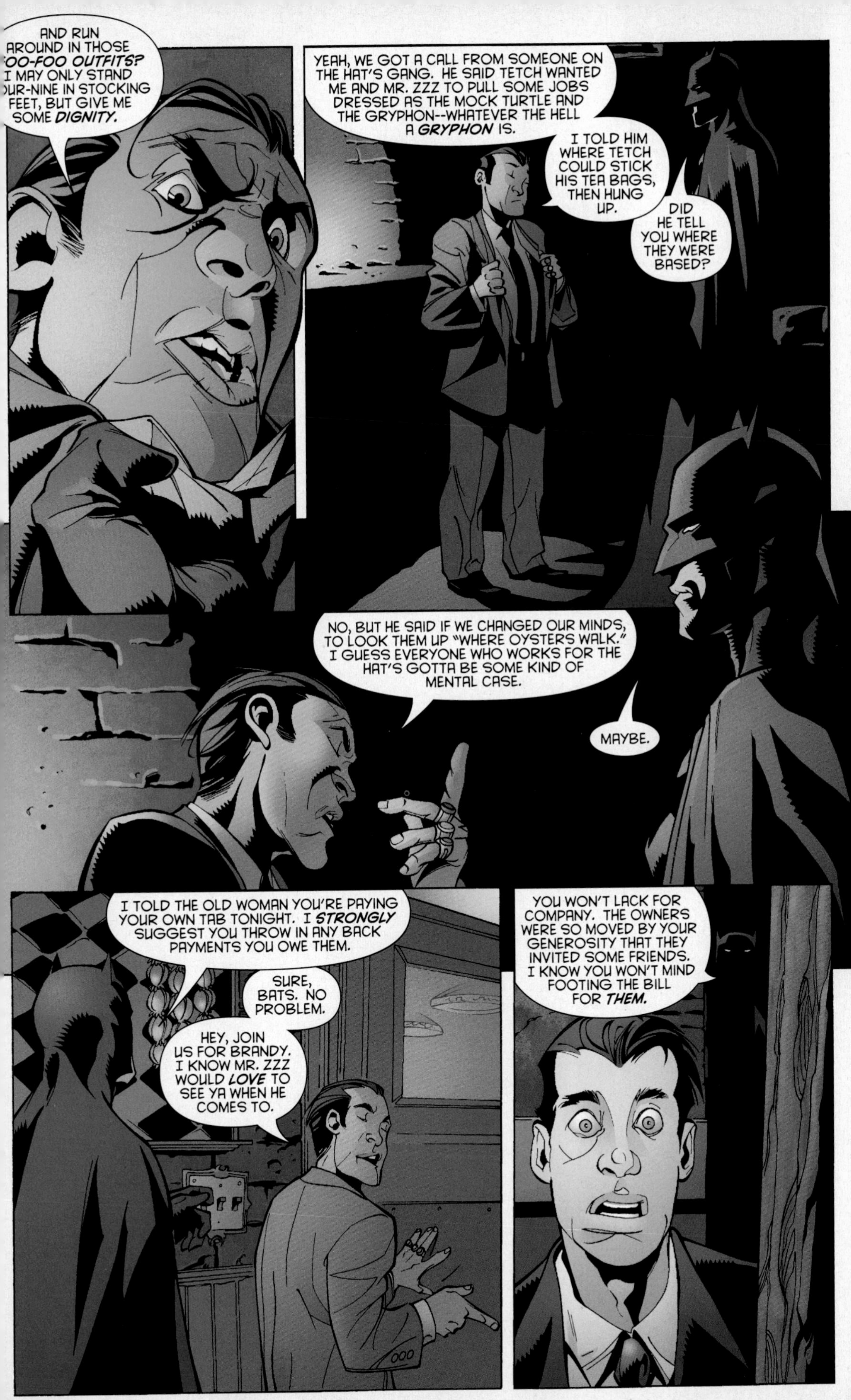

AND RUN AROUND IN THOSE FOO-FOO OUTFITS? I MAY ONLY STAND FOUR-NINE IN STOCKING FEET, BUT GIVE ME SOME DIGNITY.
YEAH, WE GOT A CALL FROM SOMEONE ON THE HAT'S GANG. HE SAID TETCH WANTED ME AND MR. ZZZ TO PULL SOME JOBS DRESSED AS THE MOCK TURTLE AND THE GRYPHON--WHATEVER THE HELL A GRYPHON IS.
I TOLD HIM WHERE TETCH COULD STICK HIS TEA BAGS, THEN HUNG UP.
DID HE TELL YOU WHERE THEY WERE BASED?
NO, BUT HE SAID IF WE CHANGED OUR MINDS, TO LOOK THEM UP "WHERE OYSTERS WALK." I GUESS EVERYONE WHO WORKS FOR THE HAT'S GOTTA BE SOME KIND OF MENTAL CASE.
MAYBE.
I TOLD THE OLD WOMAN YOU'RE PAYING YOUR OWN TAB TONIGHT. I STRONGLY SUGGEST YOU THROW IN ANY BACK PAYMENTS YOU OWE THEM.
SURE, BATS. NO PROBLEM.
HEY, JOIN US FOR BRANDY. I KNOW MR. ZZZ WOULD LOVE TO SEE YA WHEN HE COMES TO.
YOU WON'T LACK FOR COMPANY. THE OWNERS WERE SO MOVED BY YOUR GENEROSITY THAT THEY INVITED SOME FRIENDS. I KNOW YOU WON'T MIND FOOTING THE BILL FOR THEM.

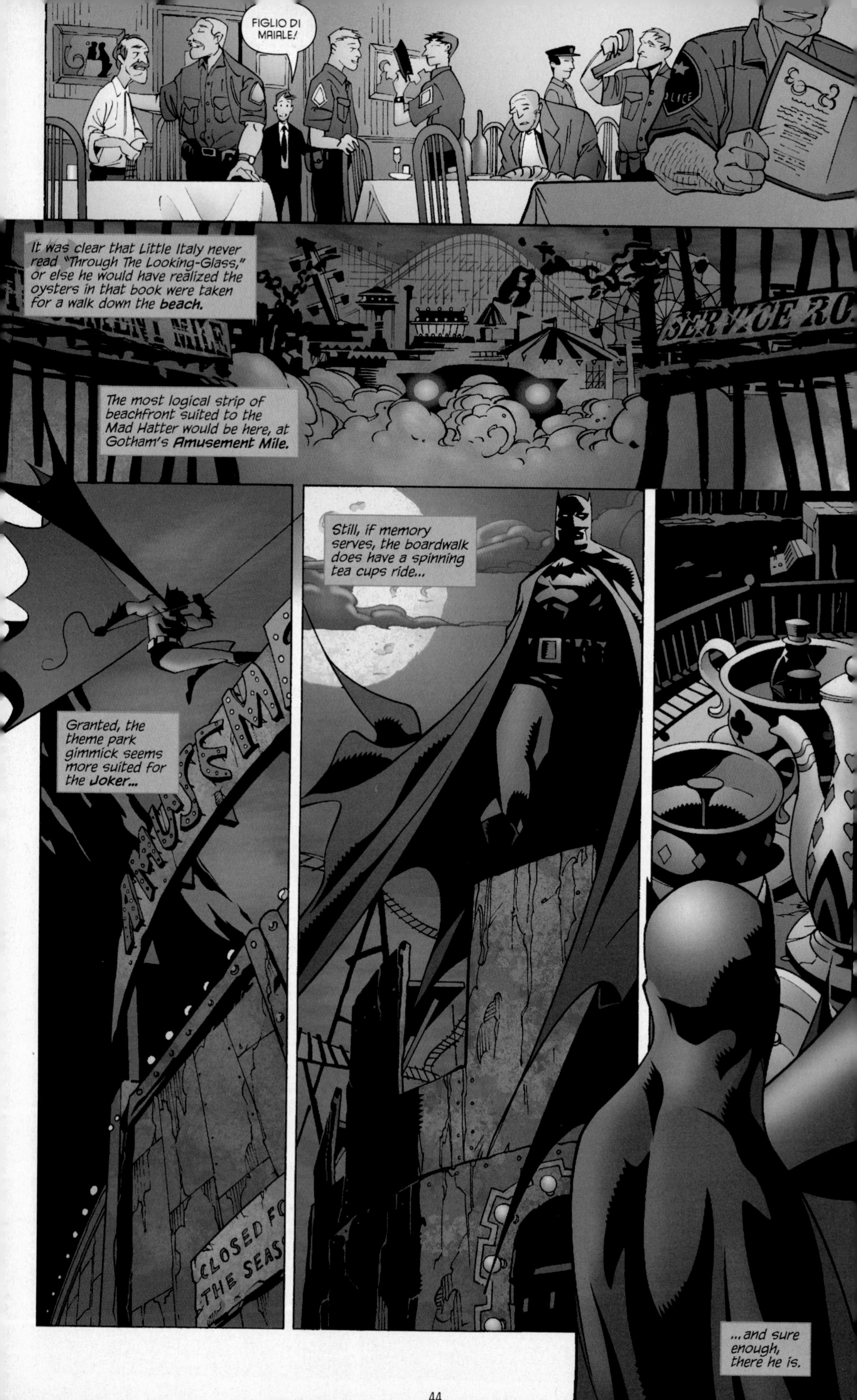

FIGLIO DI MAIALE!
It was clear that Little Italy never read "Through The Looking-Glass," or else he would have realized the oysters in that book were taken for a walk down the beach.
SERVICE RO
The most logical strip of beachfront suited to the Mad Hatter would be here, at Gotham's Amusement Mile.
Granted, the theme park gimmick seems more suited for the Joker...
CLOSED FO THE SEAS
Still, if memory serves, the boardwalk does have a spinning tea cups ride...
...and sure enough, there he is.

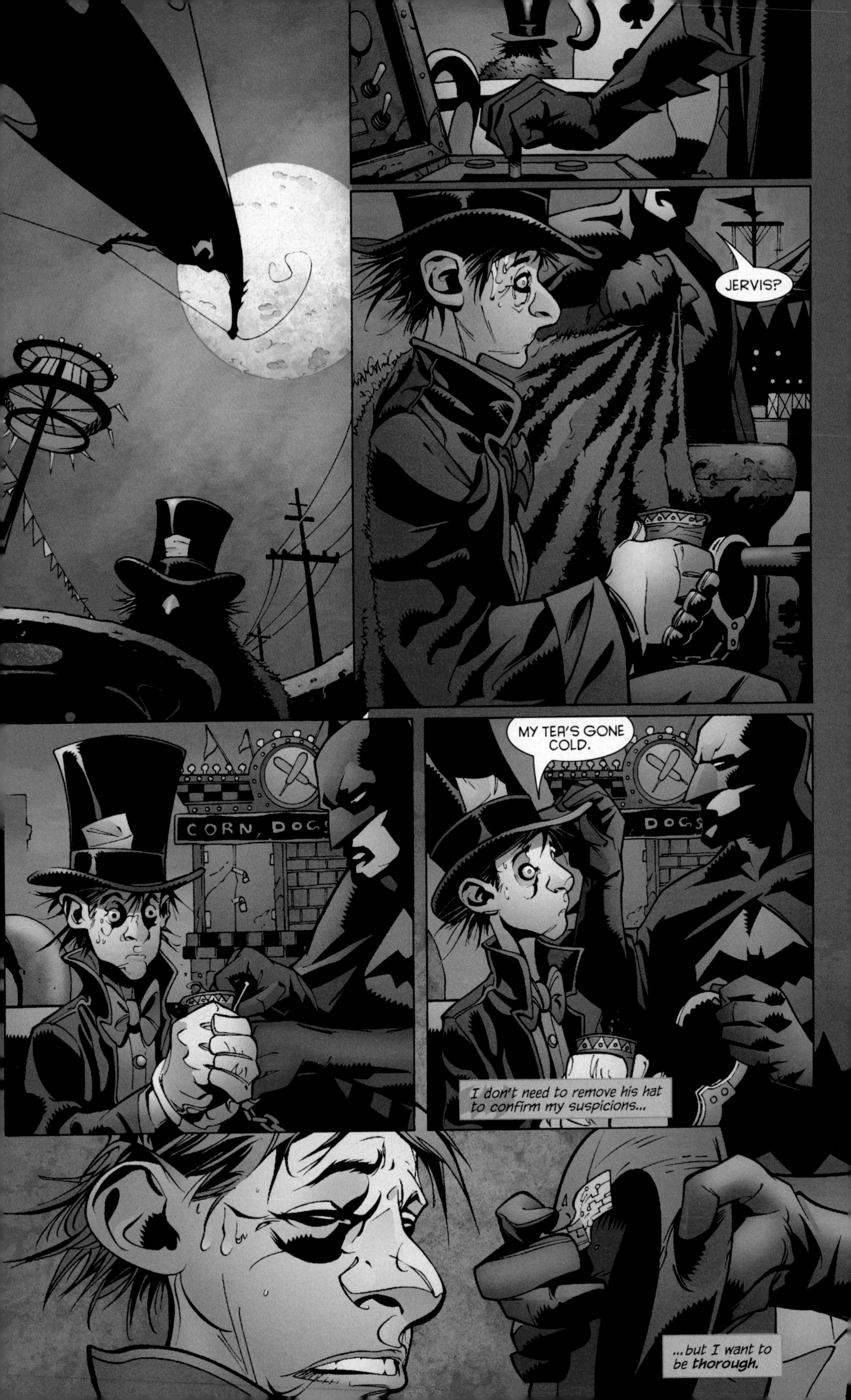
JERVIS?
CORN DOGS
MY TEA'S GONE COLD.
DOGS
I don't need to remove his hat to confirm my suspicions...
...but I want to be **thorough.**

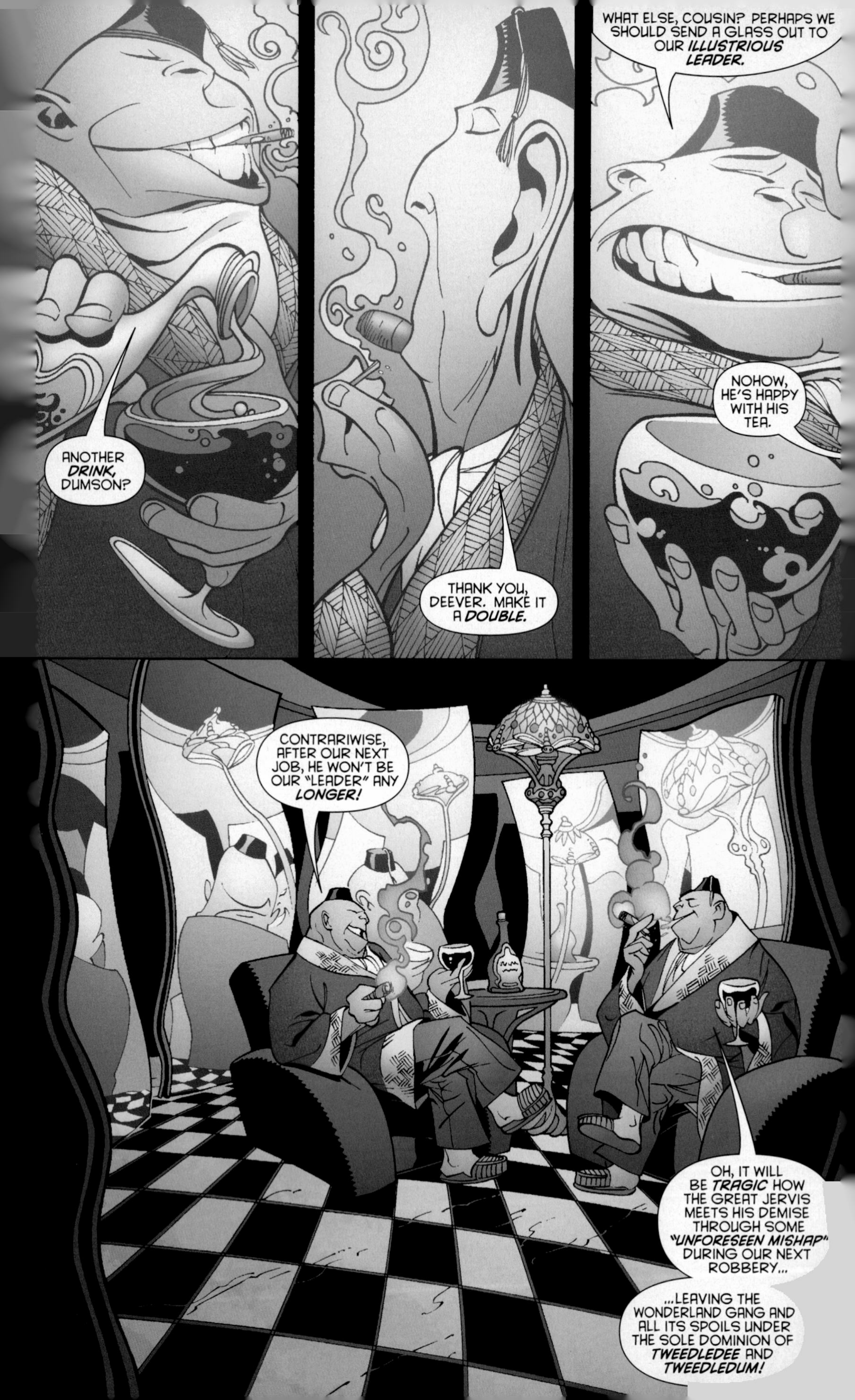
ANOTHER DRINK, DUMSON?
THANK YOU, DEEVER. MAKE IT A DOUBLE.
WHAT ELSE, COUSIN? PERHAPS WE SHOULD SEND A GLASS OUT TO OUR ILLUSTRIOUS LEADER.
NOHOW, HE'S HAPPY WITH HIS TEA.
CONTRARIWISE, AFTER OUR NEXT JOB, HE WON'T BE OUR "LEADER" ANY LONGER!
OH, IT WILL BE TRAGIC HOW THE GREAT JERVIS MEETS HIS DEMISE THROUGH SOME "UNFORESEEN MISHAP" DURING OUR NEXT ROBBERY...
...LEAVING THE WONDERLAND GANG AND ALL ITS SPOILS UNDER THE SOLE DOMINION OF TWEEDLEDEE AND TWEEDLEDUM!

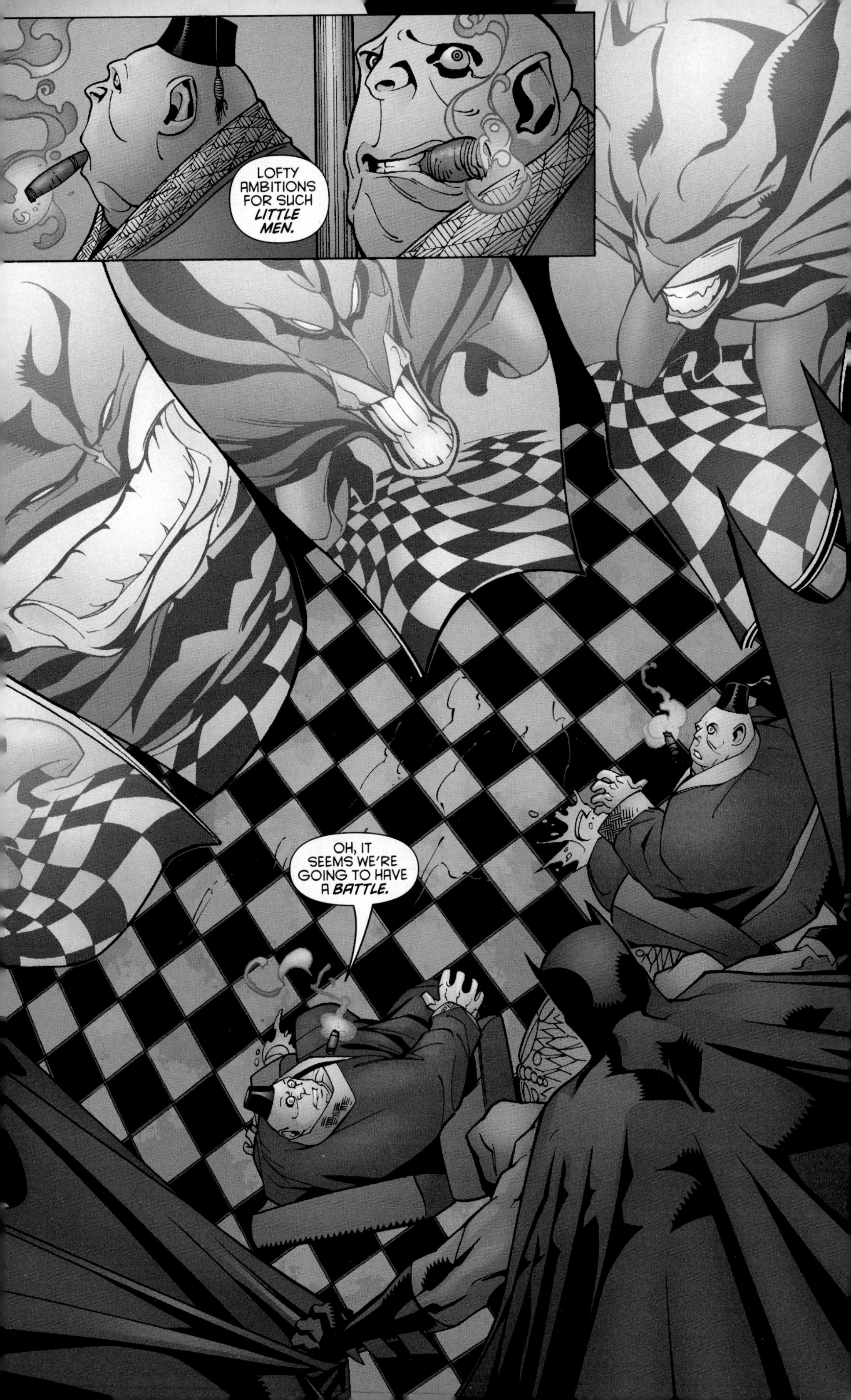
LOFTY AMBITIONS FOR SUCH LITTLE MEN.
OH, IT SEEMS WE'RE GOING TO HAVE A BATTLE.

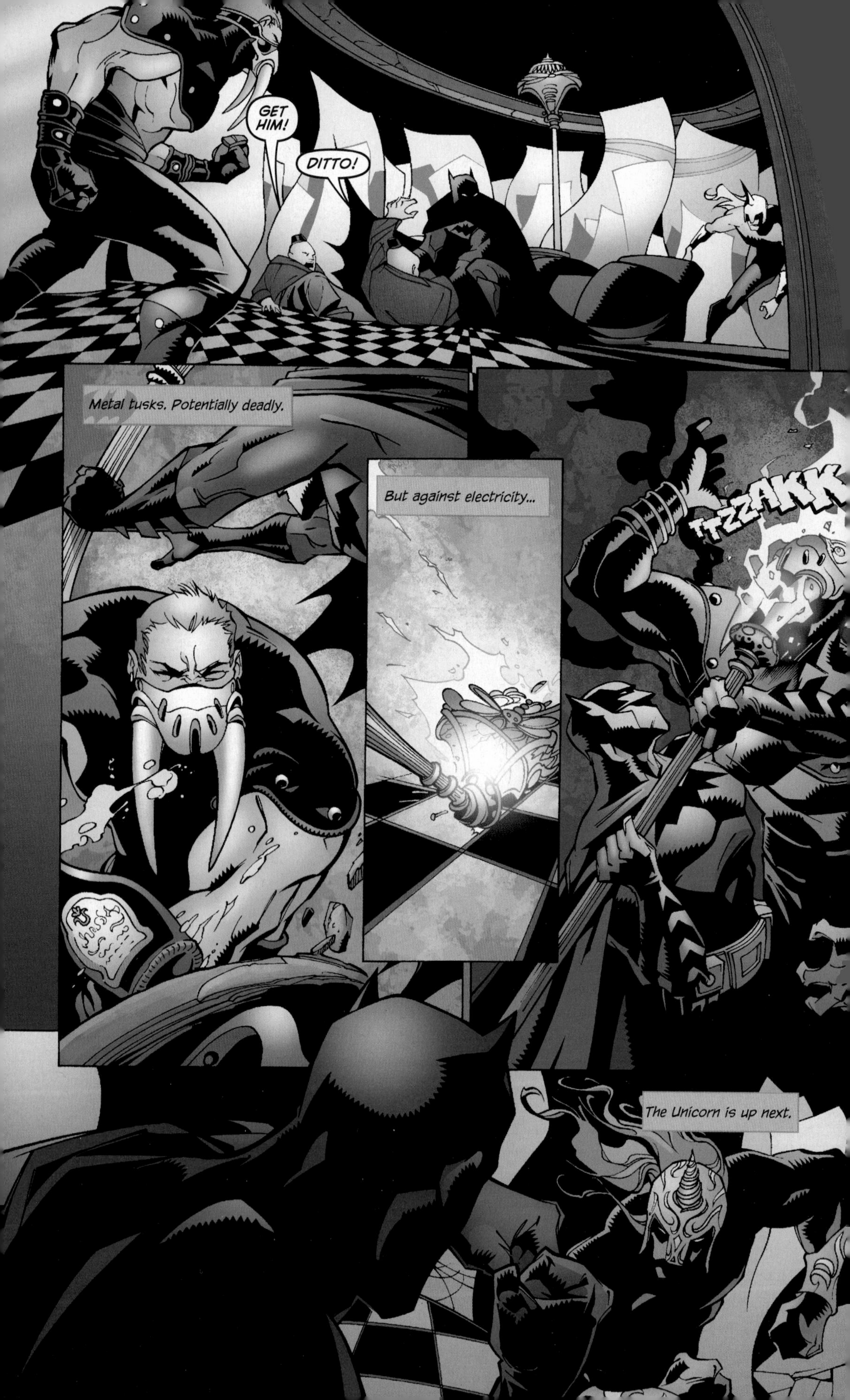
GET HIM!
DITTO!
Metal tusks. Potentially deadly.
But against electricity...
TTZZAKK
The Unicorn is up next.

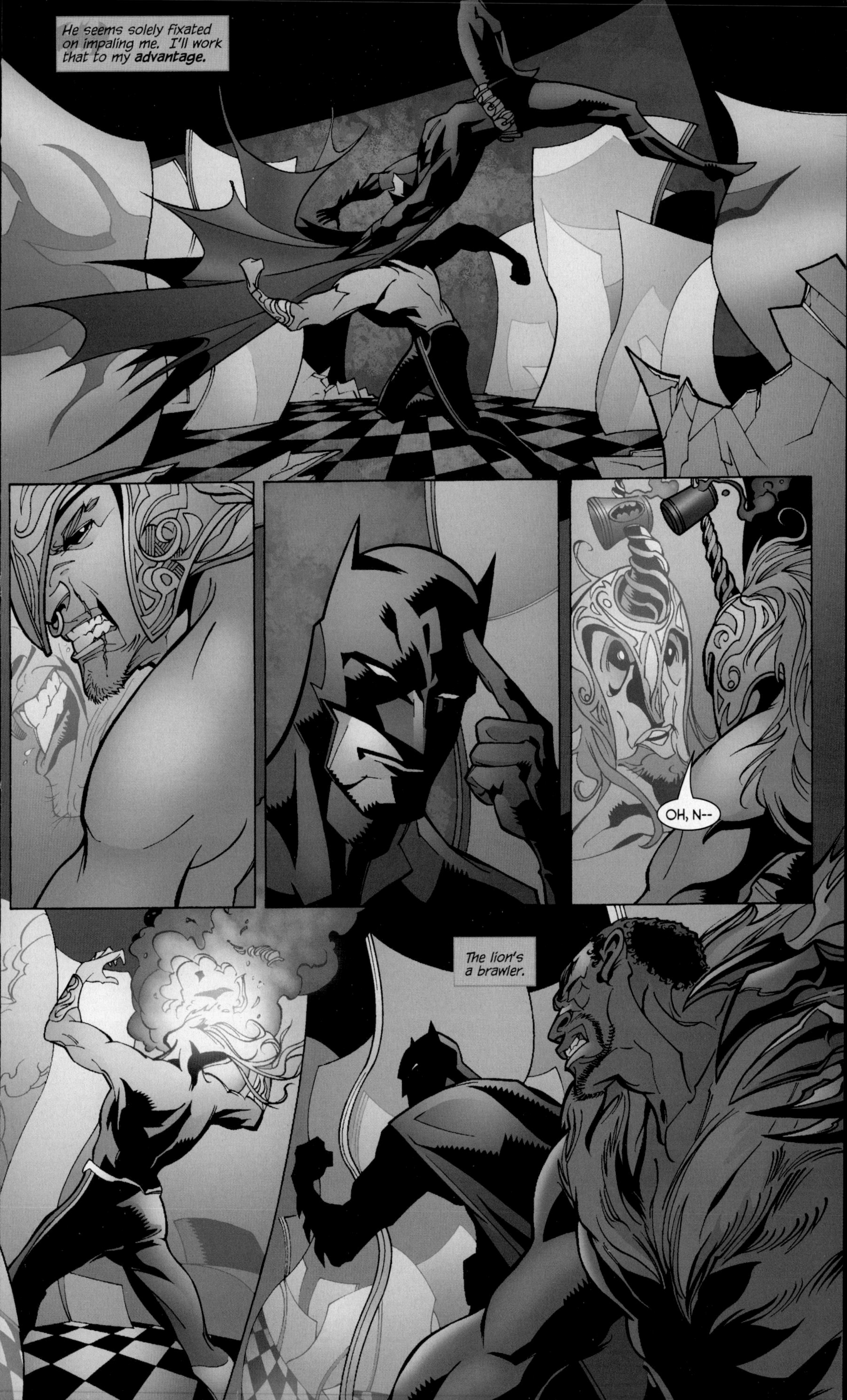
He seems solely fixated on impaling me. I'll work that to my **advantage.**
OH, N--
The lion's a brawler.

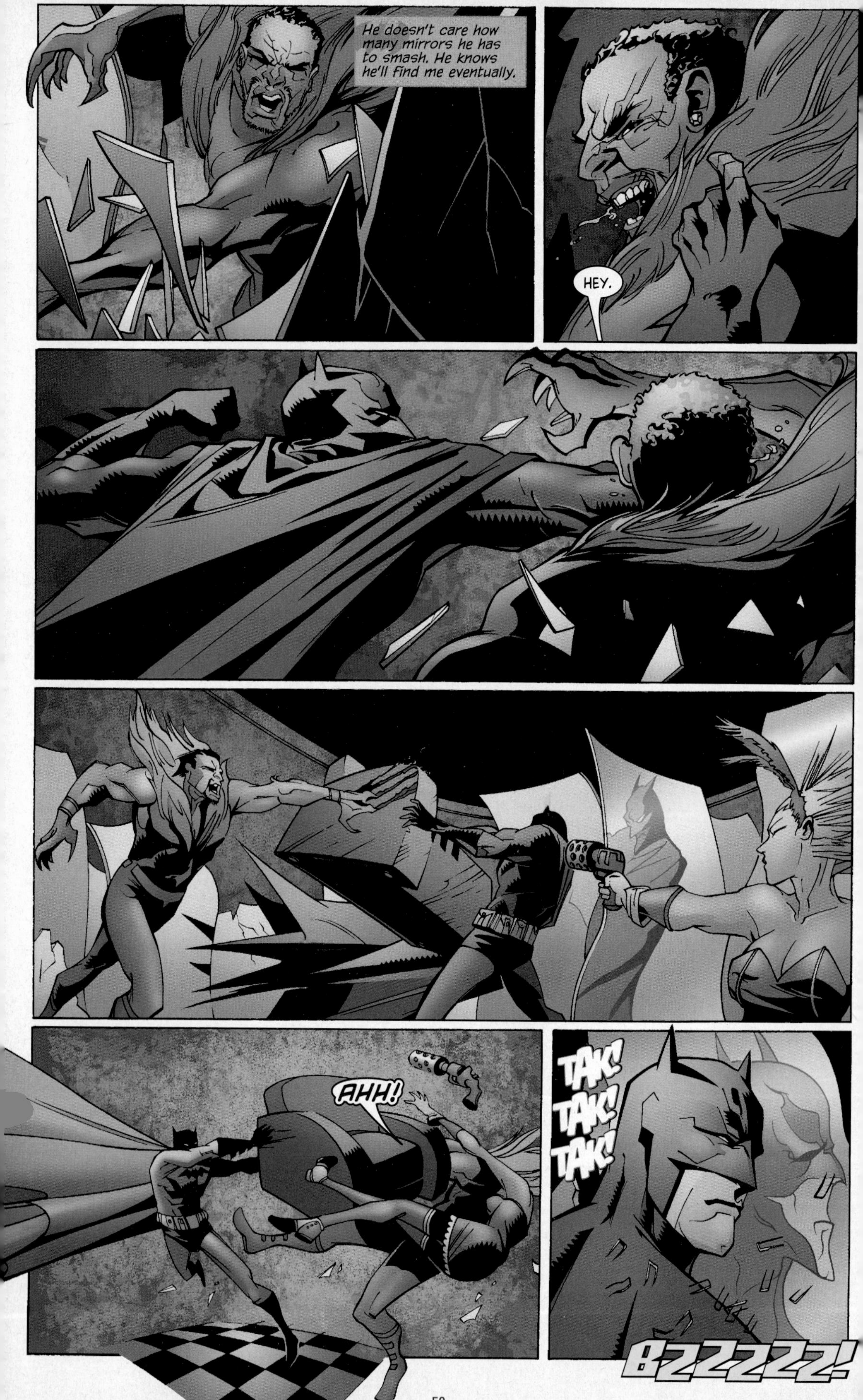
He doesn't care how many mirrors he has to smash. He knows he'll find me eventually.
HEY.
AHH!
TAK! TAK! TAK!
BZZZZZ!

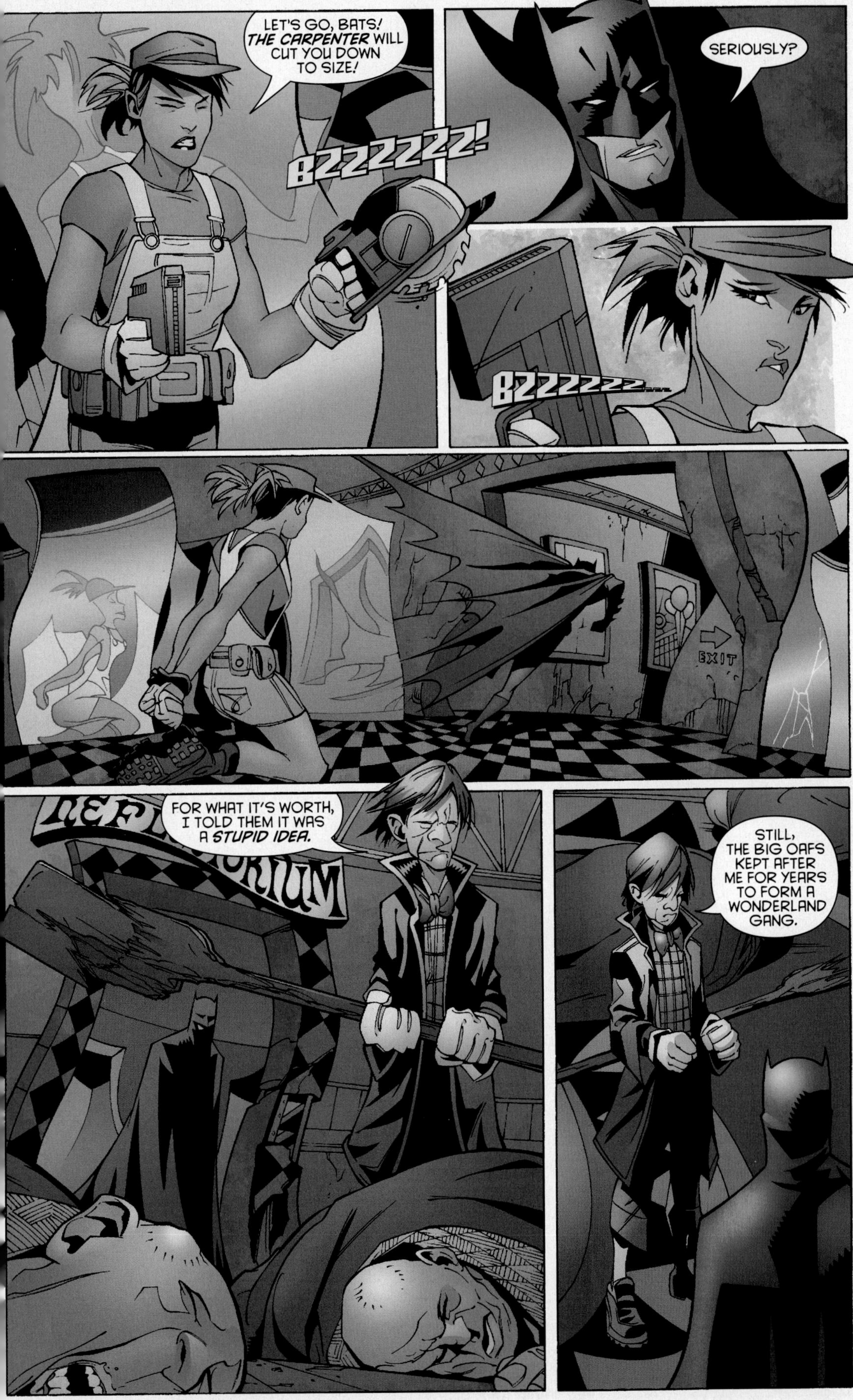
LET'S GO, BATS! THE CARPENTER WILL CUT YOU DOWN TO SIZE!
BZZZZZZZ!
SERIOUSLY?
BZZZZZZ...
EXIT
FOR WHAT IT'S WORTH, I TOLD THEM IT WAS A STUPID IDEA.
STILL, THE BIG OAFS KEPT AFTER ME FOR YEARS TO FORM A WONDERLAND GANG.

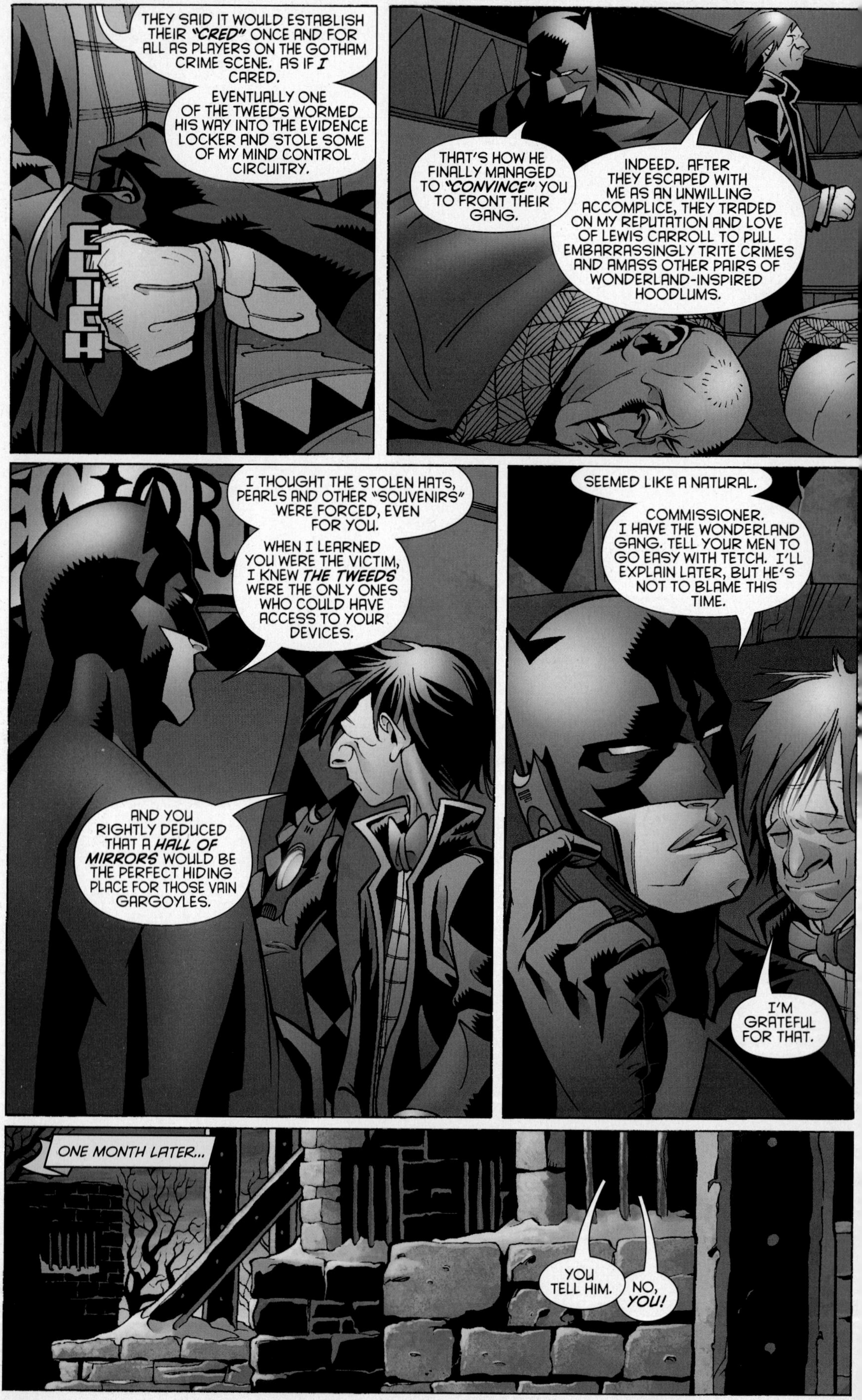
THEY SAID IT WOULD ESTABLISH THEIR "CRED" ONCE AND FOR ALL AS PLAYERS ON THE GOTHAM CRIME SCENE. AS IF I CARED.
EVENTUALLY ONE OF THE TWEEDS WORMED HIS WAY INTO THE EVIDENCE LOCKER AND STOLE SOME OF MY MIND CONTROL CIRCUITRY.
CLICK
THAT'S HOW HE FINALLY MANAGED TO "CONVINCE" YOU TO FRONT THEIR GANG.
INDEED. AFTER THEY ESCAPED WITH ME AS AN UNWILLING ACCOMPLICE, THEY TRADED ON MY REPUTATION AND LOVE OF LEWIS CARROLL TO PULL EMBARRASSINGLY TRITE CRIMES AND AMASS OTHER PAIRS OF WONDERLAND-INSPIRED HOODLUMS.
I THOUGHT THE STOLEN HATS, PEARLS AND OTHER "SOUVENIRS" WERE FORCED, EVEN FOR YOU.
WHEN I LEARNED YOU WERE THE VICTIM, I KNEW THE TWEEDS WERE THE ONLY ONES WHO COULD HAVE ACCESS TO YOUR DEVICES.
AND YOU RIGHTLY DEDUCED THAT A HALL OF MIRRORS WOULD BE THE PERFECT HIDING PLACE FOR THOSE VAIN GARGOYLES.
SEEMED LIKE A NATURAL.
COMMISSIONER. I HAVE THE WONDERLAND GANG. TELL YOUR MEN TO GO EASY WITH TETCH. I'LL EXPLAIN LATER, BUT HE'S NOT TO BLAME THIS TIME.
I'M GRATEFUL FOR THAT.
ONE MONTH LATER...
YOU TELL HIM.
NO, YOU!

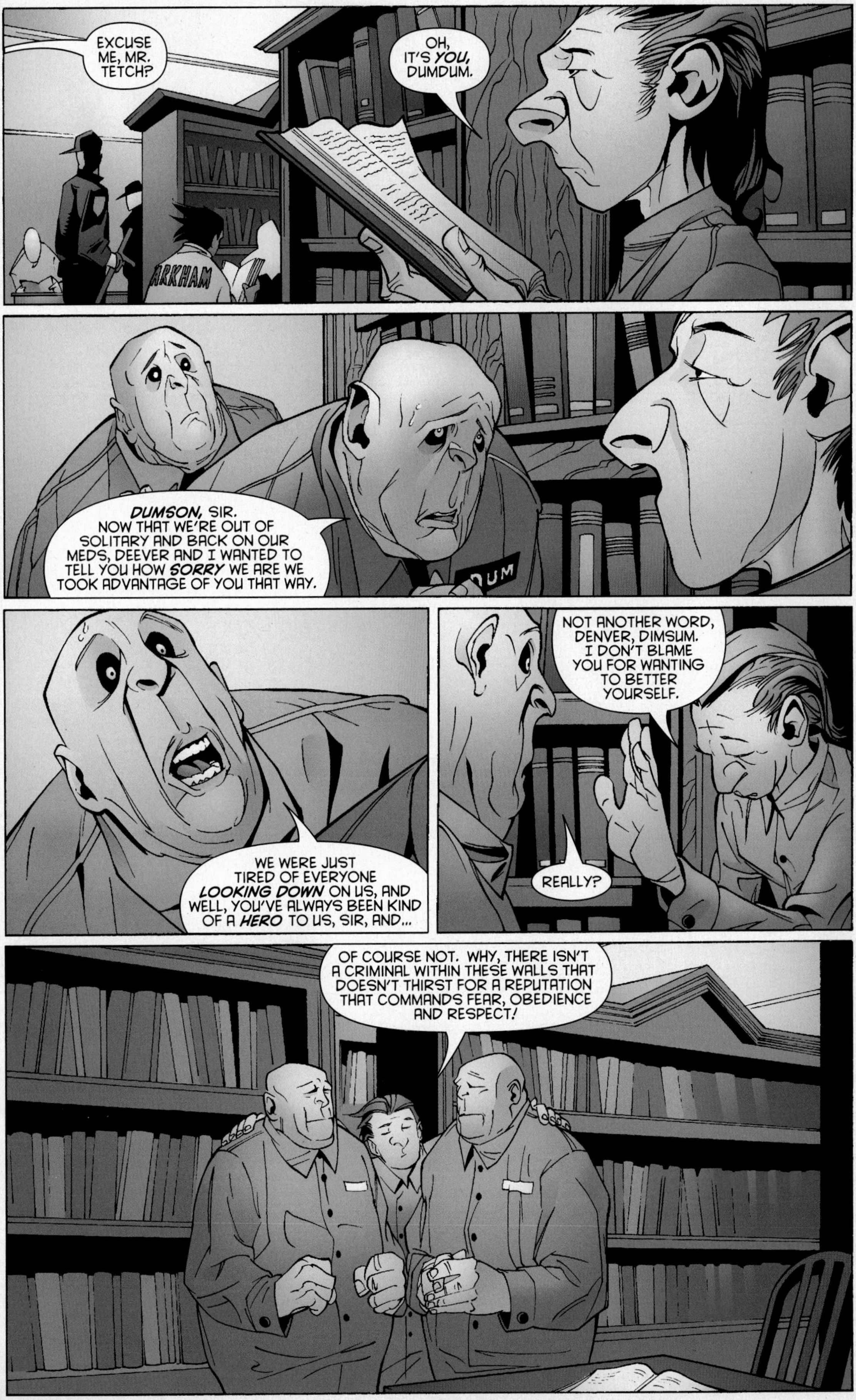
EXCUSE ME, MR. TETCH?
OH, IT'S *YOU,* DUMDUM.
DUMSON, SIR. NOW THAT WE'RE OUT OF SOLITARY AND BACK ON OUR MEDS, DEEVER AND I WANTED TO TELL YOU HOW *SORRY* WE ARE WE TOOK ADVANTAGE OF YOU THAT WAY.
DUM
WE WERE JUST TIRED OF EVERYONE *LOOKING DOWN* ON US, AND WELL, YOU'VE ALWAYS BEEN KIND OF A *HERO* TO US, SIR, AND...
NOT ANOTHER WORD, DENVER, DIMSUM. I DON'T BLAME YOU FOR WANTING TO BETTER YOURSELF.
REALLY?
OF COURSE NOT. WHY, THERE ISN'T A CRIMINAL WITHIN THESE WALLS THAT DOESN'T THIRST FOR A REPUTATION THAT COMMANDS FEAR, OBEDIENCE AND RESPECT!

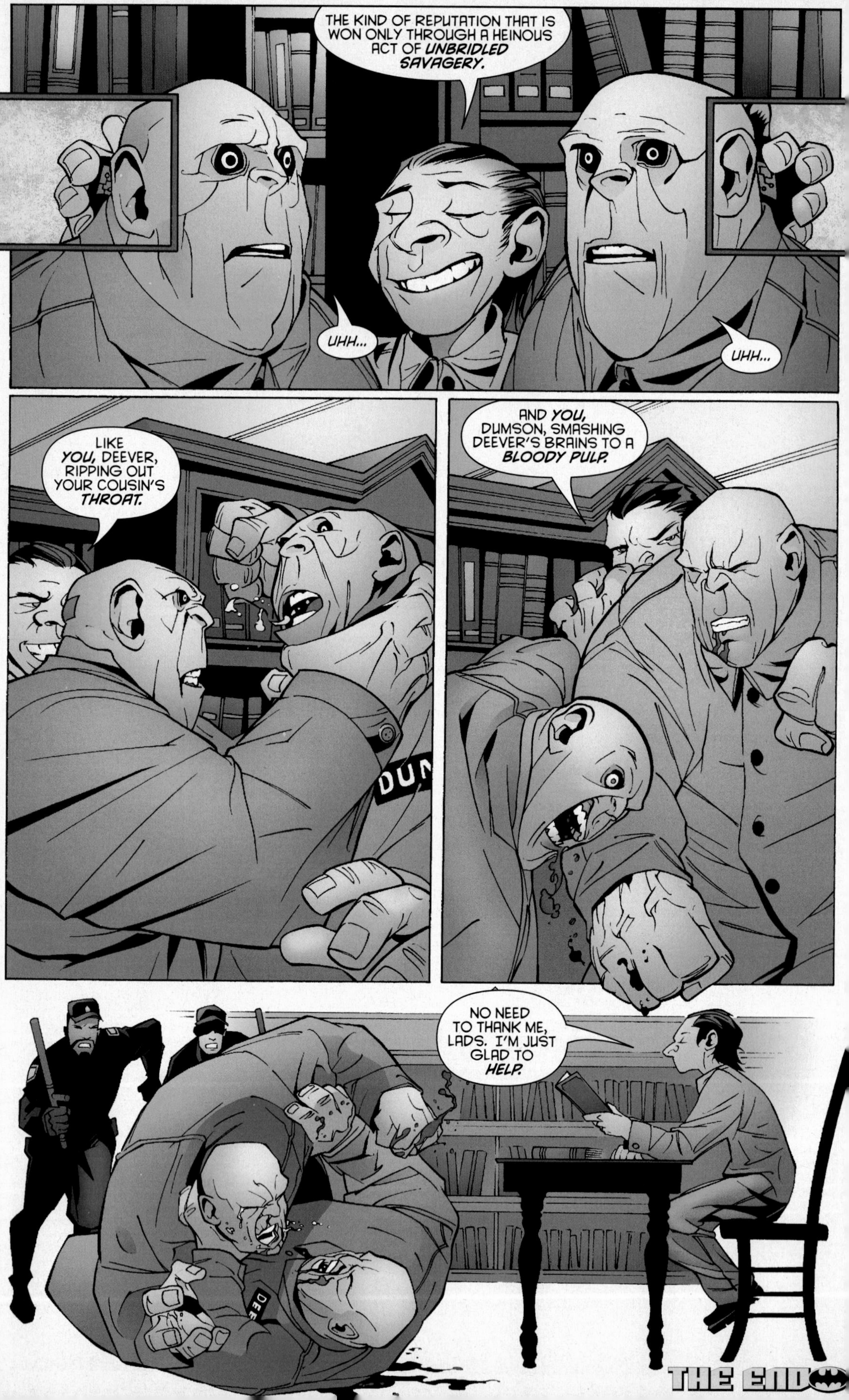

THE KIND OF REPUTATION THAT IS WON ONLY THROUGH A HEINOUS ACT OF UNBRIDLED SAVAGERY.
UHH...
UHH...
LIKE YOU, DEEVER, RIPPING OUT YOUR COUSIN'S THROAT.
DUN
AND YOU, DUMSON, SMASHING DEEVER'S BRAINS TO A BLOODY PULP.
NO NEED TO THANK ME, LADS. I'M JUST GLAD TO HELP.
DEE
THE END

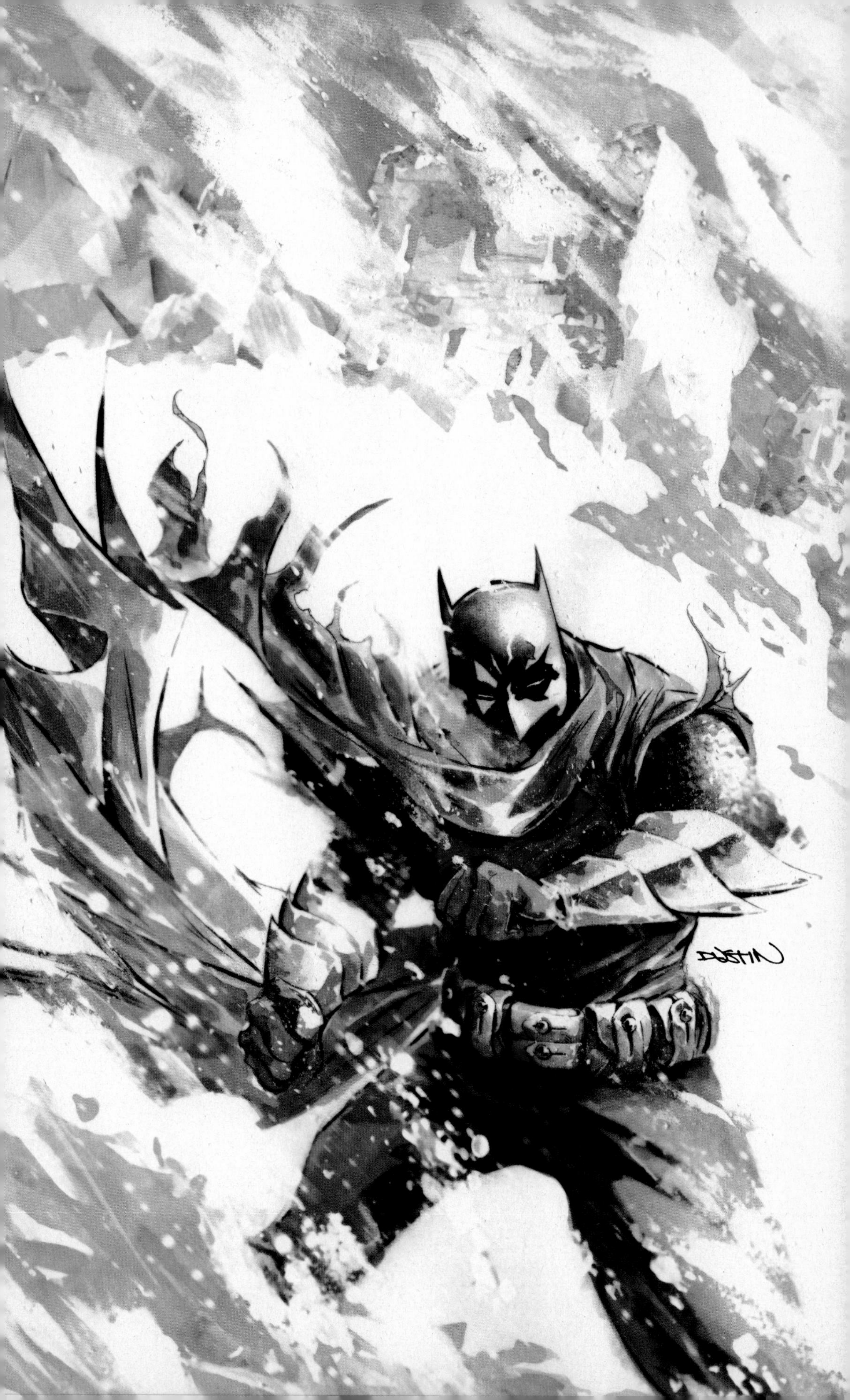
DUSTIN

The Suit of Sorrows

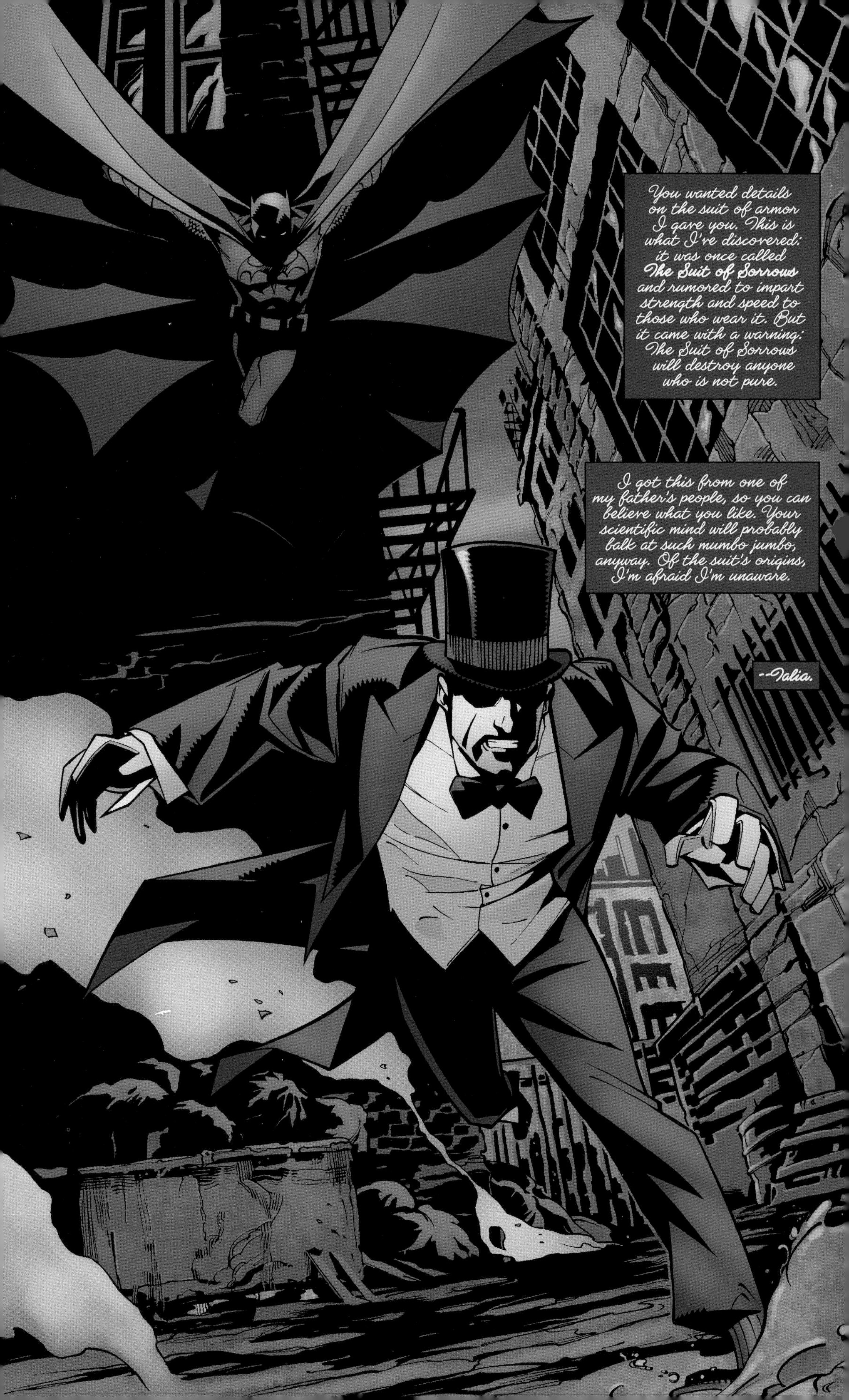
You wanted details on the suit of armor I gave you. This is what I've discovered: it was once called **The Suit of Sorrows** and rumored to impart strength and speed to those who wear it. But it came with a warning: The Suit of Sorrows will destroy anyone who is not pure.
I got this from one of my father's people, so you can believe what you like. Your scientific mind will probably balk at such mumbo jumbo, anyway. Of the suit's origins, I'm afraid I'm unaware.
--Talia.

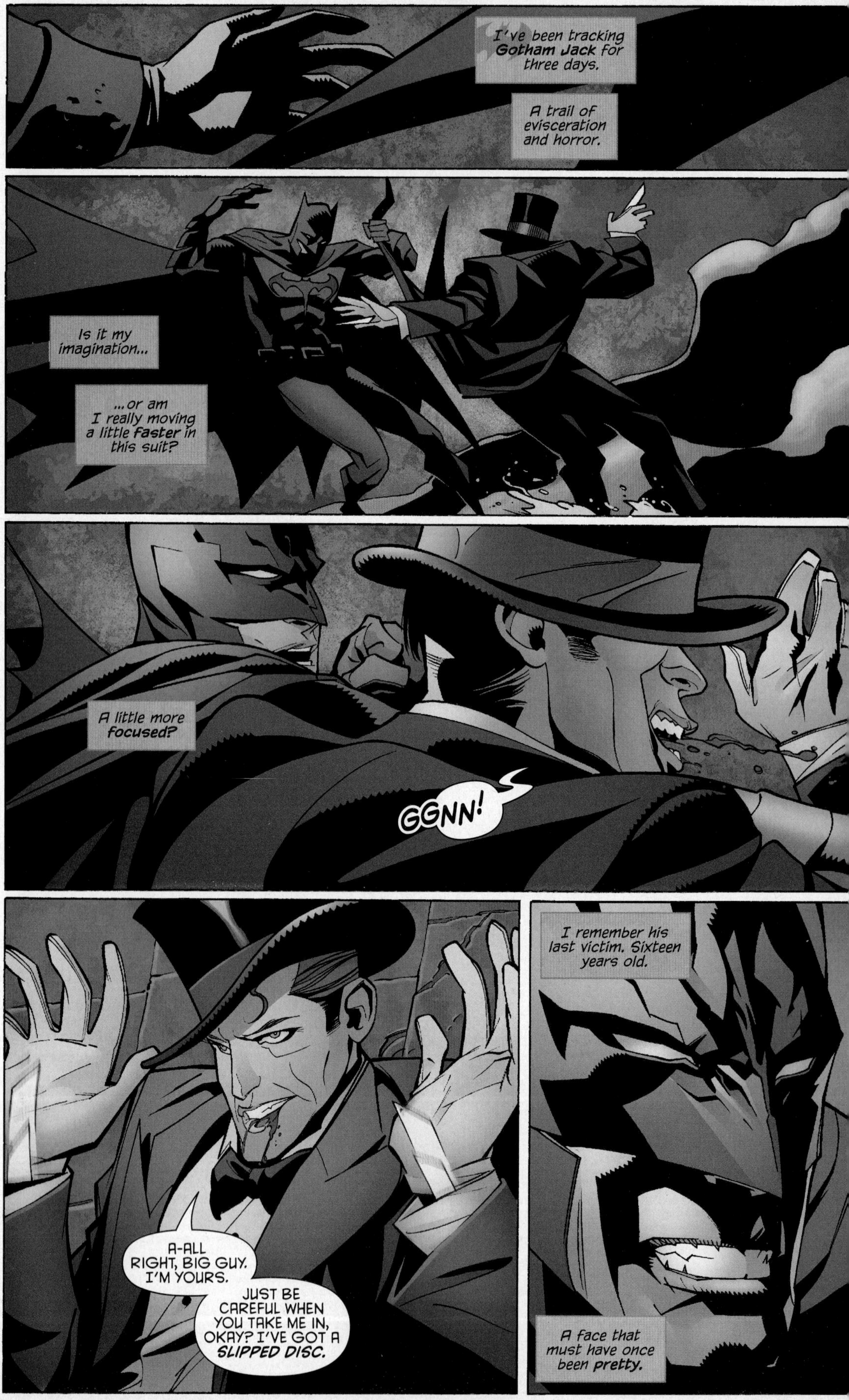
I've been tracking Gotham Jack for three days.
A trail of evisceration and horror.
Is it my imagination...
...or am I really moving a little faster in this suit?
A little more focused?
GGNN!
A-ALL RIGHT, BIG GUY. I'M YOURS.
JUST BE CAREFUL WHEN YOU TAKE ME IN, OKAY? I'VE GOT A SLIPPED DISC.
I remember his last victim. Sixteen years old.
A face that must have once been pretty.

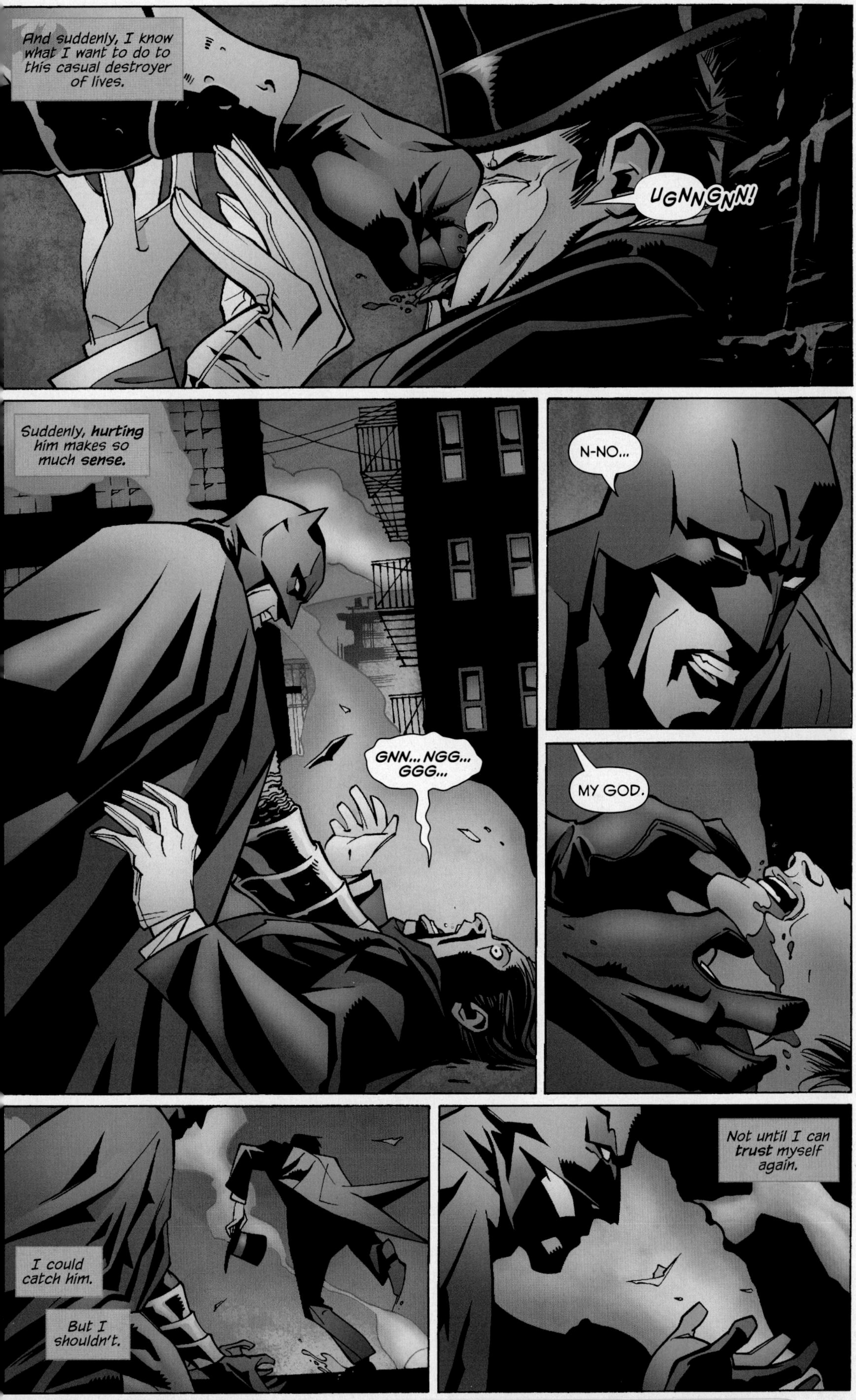

And suddenly, I know what I want to do to this casual destroyer of lives.
UGNNGNN!
Suddenly, **hurting** him makes so much **sense.**
N-NO...
GNN... NGG... GGG...
MY GOD.
I could catch him.
But I shouldn't.
Not until I can **trust** myself again.

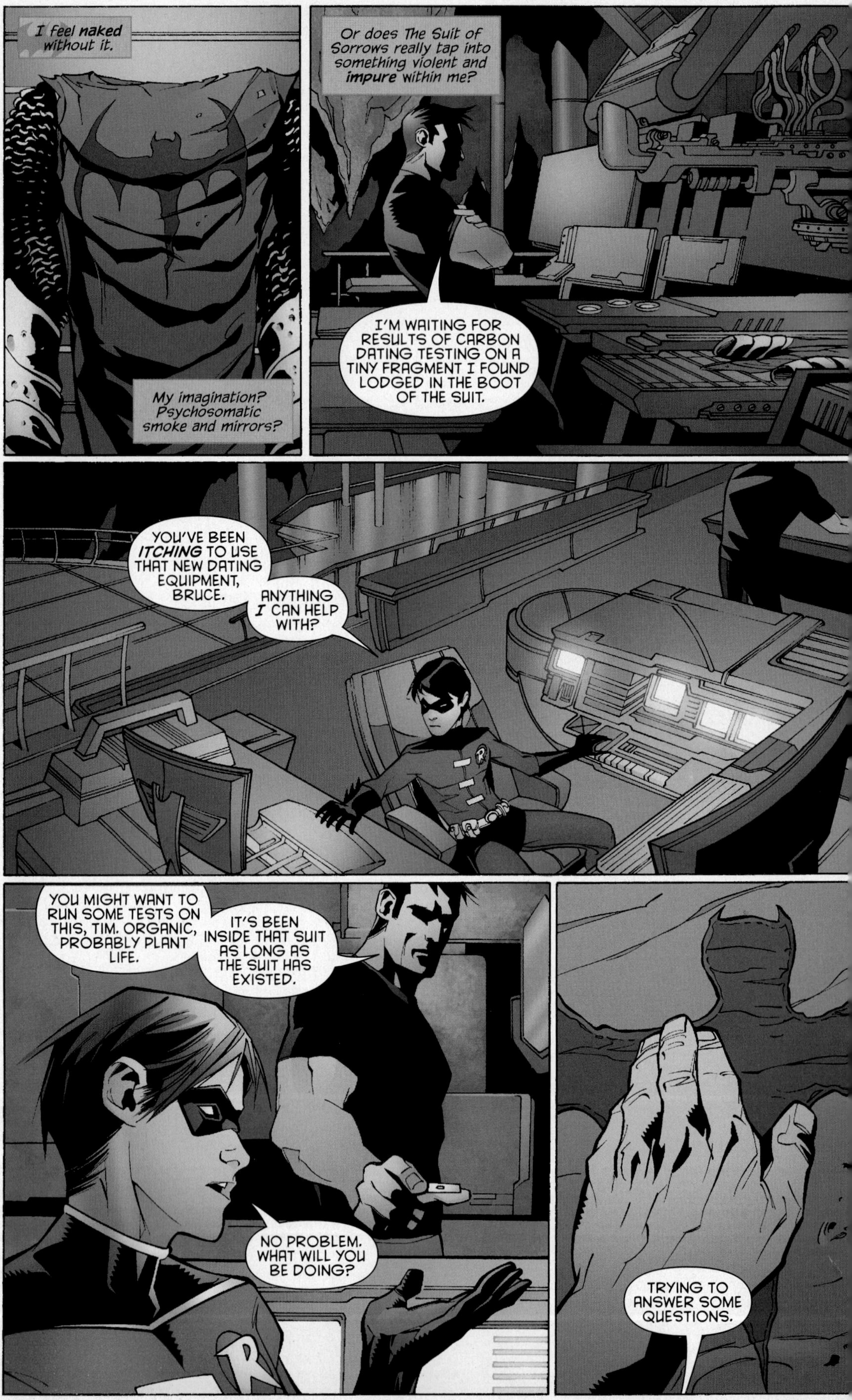
I feel naked without it.
My imagination? Psychosomatic smoke and mirrors?
Or does The Suit of Sorrows really tap into something violent and impure within me?
I'M WAITING FOR RESULTS OF CARBON DATING TESTING ON A TINY FRAGMENT I FOUND LODGED IN THE BOOT OF THE SUIT.
YOU'VE BEEN ITCHING TO USE THAT NEW DATING EQUIPMENT, BRUCE.
ANYTHING I CAN HELP WITH?
YOU MIGHT WANT TO RUN SOME TESTS ON THIS, TIM. ORGANIC, PROBABLY PLANT LIFE.
IT'S BEEN INSIDE THAT SUIT AS LONG AS THE SUIT HAS EXISTED.
NO PROBLEM. WHAT WILL YOU BE DOING?
TRYING TO ANSWER SOME QUESTIONS.

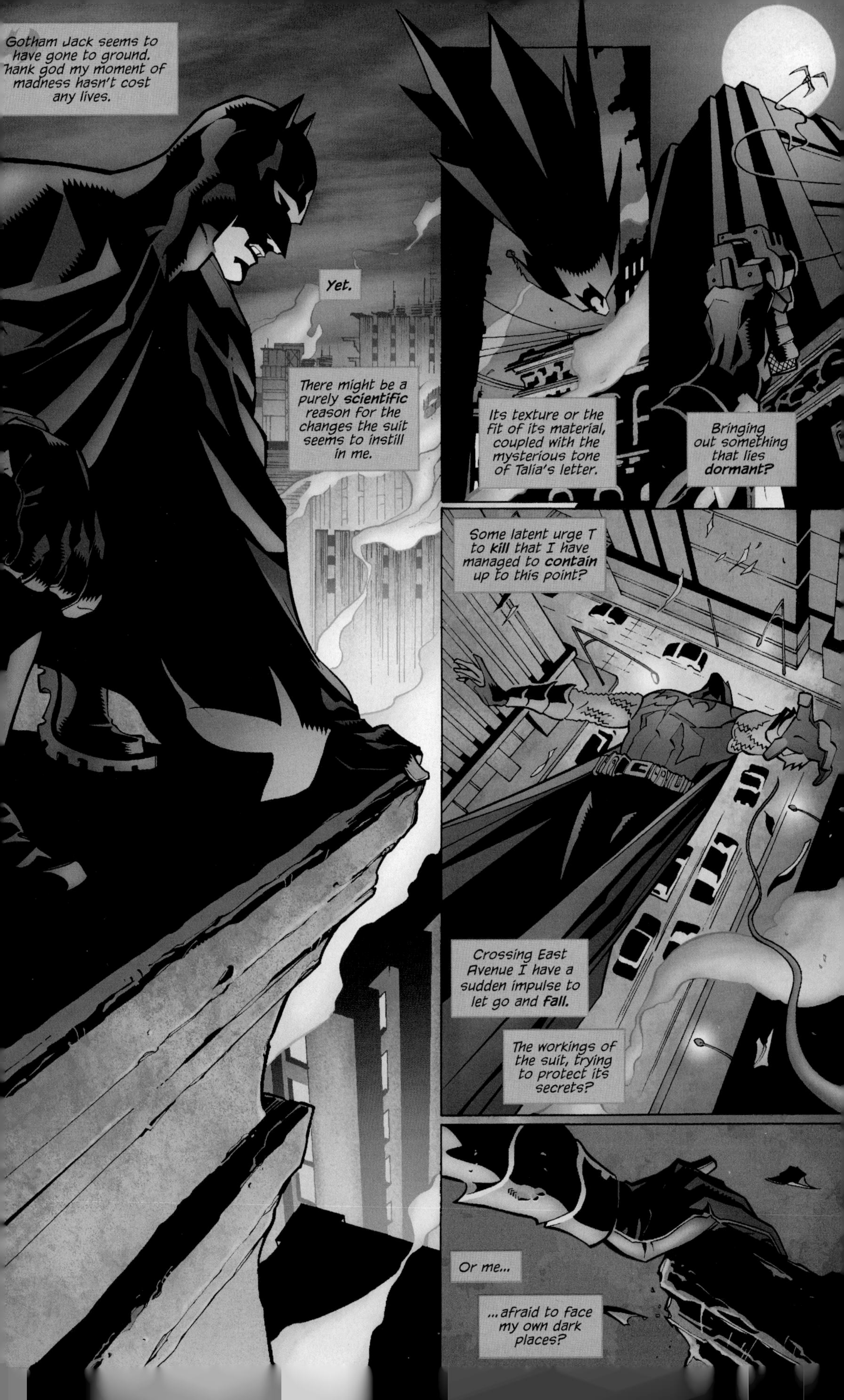
Gotham Jack seems to have gone to ground. 'hank god my moment of madness hasn't cost any lives.
Yet.
There might be a purely scientific reason for the changes the suit seems to instill in me.
Its texture or the fit of its material, coupled with the mysterious tone of Talia's letter.
Bringing out something that lies dormant?
Some latent urge T to kill that I have managed to contain up to this point?
Crossing East Avenue I have a sudden impulse to let go and fall.
The workings of the suit, trying to protect its secrets?
Or me...
...afraid to face my own dark places?

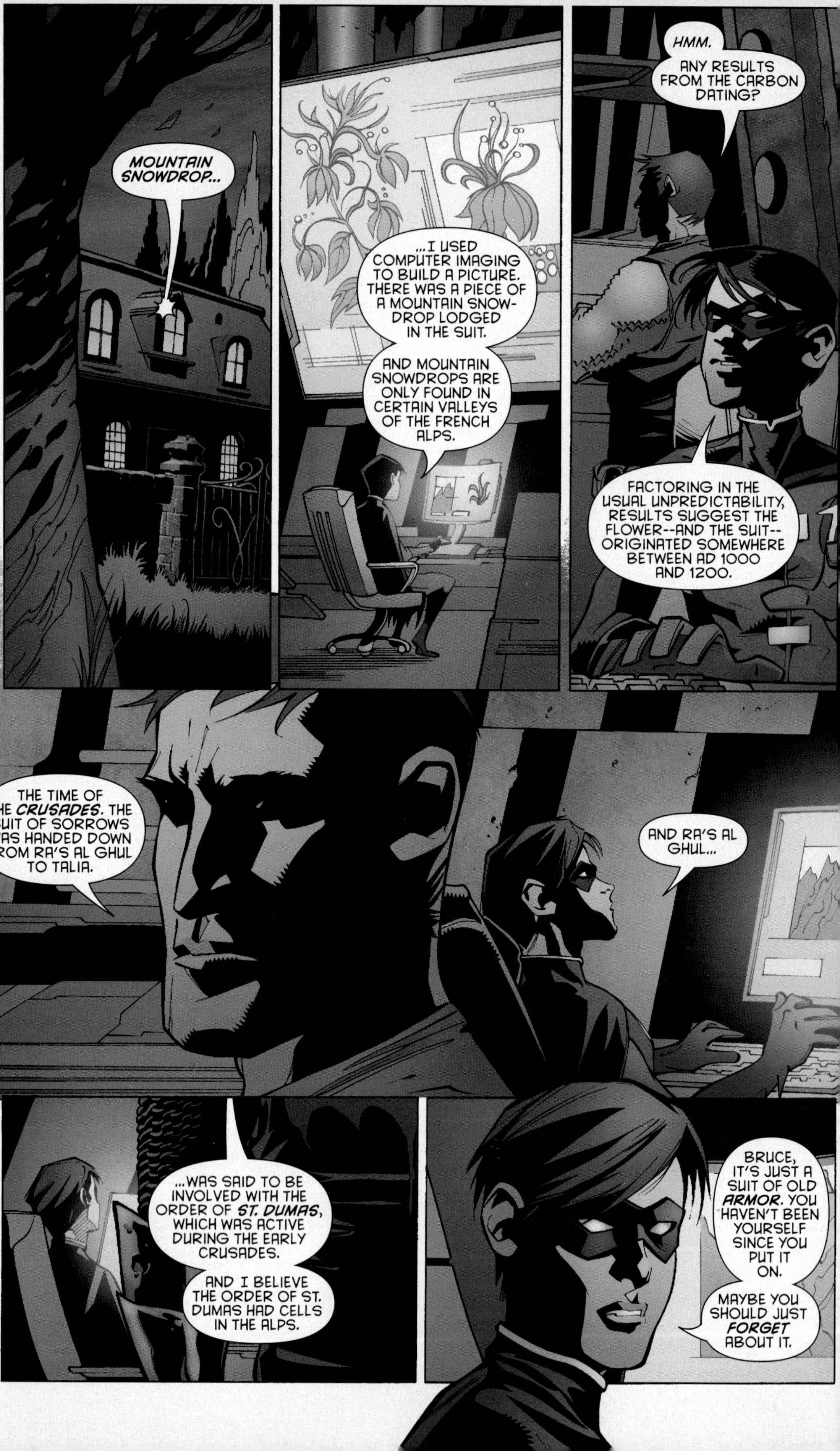
MOUNTAIN SNOWDROP...
...I USED COMPUTER IMAGING TO BUILD A PICTURE. THERE WAS A PIECE OF A MOUNTAIN SNOW-DROP LODGED IN THE SUIT.
AND MOUNTAIN SNOWDROPS ARE ONLY FOUND IN CERTAIN VALLEYS OF THE FRENCH ALPS.
HMM.
ANY RESULTS FROM THE CARBON DATING?
FACTORING IN THE USUAL UNPREDICTABILITY, RESULTS SUGGEST THE FLOWER--AND THE SUIT--ORIGINATED SOMEWHERE BETWEEN AD 1000 AND 1200.
THE TIME OF THE CRUSADES. THE SUIT OF SORROWS WAS HANDED DOWN FROM RA'S AL GHUL TO TALIA.
AND RA'S AL GHUL...
...WAS SAID TO BE INVOLVED WITH THE ORDER OF ST. DUMAS, WHICH WAS ACTIVE DURING THE EARLY CRUSADES.
AND I BELIEVE THE ORDER OF ST. DUMAS HAD CELLS IN THE ALPS.
BRUCE, IT'S JUST A SUIT OF OLD ARMOR. YOU HAVEN'T BEEN YOURSELF SINCE YOU PUT IT ON.
MAYBE YOU SHOULD JUST FORGET ABOUT IT.

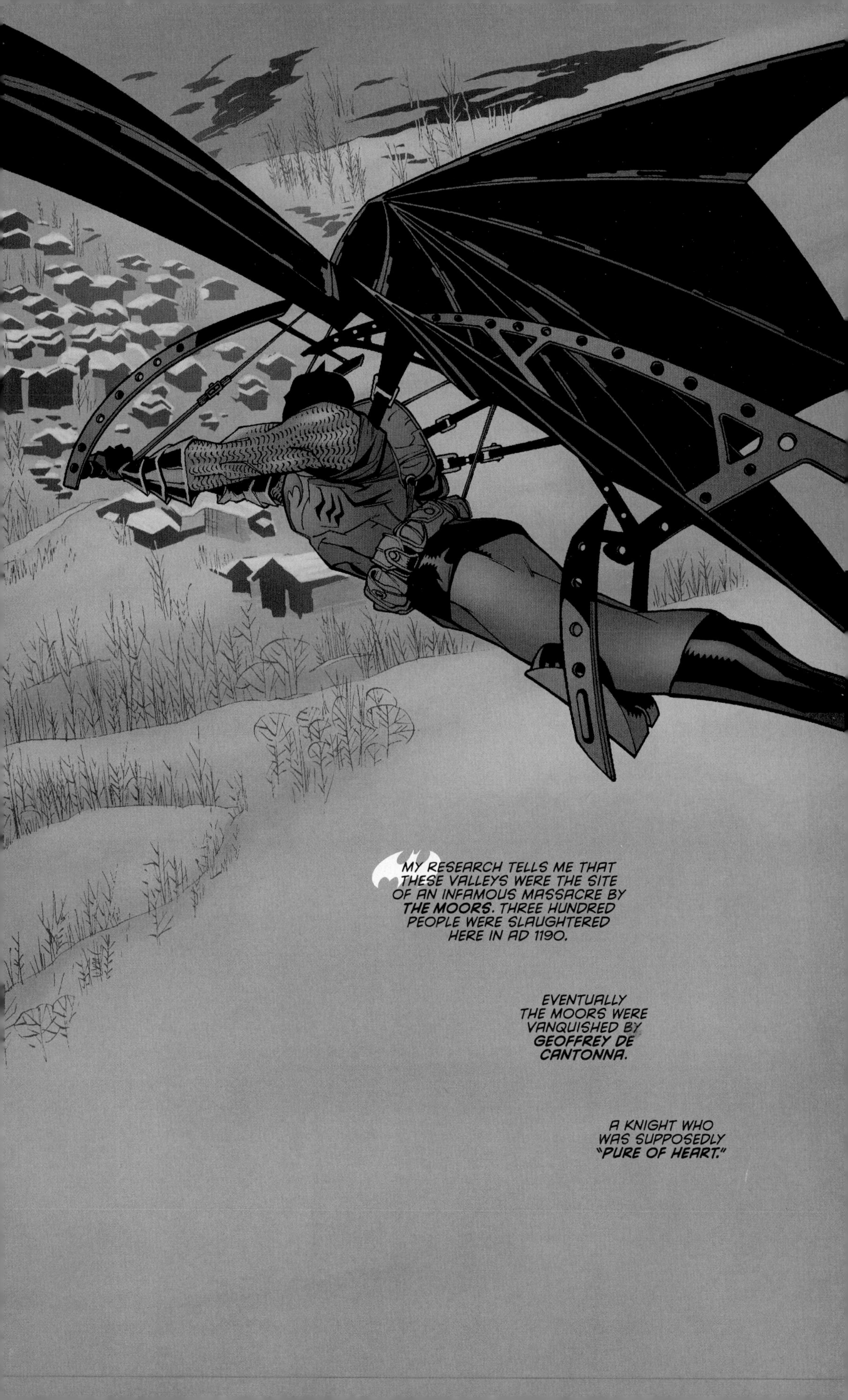
MY RESEARCH TELLS ME THAT THESE VALLEYS WERE THE SITE OF AN INFAMOUS MASSACRE BY THE MOORS. THREE HUNDRED PEOPLE WERE SLAUGHTERED HERE IN AD 1190.
EVENTUALLY THE MOORS WERE VANQUISHED BY GEOFFREY DE CANTONNA.
A KNIGHT WHO WAS SUPPOSEDLY "PURE OF HEART."

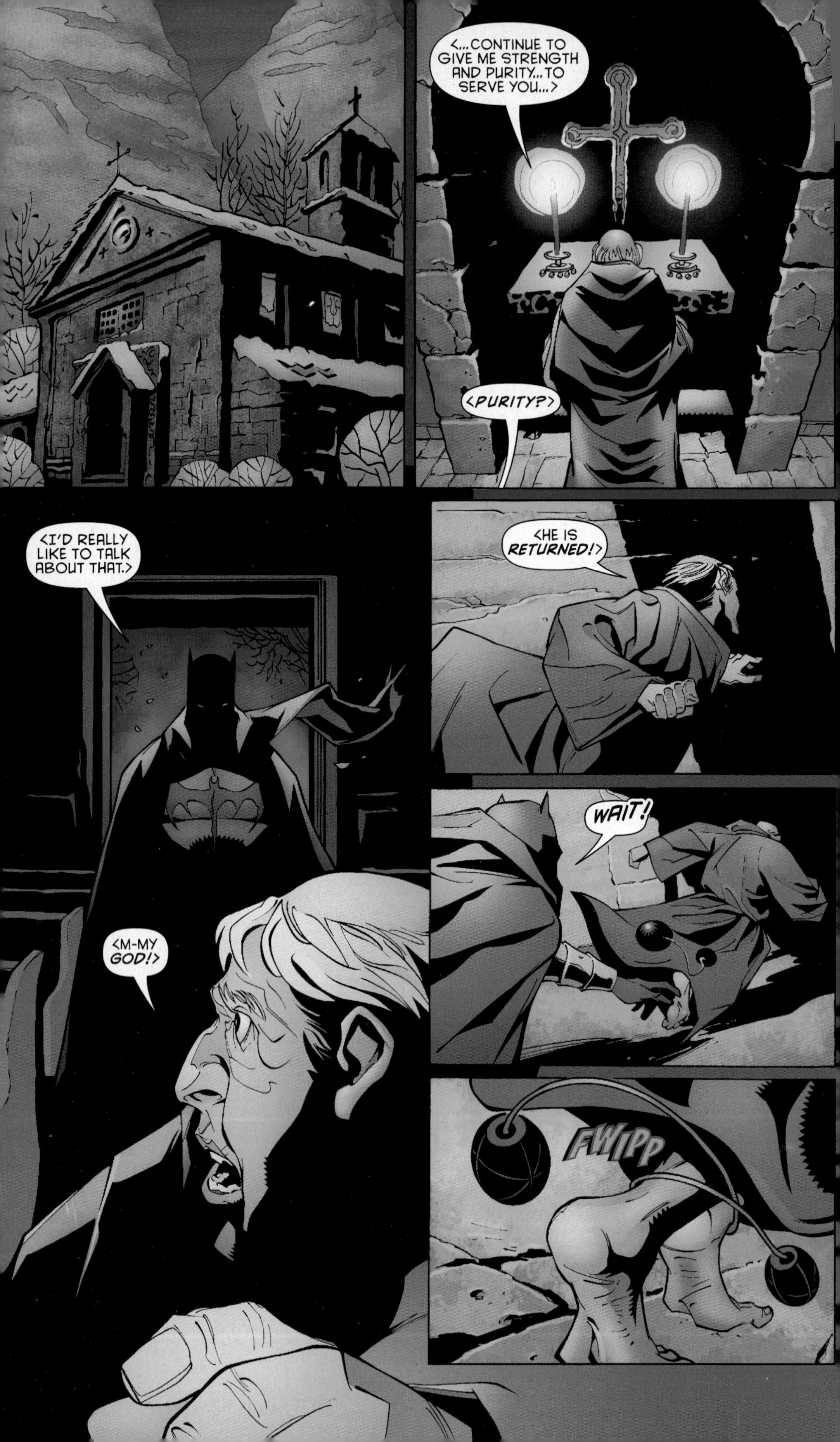
<...CONTINUE TO GIVE ME STRENGTH AND PURITY... TO SERVE YOU...>
<PURITY?>
<I'D REALLY LIKE TO TALK ABOUT THAT.>
<M-MY GOD!>
<HE IS RETURNED!>
WAIT!
FWIPP

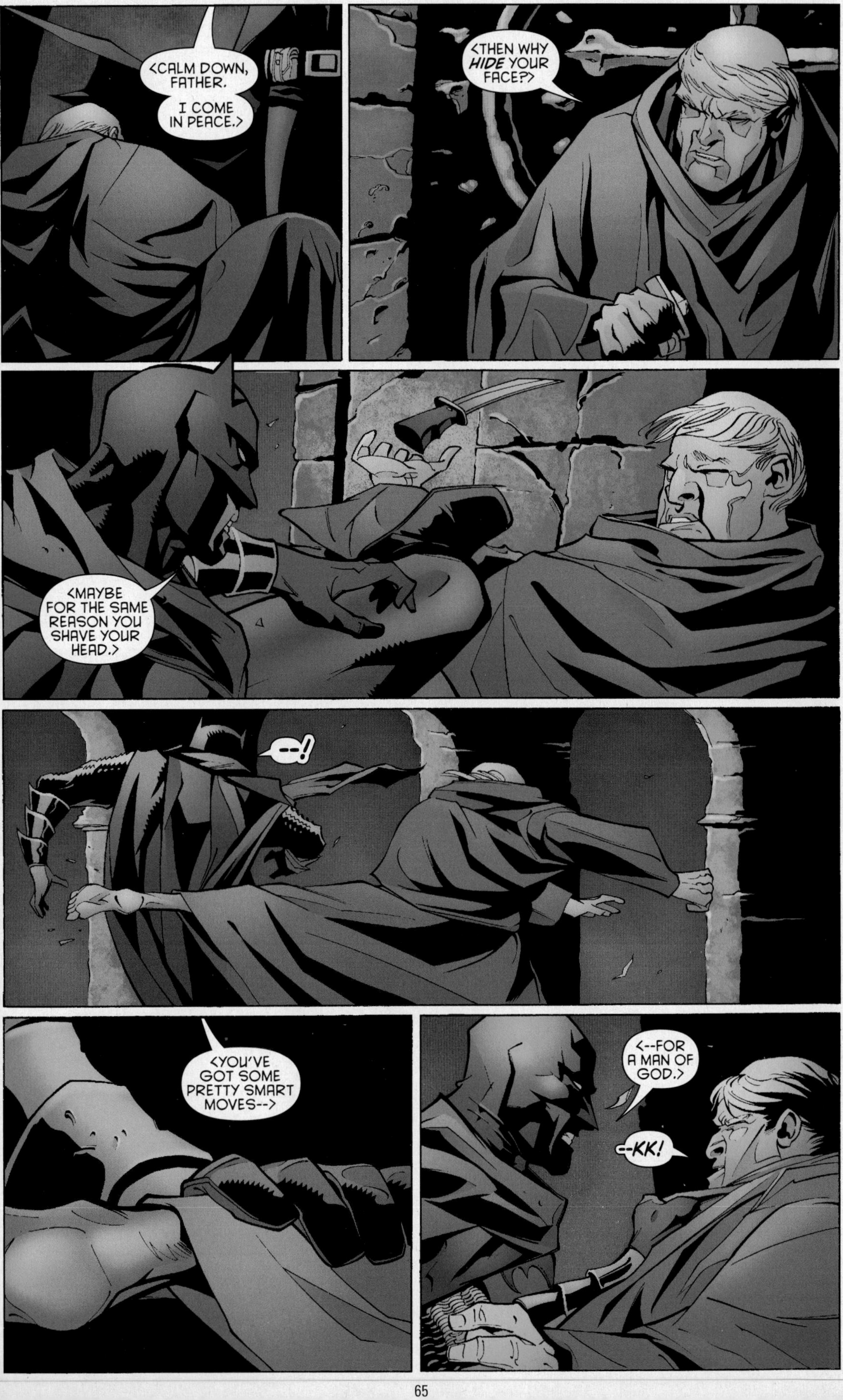
<CALM DOWN, FATHER.
I COME IN PEACE.>
<THEN WHY *HIDE* YOUR FACE?>
<MAYBE FOR THE SAME REASON YOU SHAVE YOUR HEAD.>
--!
<YOU'VE GOT SOME PRETTY SMART MOVES-->
<--FOR A MAN OF GOD.>
--KK!

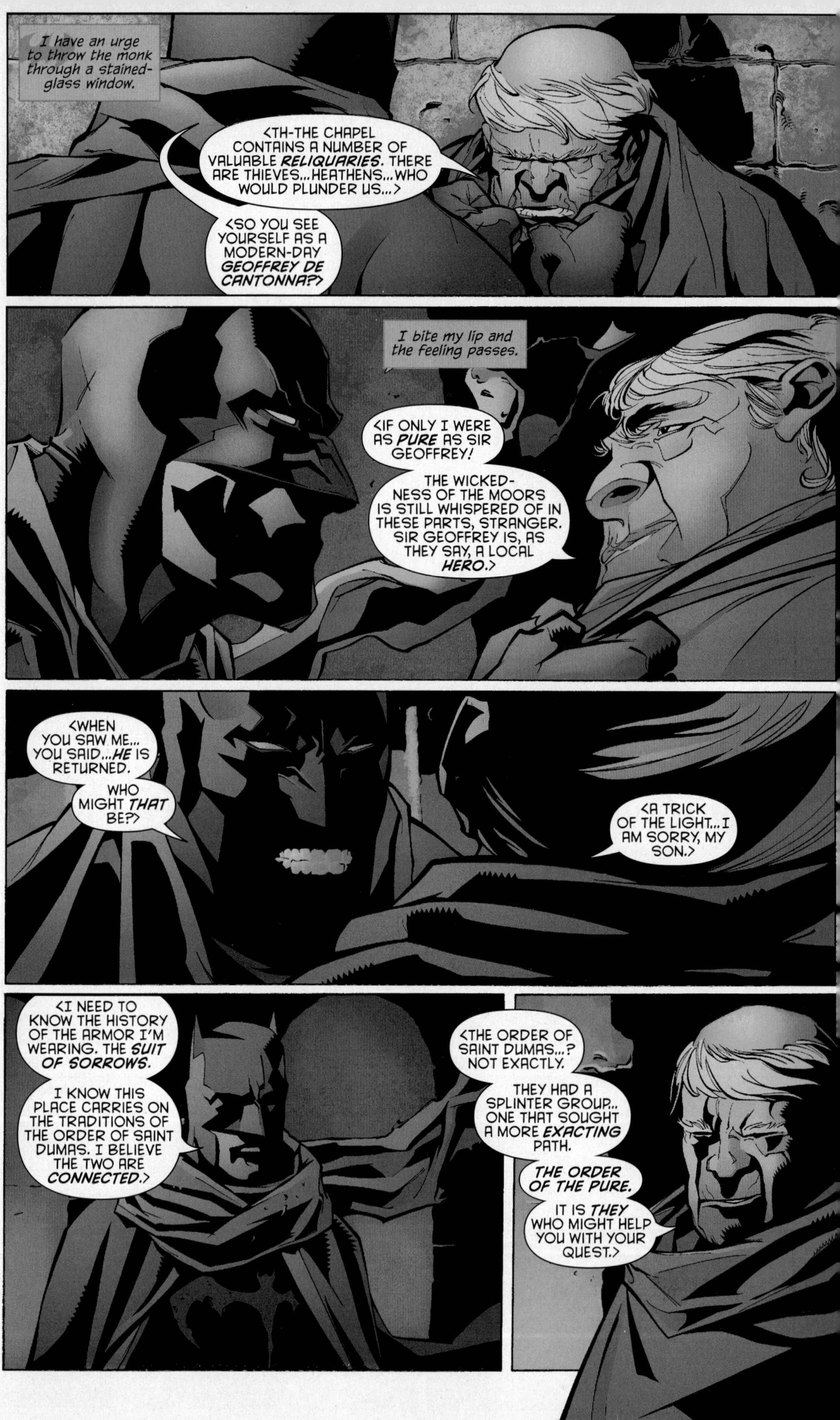
I have an urge to throw the monk through a stained-glass window.
<TH-THE CHAPEL CONTAINS A NUMBER OF VALUABLE RELIQUARIES. THERE ARE THIEVES... HEATHENS... WHO WOULD PLUNDER US...>
<SO YOU SEE YOURSELF AS A MODERN-DAY GEOFFREY DE CANTONNA?>
I bite my lip and the feeling passes.
<IF ONLY I WERE AS PURE AS SIR GEOFFREY!
THE WICKED-NESS OF THE MOORS IS STILL WHISPERED OF IN THESE PARTS, STRANGER. SIR GEOFFREY IS, AS THEY SAY, A LOCAL HERO.>
<WHEN YOU SAW ME... YOU SAID... HE IS RETURNED.
WHO MIGHT THAT BE?>
<A TRICK OF THE LIGHT... I AM SORRY, MY SON.>
<I NEED TO KNOW THE HISTORY OF THE ARMOR I'M WEARING. THE SUIT OF SORROWS.
I KNOW THIS PLACE CARRIES ON THE TRADITIONS OF THE ORDER OF SAINT DUMAS. I BELIEVE THE TWO ARE CONNECTED.>
<THE ORDER OF SAINT DUMAS...? NOT EXACTLY.
THEY HAD A SPLINTER GROUP... ONE THAT SOUGHT A MORE EXACTING PATH.
THE ORDER OF THE PURE.
IT IS THEY WHO MIGHT HELP YOU WITH YOUR QUEST.>

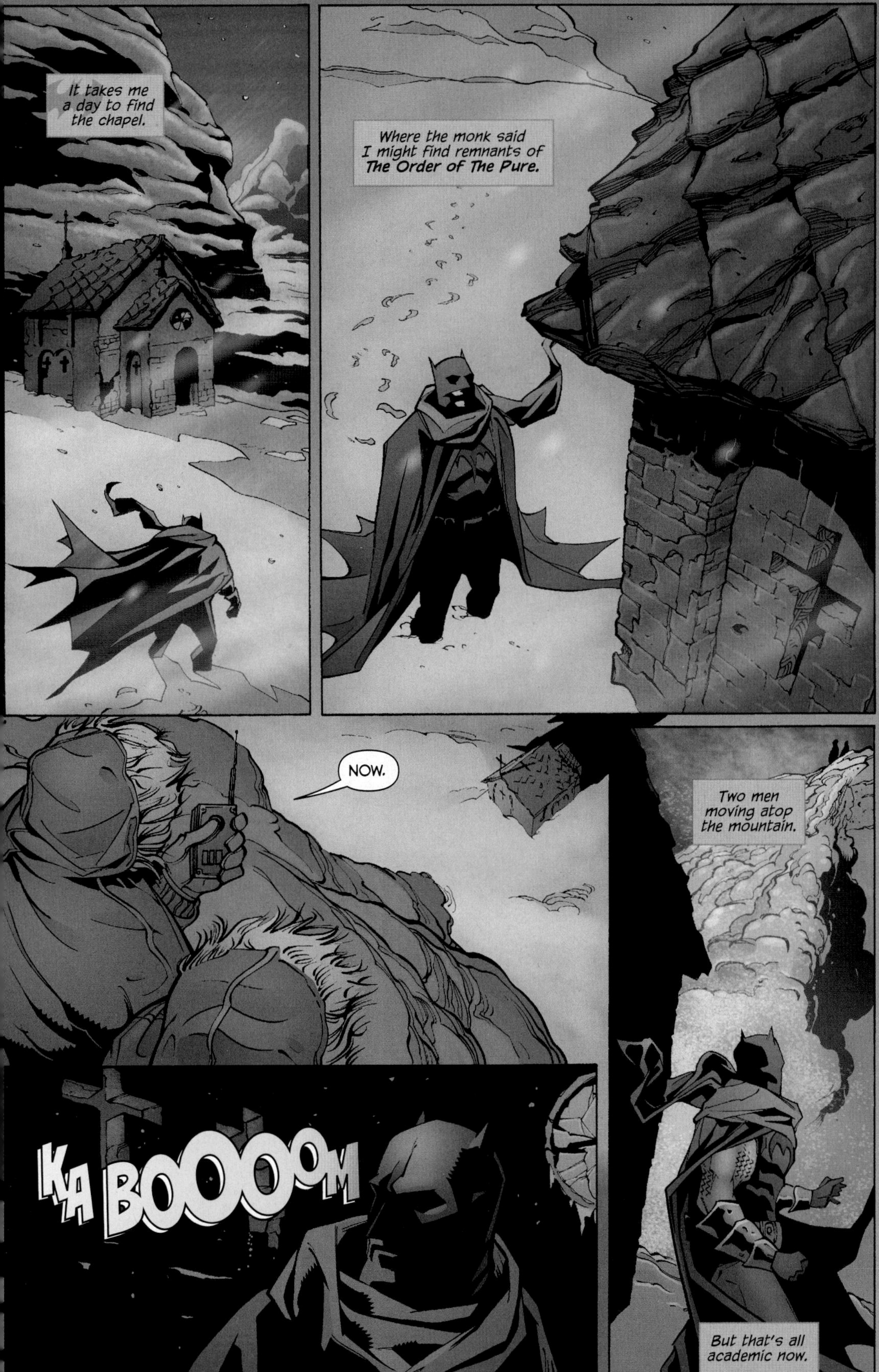
It takes me a day to find the chapel.
Where the monk said I might find remnants of The Order of The Pure.
NOW.
Two men moving atop the mountain.
KA BOOOOOM
But that's all academic now.

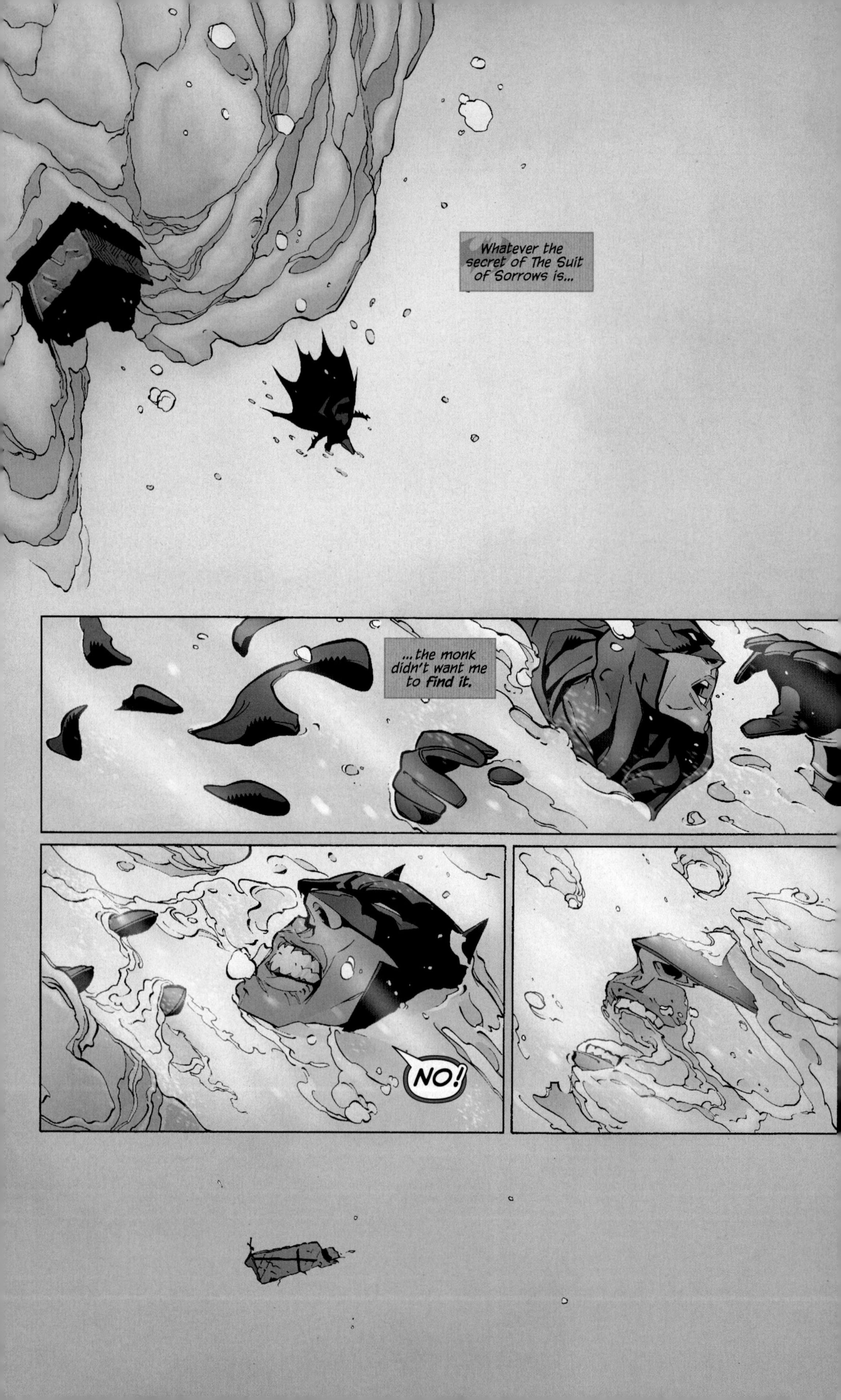

Whatever the secret of The Suit of Sorrows is...
...the monk didn't want me to find it.
NO!

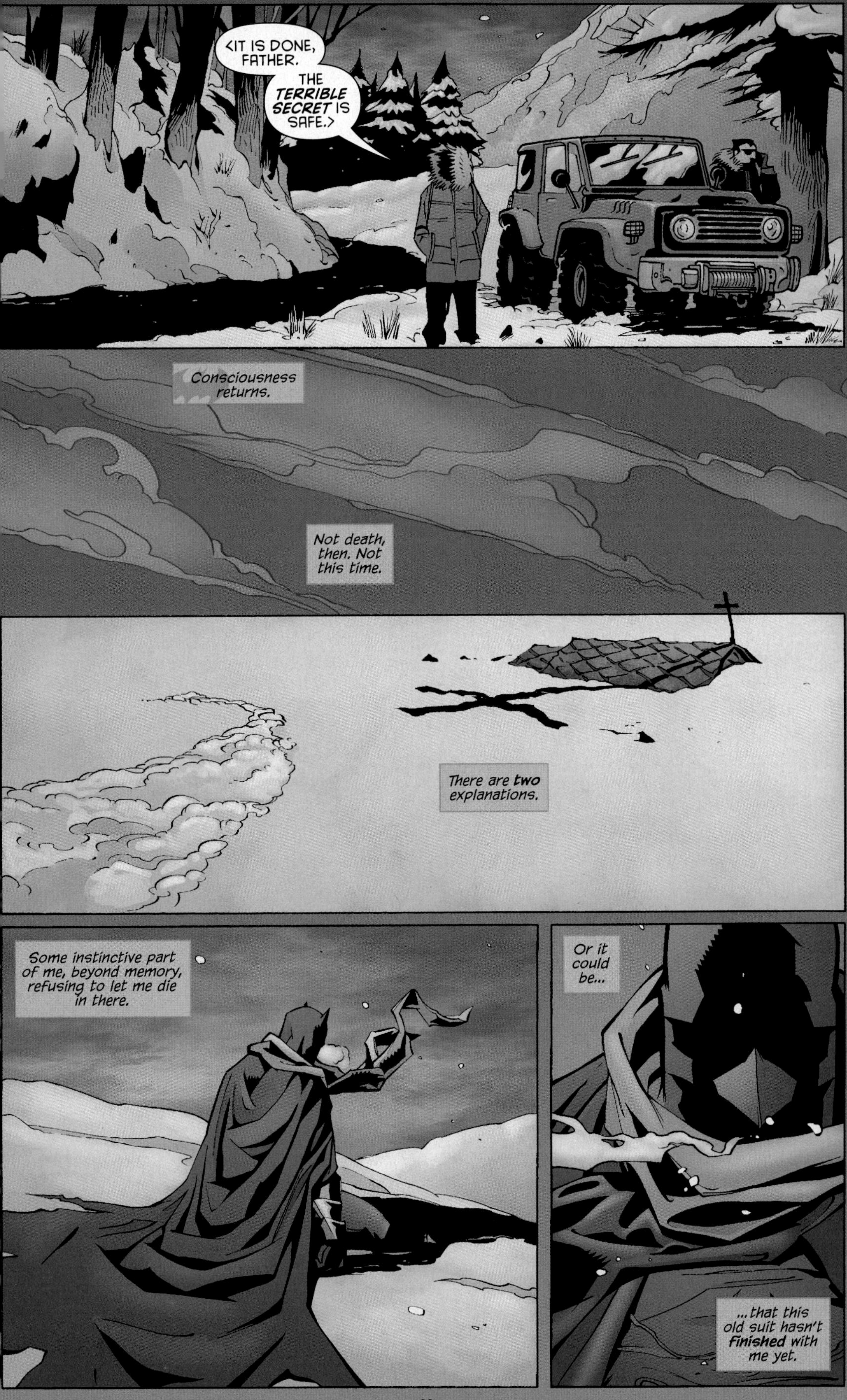
<IT IS DONE, FATHER.
THE TERRIBLE SECRET IS SAFE.>
Consciousness returns.
Not death, then. Not this time.
There are two explanations.
Some instinctive part of me, beyond memory, refusing to let me die in there.
Or it could be...
...that this old suit hasn't finished with me yet.

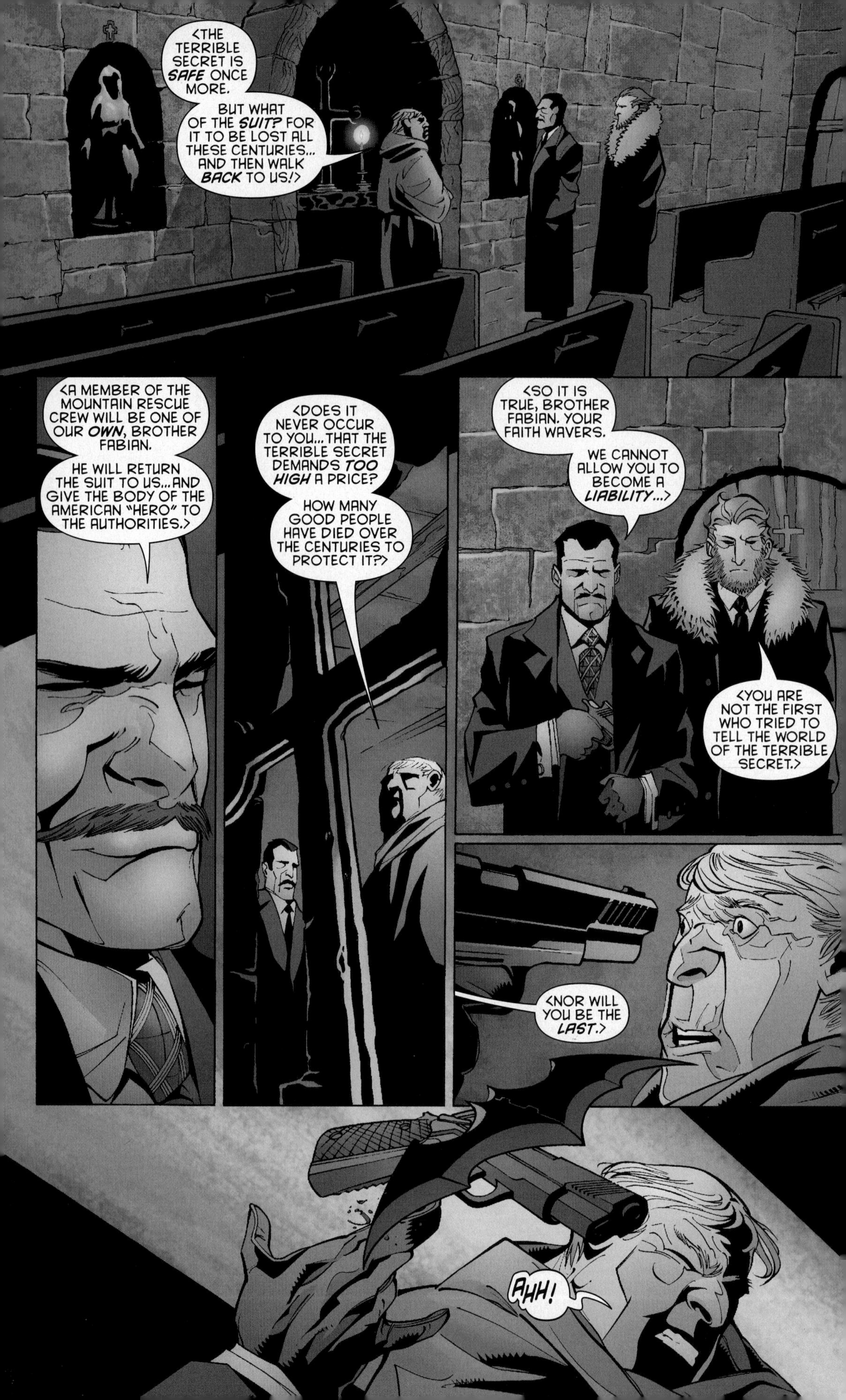
<THE TERRIBLE SECRET IS SAFE ONCE MORE.
BUT WHAT OF THE SUIT? FOR IT TO BE LOST ALL THESE CENTURIES... AND THEN WALK BACK TO US!>
<A MEMBER OF THE MOUNTAIN RESCUE CREW WILL BE ONE OF OUR OWN, BROTHER FABIAN.
HE WILL RETURN THE SUIT TO US... AND GIVE THE BODY OF THE AMERICAN "HERO" TO THE AUTHORITIES.>
<DOES IT NEVER OCCUR TO YOU... THAT THE TERRIBLE SECRET DEMANDS TOO HIGH A PRICE?
HOW MANY GOOD PEOPLE HAVE DIED OVER THE CENTURIES TO PROTECT IT?>
<SO IT IS TRUE, BROTHER FABIAN. YOUR FAITH WAVERS.
WE CANNOT ALLOW YOU TO BECOME A LIABILITY...>
<YOU ARE NOT THE FIRST WHO TRIED TO TELL THE WORLD OF THE TERRIBLE SECRET.>
<NOR WILL YOU BE THE LAST.>
AHH!

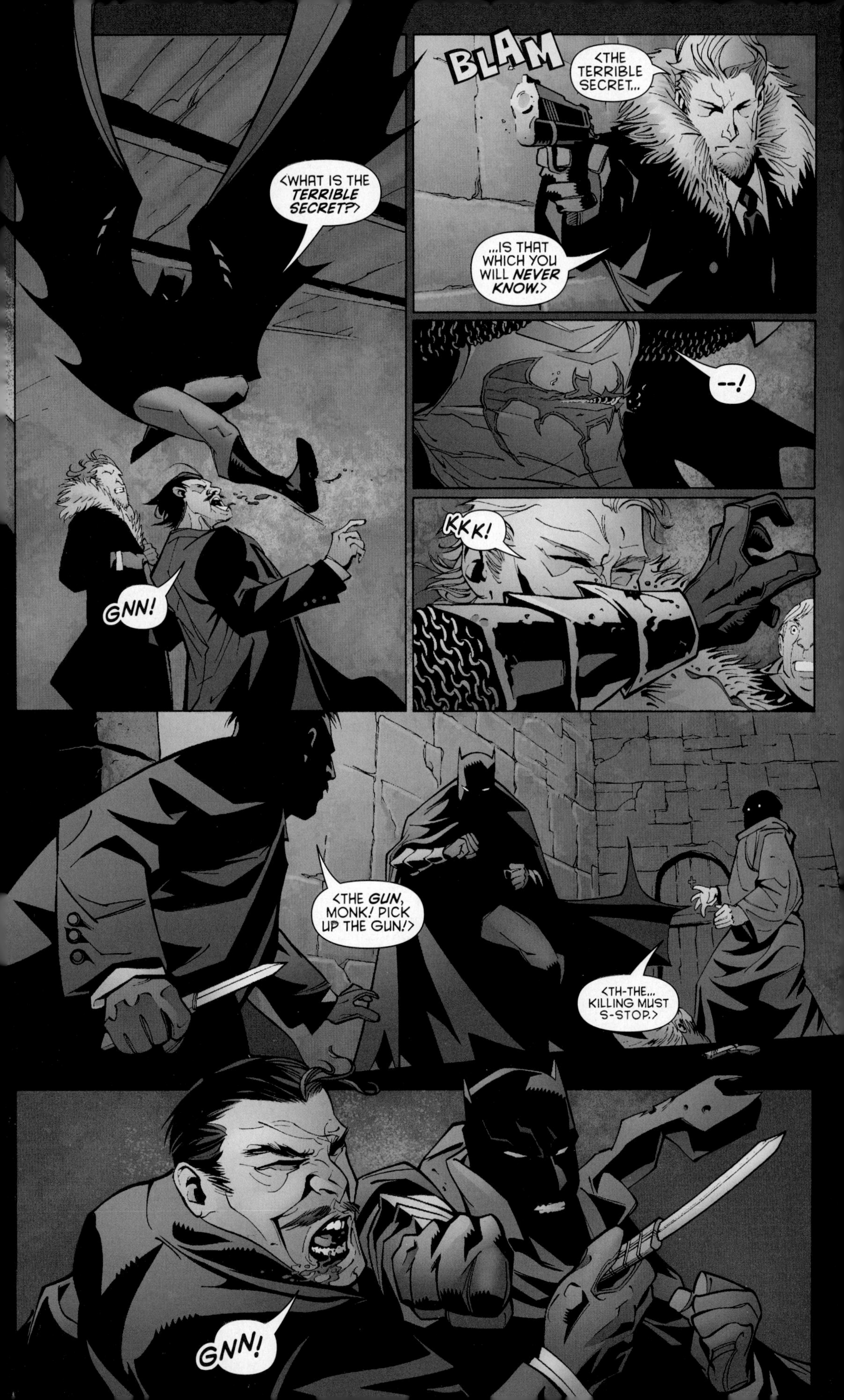
<WHAT IS THE TERRIBLE SECRET?>
BLAM
<THE TERRIBLE SECRET...
...IS THAT WHICH YOU WILL NEVER KNOW.>
GNN!
--!
KKK!
<THE GUN, MONK! PICK UP THE GUN!>
<TH-THE... KILLING MUST S-STOP.>
GNN!

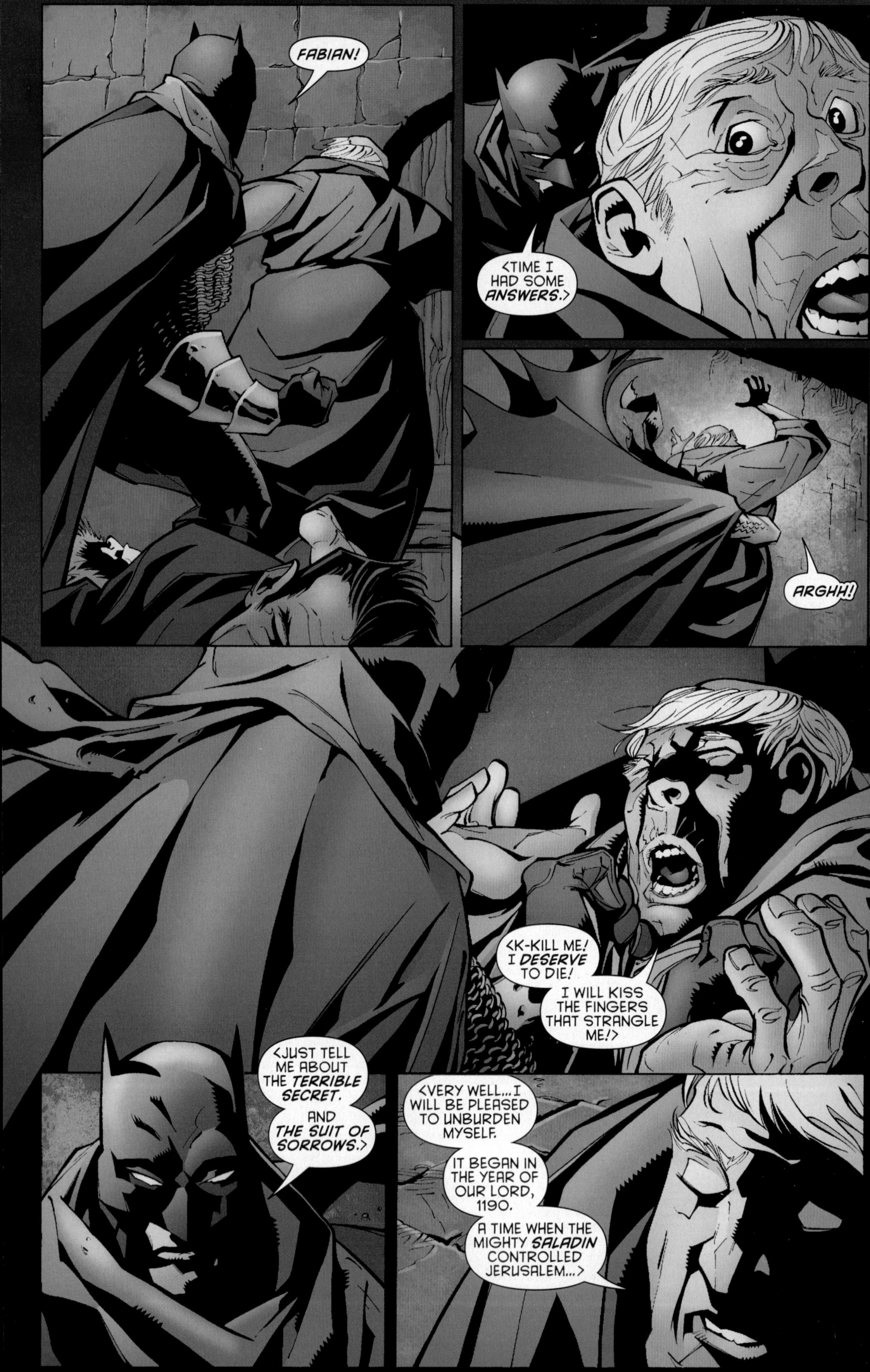
FABIAN!
<TIME I HAD SOME ANSWERS.>
ARGHH!
<K-KILL ME! I DESERVE TO DIE!
I WILL KISS THE FINGERS THAT STRANGLE ME!>
<JUST TELL ME ABOUT THE TERRIBLE SECRET.
AND THE SUIT OF SORROWS.>
<VERY WELL...I WILL BE PLEASED TO UNBURDEN MYSELF.
IT BEGAN IN THE YEAR OF OUR LORD, 1190.
A TIME WHEN THE MIGHTY SALADIN CONTROLLED JERUSALEM...>

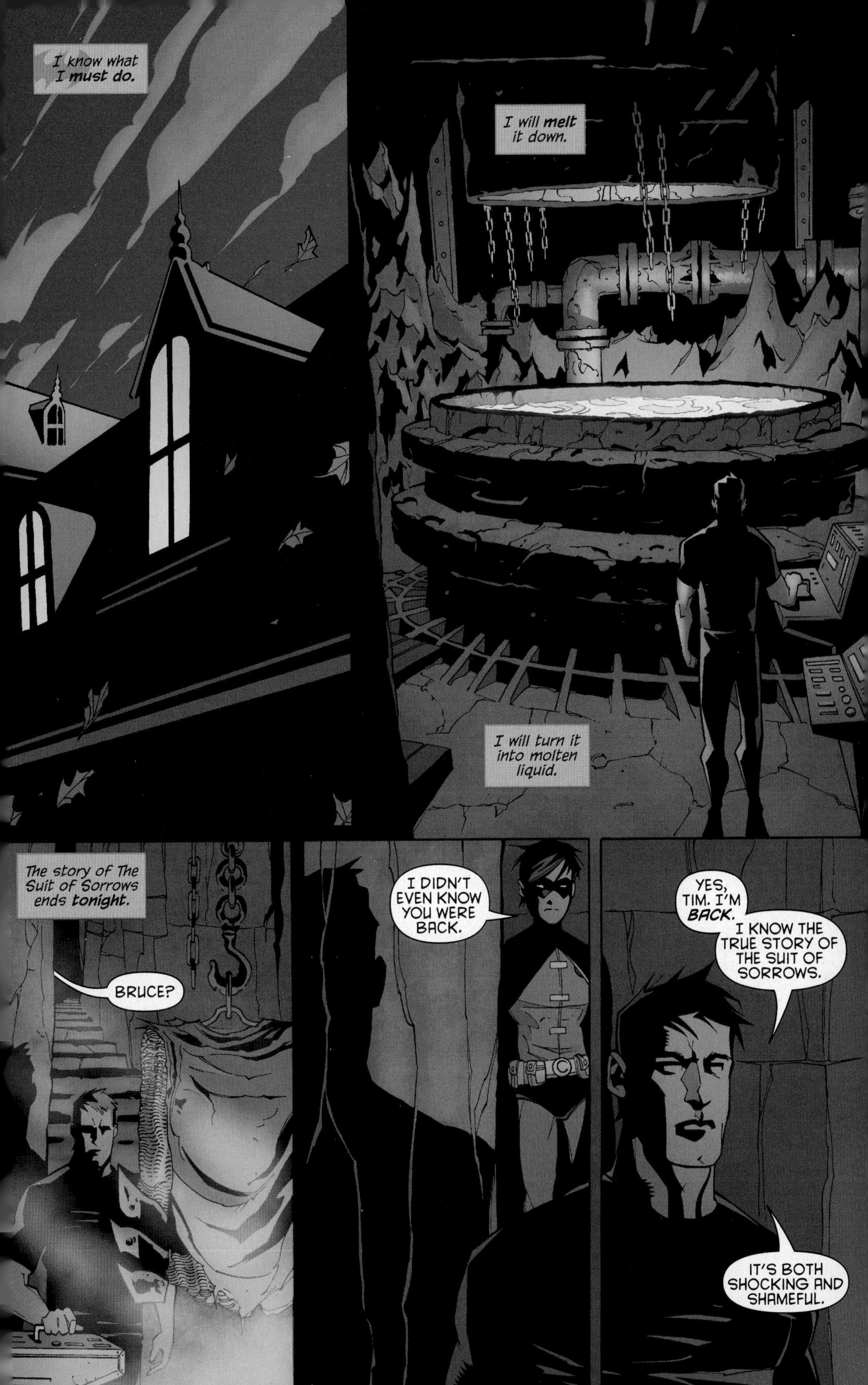
I know what I must do.
I will melt it down.
I will turn it into molten liquid.
The story of The Suit of Sorrows ends tonight.
BRUCE?
I DIDN'T EVEN KNOW YOU WERE BACK.
YES, TIM. I'M BACK.
I KNOW THE TRUE STORY OF THE SUIT OF SORROWS.
IT'S BOTH SHOCKING AND SHAMEFUL.

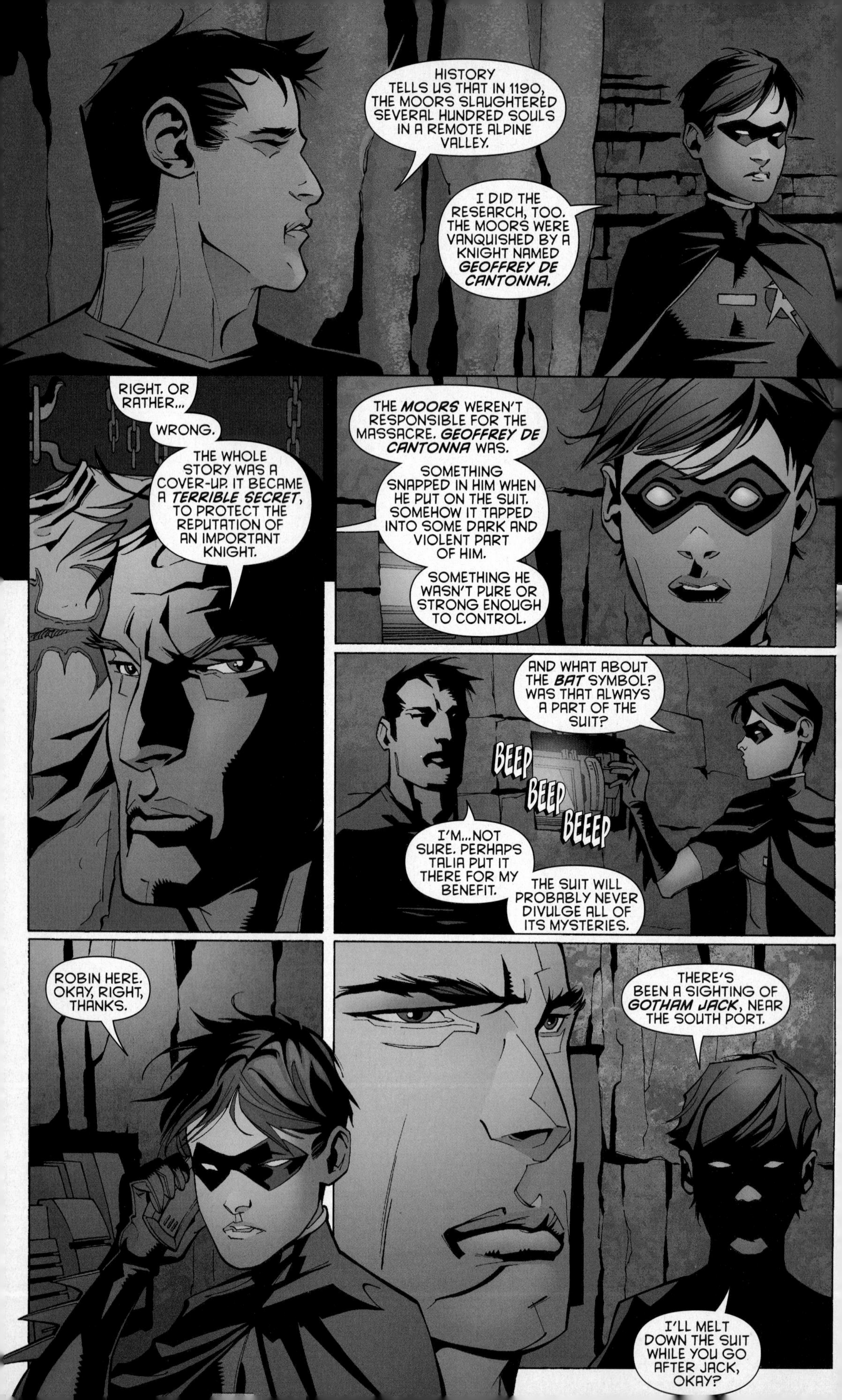
HISTORY TELLS US THAT IN 1190, THE MOORS SLAUGHTERED SEVERAL HUNDRED SOULS IN A REMOTE ALPINE VALLEY.
I DID THE RESEARCH, TOO. THE MOORS WERE VANQUISHED BY A KNIGHT NAMED GEOFFREY DE CANTONNA.
RIGHT. OR RATHER...
WRONG.
THE WHOLE STORY WAS A COVER-UP. IT BECAME A TERRIBLE SECRET, TO PROTECT THE REPUTATION OF AN IMPORTANT KNIGHT.
THE MOORS WEREN'T RESPONSIBLE FOR THE MASSACRE. GEOFFREY DE CANTONNA WAS.
SOMETHING SNAPPED IN HIM WHEN HE PUT ON THE SUIT. SOMEHOW IT TAPPED INTO SOME DARK AND VIOLENT PART OF HIM.
SOMETHING HE WASN'T PURE OR STRONG ENOUGH TO CONTROL.
AND WHAT ABOUT THE BAT SYMBOL? WAS THAT ALWAYS A PART OF THE SUIT?
BEEP
BEEP
BEEEP
I'M...NOT SURE. PERHAPS TALIA PUT IT THERE FOR MY BENEFIT.
THE SUIT WILL PROBABLY NEVER DIVULGE ALL OF ITS MYSTERIES.
ROBIN HERE. OKAY, RIGHT, THANKS.
THERE'S BEEN A SIGHTING OF GOTHAM JACK, NEAR THE SOUTH PORT.
I'LL MELT DOWN THE SUIT WHILE YOU GO AFTER JACK, OKAY?

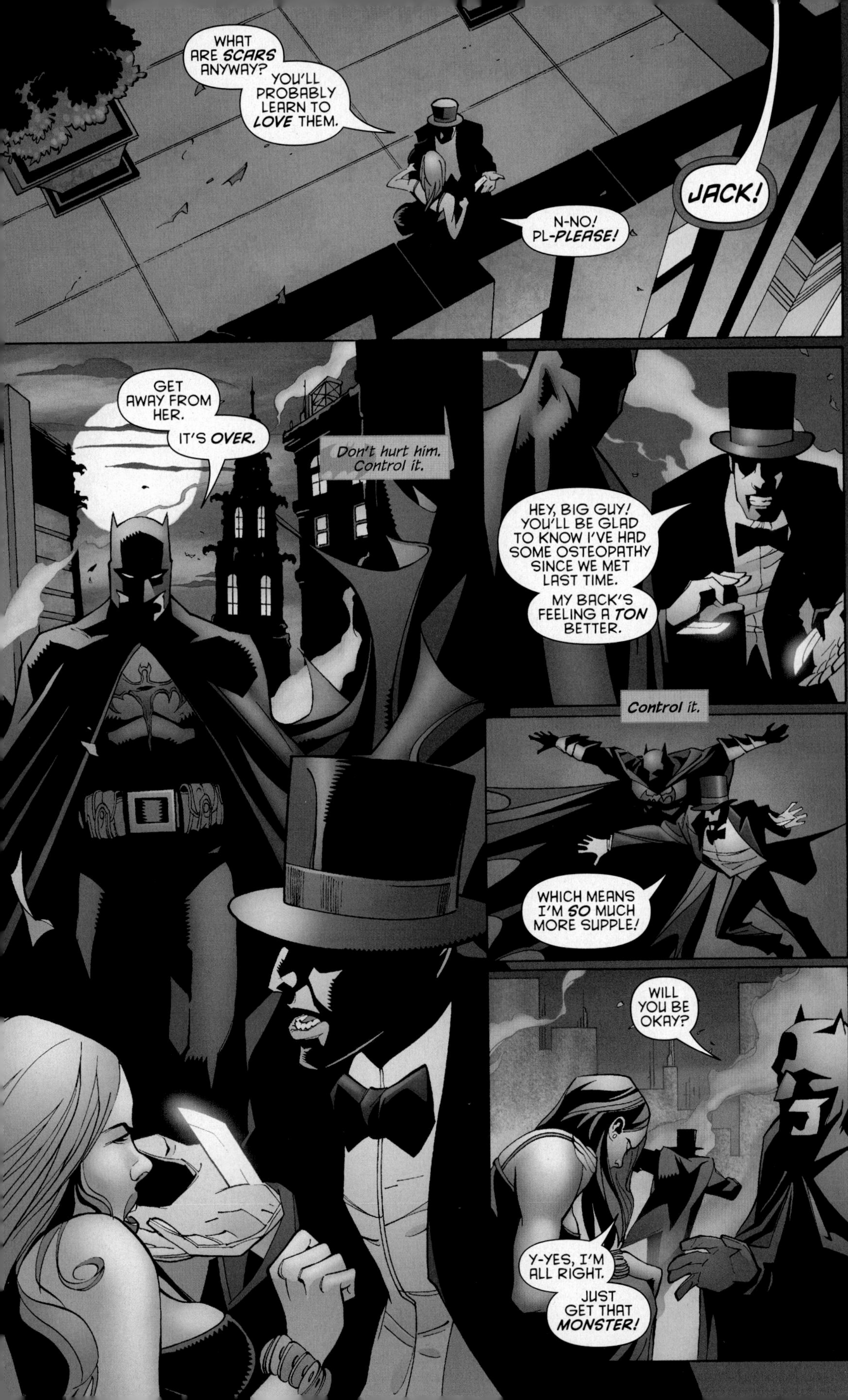
WHAT ARE SCARS ANYWAY? YOU'LL PROBABLY LEARN TO LOVE THEM.
N-NO! PL-PLEASE!
JACK!
GET AWAY FROM HER.
IT'S OVER.
Don't hurt him. Control it.
HEY, BIG GUY! YOU'LL BE GLAD TO KNOW I'VE HAD SOME OSTEOPATHY SINCE WE MET LAST TIME.
MY BACK'S FEELING A TON BETTER.
Control it.
WHICH MEANS I'M SO MUCH MORE SUPPLE!
WILL YOU BE OKAY?
Y-YES, I'M ALL RIGHT.
JUST GET THAT MONSTER!

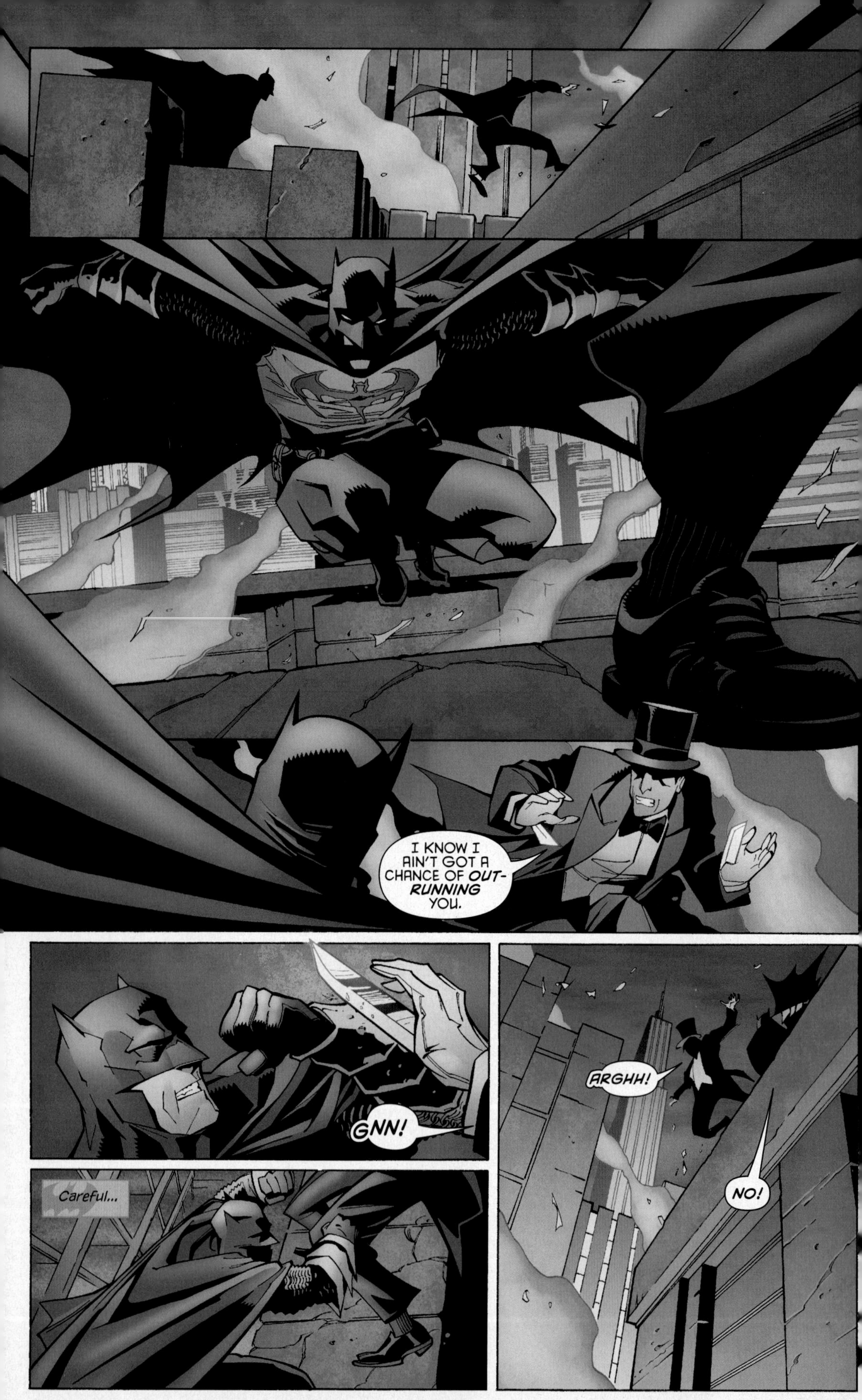
I KNOW I AIN'T GOT A CHANCE OF OUT-RUNNING YOU.
GNN!
Careful...
ARGHH!
NO!

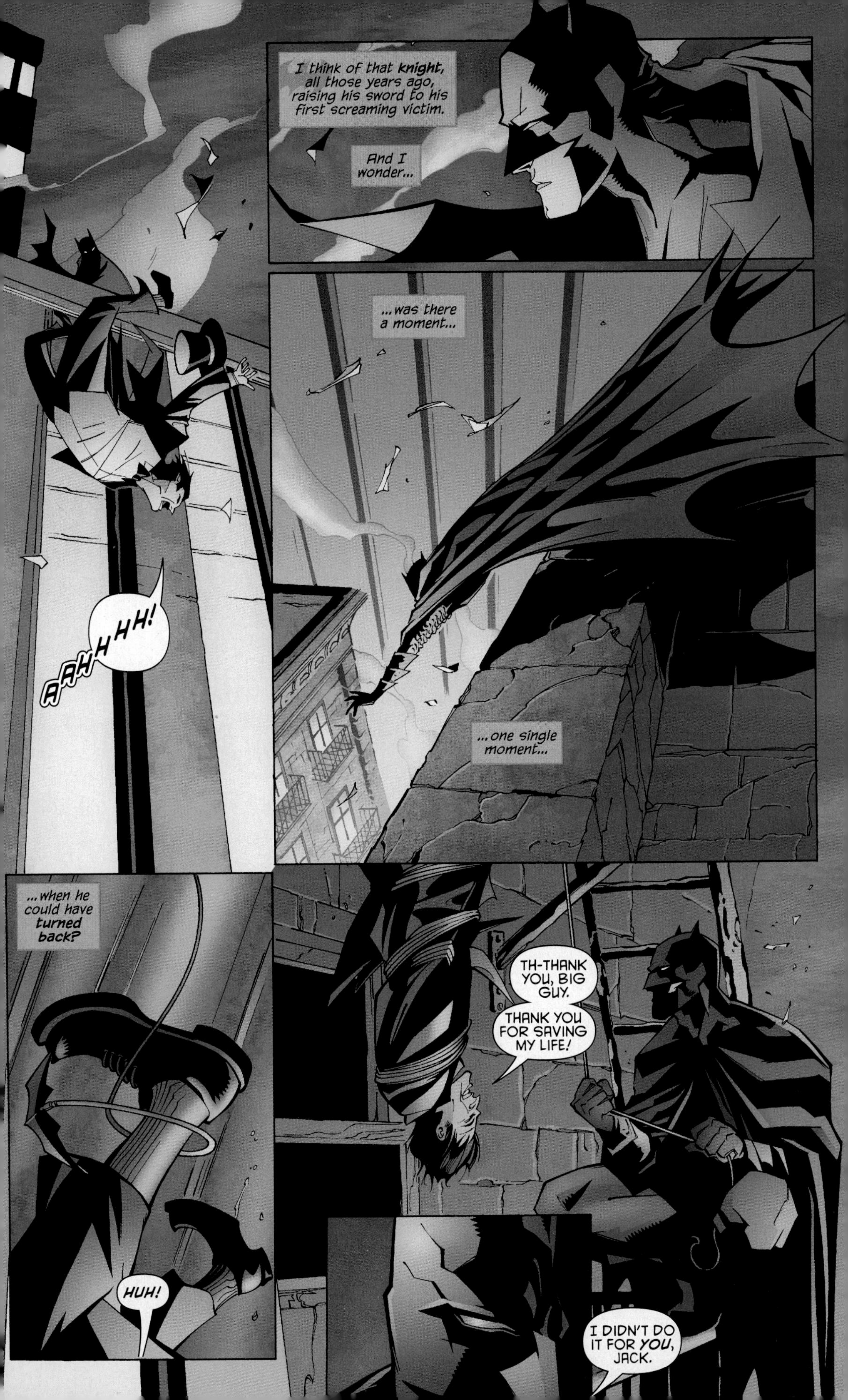
I think of that knight, all those years ago, raising his sword to his first screaming victim.
And I wonder...
AAHHHH!
...was there a moment...
...one single moment...
...when he could have turned back?
HUH!
TH-THANK YOU, BIG GUY.
THANK YOU FOR SAVING MY LIFE!
I DIDN'T DO IT FOR YOU, JACK.

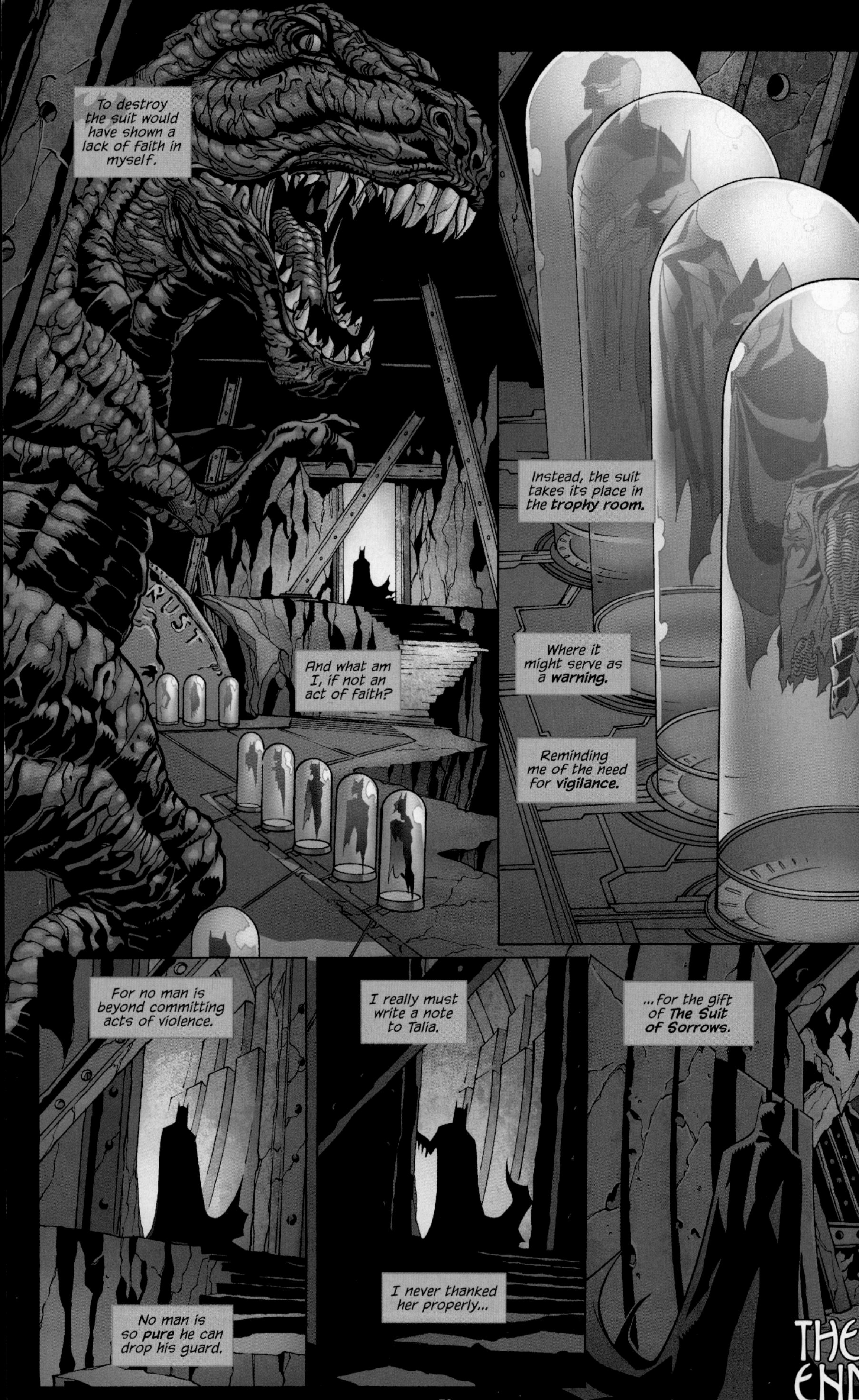

To destroy the suit would have shown a lack of faith in myself.
RUST
And what am I, if not an act of faith?
Instead, the suit takes its place in the **trophy room.**
Where it might serve as a **warning.**
Reminding me of the need for **vigilance.**
For no man is beyond committing acts of violence.
No man is so **pure** he can drop his guard.
I really must write a note to Talia.
I never thanked her properly...
...for the gift of **The Suit of Sorrows.**

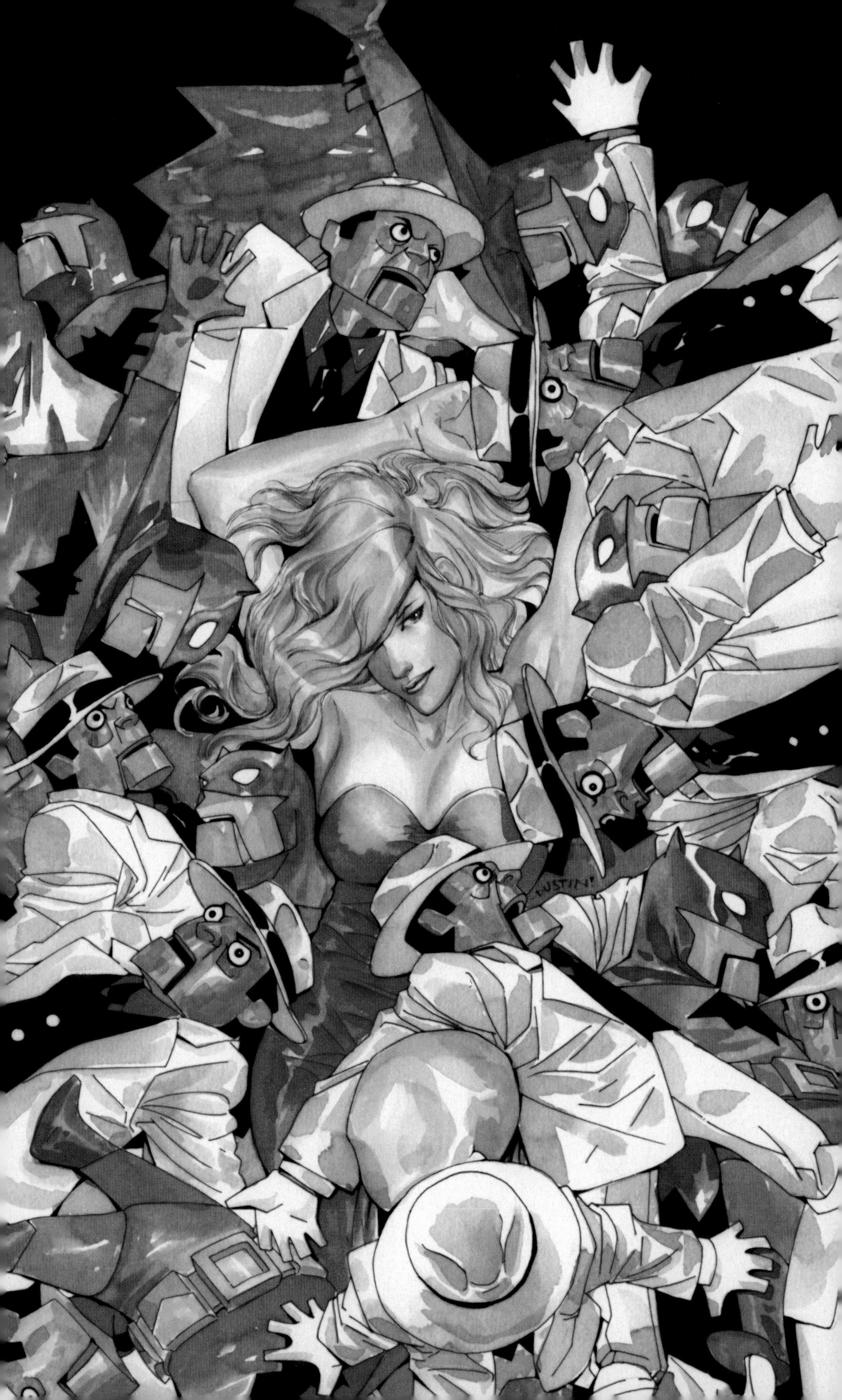

Opening Night

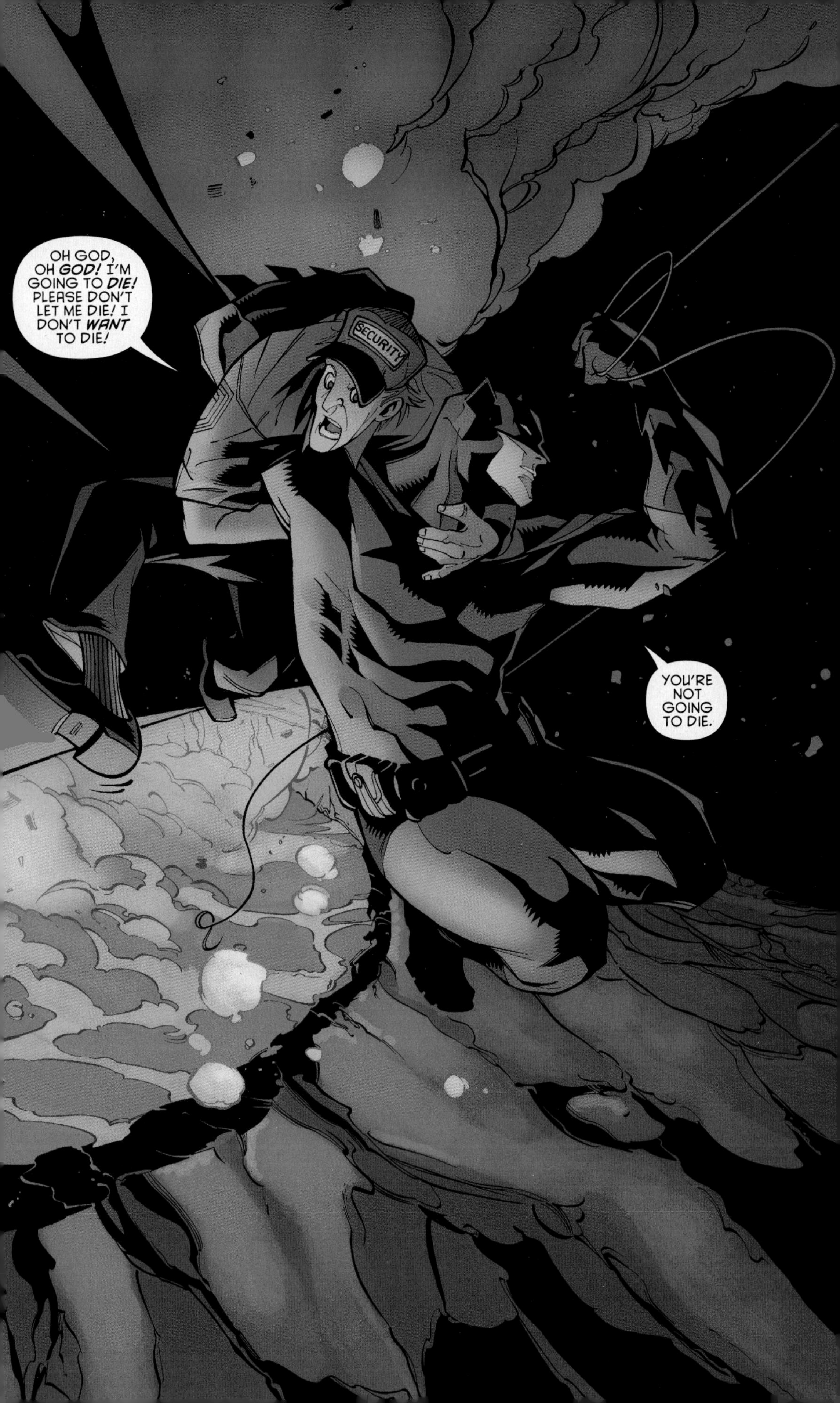
OH GOD, OH GOD! I'M GOING TO DIE! PLEASE DON'T LET ME DIE! I DON'T WANT TO DIE!
YOU'RE NOT GOING TO DIE.
SECURITY

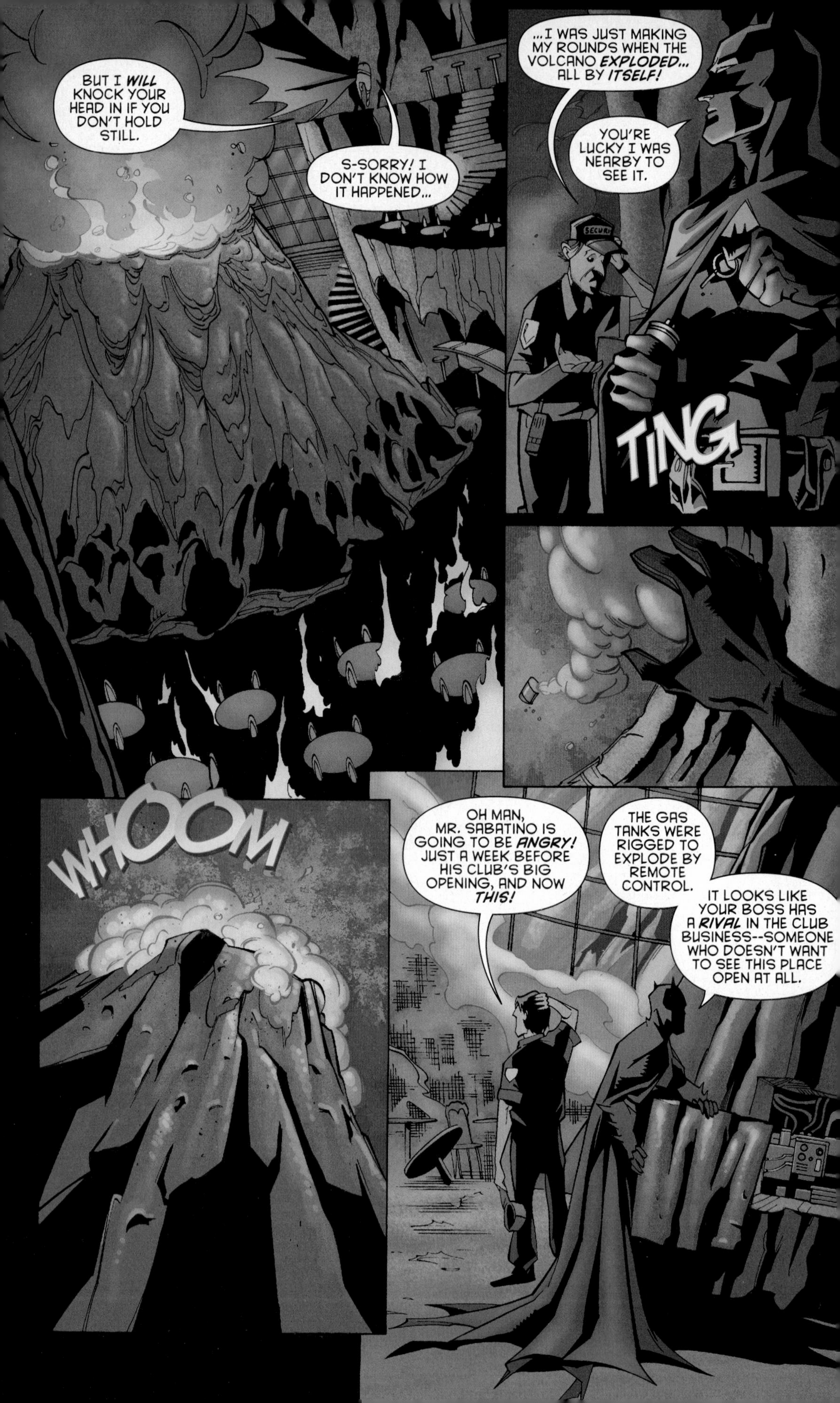

BUT I WILL KNOCK YOUR HEAD IN IF YOU DON'T HOLD STILL.
S-SORRY! I DON'T KNOW HOW IT HAPPENED...
...I WAS JUST MAKING MY ROUNDS WHEN THE VOLCANO EXPLODED... ALL BY ITSELF!
YOU'RE LUCKY I WAS NEARBY TO SEE IT.
SECURITY
TING
WHOOM
OH MAN, MR. SABATINO IS GOING TO BE ANGRY! JUST A WEEK BEFORE HIS CLUB'S BIG OPENING, AND NOW THIS!
THE GAS TANKS WERE RIGGED TO EXPLODE BY REMOTE CONTROL.
IT LOOKS LIKE YOUR BOSS HAS A RIVAL IN THE CLUB BUSINESS--SOMEONE WHO DOESN'T WANT TO SEE THIS PLACE OPEN AT ALL.

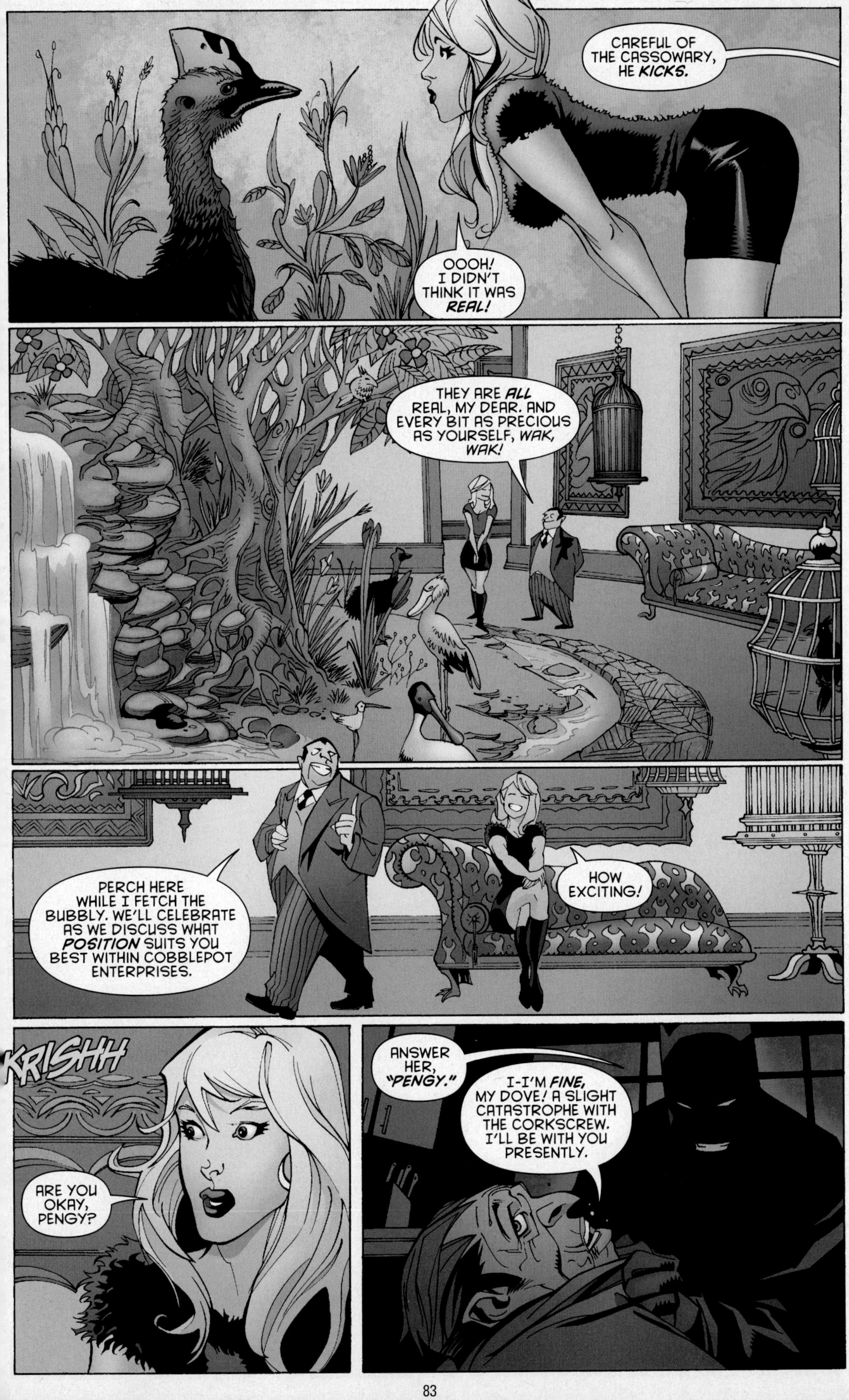
CAREFUL OF THE CASSOWARY, HE KICKS.
OOOH! I DIDN'T THINK IT WAS REAL!
THEY ARE ALL REAL, MY DEAR. AND EVERY BIT AS PRECIOUS AS YOURSELF, WAK, WAK!
PERCH HERE WHILE I FETCH THE BUBBLY. WE'LL CELEBRATE AS WE DISCUSS WHAT POSITION SUITS YOU BEST WITHIN COBBLEPOT ENTERPRISES.
HOW EXCITING!
KRISHH
ARE YOU OKAY, PENGY?
ANSWER HER, "PENGY."
I-I'M FINE, MY DOVE! A SLIGHT CATASTROPHE WITH THE CORKSCREW. I'LL BE WITH YOU PRESENTLY.

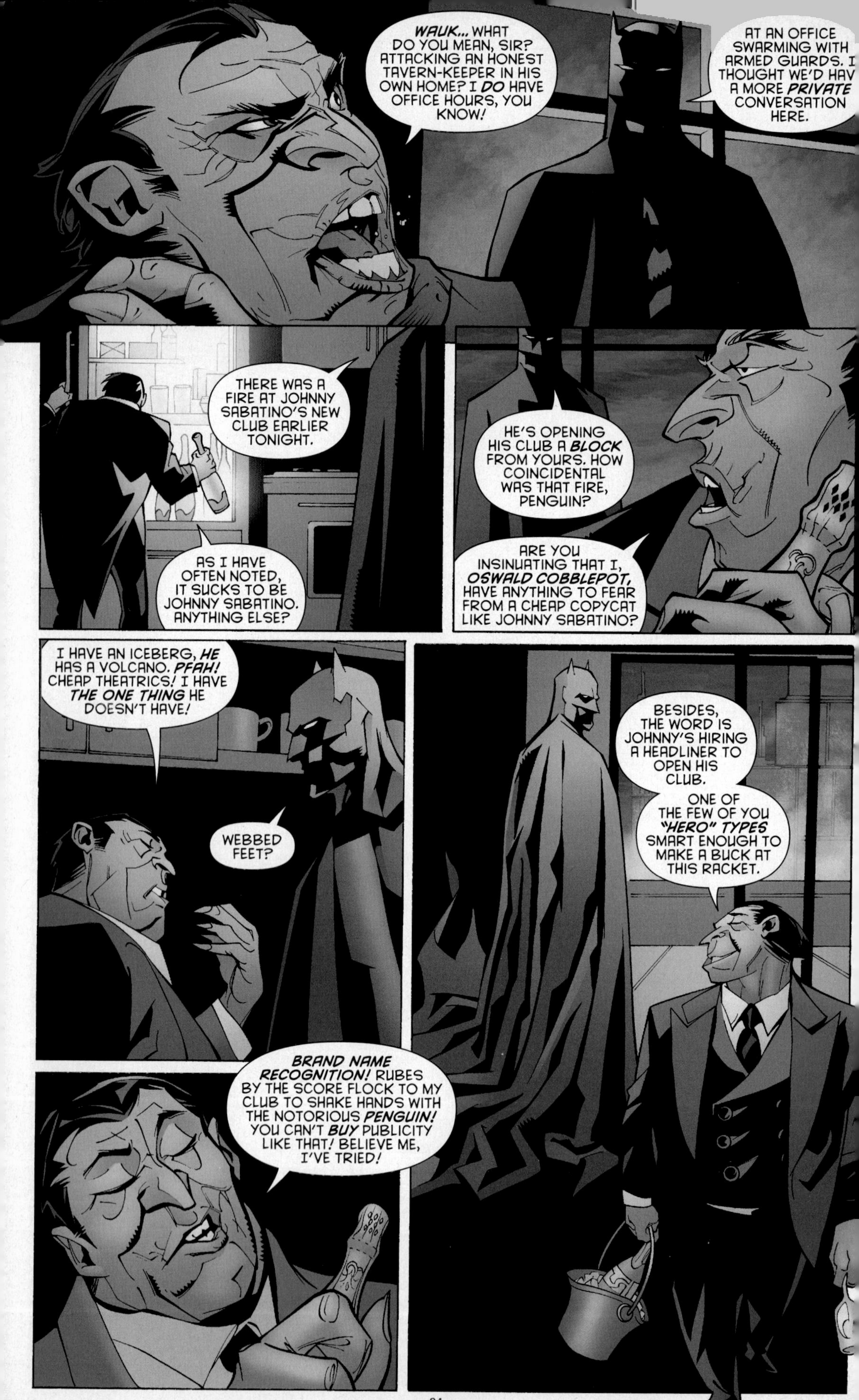
WAUK... WHAT DO YOU MEAN, SIR? ATTACKING AN HONEST TAVERN-KEEPER IN HIS OWN HOME? I DO HAVE OFFICE HOURS, YOU KNOW!
AT AN OFFICE SWARMING WITH ARMED GUARDS. I THOUGHT WE'D HAV A MORE PRIVATE CONVERSATION HERE.
THERE WAS A FIRE AT JOHNNY SABATINO'S NEW CLUB EARLIER TONIGHT.
AS I HAVE OFTEN NOTED, IT SUCKS TO BE JOHNNY SABATINO. ANYTHING ELSE?
HE'S OPENING HIS CLUB A BLOCK FROM YOURS. HOW COINCIDENTAL WAS THAT FIRE, PENGUIN?
ARE YOU INSINUATING THAT I, OSWALD COBBLEPOT, HAVE ANYTHING TO FEAR FROM A CHEAP COPYCAT LIKE JOHNNY SABATINO?
I HAVE AN ICEBERG, HE HAS A VOLCANO. PFAH! CHEAP THEATRICS! I HAVE THE ONE THING HE DOESN'T HAVE!
WEBBED FEET?
BRAND NAME RECOGNITION! RUBES BY THE SCORE FLOCK TO MY CLUB TO SHAKE HANDS WITH THE NOTORIOUS PENGUIN! YOU CAN'T BUY PUBLICITY LIKE THAT! BELIEVE ME, I'VE TRIED!
BESIDES, THE WORD IS JOHNNY'S HIRING A HEADLINER TO OPEN HIS CLUB.
ONE OF THE FEW OF YOU "HERO" TYPES SMART ENOUGH TO MAKE A BUCK AT THIS RACKET.

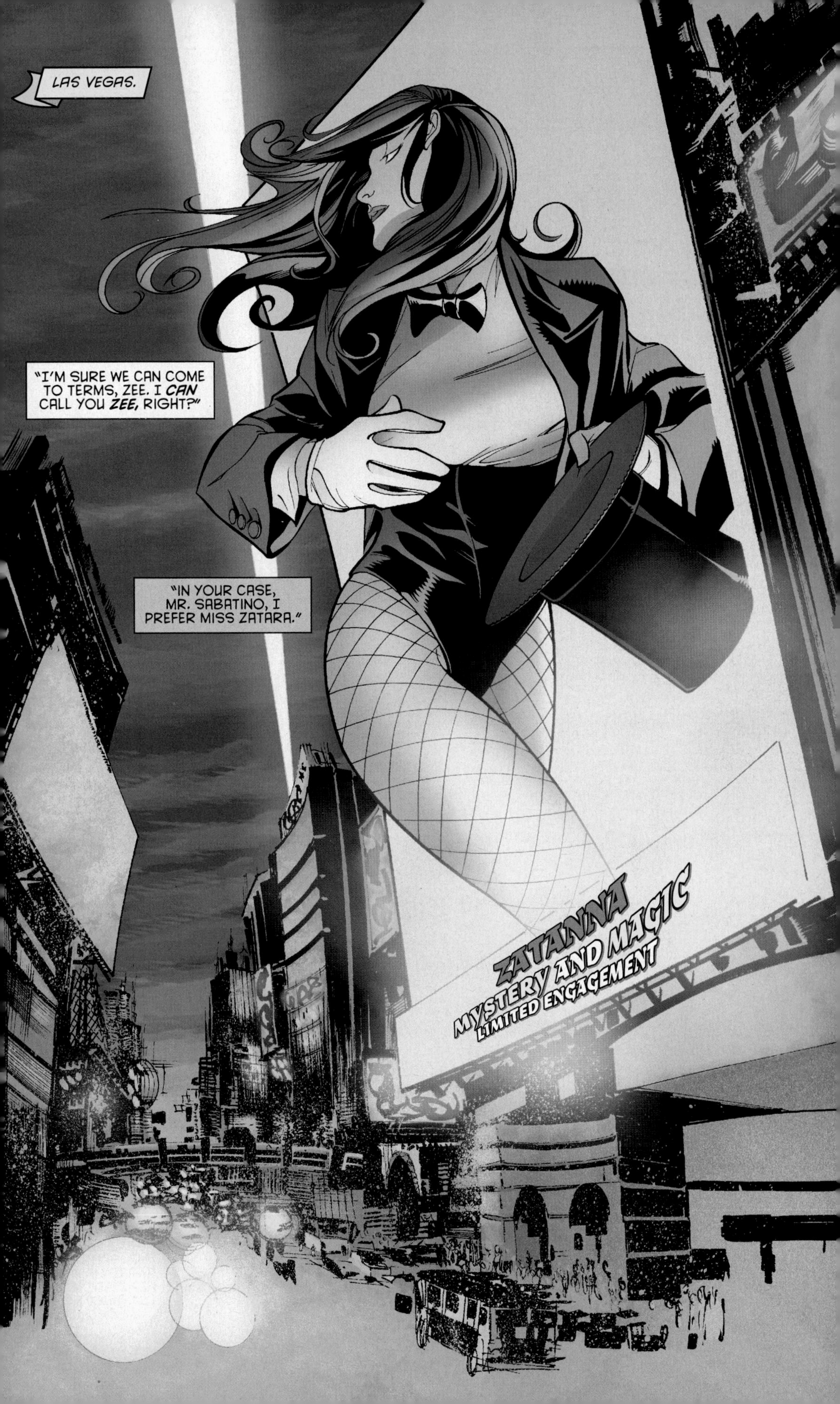
LAS VEGAS.
"I'M SURE WE CAN COME TO TERMS, ZEE. I *CAN* CALL YOU *ZEE,* RIGHT?"
"IN YOUR CASE, MR. SABATINO, I PREFER MISS ZATARA."
ZATANNA
MYSTERY AND MAGIC
LIMITED ENGAGEMENT

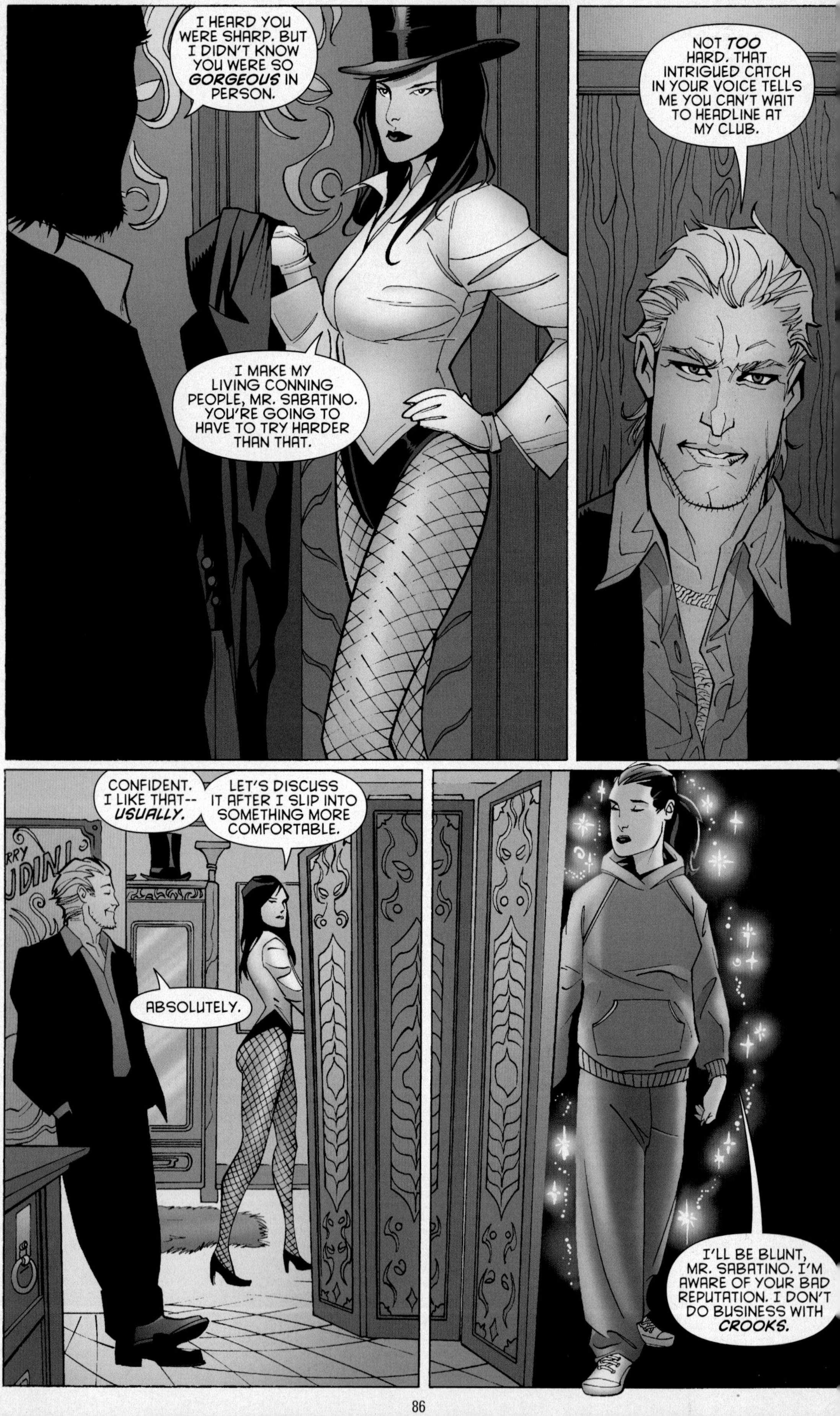
I HEARD YOU WERE SHARP. BUT I DIDN'T KNOW YOU WERE SO **GORGEOUS** IN PERSON.
I MAKE MY LIVING CONNING PEOPLE, MR. SABATINO. YOU'RE GOING TO HAVE TO TRY HARDER THAN THAT.
NOT ***TOO*** HARD. THAT INTRIGUED CATCH IN YOUR VOICE TELLS ME YOU CAN'T WAIT TO HEADLINE AT MY CLUB.
CONFIDENT. I LIKE THAT-- ***USUALLY.***
LET'S DISCUSS IT AFTER I SLIP INTO SOMETHING MORE COMFORTABLE.
ABSOLUTELY.
I'LL BE BLUNT, MR. SABATINO. I'M AWARE OF YOUR BAD REPUTATION. I DON'T DO BUSINESS WITH ***CROOKS.***

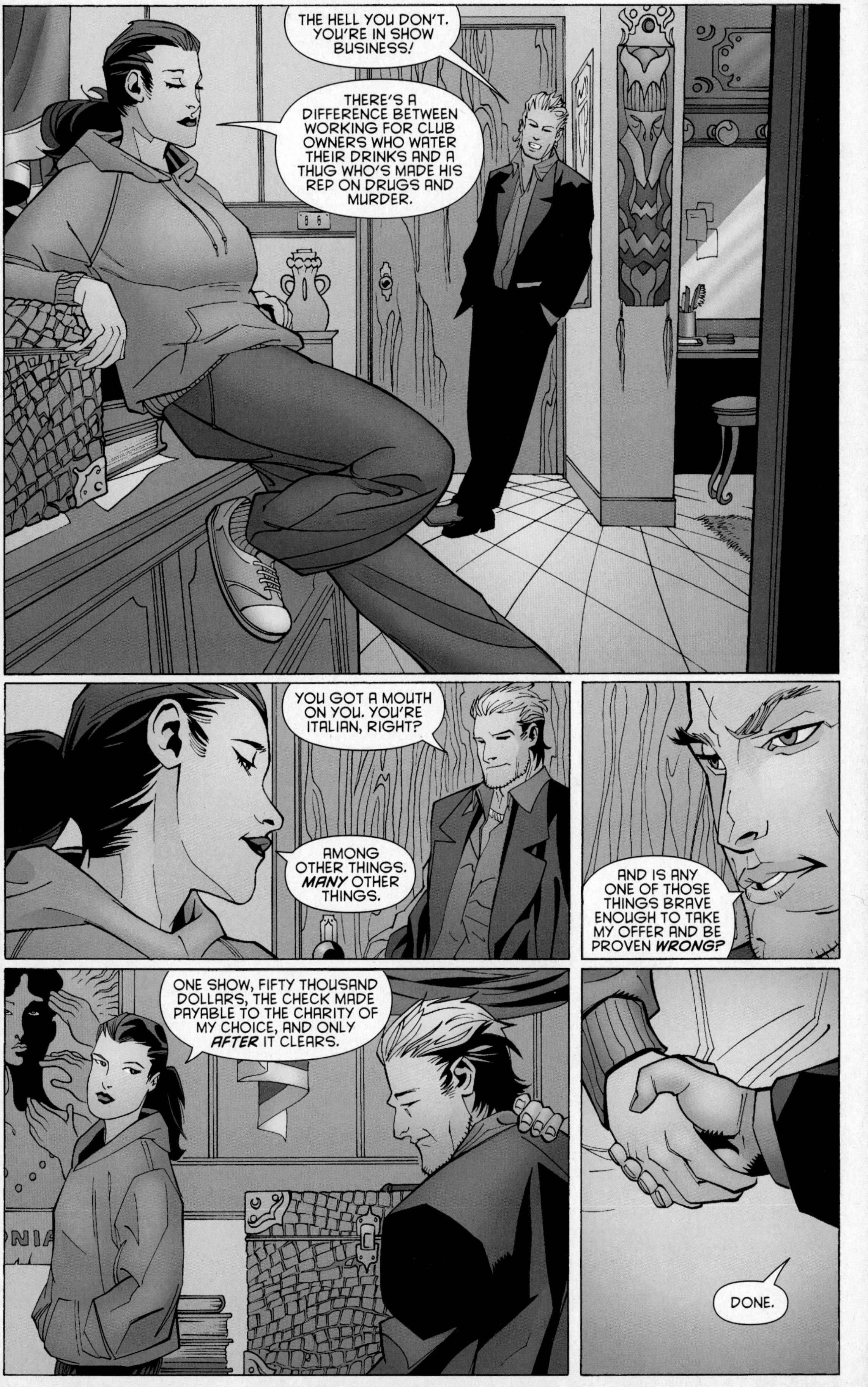
THE HELL YOU DON'T. YOU'RE IN SHOW BUSINESS!
THERE'S A DIFFERENCE BETWEEN WORKING FOR CLUB OWNERS WHO WATER THEIR DRINKS AND A THUG WHO'S MADE HIS REP ON DRUGS AND MURDER.
YOU GOT A MOUTH ON YOU. YOU'RE ITALIAN, RIGHT?
AMONG OTHER THINGS. *MANY* OTHER THINGS.
AND IS ANY ONE OF THOSE THINGS BRAVE ENOUGH TO TAKE MY OFFER AND BE PROVEN *WRONG?*
ONE SHOW, FIFTY THOUSAND DOLLARS, THE CHECK MADE PAYABLE TO THE CHARITY OF MY CHOICE, AND ONLY *AFTER* IT CLEARS.
DONE.

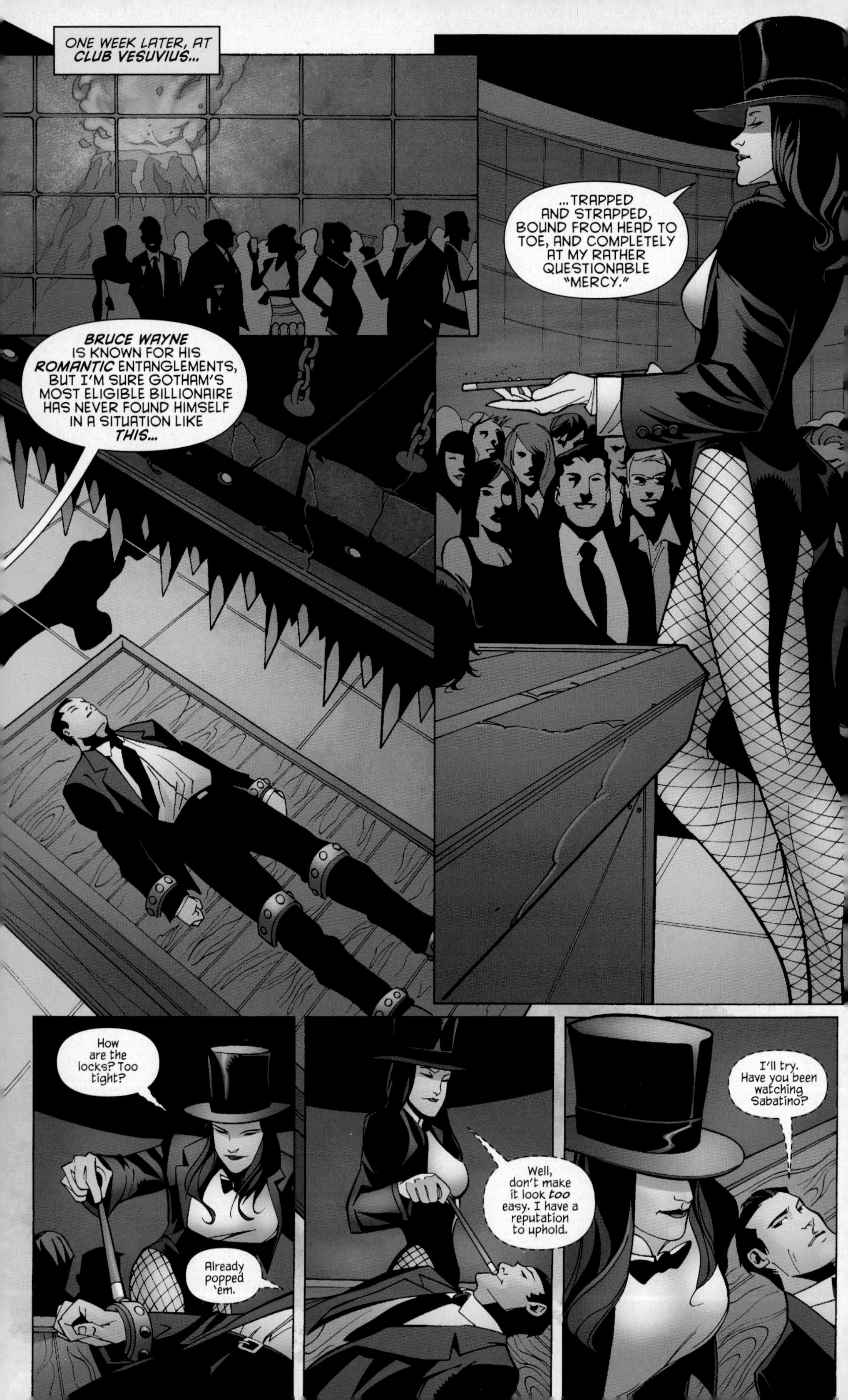
ONE WEEK LATER, AT CLUB VESUVIUS...
BRUCE WAYNE IS KNOWN FOR HIS ROMANTIC ENTANGLEMENTS, BUT I'M SURE GOTHAM'S MOST ELIGIBLE BILLIONAIRE HAS NEVER FOUND HIMSELF IN A SITUATION LIKE THIS...
...TRAPPED AND STRAPPED, BOUND FROM HEAD TO TOE, AND COMPLETELY AT MY RATHER QUESTIONABLE "MERCY."
How are the locks? Too tight?
Already popped 'em.
Well, don't make it look too easy. I have a reputation to uphold.
I'll try. Have you been watching Sabatino?

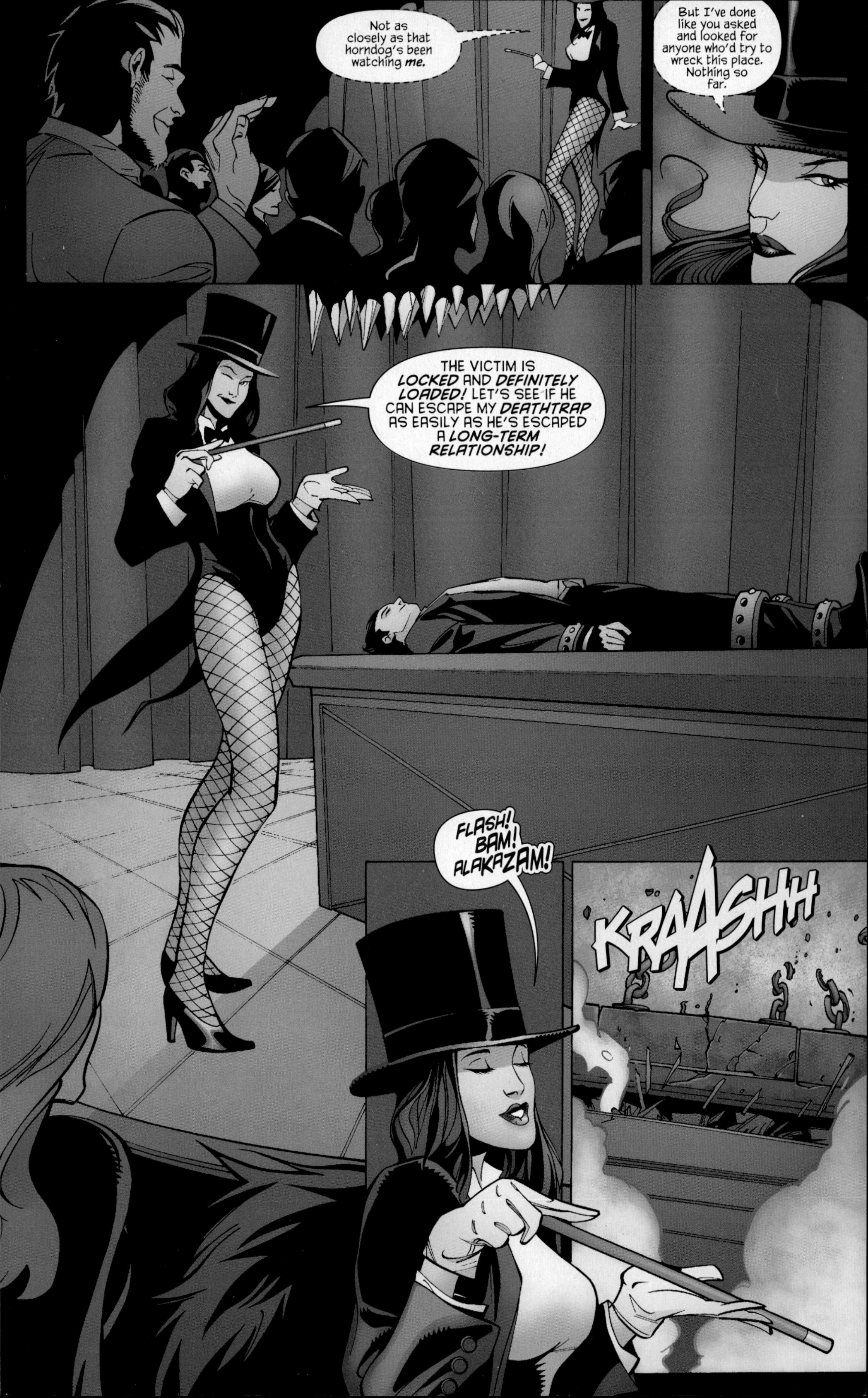
Not as closely as that horndog's been watching *me.*
But I've done like you asked and looked for anyone who'd try to wreck this place. Nothing so far.
THE VICTIM IS *LOCKED* AND *DEFINITELY LOADED!* LET'S SEE IF HE CAN ESCAPE MY *DEATHTRAP* AS EASILY AS HE'S ESCAPED A *LONG-TERM RELATIONSHIP!*
FLASH! BAM! ALAKAZAM!
KRAASHH

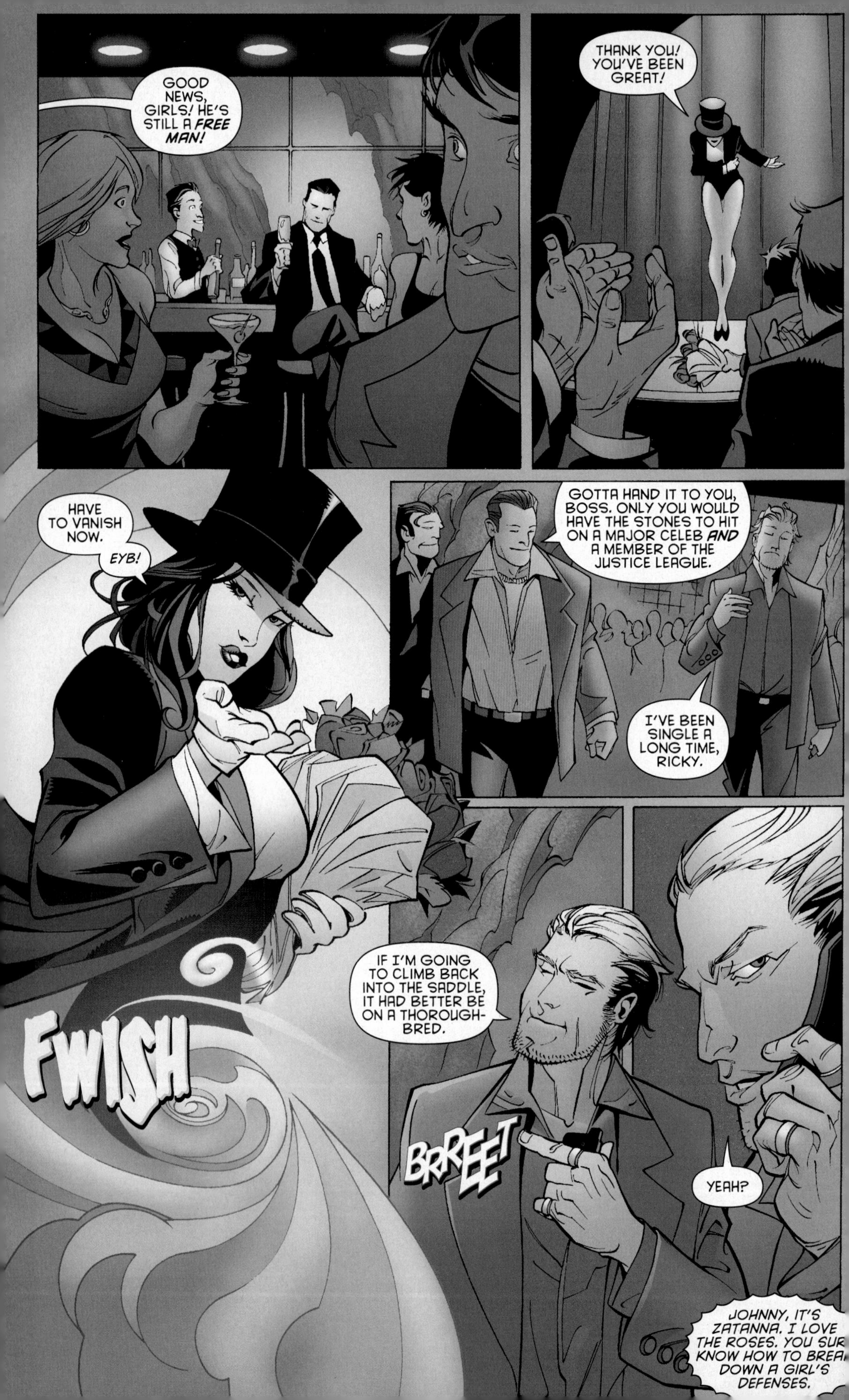
GOOD NEWS, GIRLS! HE'S STILL A *FREE MAN!*
THANK YOU! YOU'VE BEEN GREAT!
HAVE TO VANISH NOW.
EYB!
GOTTA HAND IT TO YOU, BOSS. ONLY YOU WOULD HAVE THE STONES TO HIT ON A MAJOR CELEB *AND* A MEMBER OF THE JUSTICE LEAGUE.
I'VE BEEN SINGLE A LONG TIME, RICKY.
FWISH
IF I'M GOING TO CLIMB BACK INTO THE SADDLE, IT HAD BETTER BE ON A THOROUGH-BRED.
BRREEET
YEAH?
JOHNNY, IT'S ZATANNA. I LOVE THE ROSES. YOU SUR KNOW HOW TO BREA DOWN A GIRL'S DEFENSES.

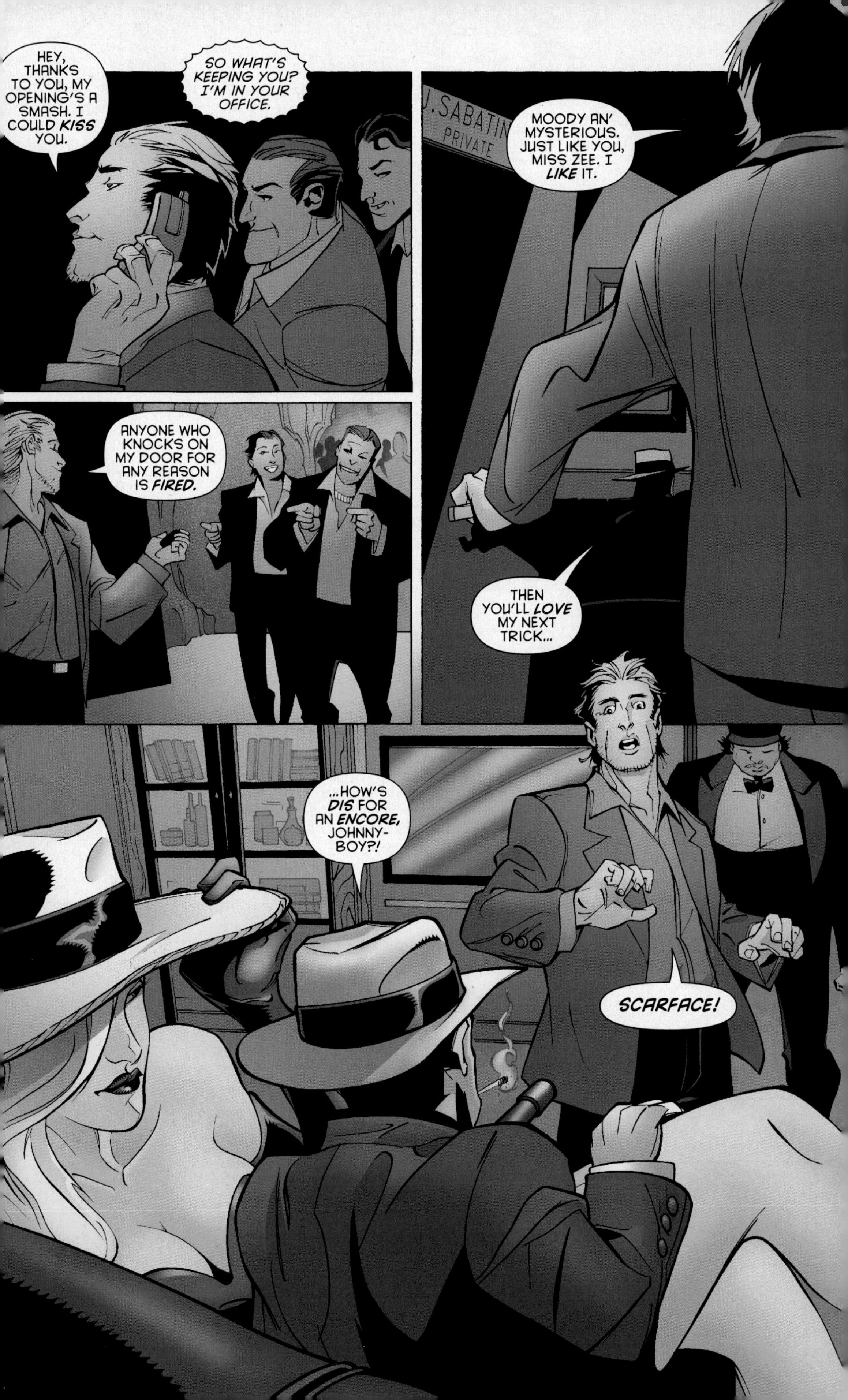
HEY, THANKS TO YOU, MY OPENING'S A SMASH. I COULD KISS YOU.
SO WHAT'S KEEPING YOU? I'M IN YOUR OFFICE.
ANYONE WHO KNOCKS ON MY DOOR FOR ANY REASON IS FIRED.
J. SABATIN
PRIVATE
MOODY AN' MYSTERIOUS. JUST LIKE YOU, MISS ZEE. I LIKE IT.
THEN YOU'LL LOVE MY NEXT TRICK...
...HOW'S DIS FOR AN ENCORE, JOHNNY-BOY?!
SCARFACE!

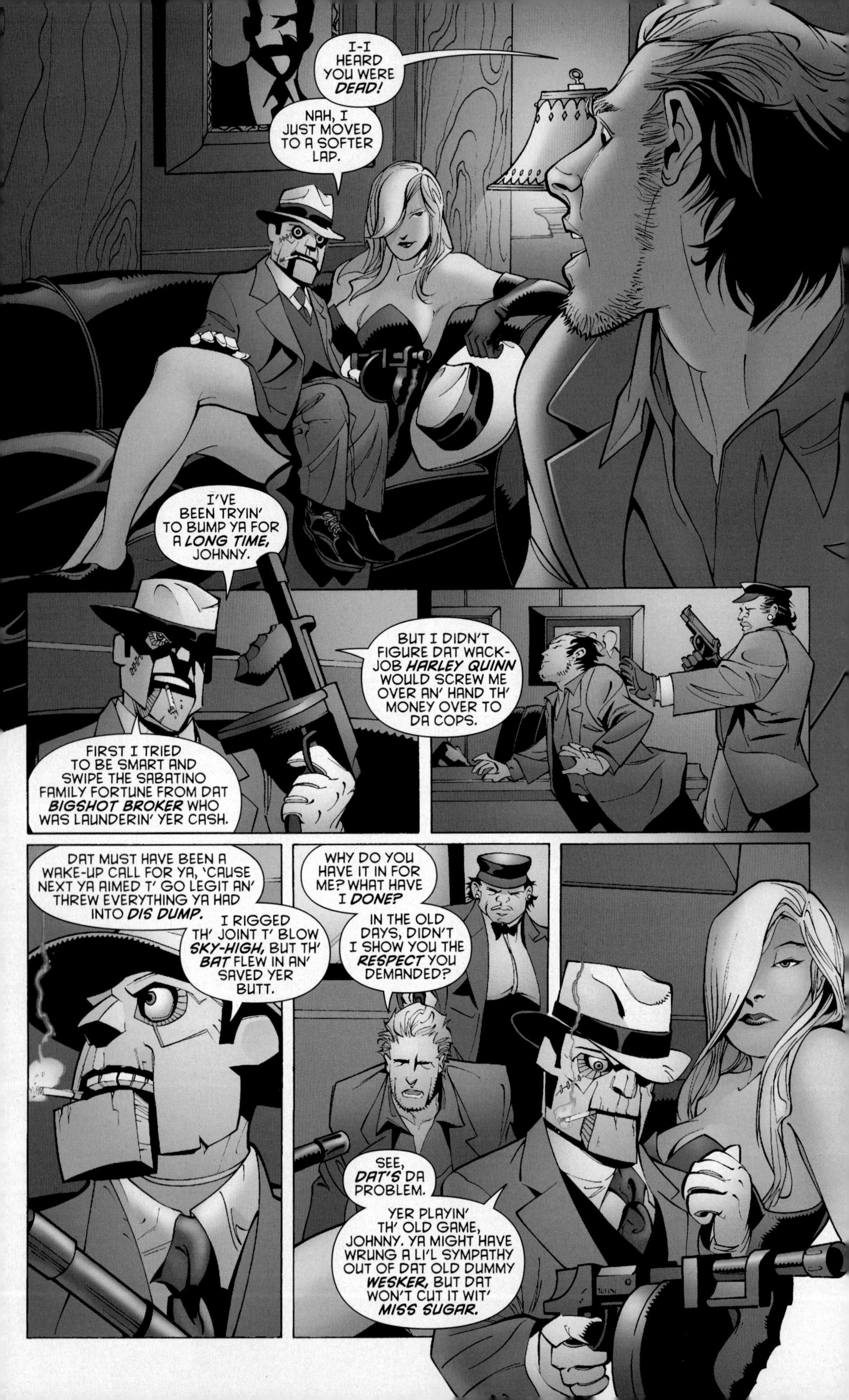
I-I HEARD YOU WERE DEAD!
NAH, I JUST MOVED TO A SOFTER LAP.
I'VE BEEN TRYIN' TO BUMP YA FOR A LONG TIME, JOHNNY.
FIRST I TRIED TO BE SMART AND SWIPE THE SABATINO FAMILY FORTUNE FROM DAT BIGSHOT BROKER WHO WAS LAUNDERIN' YER CASH.
BUT I DIDN'T FIGURE DAT WACK-JOB HARLEY QUINN WOULD SCREW ME OVER AN' HAND TH' MONEY OVER TO DA COPS.
DAT MUST HAVE BEEN A WAKE-UP CALL FOR YA, 'CAUSE NEXT YA AIMED T' GO LEGIT AN' THREW EVERYTHING YA HAD INTO DIS DUMP.
I RIGGED TH' JOINT T' BLOW SKY-HIGH, BUT TH' BAT FLEW IN AN' SAVED YER BUTT.
WHY DO YOU HAVE IT IN FOR ME? WHAT HAVE I DONE?
IN THE OLD DAYS, DIDN'T I SHOW YOU THE RESPECT YOU DEMANDED?
SEE, DAT'S DA PROBLEM.
YER PLAYIN' TH' OLD GAME, JOHNNY. YA MIGHT HAVE WRUNG A LI'L SYMPATHY OUT OF DAT OLD DUMMY WESKER, BUT DAT WON'T CUT IT WIT' MISS SUGAR.

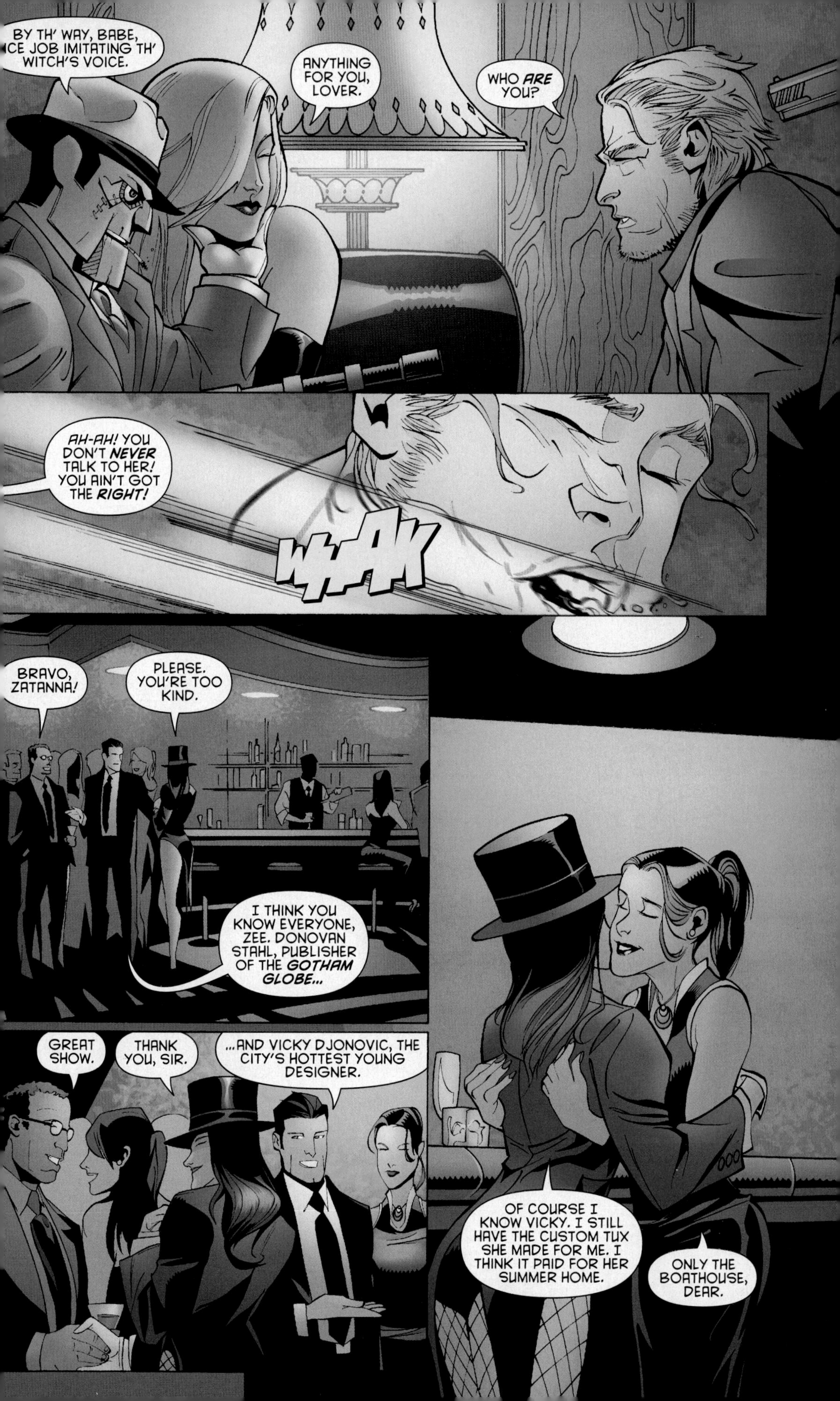
BY TH' WAY, BABE, ICE JOB IMITATING TH' WITCH'S VOICE.
ANYTHING FOR YOU, LOVER.
WHO *ARE* YOU?
AH-AH! YOU DON'T *NEVER* TALK TO HER! YOU AIN'T GOT THE *RIGHT!*
WHAK
BRAVO, ZATANNA!
PLEASE. YOU'RE TOO KIND.
I THINK YOU KNOW EVERYONE, ZEE. DONOVAN STAHL, PUBLISHER OF THE *GOTHAM GLOBE*...
GREAT SHOW.
THANK YOU, SIR.
...AND VICKY DJONOVIC, THE CITY'S HOTTEST YOUNG DESIGNER.
OF COURSE I KNOW VICKY. I STILL HAVE THE CUSTOM TUX SHE MADE FOR ME. I THINK IT PAID FOR HER SUMMER HOME.
ONLY THE BOATHOUSE, DEAR.

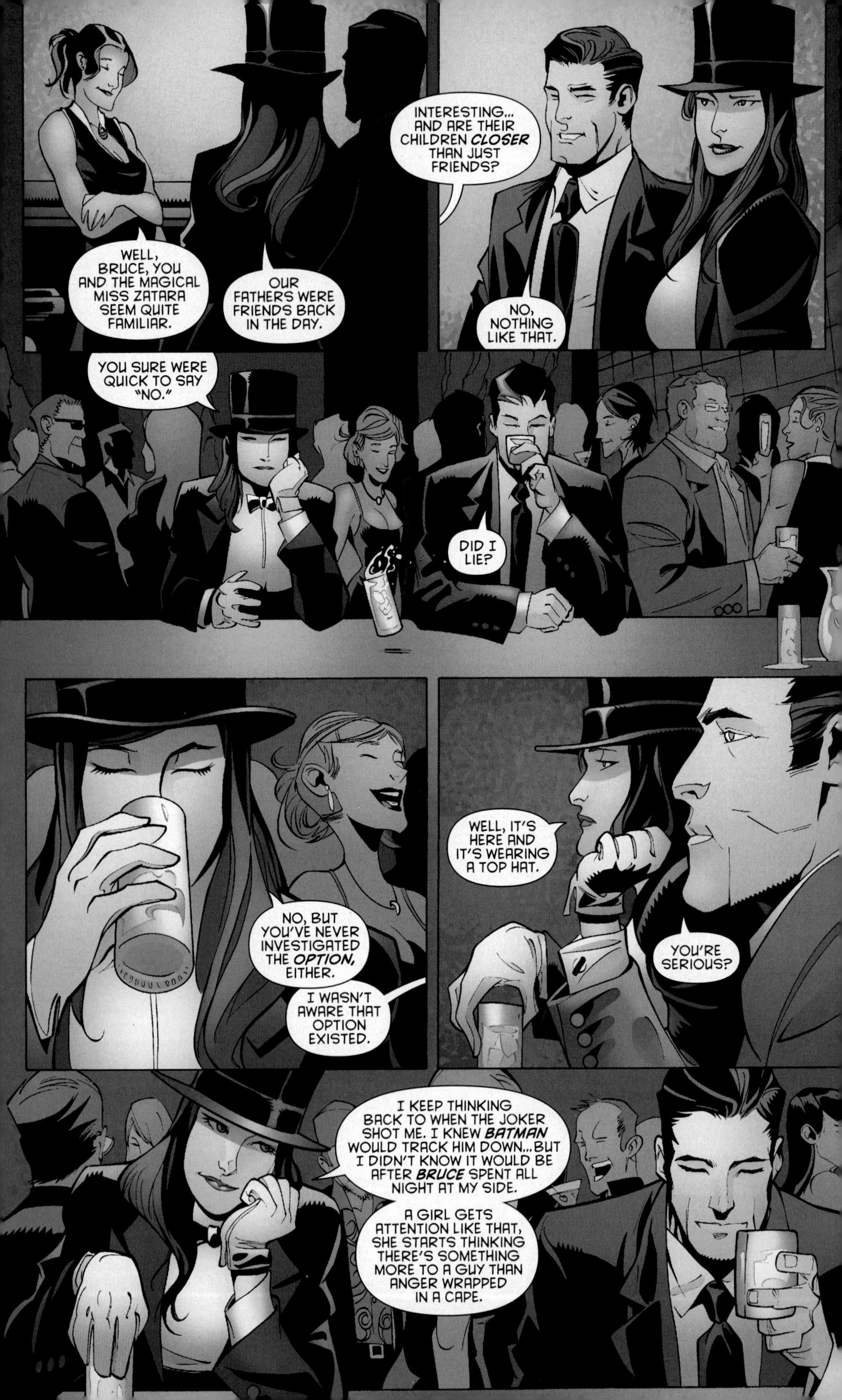
WELL, BRUCE, YOU AND THE MAGICAL MISS ZATARA SEEM QUITE FAMILIAR.
OUR FATHERS WERE FRIENDS BACK IN THE DAY.
INTERESTING... AND ARE THEIR CHILDREN CLOSER THAN JUST FRIENDS?
NO, NOTHING LIKE THAT.
YOU SURE WERE QUICK TO SAY "NO."
DID I LIE?
NO, BUT YOU'VE NEVER INVESTIGATED THE OPTION, EITHER.
I WASN'T AWARE THAT OPTION EXISTED.
WELL, IT'S HERE AND IT'S WEARING A TOP HAT.
YOU'RE SERIOUS?
I KEEP THINKING BACK TO WHEN THE JOKER SHOT ME. I KNEW BATMAN WOULD TRACK HIM DOWN...BUT I DIDN'T KNOW IT WOULD BE AFTER BRUCE SPENT ALL NIGHT AT MY SIDE.
A GIRL GETS ATTENTION LIKE THAT, SHE STARTS THINKING THERE'S SOMETHING MORE TO A GUY THAN ANGER WRAPPED IN A CAPE.

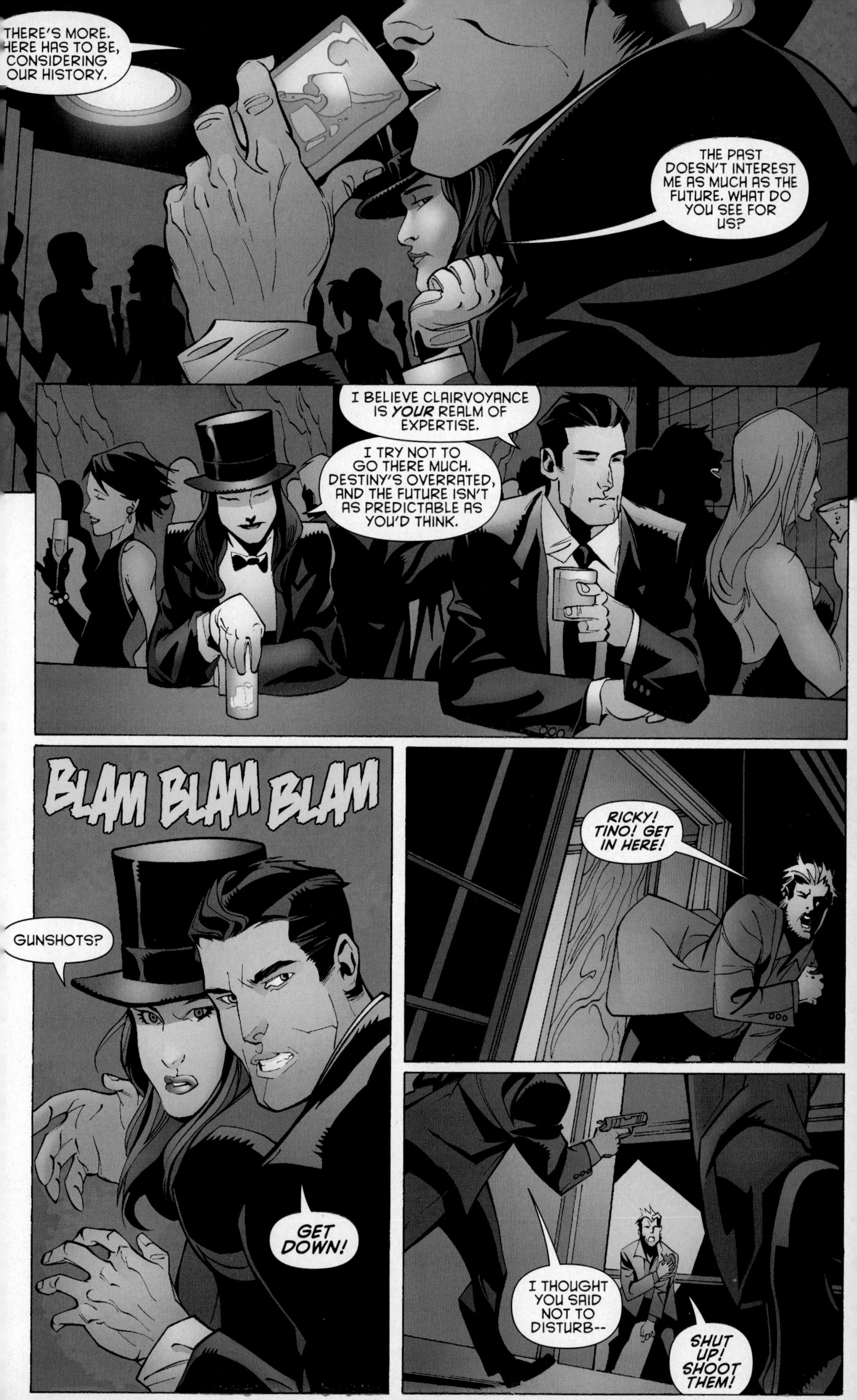

THERE'S MORE. HERE HAS TO BE, CONSIDERING OUR HISTORY.
THE PAST DOESN'T INTEREST ME AS MUCH AS THE FUTURE. WHAT DO YOU SEE FOR US?
I BELIEVE CLAIRVOYANCE IS *YOUR* REALM OF EXPERTISE.
I TRY NOT TO GO THERE MUCH. DESTINY'S OVERRATED, AND THE FUTURE ISN'T AS PREDICTABLE AS YOU'D THINK.
BLAM BLAM BLAM
GUNSHOTS?
GET DOWN!
RICKY! TINO! GET IN HERE!
I THOUGHT YOU SAID NOT TO DISTURB--
SHUT UP! SHOOT THEM!

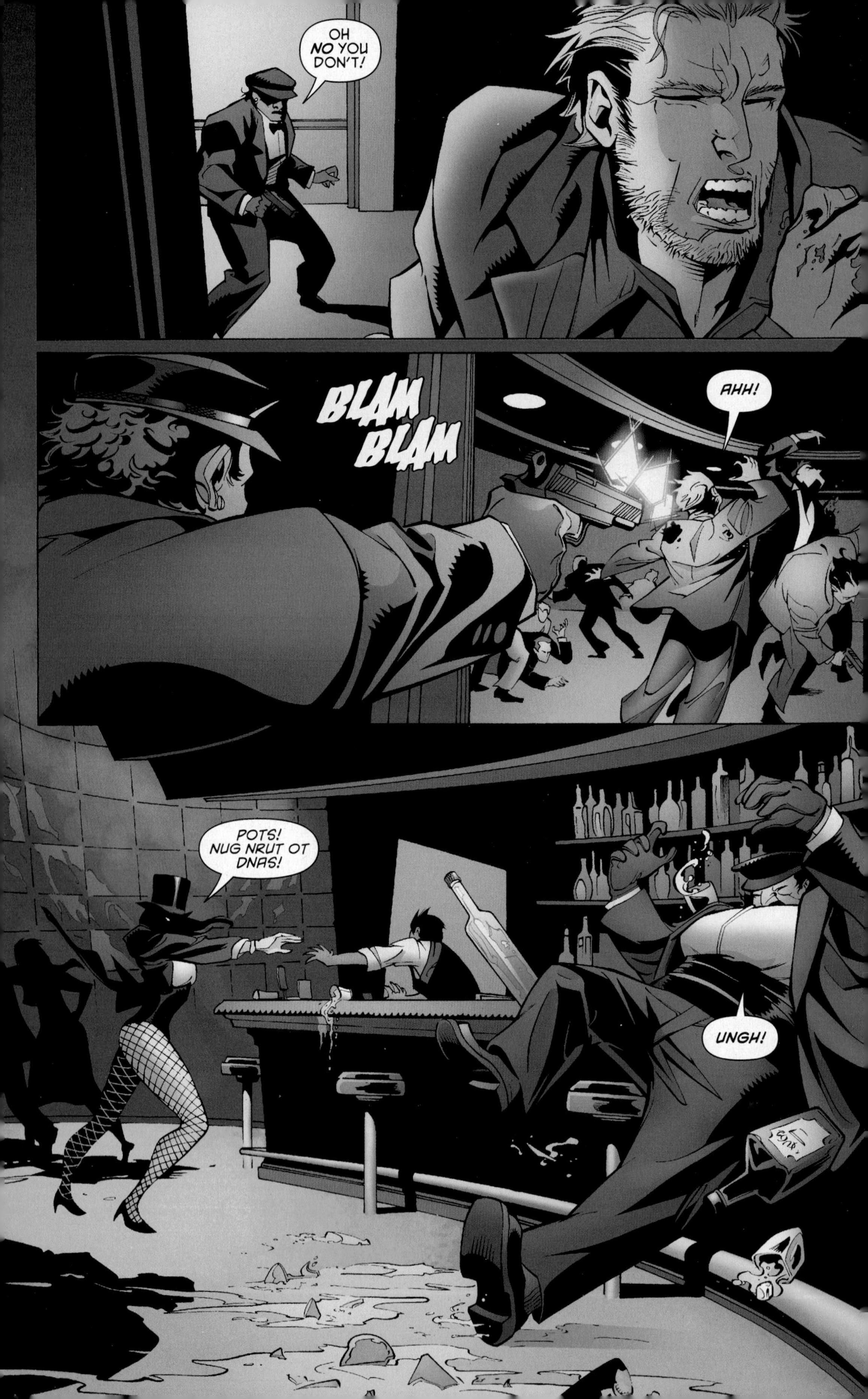
OH NO YOU DON'T!
BLAM BLAM
AHH!
POTS! NUG NRUT OT DNAS!
UNGH!

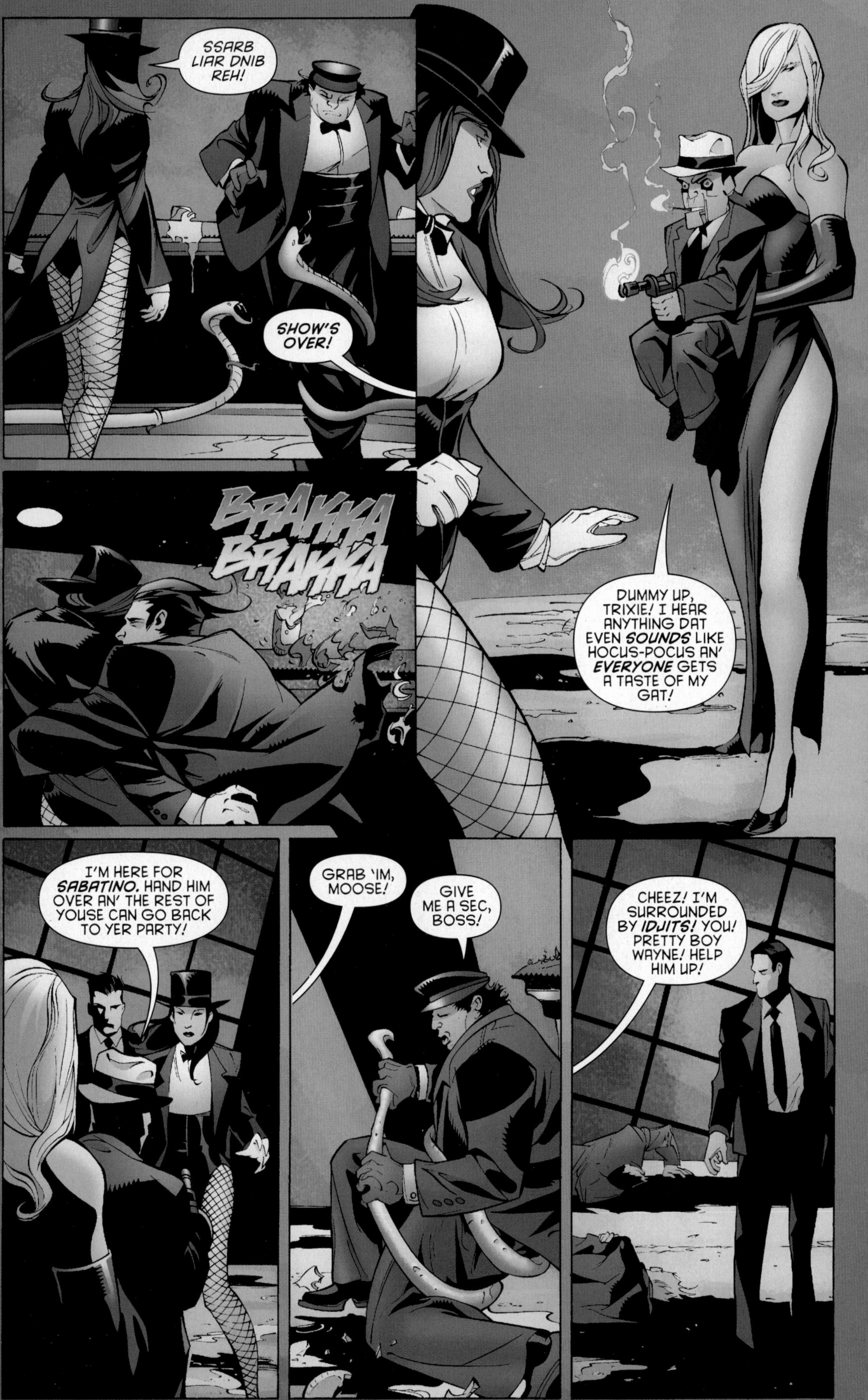
SSARB LIAR DNIB REH!
SHOW'S OVER!
BRAKKA BRAKKA
DUMMY UP, TRIXIE! I HEAR ANYTHING DAT EVEN SOUNDS LIKE HOCUS-POCUS AN' EVERYONE GETS A TASTE OF MY GAT!
I'M HERE FOR SABATINO. HAND HIM OVER AN' THE REST OF YOUSE CAN GO BACK TO YER PARTY!
GRAB 'IM, MOOSE!
GIVE ME A SEC, BOSS!
CHEEZ! I'M SURROUNDED BY IDJITS! YOU! PRETTY BOY WAYNE! HELP HIM UP!

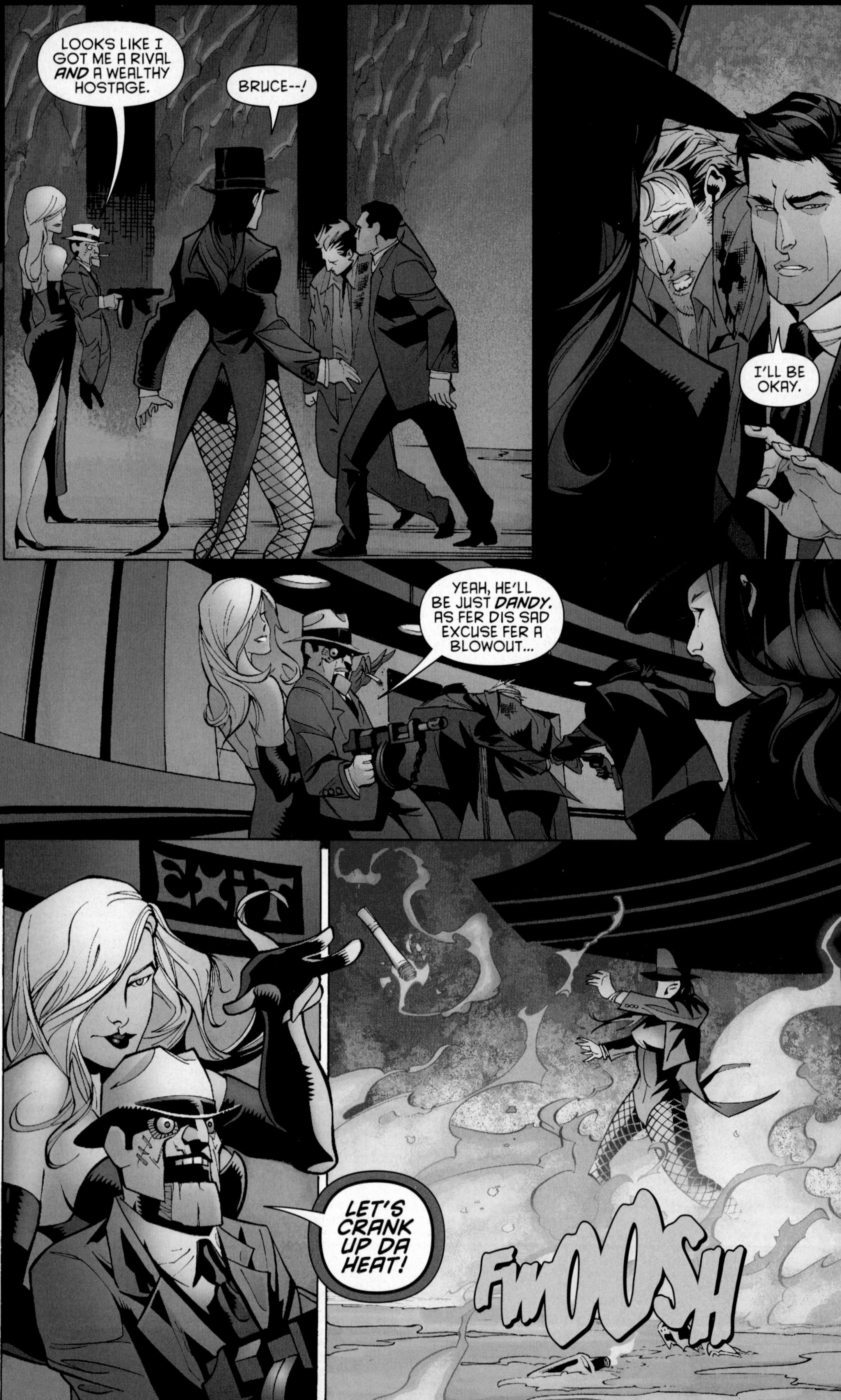
LOOKS LIKE I GOT ME A RIVAL *AND* A WEALTHY HOSTAGE.
BRUCE--!
I'LL BE OKAY.
YEAH, HE'LL BE JUST *DANDY*. AS FER DIS SAD EXCUSE FER A BLOWOUT...
LET'S CRANK UP DA HEAT!
FWOOSH

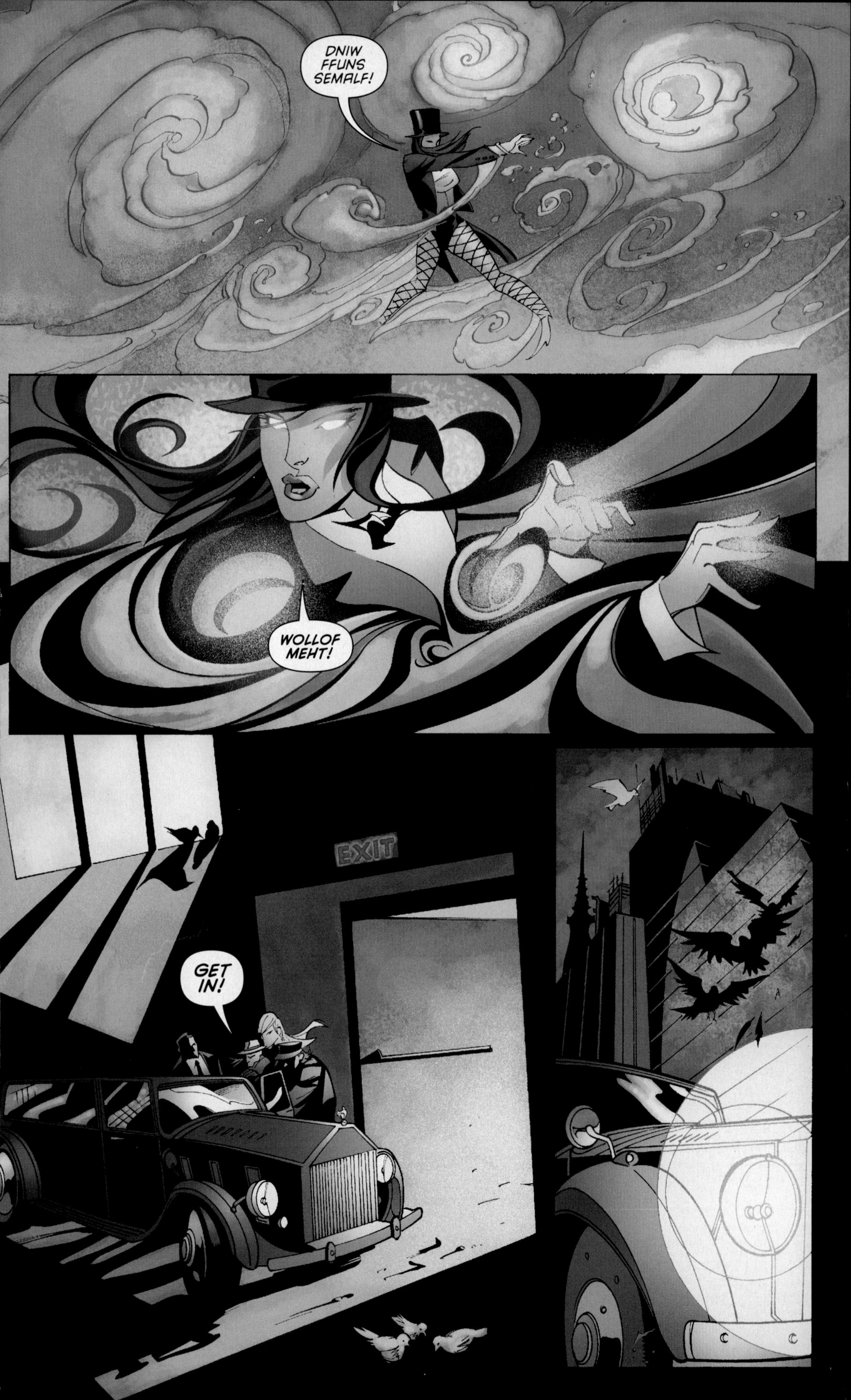
DNIW FFUNS SEMALF!
WOLLOF MEHT!
EXIT
GET IN!

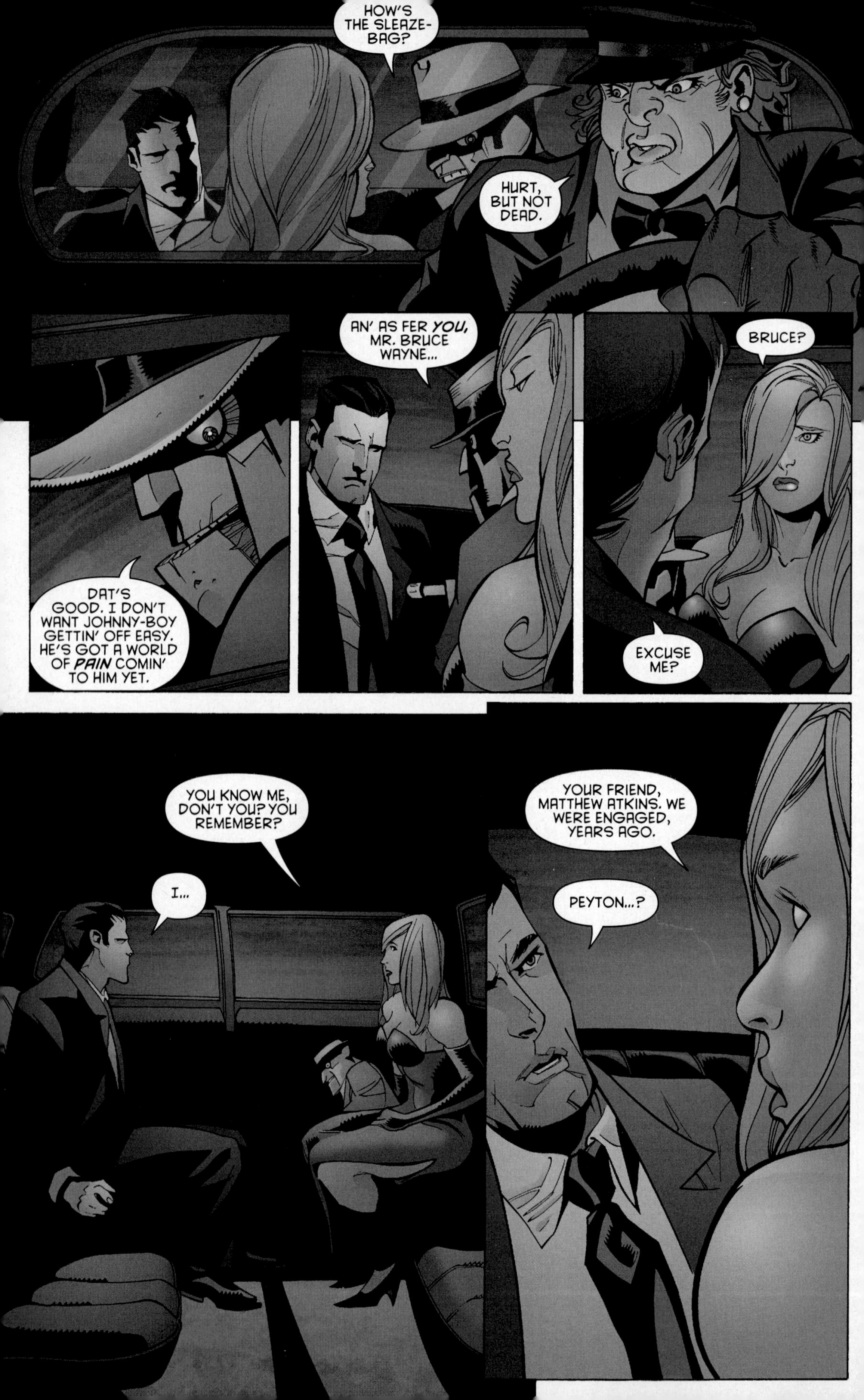
HOW'S THE SLEAZE-BAG?
HURT, BUT NOT DEAD.
DAT'S GOOD. I DON'T WANT JOHNNY-BOY GETTIN' OFF EASY. HE'S GOT A WORLD OF *PAIN* COMIN' TO HIM YET.
AN' AS FER *YOU,* MR. BRUCE WAYNE...
BRUCE?
EXCUSE ME?
YOU KNOW ME, DON'T YOU? YOU REMEMBER?
I...
YOUR FRIEND, MATTHEW ATKINS. WE WERE ENGAGED, YEARS AGO.
PEYTON...?

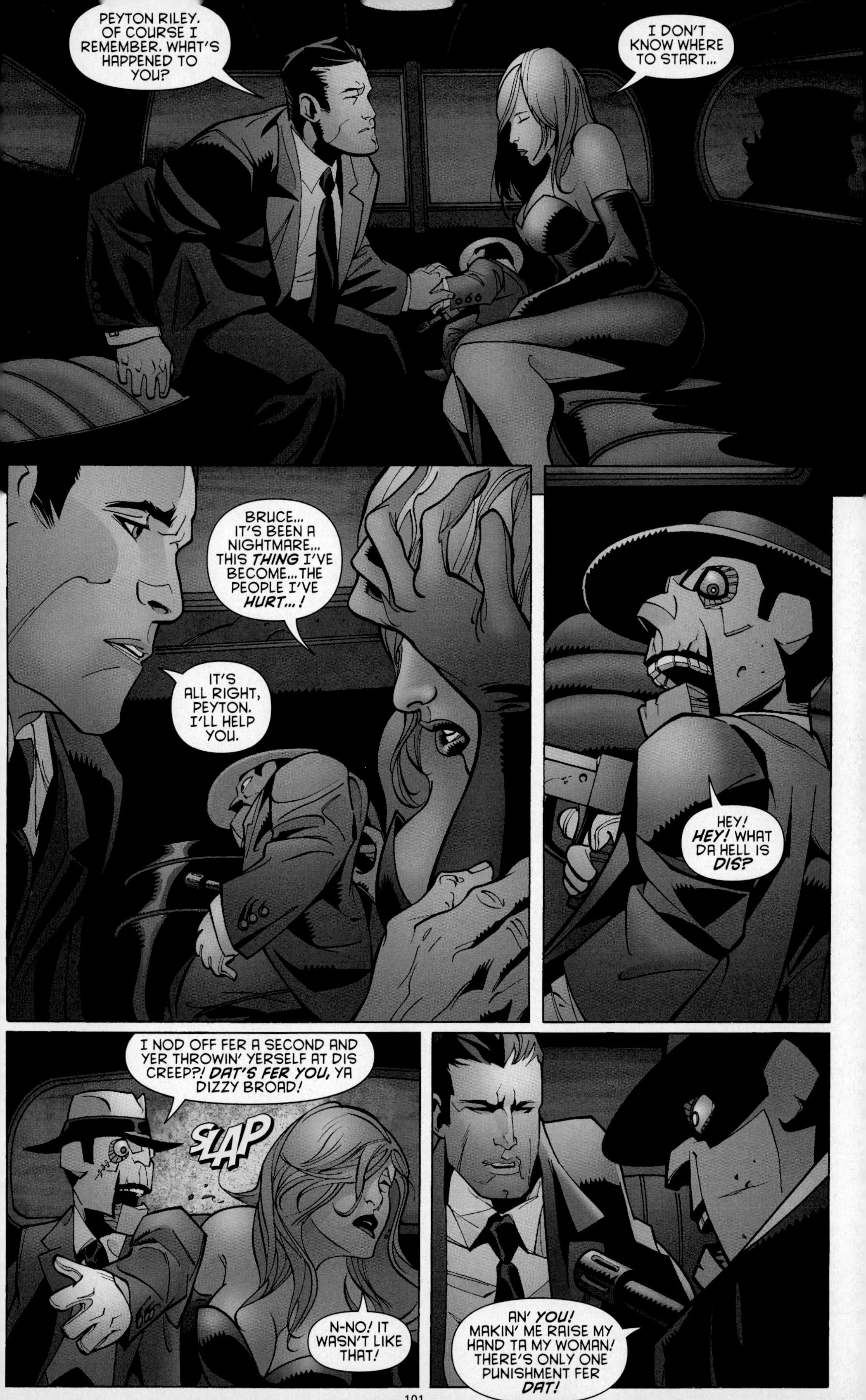
PEYTON RILEY. OF COURSE I REMEMBER. WHAT'S HAPPENED TO YOU?
I DON'T KNOW WHERE TO START...
BRUCE... IT'S BEEN A NIGHTMARE... THIS *THING* I'VE BECOME... THE PEOPLE I'VE *HURT...!*
IT'S ALL RIGHT, PEYTON. I'LL HELP YOU.
HEY! *HEY!* WHAT DA HELL IS *DIS?*
I NOD OFF FER A SECOND AND YER THROWIN' YERSELF AT DIS CREEP?! *DAT'S FER YOU,* YA DIZZY BROAD!
SLAP
N-NO! IT WASN'T LIKE THAT!
AN' *YOU!* MAKIN' ME RAISE MY HAND TA MY WOMAN! THERE'S ONLY ONE PUNISHMENT FER *DAT!*

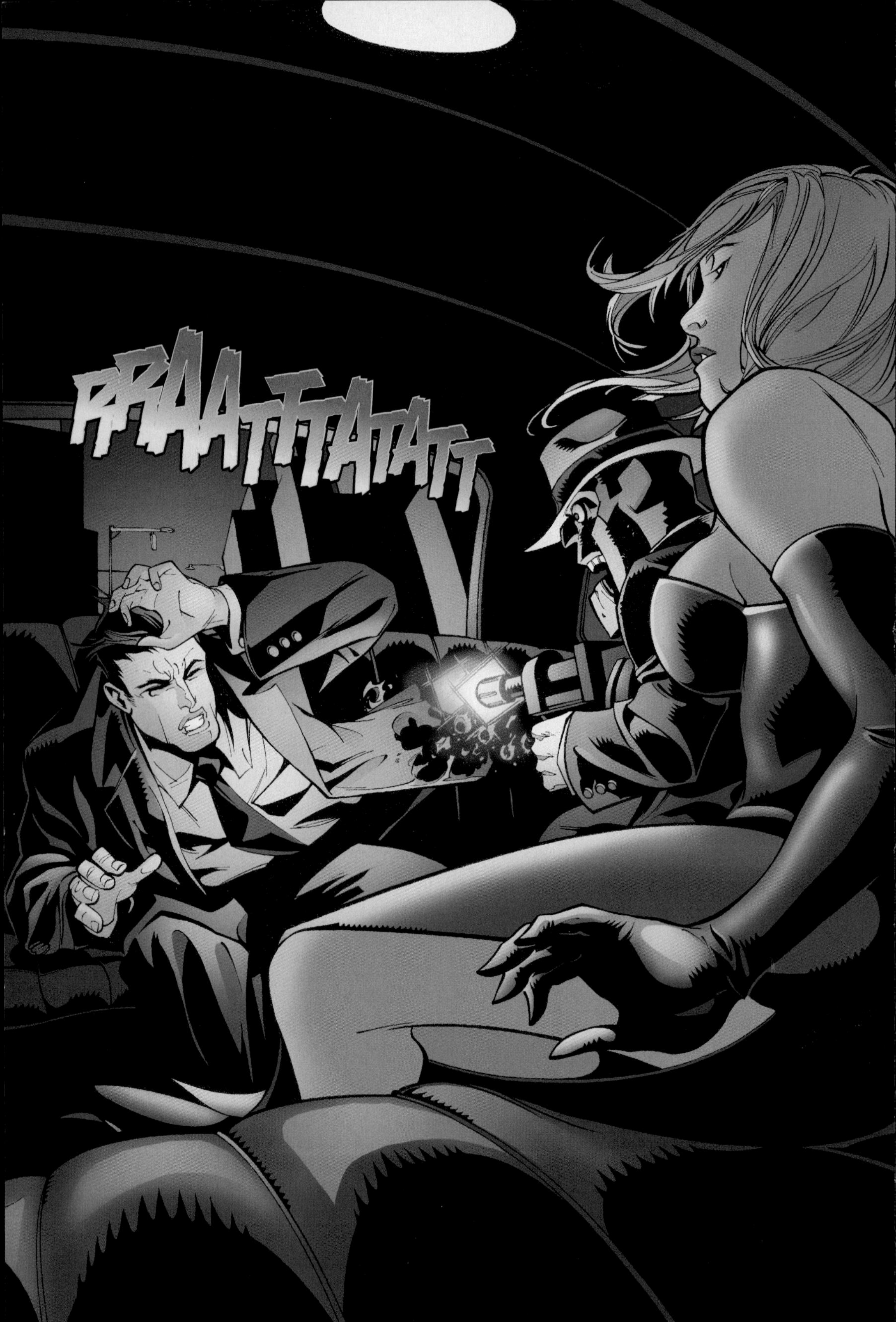
RRAATTTATATT

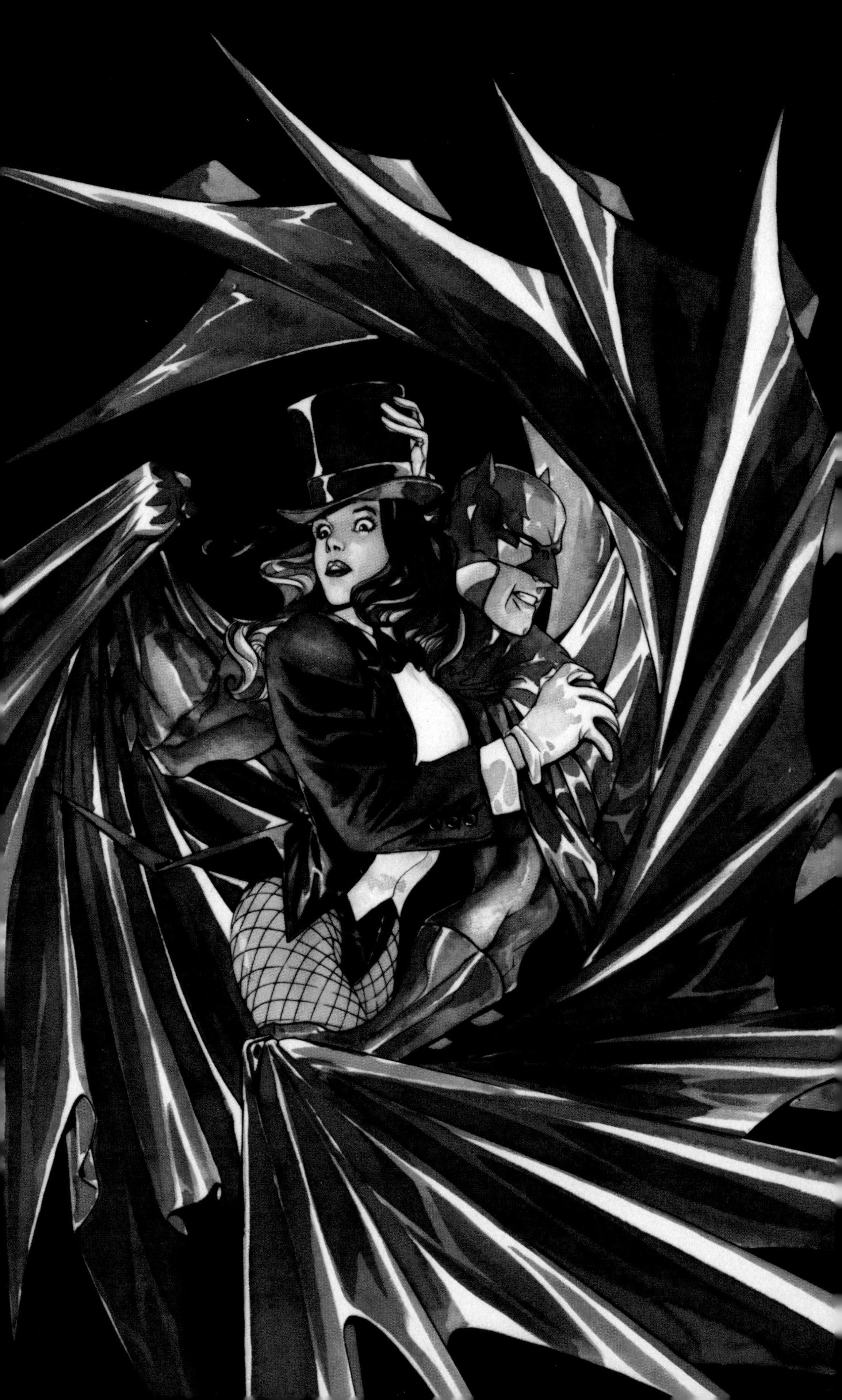

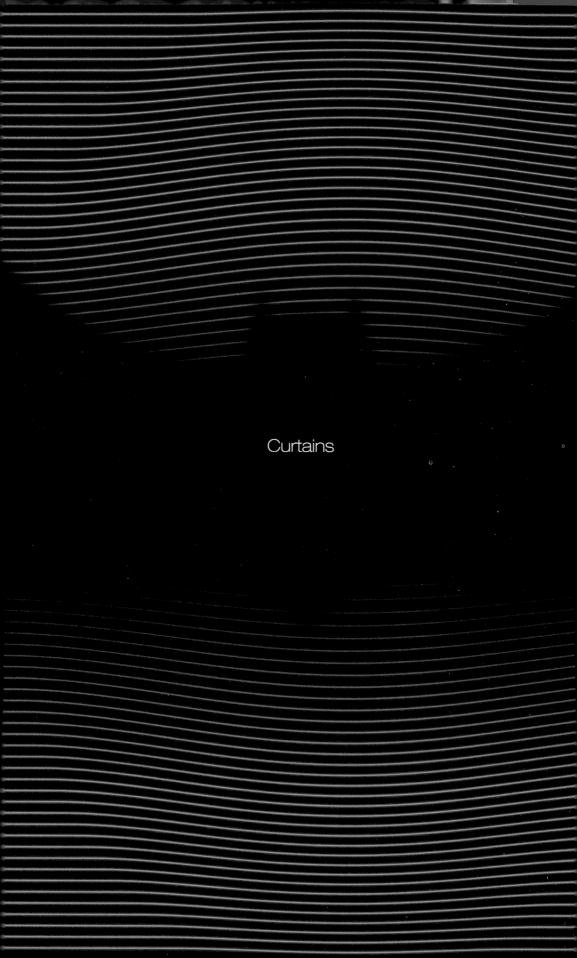

Curtains

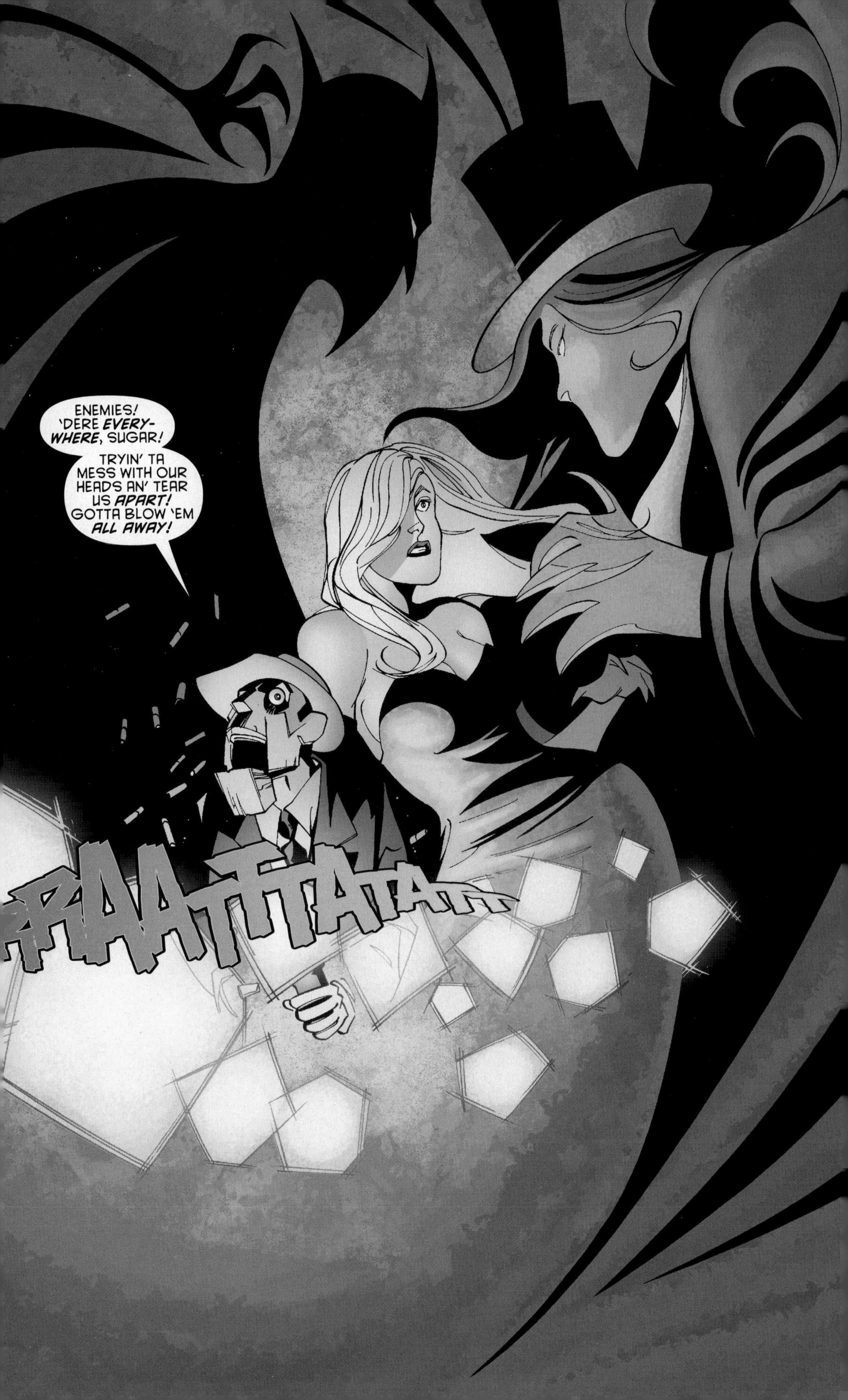

ENEMIES! 'DERE EVERY-WHERE, SUGAR!
TRYIN' TA MESS WITH OUR HEADS AN' TEAR US APART! GOTTA BLOW 'EM ALL AWAY!
RAATTTATAT...

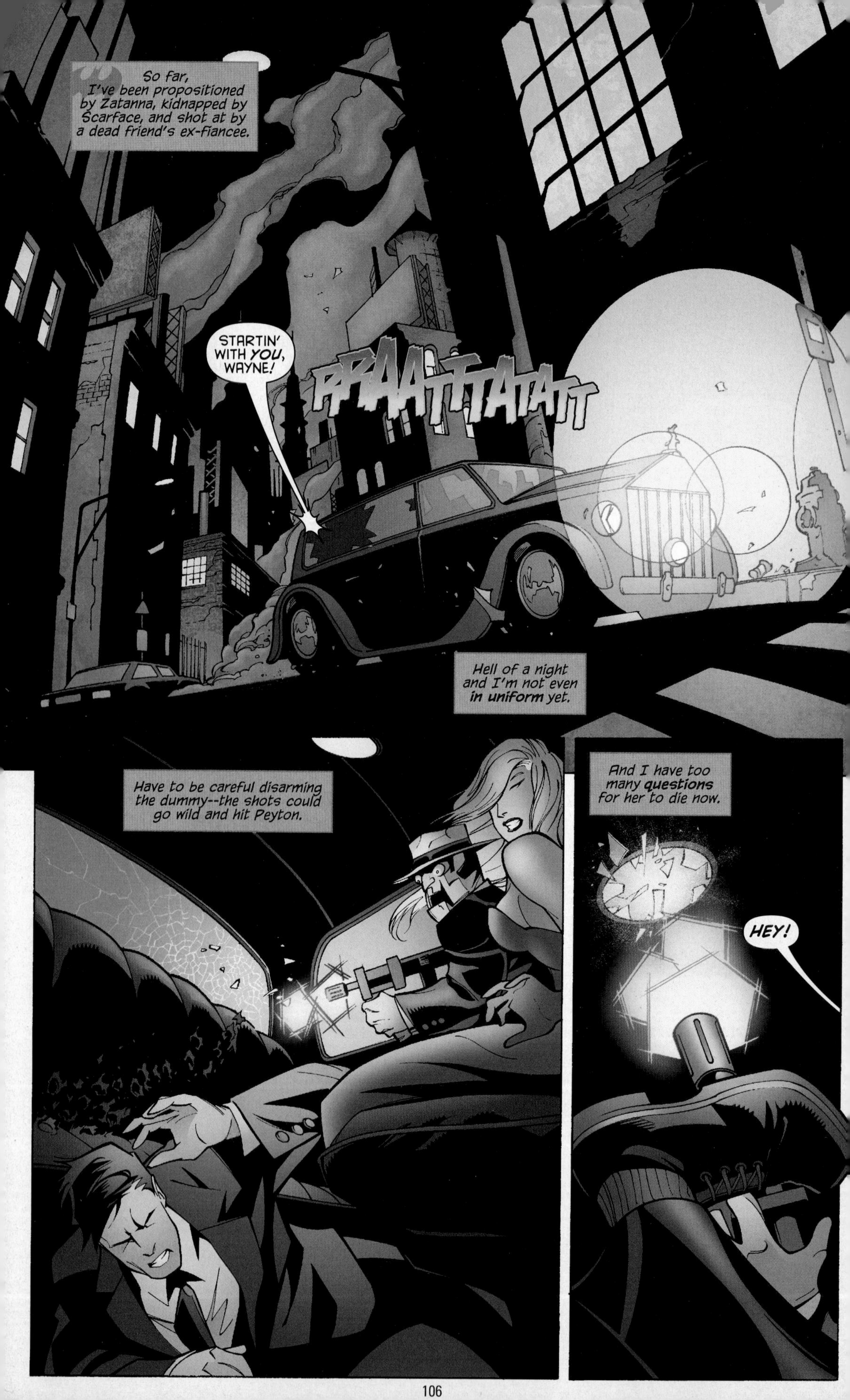
So far, I've been propositioned by Zatanna, kidnapped by Scarface, and shot at by a dead friend's ex-fiancee.
STARTIN' WITH YOU, WAYNE!
BRAATTTATATT
Hell of a night and I'm not even in uniform yet.
Have to be careful disarming the dummy--the shots could go wild and hit Peyton.
And I have too many questions for her to die now.
HEY!

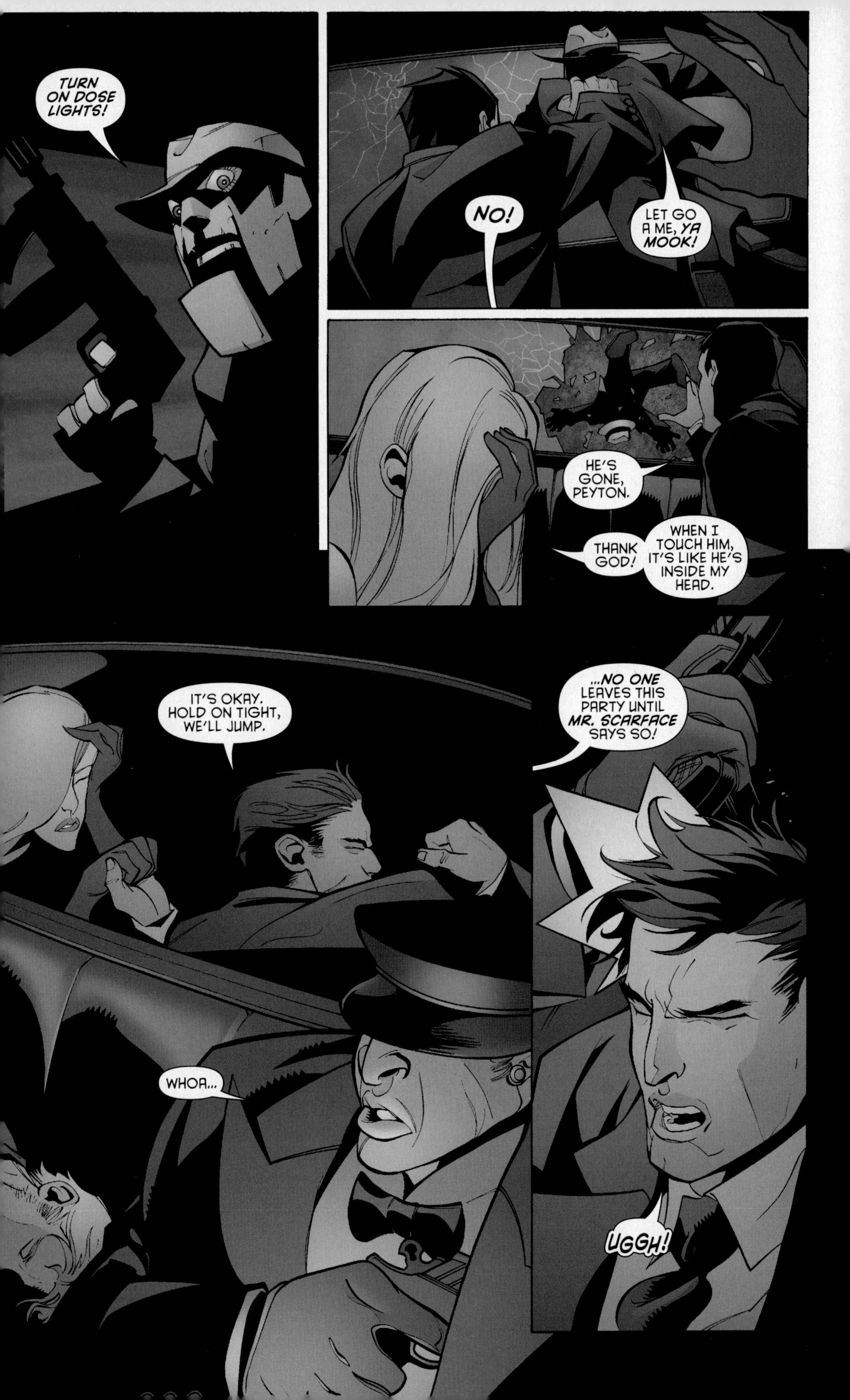
TURN ON DOSE LIGHTS!
NO!
LET GO A ME, YA MOOK!
HE'S GONE, PEYTON.
THANK GOD!
WHEN I TOUCH HIM, IT'S LIKE HE'S INSIDE MY HEAD.
IT'S OKAY. HOLD ON TIGHT, WE'LL JUMP.
WHOA...
...NO ONE LEAVES THIS PARTY UNTIL MR. SCARFACE SAYS SO!
UGGH!

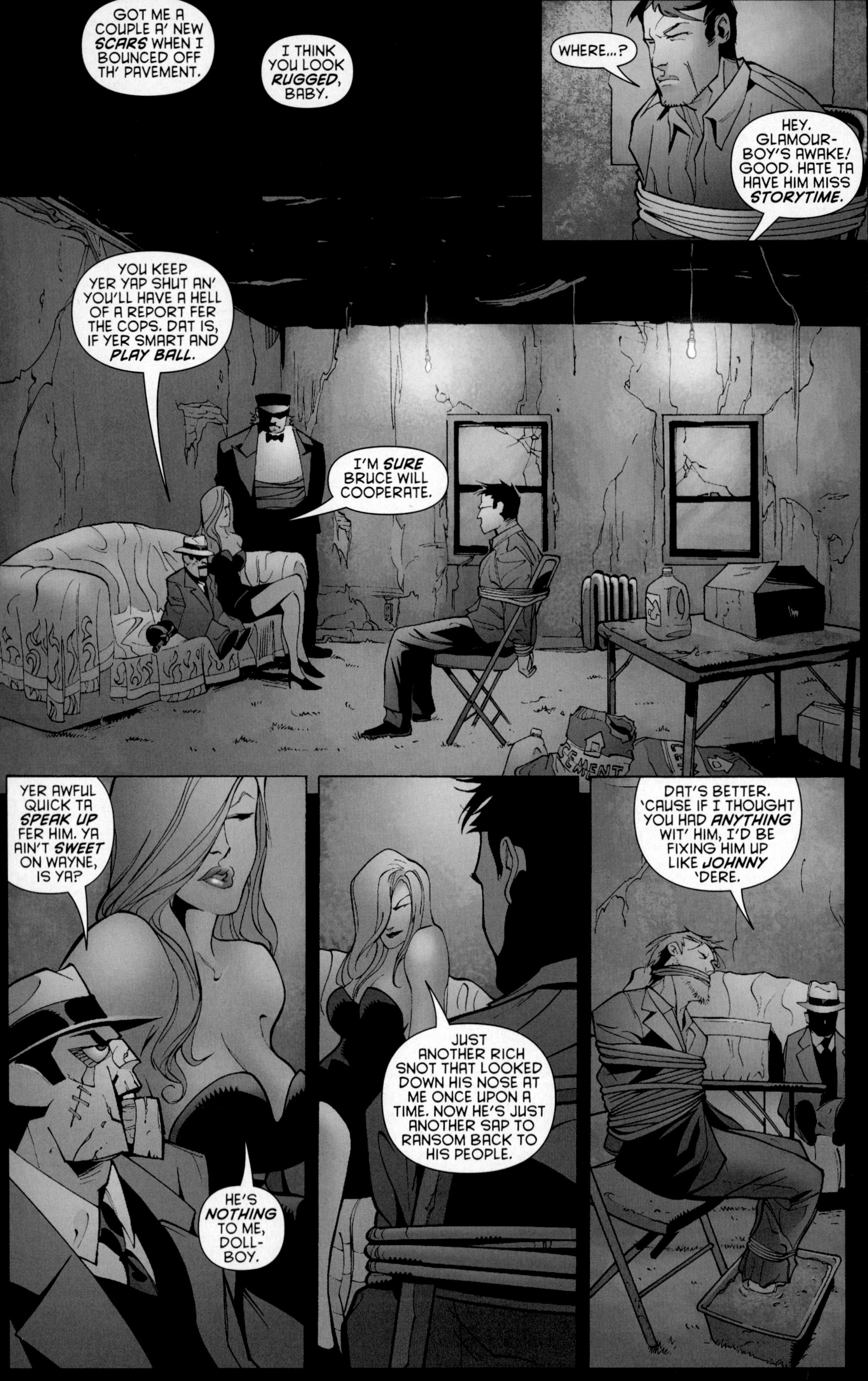
GOT ME A COUPLE A' NEW SCARS WHEN I BOUNCED OFF TH' PAVEMENT.
I THINK YOU LOOK RUGGED, BABY.
WHERE...?
HEY. GLAMOUR-BOY'S AWAKE! GOOD. HATE TA HAVE HIM MISS STORYTIME.
YOU KEEP YER YAP SHUT AN' YOU'LL HAVE A HELL OF A REPORT FER THE COPS. DAT IS, IF YER SMART AND PLAY BALL.
I'M SURE BRUCE WILL COOPERATE.
CEMENT
YER AWFUL QUICK TA SPEAK UP FER HIM. YA AIN'T SWEET ON WAYNE, IS YA?
HE'S NOTHING TO ME, DOLL-BOY.
JUST ANOTHER RICH SNOT THAT LOOKED DOWN HIS NOSE AT ME ONCE UPON A TIME. NOW HE'S JUST ANOTHER SAP TO RANSOM BACK TO HIS PEOPLE.
DAT'S BETTER. 'CAUSE IF I THOUGHT YOU HAD ANYTHING WIT' HIM, I'D BE FIXING HIM UP LIKE JOHNNY 'DERE.

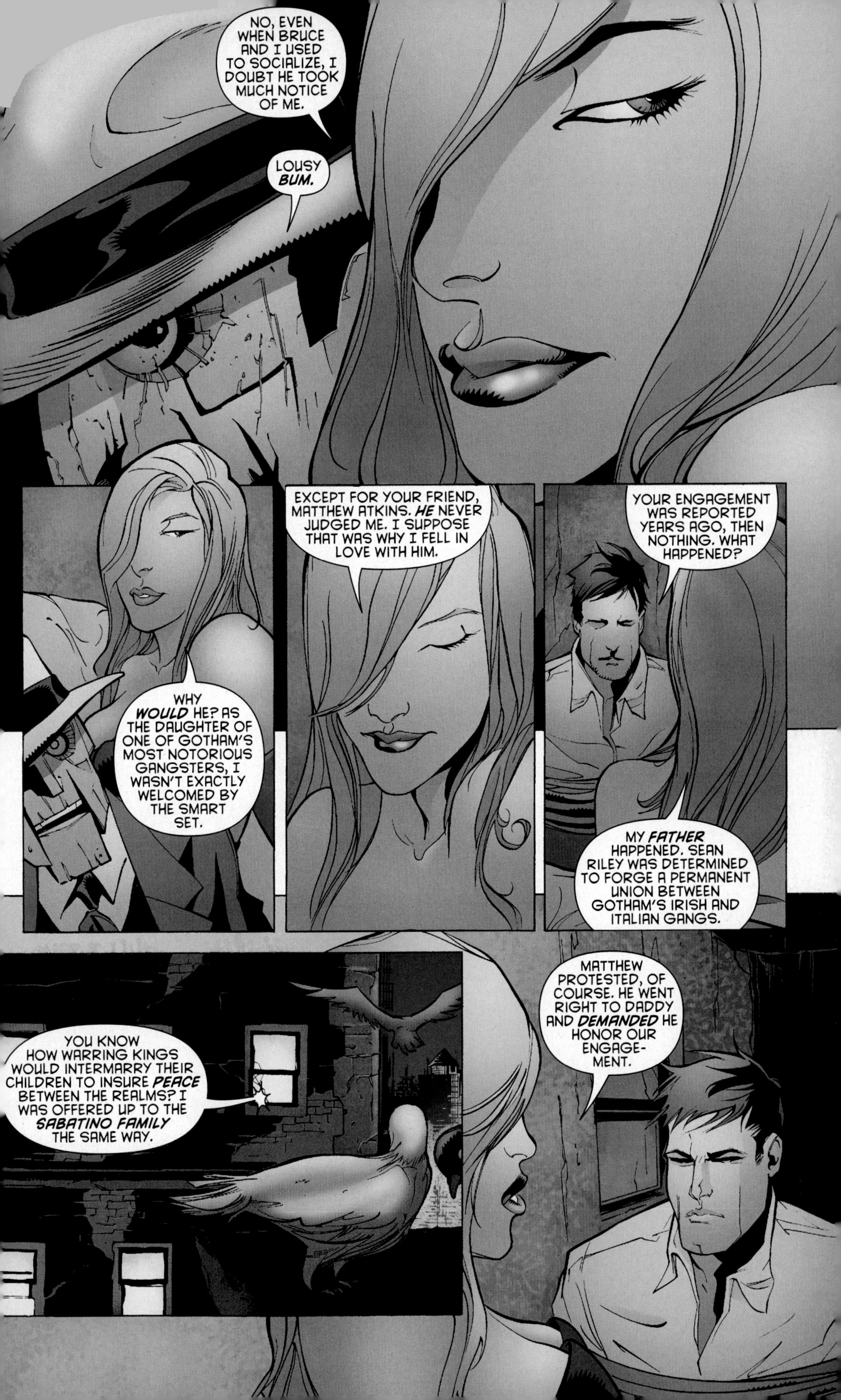

NO, EVEN WHEN BRUCE AND I USED TO SOCIALIZE, I DOUBT HE TOOK MUCH NOTICE OF ME.
LOUSY BUM.
WHY WOULD HE? AS THE DAUGHTER OF ONE OF GOTHAM'S MOST NOTORIOUS GANGSTERS, I WASN'T EXACTLY WELCOMED BY THE SMART SET.
EXCEPT FOR YOUR FRIEND, MATTHEW ATKINS. HE NEVER JUDGED ME. I SUPPOSE THAT WAS WHY I FELL IN LOVE WITH HIM.
YOUR ENGAGEMENT WAS REPORTED YEARS AGO, THEN NOTHING. WHAT HAPPENED?
MY FATHER HAPPENED. SEAN RILEY WAS DETERMINED TO FORGE A PERMANENT UNION BETWEEN GOTHAM'S IRISH AND ITALIAN GANGS.
YOU KNOW HOW WARRING KINGS WOULD INTERMARRY THEIR CHILDREN TO INSURE PEACE BETWEEN THE REALMS? I WAS OFFERED UP TO THE SABATINO FAMILY THE SAME WAY.
MATTHEW PROTESTED, OF COURSE. HE WENT RIGHT TO DADDY AND DEMANDED HE HONOR OUR ENGAGE-MENT.

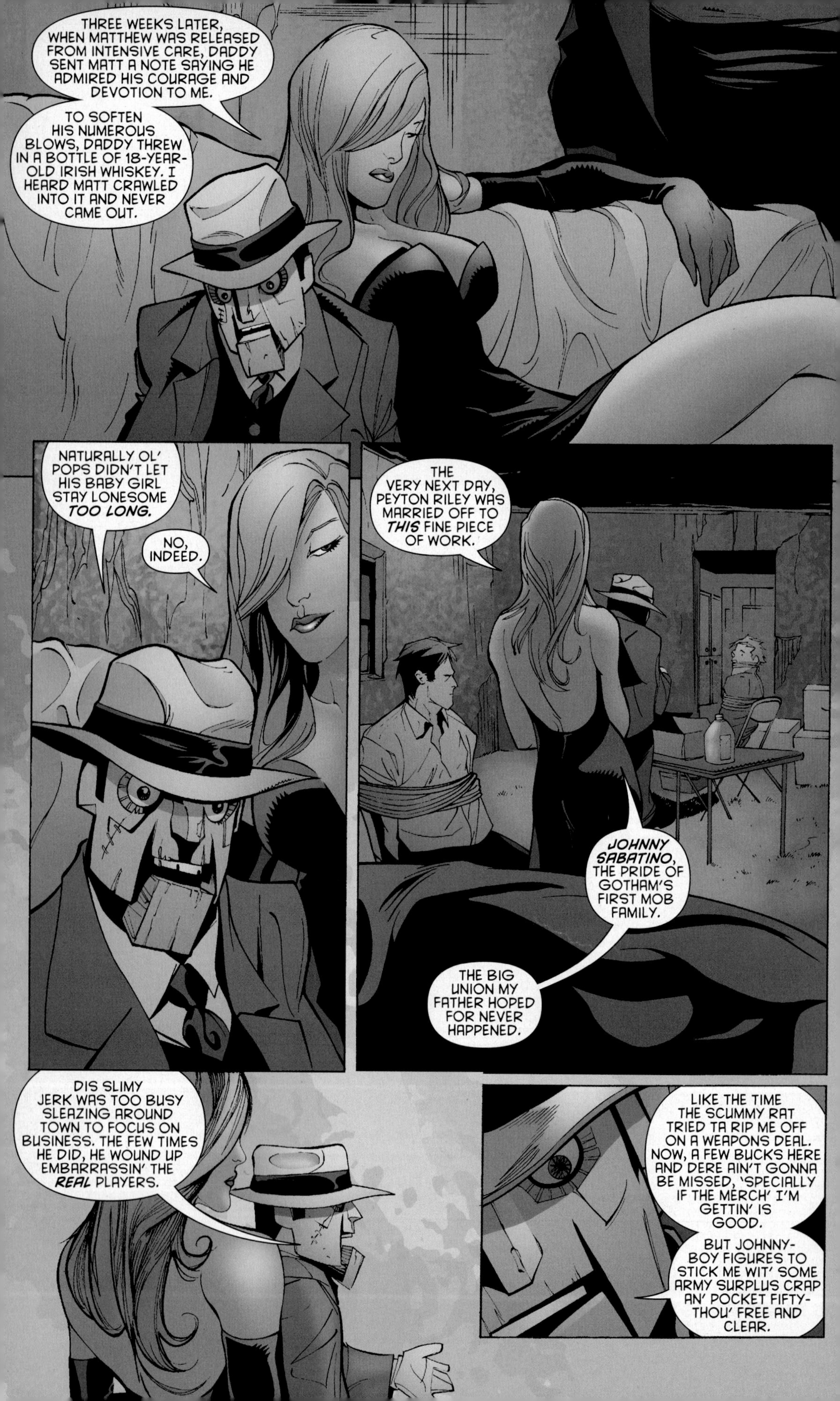
THREE WEEKS LATER, WHEN MATTHEW WAS RELEASED FROM INTENSIVE CARE, DADDY SENT MATT A NOTE SAYING HE ADMIRED HIS COURAGE AND DEVOTION TO ME.
TO SOFTEN HIS NUMEROUS BLOWS, DADDY THREW IN A BOTTLE OF 18-YEAR-OLD IRISH WHISKEY. I HEARD MATT CRAWLED INTO IT AND NEVER CAME OUT.
NATURALLY OL' POPS DIDN'T LET HIS BABY GIRL STAY LONESOME *TOO LONG.*
NO, INDEED.
THE VERY NEXT DAY, PEYTON RILEY WAS MARRIED OFF TO *THIS* FINE PIECE OF WORK.
JOHNNY SABATINO, THE PRIDE OF GOTHAM'S FIRST MOB FAMILY.
THE BIG UNION MY FATHER HOPED FOR NEVER HAPPENED.
DIS SLIMY JERK WAS TOO BUSY SLEAZING AROUND TOWN TO FOCUS ON BUSINESS. THE FEW TIMES HE DID, HE WOUND UP EMBARRASSIN' THE *REAL* PLAYERS.
LIKE THE TIME THE SCUMMY RAT TRIED TA RIP ME OFF ON A WEAPONS DEAL. NOW, A FEW BUCKS HERE AND DERE AIN'T GONNA BE MISSED, 'SPECIALLY IF THE MERCH' I'M GETTIN' IS GOOD.
BUT JOHNNY-BOY FIGURES TO STICK ME WIT' SOME ARMY SURPLUS CRAP AN' POCKET FIFTY-THOU' FREE AND CLEAR.

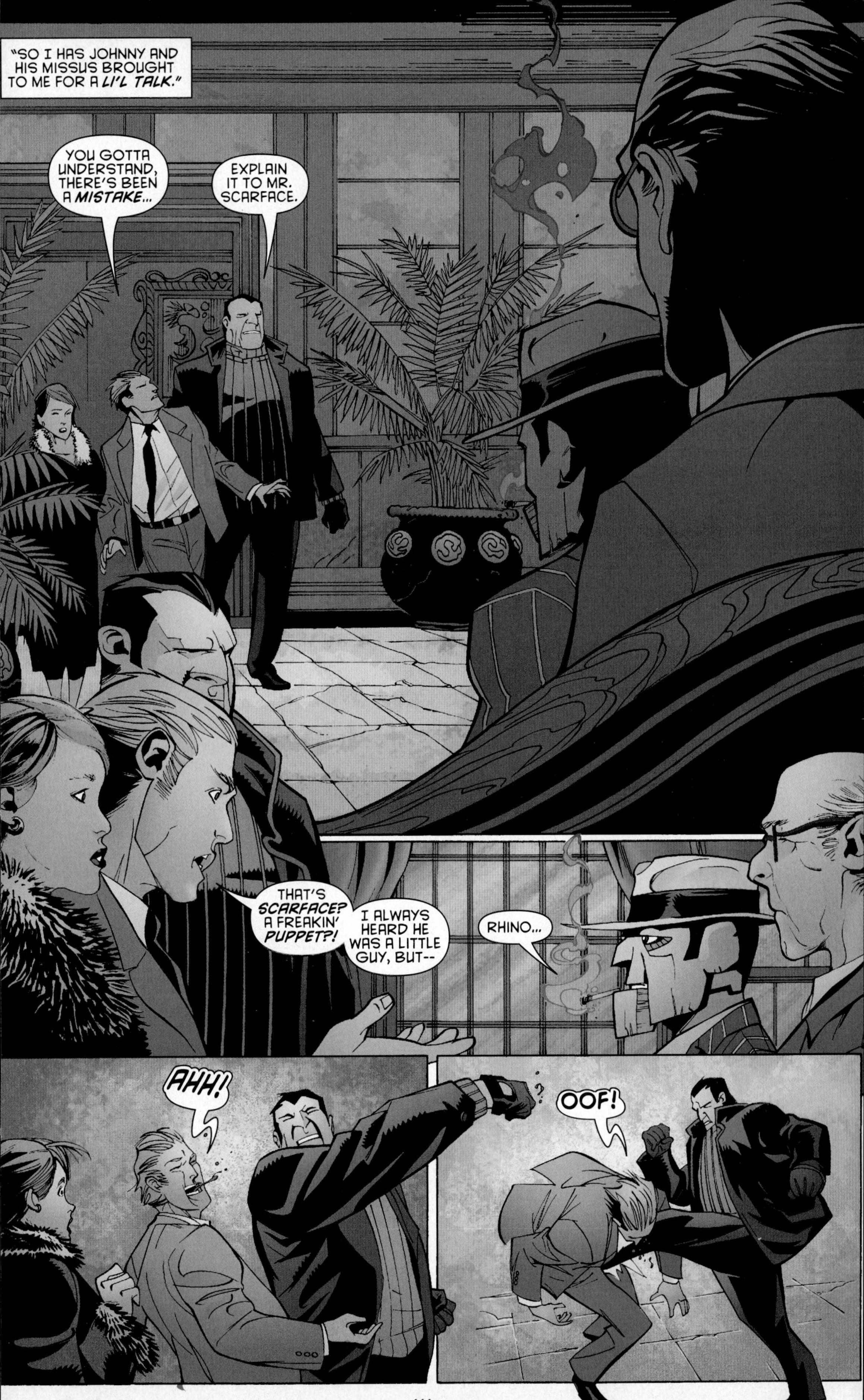
"SO I HAS JOHNNY AND HIS MISSUS BROUGHT TO ME FOR A *LI'L TALK.*"
YOU GOTTA UNDERSTAND, THERE'S BEEN A *MISTAKE*...
EXPLAIN IT TO MR. SCARFACE.
THAT'S *SCARFACE?* A FREAKIN' *PUPPET?!*
I ALWAYS HEARD HE WAS A LITTLE GUY, BUT--
RHINO...
AHH!
OOF!

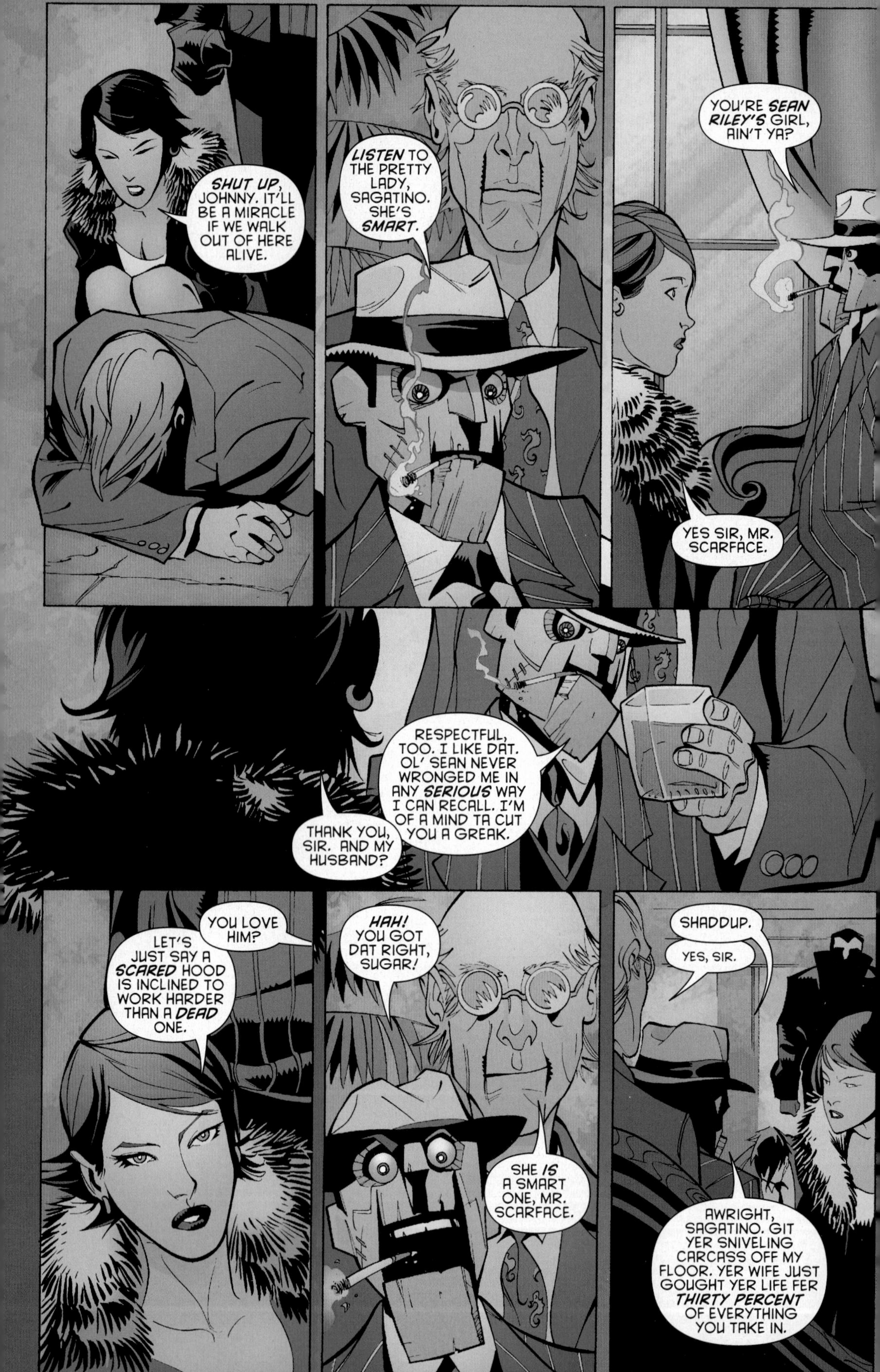
SHUT UP, JOHNNY. IT'LL BE A MIRACLE IF WE WALK OUT OF HERE ALIVE.
LISTEN TO THE PRETTY LADY, SAGATINO. SHE'S SMART.
YOU'RE SEAN RILEY'S GIRL, AIN'T YA?
YES SIR, MR. SCARFACE.
RESPECTFUL, TOO. I LIKE DAT. OL' SEAN NEVER WRONGED ME IN ANY SERIOUS WAY I CAN RECALL. I'M OF A MIND TA CUT YOU A BREAK.
THANK YOU, SIR. AND MY HUSBAND?
YOU LOVE HIM?
LET'S JUST SAY A SCARED HOOD IS INCLINED TO WORK HARDER THAN A DEAD ONE.
HAH! YOU GOT DAT RIGHT, SUGAR!
SHE IS A SMART ONE, MR. SCARFACE.
SHADDUP.
YES, SIR.
AWRIGHT, SAGATINO. GIT YER SNIVELING CARCASS OFF MY FLOOR. YER WIFE JUST BOUGHT YER LIFE FER THIRTY PERCENT OF EVERYTHING YOU TAKE IN.

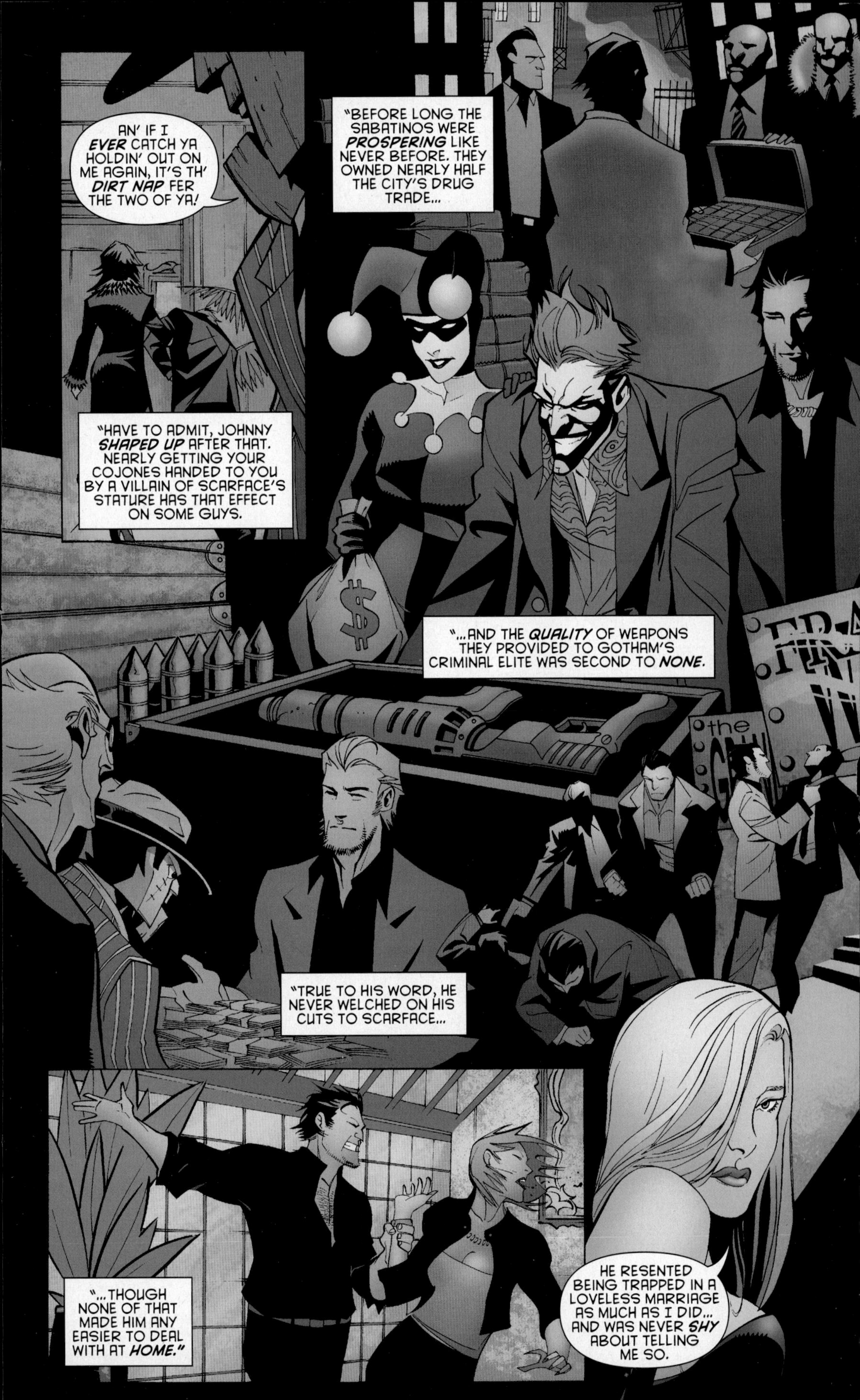
AN' IF I EVER CATCH YA HOLDIN' OUT ON ME AGAIN, IT'S TH' DIRT NAP FER THE TWO OF YA!
"BEFORE LONG THE SABATINOS WERE PROSPERING LIKE NEVER BEFORE. THEY OWNED NEARLY HALF THE CITY'S DRUG TRADE...
"HAVE TO ADMIT, JOHNNY SHAPED UP AFTER THAT. NEARLY GETTING YOUR COJONES HANDED TO YOU BY A VILLAIN OF SCARFACE'S STATURE HAS THAT EFFECT ON SOME GUYS.
"...AND THE QUALITY OF WEAPONS THEY PROVIDED TO GOTHAM'S CRIMINAL ELITE WAS SECOND TO NONE.
"TRUE TO HIS WORD, HE NEVER WELCHED ON HIS CUTS TO SCARFACE...
"...THOUGH NONE OF THAT MADE HIM ANY EASIER TO DEAL WITH AT HOME."
HE RESENTED BEING TRAPPED IN A LOVELESS MARRIAGE AS MUCH AS I DID... AND WAS NEVER SHY ABOUT TELLING ME SO.

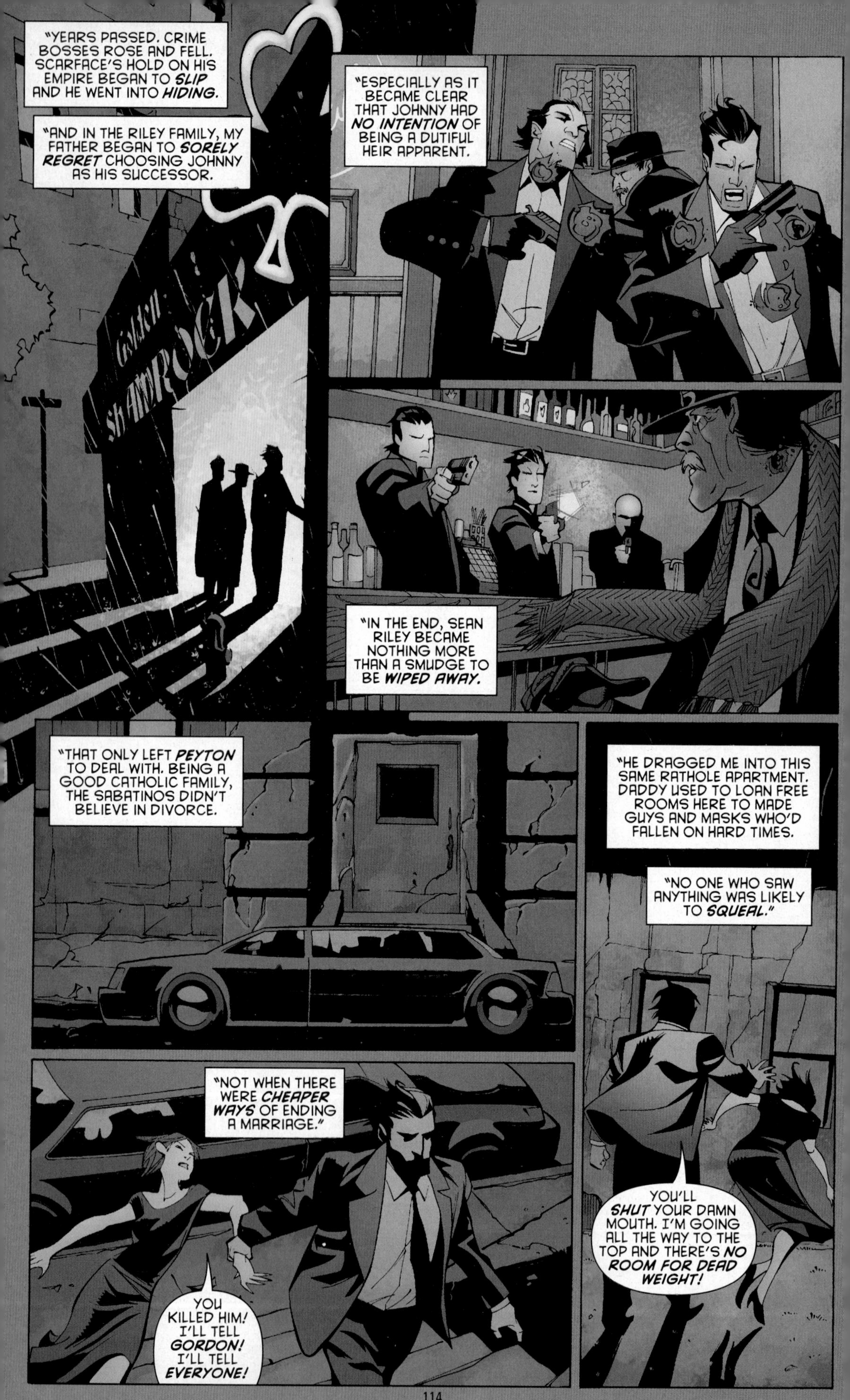

"YEARS PASSED. CRIME BOSSES ROSE AND FELL. SCARFACE'S HOLD ON HIS EMPIRE BEGAN TO SLIP AND HE WENT INTO HIDING.
"AND IN THE RILEY FAMILY, MY FATHER BEGAN TO SORELY REGRET CHOOSING JOHNNY AS HIS SUCCESSOR.
Golden Shamrock
"ESPECIALLY AS IT BECAME CLEAR THAT JOHNNY HAD NO INTENTION OF BEING A DUTIFUL HEIR APPARENT.
"IN THE END, SEAN RILEY BECAME NOTHING MORE THAN A SMUDGE TO BE WIPED AWAY.
"THAT ONLY LEFT PEYTON TO DEAL WITH. BEING A GOOD CATHOLIC FAMILY, THE SABATINOS DIDN'T BELIEVE IN DIVORCE.
"HE DRAGGED ME INTO THIS SAME RATHOLE APARTMENT. DADDY USED TO LOAN FREE ROOMS HERE TO MADE GUYS AND MASKS WHO'D FALLEN ON HARD TIMES.
"NO ONE WHO SAW ANYTHING WAS LIKELY TO SQUEAL."
"NOT WHEN THERE WERE CHEAPER WAYS OF ENDING A MARRIAGE."
YOU KILLED HIM! I'LL TELL GORDON! I'LL TELL EVERYONE!
YOU'LL SHUT YOUR DAMN MOUTH. I'M GOING ALL THE WAY TO THE TOP AND THERE'S NO ROOM FOR DEAD WEIGHT!

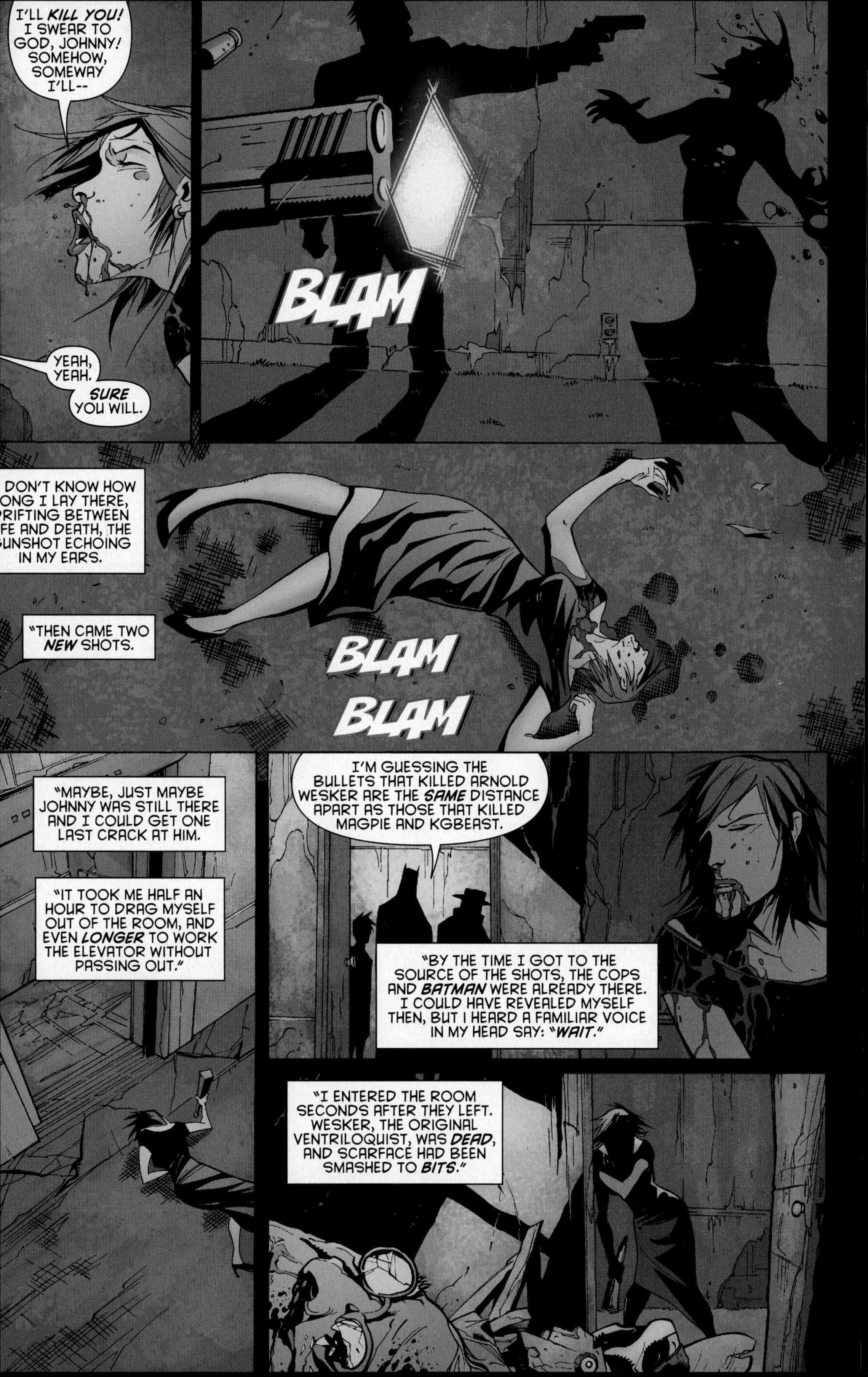

I'LL KILL YOU! I SWEAR TO GOD, JOHNNY! SOMEHOW, SOMEWAY I'LL--
YEAH, YEAH. SURE YOU WILL.
BLAM
DON'T KNOW HOW ONG I LAY THERE, RIFTING BETWEEN FE AND DEATH, THE GUNSHOT ECHOING IN MY EARS.
"THEN CAME TWO NEW SHOTS.
BLAM
BLAM
"MAYBE, JUST MAYBE JOHNNY WAS STILL THERE AND I COULD GET ONE LAST CRACK AT HIM.
"IT TOOK ME HALF AN HOUR TO DRAG MYSELF OUT OF THE ROOM, AND EVEN LONGER TO WORK THE ELEVATOR WITHOUT PASSING OUT."
I'M GUESSING THE BULLETS THAT KILLED ARNOLD WESKER ARE THE SAME DISTANCE APART AS THOSE THAT KILLED MAGPIE AND KGBEAST.
"BY THE TIME I GOT TO THE SOURCE OF THE SHOTS, THE COPS AND BATMAN WERE ALREADY THERE. I COULD HAVE REVEALED MYSELF THEN, BUT I HEARD A FAMILIAR VOICE IN MY HEAD SAY: "WAIT."
"I ENTERED THE ROOM SECONDS AFTER THEY LEFT. WESKER, THE ORIGINAL VENTRILOQUIST, WAS DEAD, AND SCARFACE HAD BEEN SMASHED TO BITS."

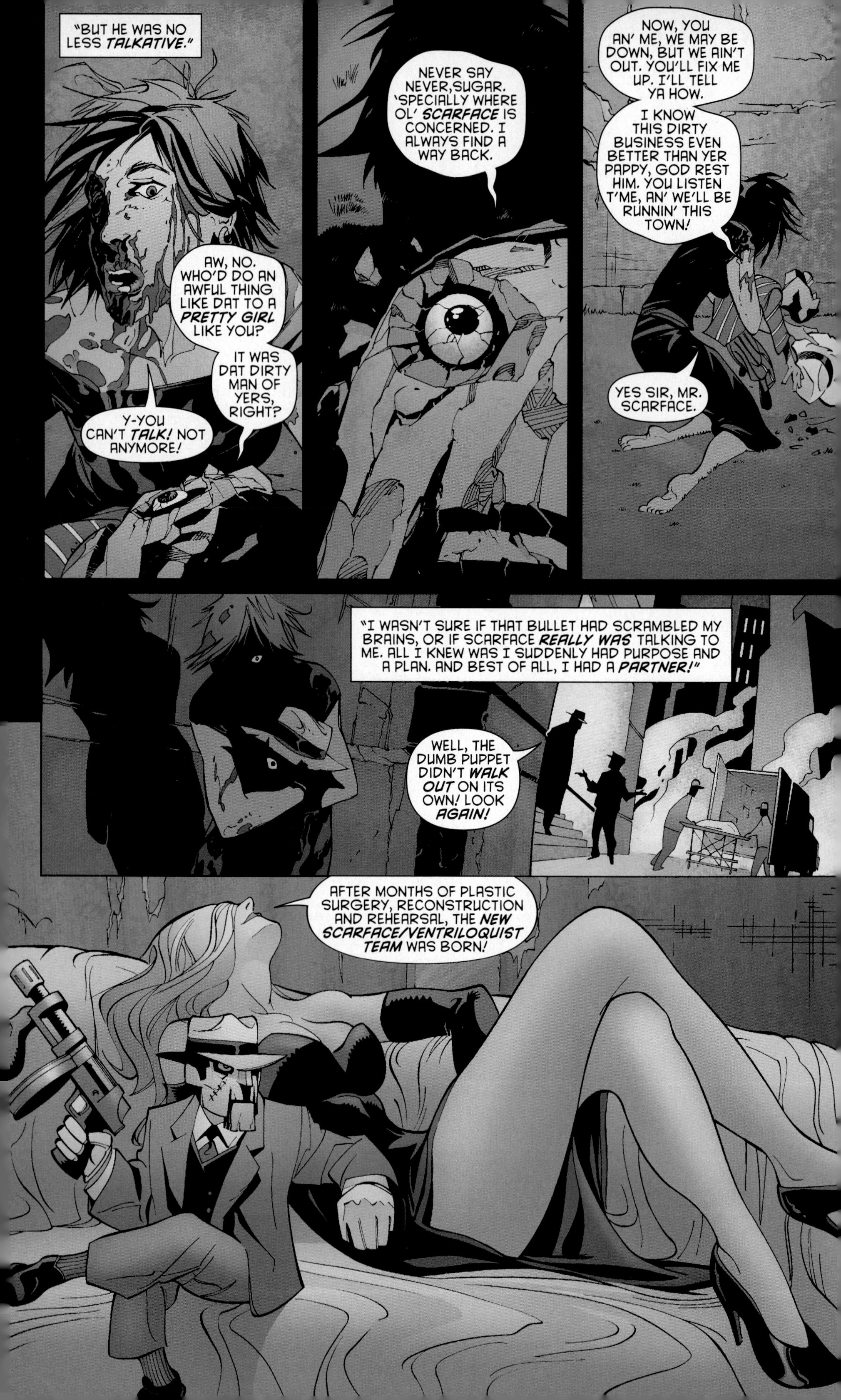
"BUT HE WAS NO LESS TALKATIVE."
AW, NO. WHO'D DO AN AWFUL THING LIKE DAT TO A PRETTY GIRL LIKE YOU?
IT WAS DAT DIRTY MAN OF YERS, RIGHT?
Y-YOU CAN'T TALK! NOT ANYMORE!
NEVER SAY NEVER, SUGAR. 'SPECIALLY WHERE OL' SCARFACE IS CONCERNED. I ALWAYS FIND A WAY BACK.
NOW, YOU AN' ME, WE MAY BE DOWN, BUT WE AIN'T OUT. YOU'LL FIX ME UP. I'LL TELL YA HOW.
I KNOW THIS DIRTY BUSINESS EVEN BETTER THAN YER PAPPY, GOD REST HIM. YOU LISTEN T'ME, AN' WE'LL BE RUNNIN' THIS TOWN!
YES SIR, MR. SCARFACE.
"I WASN'T SURE IF THAT BULLET HAD SCRAMBLED MY BRAINS, OR IF SCARFACE REALLY WAS TALKING TO ME. ALL I KNEW WAS I SUDDENLY HAD PURPOSE AND A PLAN. AND BEST OF ALL, I HAD A PARTNER!"
WELL, THE DUMB PUPPET DIDN'T WALK OUT ON ITS OWN! LOOK AGAIN!
AFTER MONTHS OF PLASTIC SURGERY, RECONSTRUCTION AND REHEARSAL, THE NEW SCARFACE/VENTRILOQUIST TEAM WAS BORN!

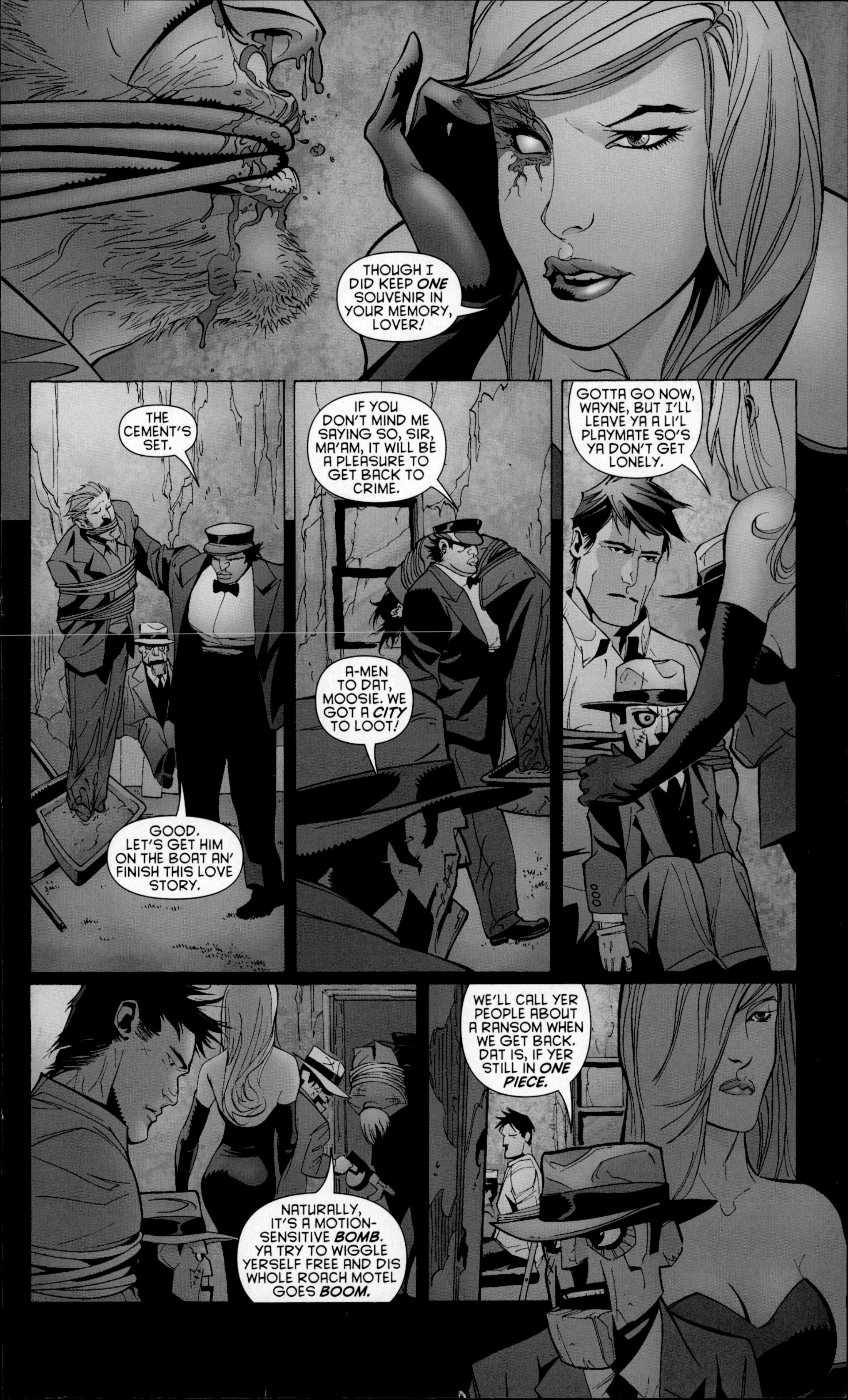
THOUGH I DID KEEP ONE SOUVENIR IN YOUR MEMORY, LOVER!
THE CEMENT'S SET.
GOOD. LET'S GET HIM ON THE BOAT AN' FINISH THIS LOVE STORY.
IF YOU DON'T MIND ME SAYING SO, SIR, MA'AM, IT WILL BE A PLEASURE TO GET BACK TO CRIME.
A-MEN TO DAT, MOOSIE. WE GOT A CITY TO LOOT!
GOTTA GO NOW, WAYNE, BUT I'LL LEAVE YA A LI'L PLAYMATE SO'S YA DON'T GET LONELY.
NATURALLY, IT'S A MOTION-SENSITIVE BOMB. YA TRY TO WIGGLE YERSELF FREE AND DIS WHOLE ROACH MOTEL GOES BOOM.
WE'LL CALL YER PEOPLE ABOUT A RANSOM WHEN WE GET BACK. DAT IS, IF YER STILL IN ONE PIECE.

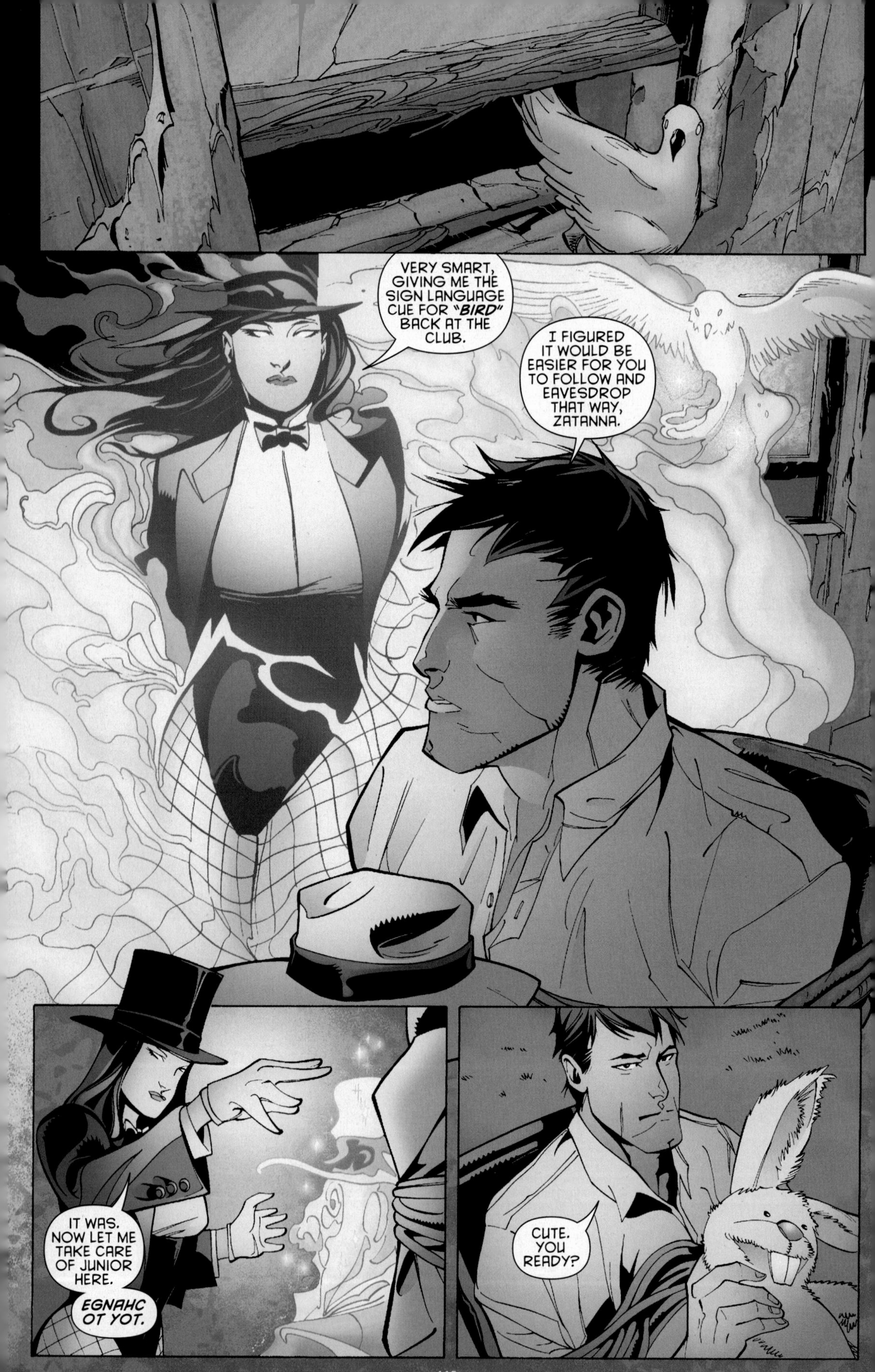
VERY SMART, GIVING ME THE SIGN LANGUAGE CUE FOR "BIRD" BACK AT THE CLUB.
I FIGURED IT WOULD BE EASIER FOR YOU TO FOLLOW AND EAVESDROP THAT WAY, ZATANNA.
IT WAS. NOW LET ME TAKE CARE OF JUNIOR HERE.
EGNAHC OT YOT.
CUTE. YOU READY?

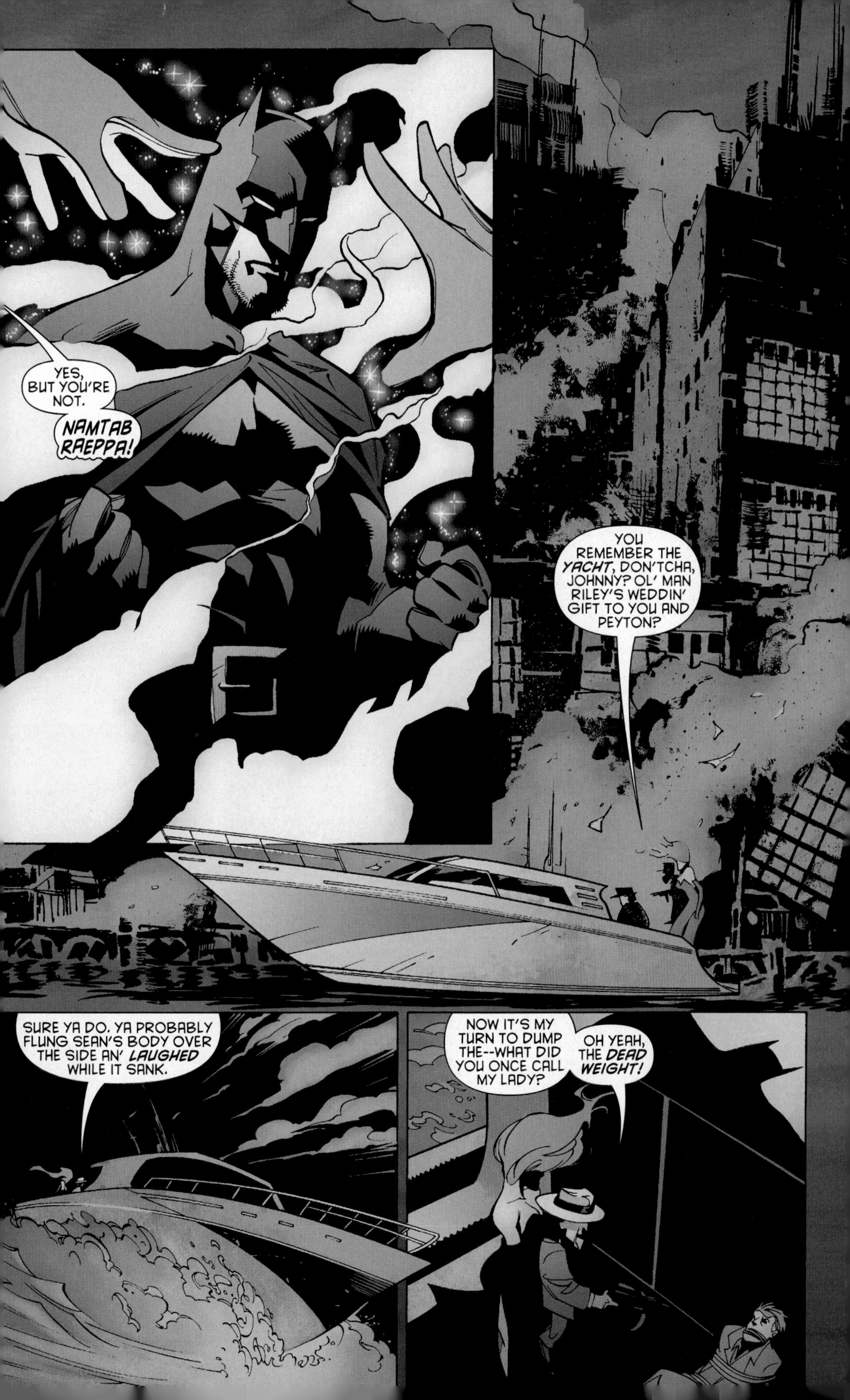
YES, BUT YOU'RE NOT.
NAMTAB RAEPPA!
YOU REMEMBER THE YACHT, DON'TCHA, JOHNNY? OL' MAN RILEY'S WEDDIN' GIFT TO YOU AND PEYTON?
SURE YA DO. YA PROBABLY FLUNG SEAN'S BODY OVER THE SIDE AN' LAUGHED WHILE IT SANK.
NOW IT'S MY TURN TO DUMP THE--WHAT DID YOU ONCE CALL MY LADY?
OH YEAH, THE DEAD WEIGHT!

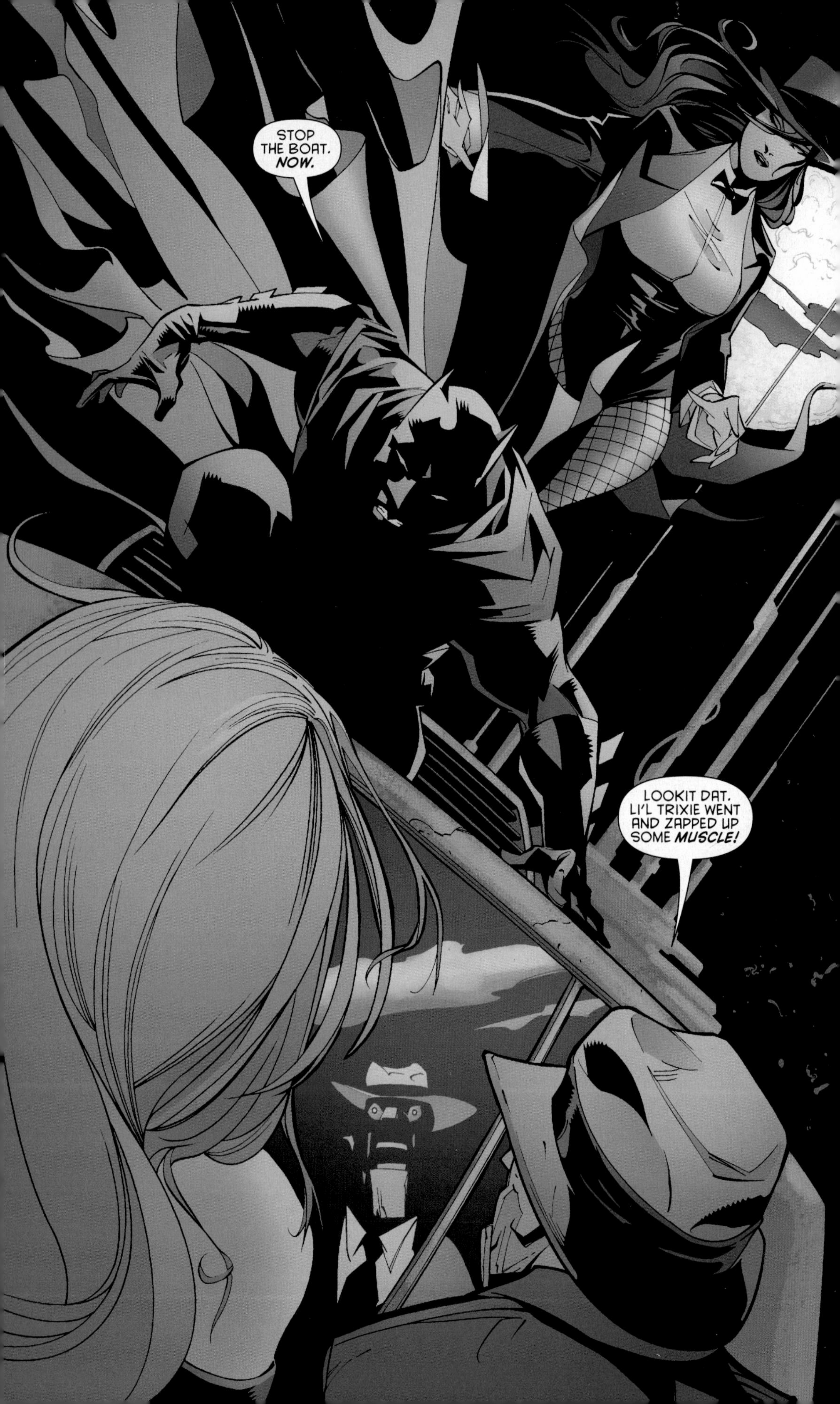
STOP THE BOAT. *NOW.*
LOOKIT DAT. LI'L TRIXIE WENT AND ZAPPED UP SOME *MUSCLE!*

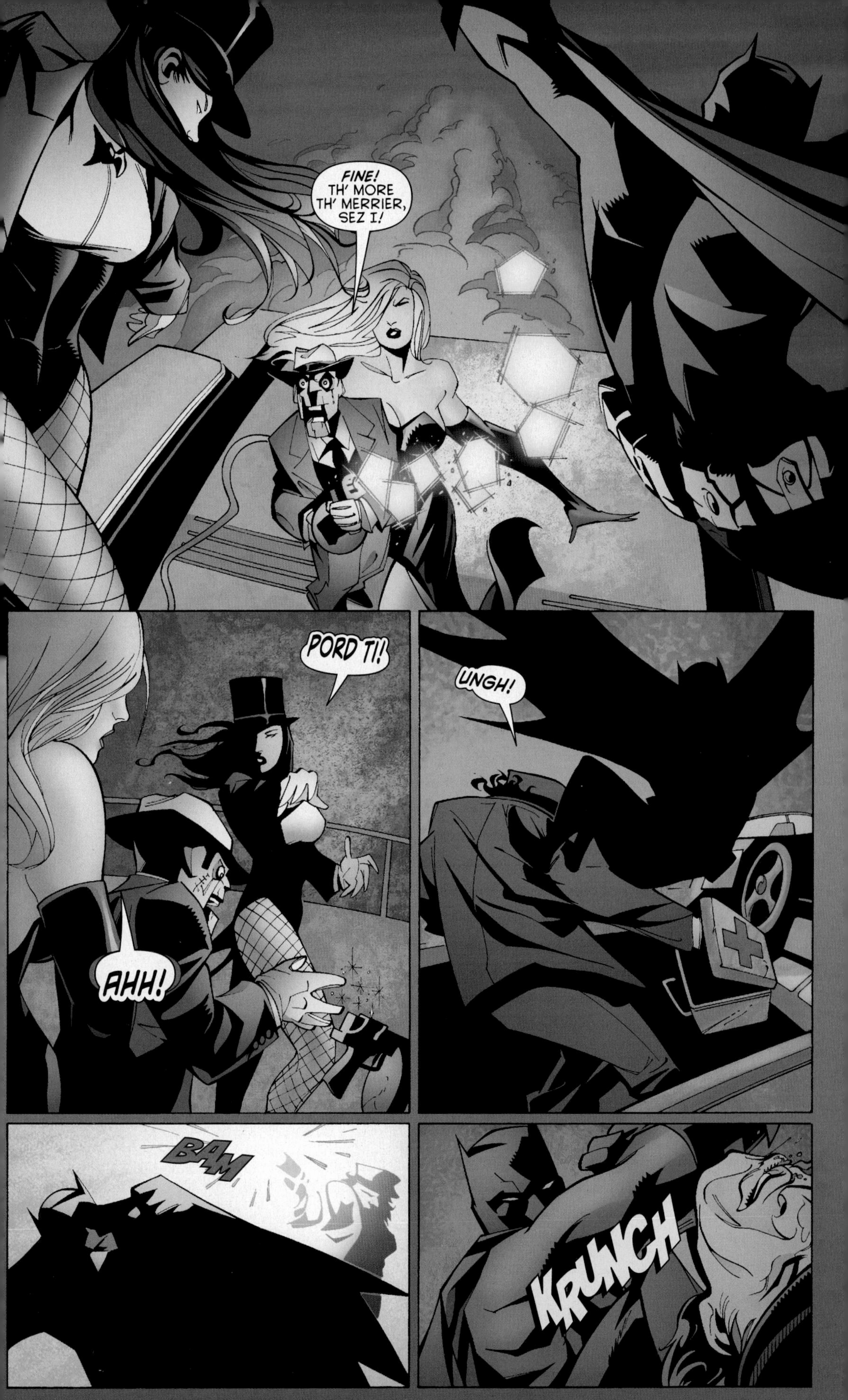
FINE! TH' MORE TH' MERRIER, SEZ I!
PORD TI!
AHH!
UNGH!
BAM
KRUNCH

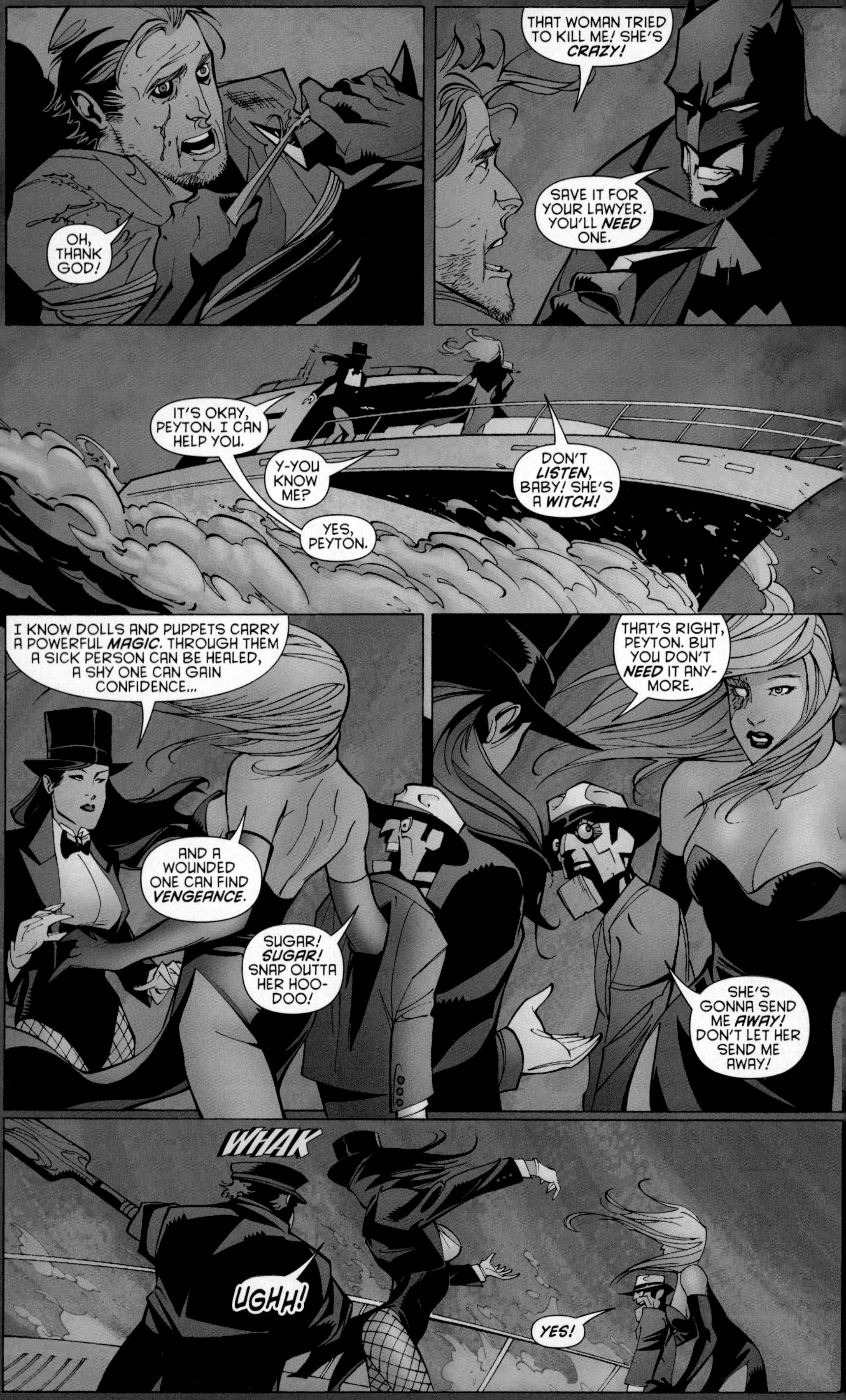
OH, THANK GOD!
THAT WOMAN TRIED TO KILL ME! SHE'S CRAZY!
SAVE IT FOR YOUR LAWYER. YOU'LL NEED ONE.
IT'S OKAY, PEYTON. I CAN HELP YOU.
Y-YOU KNOW ME?
YES, PEYTON.
DON'T LISTEN, BABY! SHE'S A WITCH!
I KNOW DOLLS AND PUPPETS CARRY A POWERFUL MAGIC. THROUGH THEM A SICK PERSON CAN BE HEALED, A SHY ONE CAN GAIN CONFIDENCE...
AND A WOUNDED ONE CAN FIND VENGEANCE.
SUGAR! SUGAR! SNAP OUTTA HER HOO-DOO!
THAT'S RIGHT, PEYTON. BUT YOU DON'T NEED IT ANY-MORE.
SHE'S GONNA SEND ME AWAY! DON'T LET HER SEND ME AWAY!
WHAK
UGHH!
YES!

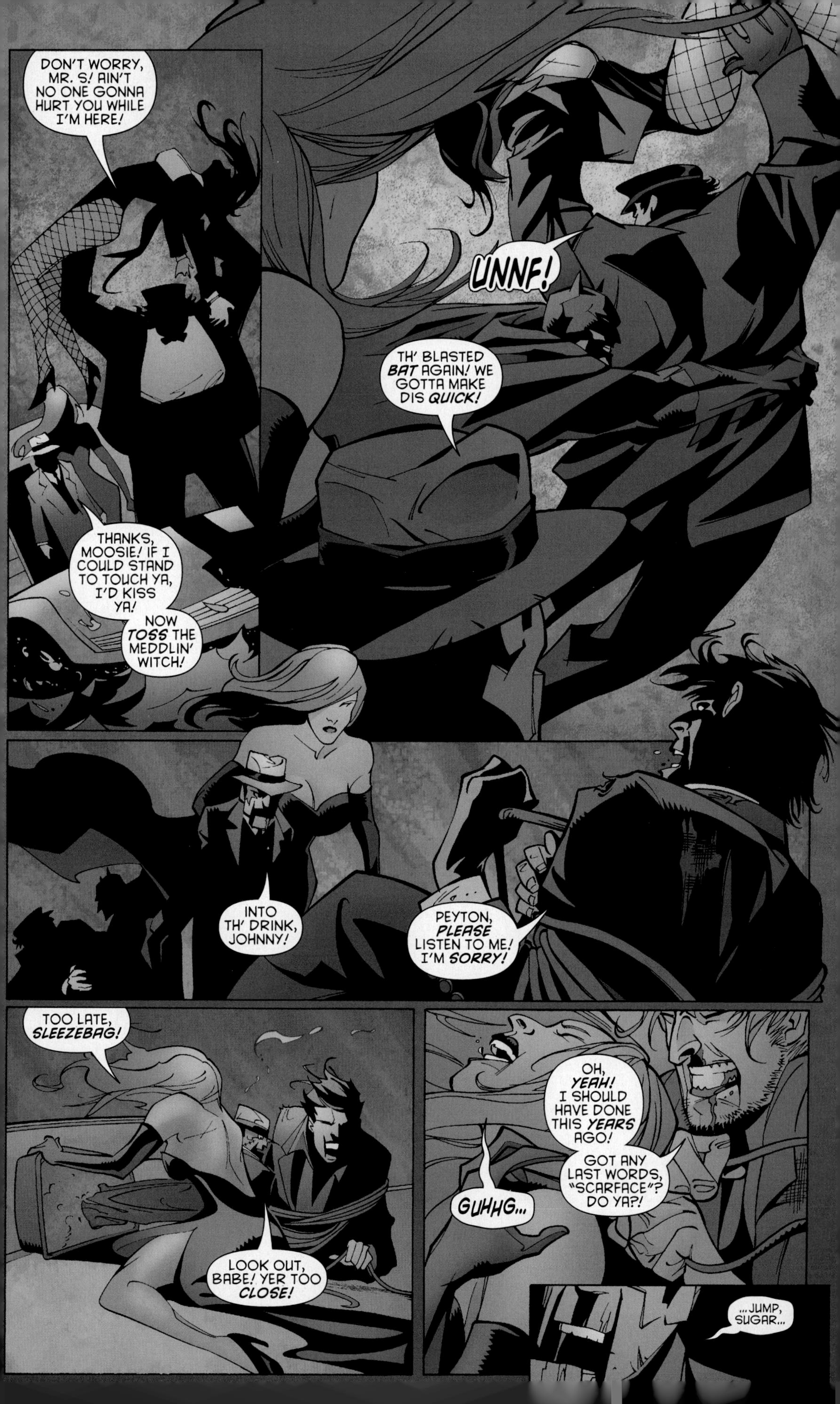
DON'T WORRY, MR. S! AIN'T NO ONE GONNA HURT YOU WHILE I'M HERE!
UNNF!
TH' BLASTED BAT AGAIN! WE GOTTA MAKE DIS QUICK!
THANKS, MOOSIE! IF I COULD STAND TO TOUCH YA, I'D KISS YA!
NOW TOSS THE MEDDLIN' WITCH!
INTO TH' DRINK, JOHNNY!
PEYTON, PLEASE LISTEN TO ME! I'M SORRY!
TOO LATE, SLEEZEBAG!
LOOK OUT, BABE! YER TOO CLOSE!
OH, YEAH! I SHOULD HAVE DONE THIS YEARS AGO!
GUHHG...
GOT ANY LAST WORDS, "SCARFACE"? DO YA?!
...JUMP, SUGAR...

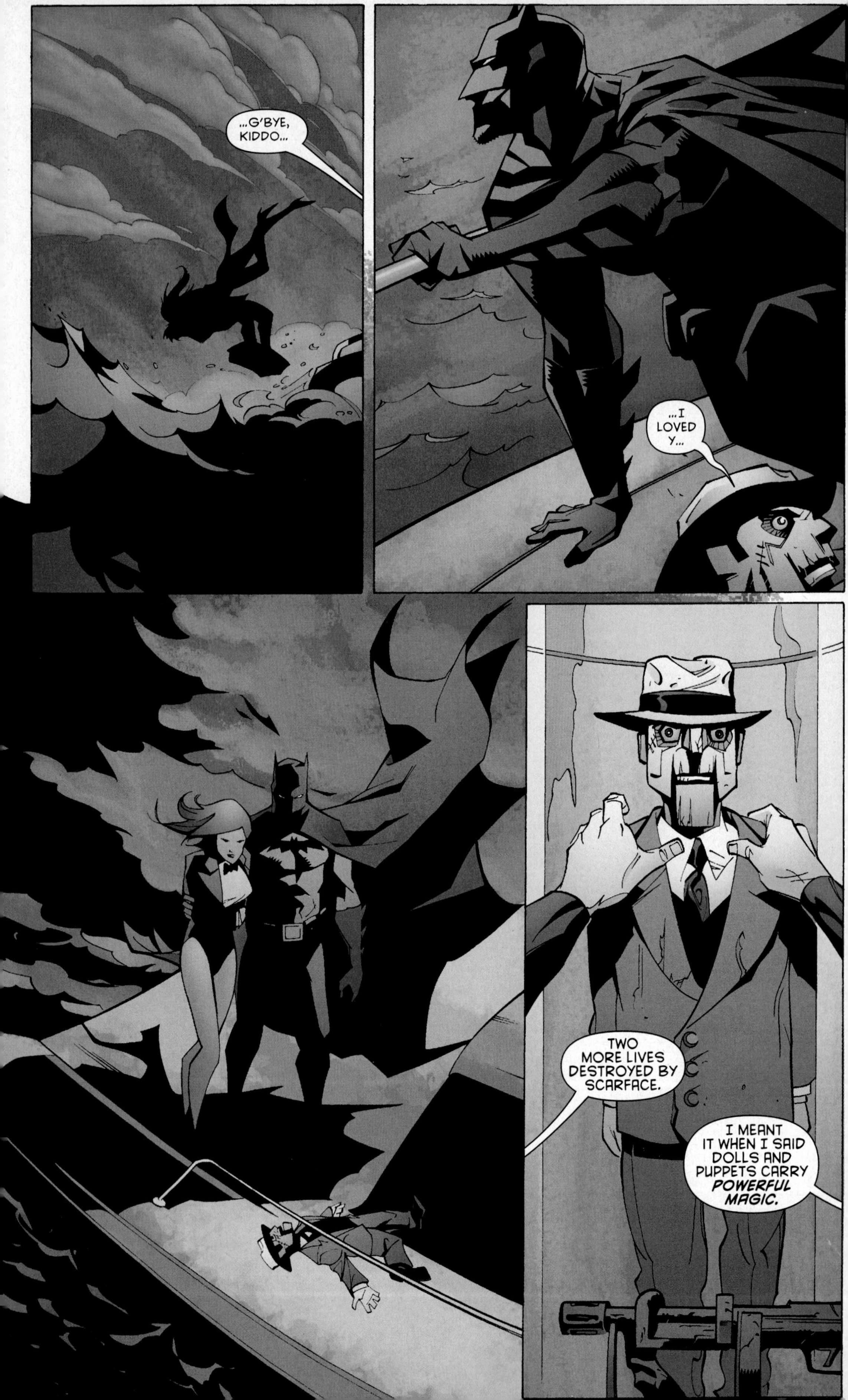
...G'BYE, KIDDO...
...I LOVED Y...
TWO MORE LIVES DESTROYED BY SCARFACE.
I MEANT IT WHEN I SAID DOLLS AND PUPPETS CARRY ***POWERFUL MAGIC.***

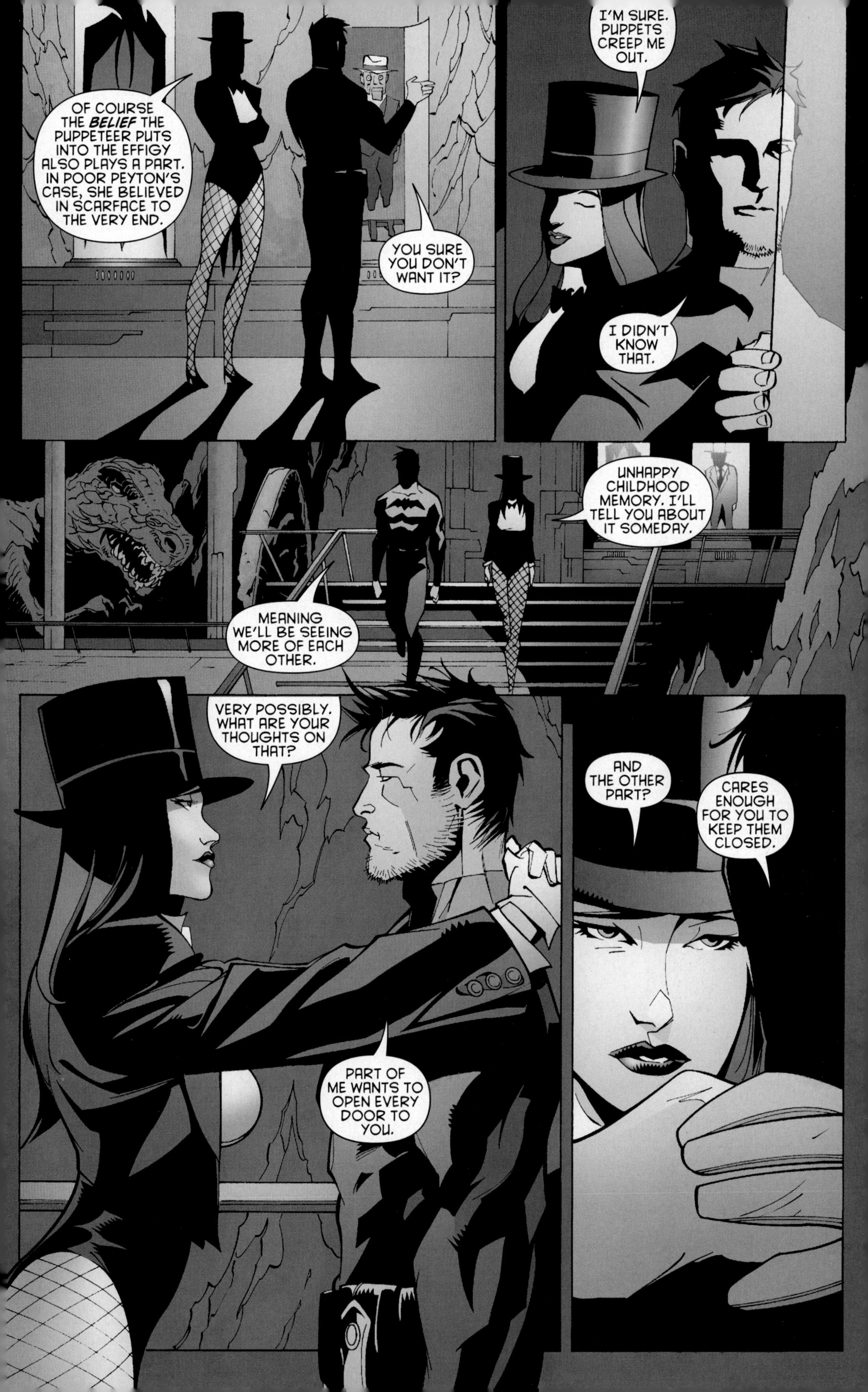
OF COURSE THE *BELIEF* THE PUPPETEER PUTS INTO THE EFFIGY ALSO PLAYS A PART. IN POOR PEYTON'S CASE, SHE BELIEVED IN SCARFACE TO THE VERY END.
YOU SURE YOU DON'T WANT IT?
I'M SURE. PUPPETS CREEP ME OUT.
I DIDN'T KNOW THAT.
UNHAPPY CHILDHOOD MEMORY. I'LL TELL YOU ABOUT IT SOMEDAY.
MEANING WE'LL BE SEEING MORE OF EACH OTHER.
VERY POSSIBLY. WHAT ARE YOUR THOUGHTS ON THAT?
PART OF ME WANTS TO OPEN EVERY DOOR TO YOU.
AND THE OTHER PART?
CARES ENOUGH FOR YOU TO KEEP THEM CLOSED.

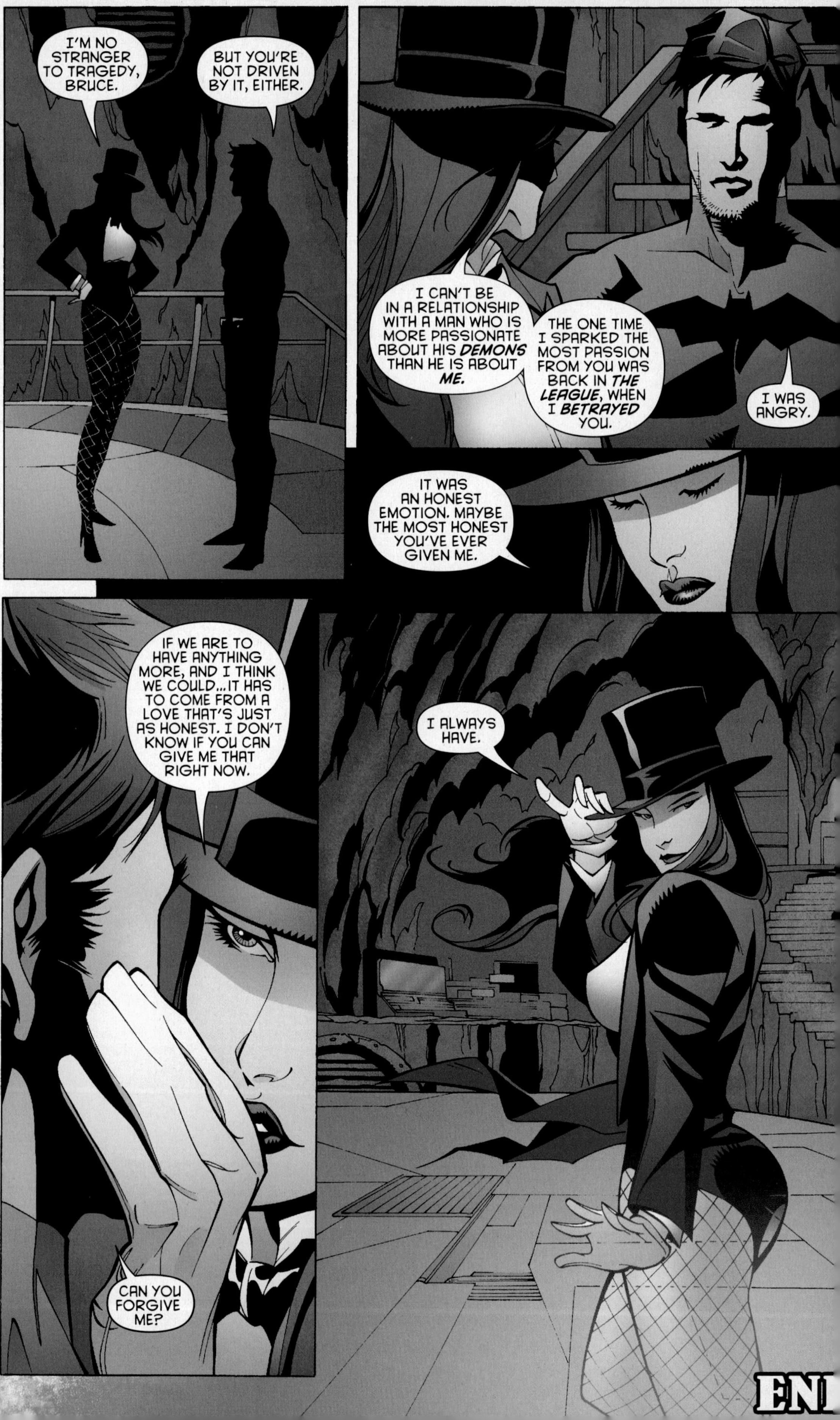
I'M NO STRANGER TO TRAGEDY, BRUCE.
BUT YOU'RE NOT DRIVEN BY IT, EITHER.
I CAN'T BE IN A RELATIONSHIP WITH A MAN WHO IS MORE PASSIONATE ABOUT HIS DEMONS THAN HE IS ABOUT ME.
THE ONE TIME I SPARKED THE MOST PASSION FROM YOU WAS BACK IN THE LEAGUE, WHEN I BETRAYED YOU.
I WAS ANGRY.
IT WAS AN HONEST EMOTION. MAYBE THE MOST HONEST YOU'VE EVER GIVEN ME.
IF WE ARE TO HAVE ANYTHING MORE, AND I THINK WE COULD...IT HAS TO COME FROM A LOVE THAT'S JUST AS HONEST. I DON'T KNOW IF YOU CAN GIVE ME THAT RIGHT NOW.
CAN YOU FORGIVE ME?
I ALWAYS HAVE.

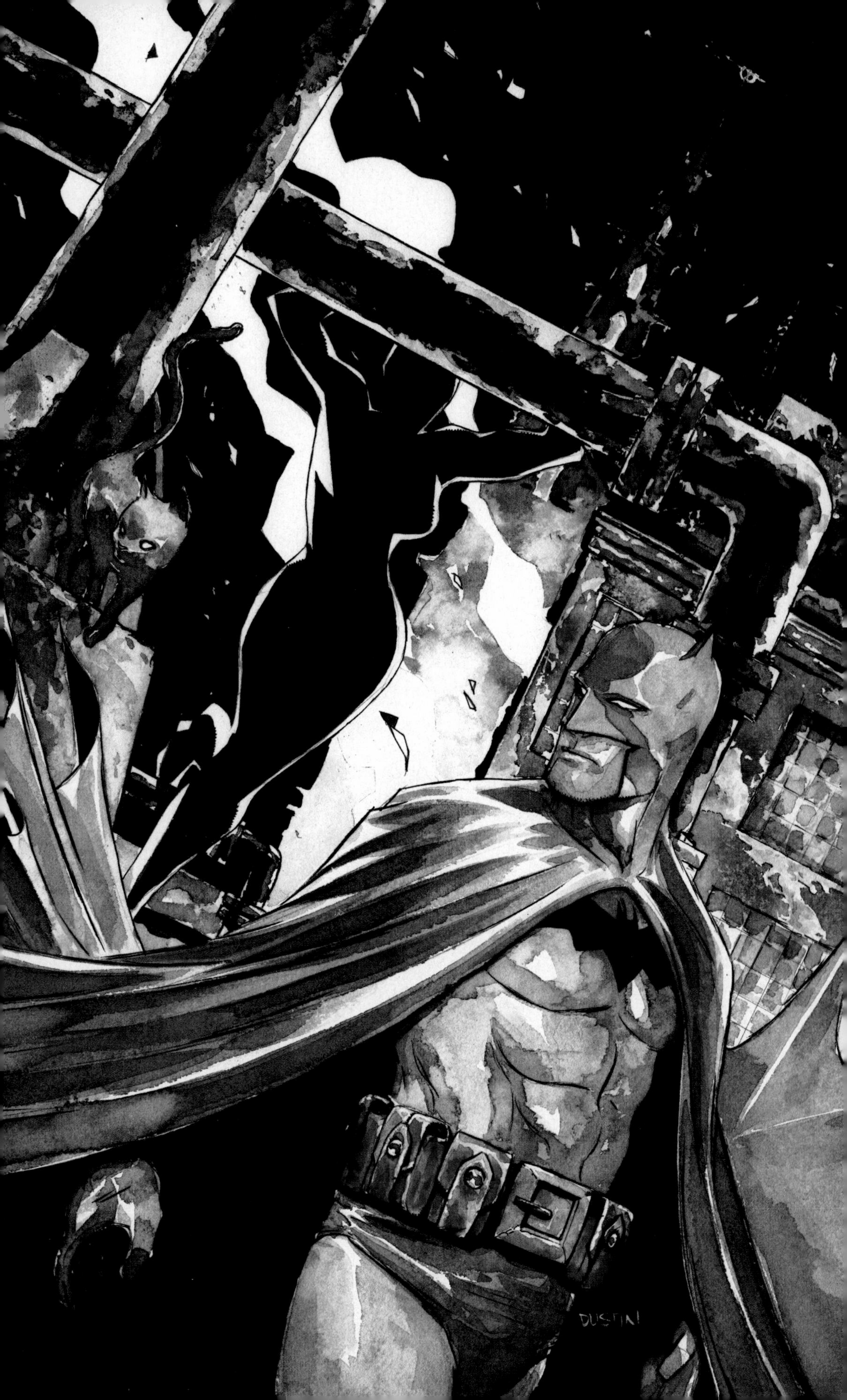
DUSTIN

The Riddle Unanswered

"Based on the victim's clothing, we can assume he was out for a morning walk. The fact that he was drinking a large mocha with whipped cream indicates he was less interested in exercise than enjoying a *treat*.

"The faint ink smudge on his right thumb tells us he was probably reading his paper at the time he was accosted.

"The killer came upon him **suddenly**, thrusting himself out of concealment directly into the victim's path. Coffee stains on the victim's sweatshirt reveal he jumped back, startled. It's likely the attacker bumped him, as well.

"Chloroform residue on the victim's face tells us he was taken in the same way as the **other two** victims.

"Startled, losing consciousness, the victim would offer virtually **no resistance** to the killer's blade. The oddly curved angle of the cut, when matched with those found on the other victims, identifies the weapon as a **ghurka khukri** knife.

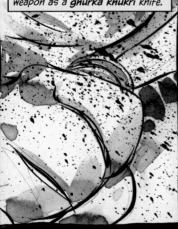

"This is also confirmed with the cut used in each murder to sever the victim's **left hand.**

"And as a final cryptic touch, a single **white lily** left floating in a widening pool of the victim's blood..."

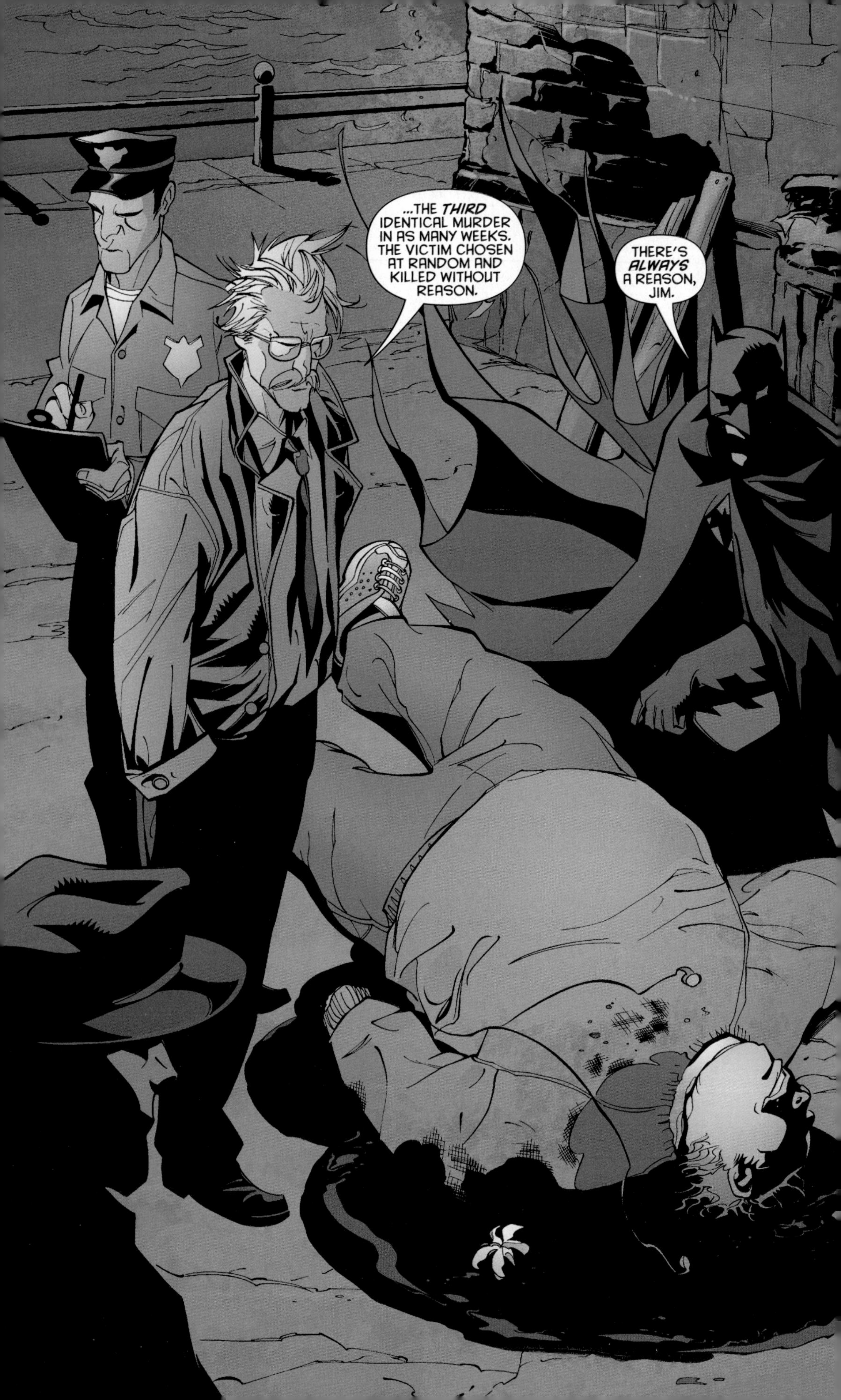
...THE THIRD IDENTICAL MURDER IN AS MANY WEEKS. THE VICTIM CHOSEN AT RANDOM AND KILLED WITHOUT REASON.
THERE'S ALWAYS A REASON, JIM.

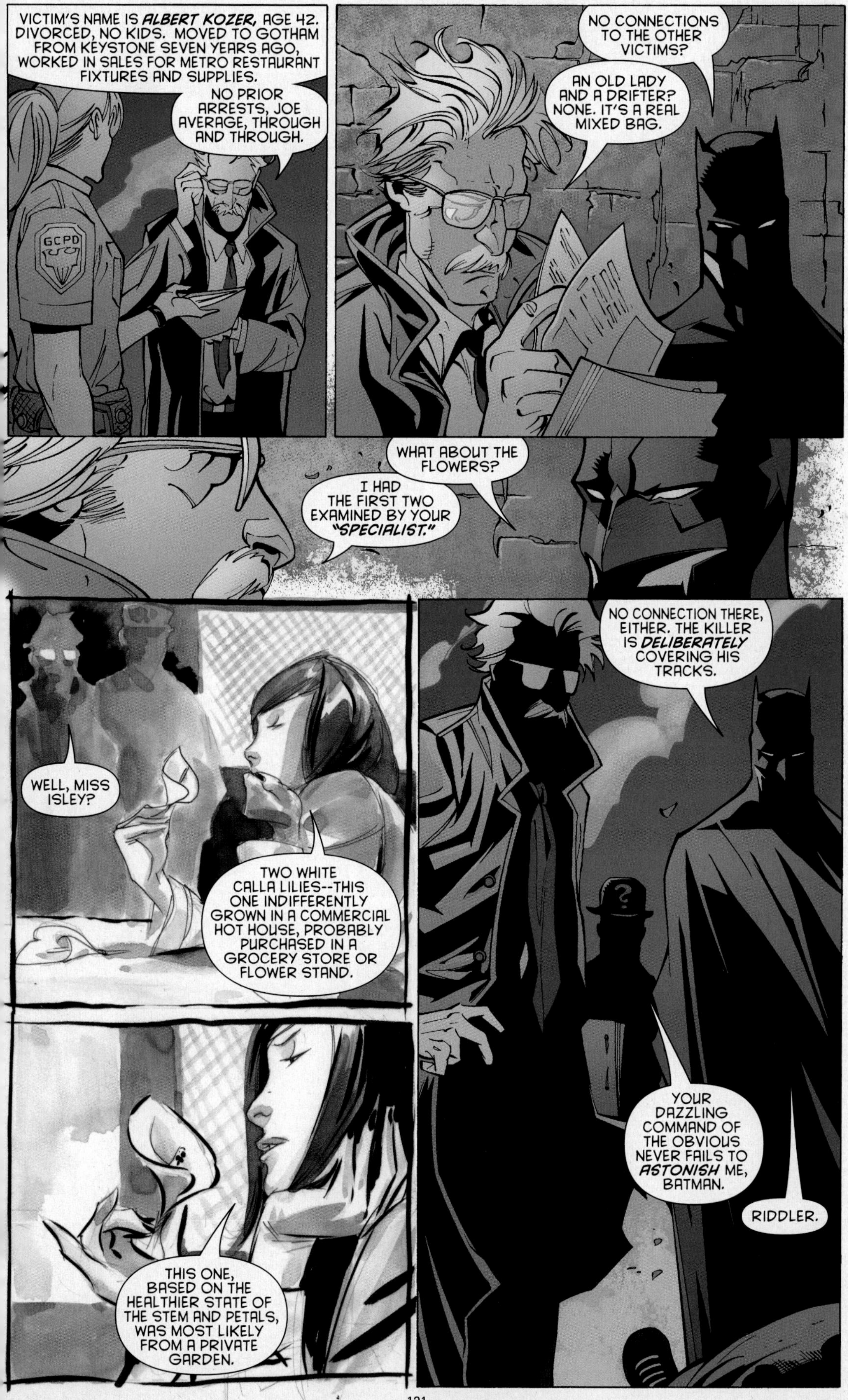
VICTIM'S NAME IS ALBERT KOZER, AGE 42. DIVORCED, NO KIDS. MOVED TO GOTHAM FROM KEYSTONE SEVEN YEARS AGO, WORKED IN SALES FOR METRO RESTAURANT FIXTURES AND SUPPLIES.
NO PRIOR ARRESTS, JOE AVERAGE, THROUGH AND THROUGH.
GCPD
NO CONNECTIONS TO THE OTHER VICTIMS?
AN OLD LADY AND A DRIFTER? NONE. IT'S A REAL MIXED BAG.
WHAT ABOUT THE FLOWERS?
I HAD THE FIRST TWO EXAMINED BY YOUR "SPECIALIST."
WELL, MISS ISLEY?
TWO WHITE CALLA LILIES--THIS ONE INDIFFERENTLY GROWN IN A COMMERCIAL HOT HOUSE, PROBABLY PURCHASED IN A GROCERY STORE OR FLOWER STAND.
THIS ONE, BASED ON THE HEALTHIER STATE OF THE STEM AND PETALS, WAS MOST LIKELY FROM A PRIVATE GARDEN.
NO CONNECTION THERE, EITHER. THE KILLER IS DELIBERATELY COVERING HIS TRACKS.
YOUR DAZZLING COMMAND OF THE OBVIOUS NEVER FAILS TO ASTONISH ME, BATMAN.
RIDDLER.

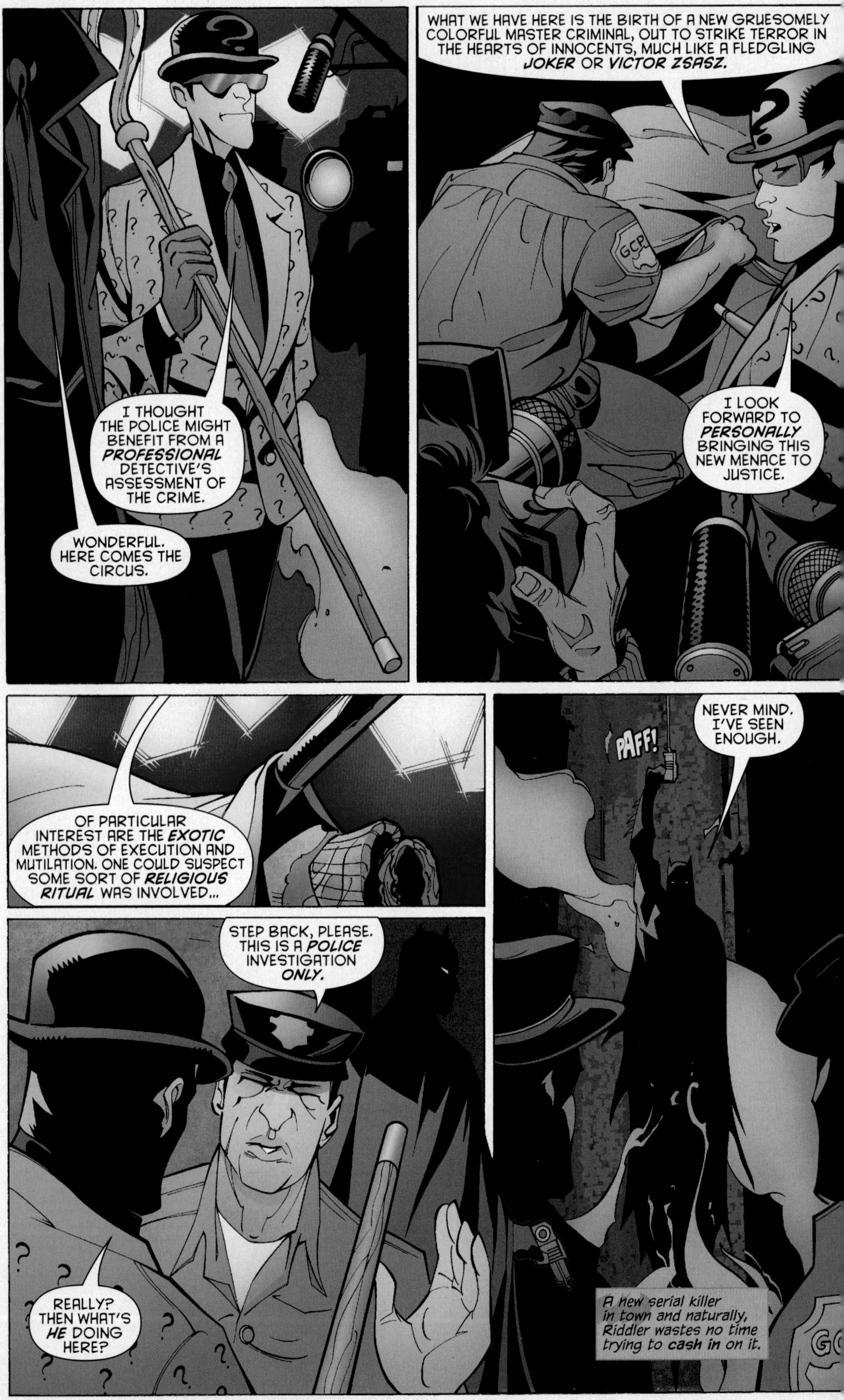
WONDERFUL. HERE COMES THE CIRCUS.
I THOUGHT THE POLICE MIGHT BENEFIT FROM A PROFESSIONAL DETECTIVE'S ASSESSMENT OF THE CRIME.
WHAT WE HAVE HERE IS THE BIRTH OF A NEW GRUESOMELY COLORFUL MASTER CRIMINAL, OUT TO STRIKE TERROR IN THE HEARTS OF INNOCENTS, MUCH LIKE A FLEDGLING JOKER OR VICTOR ZSASZ.
GCPD
I LOOK FORWARD TO PERSONALLY BRINGING THIS NEW MENACE TO JUSTICE.
OF PARTICULAR INTEREST ARE THE EXOTIC METHODS OF EXECUTION AND MUTILATION. ONE COULD SUSPECT SOME SORT OF RELIGIOUS RITUAL WAS INVOLVED...
STEP BACK, PLEASE. THIS IS A POLICE INVESTIGATION ONLY.
REALLY? THEN WHAT'S HE DOING HERE?
PAFF!
NEVER MIND. I'VE SEEN ENOUGH.
A new serial killer in town and naturally, Riddler wastes no time trying to cash in on it.

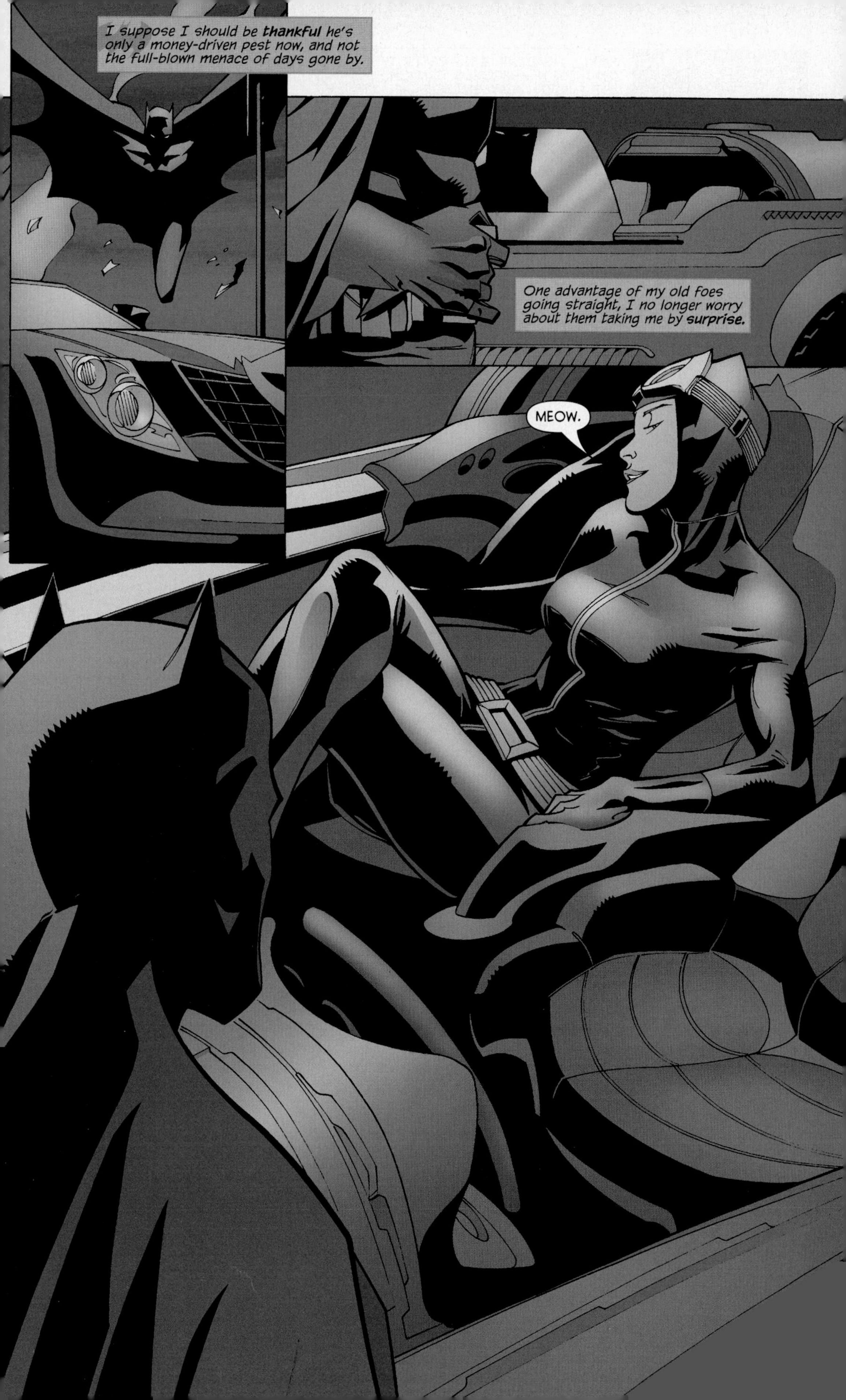
I suppose I should be **thankful** he's only a money-driven pest now, and not the full-blown menace of days gone by.
One advantage of my old foes going straight, I no longer worry about them taking me by **surprise.**
MEOW.

YOU'RE TIGHTENING THE SECURITY ON THESE NEW MODELS. IT TOOK ME *TWENTY MINUTES* TO PICK THE LOCK THIS TIME.

I'M GLAD YOU'RE BACK SAFELY FROM THE PRISON PLANET. NO ONE COULD HAVE FORESEEN HOW *BADLY* THAT WOULD END.

I'M HOME NOW. THAT'S WHAT COUNTS.

SO, NEW KILLER IN TOWN, I HEAR. WITH A FETISH FOR INDIAN KNIVES AND SEVERED LEFT HANDS, YET.

HAVE YOU HEARD ANY OTHER SPECIFICS?

ABOUT THE KILLER, NO. ABOUT YOUR BLOSSOMING ROMANCES WITH JEZEBEL JET AND ZATANNA, PLENTY.

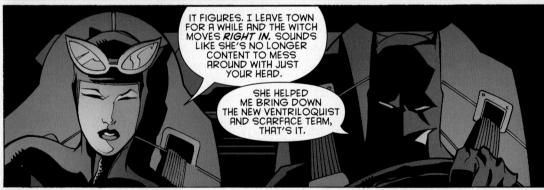

IT FIGURES. I LEAVE TOWN FOR A WHILE AND THE WITCH MOVES *RIGHT IN*. SOUNDS LIKE SHE'S NO LONGER CONTENT TO MESS AROUND WITH JUST YOUR HEAD.

SHE HELPED ME BRING DOWN THE NEW VENTRILOQUIST AND SCARFACE TEAM, THAT'S IT.

NEXT THING YOU KNOW SHE'LL BE TRADING IN HER TOP HAT AND FISHNETS FOR A CAPE AND COWL.

"BAT-ANNA." IT HAS A RING TO IT.

SELINA...

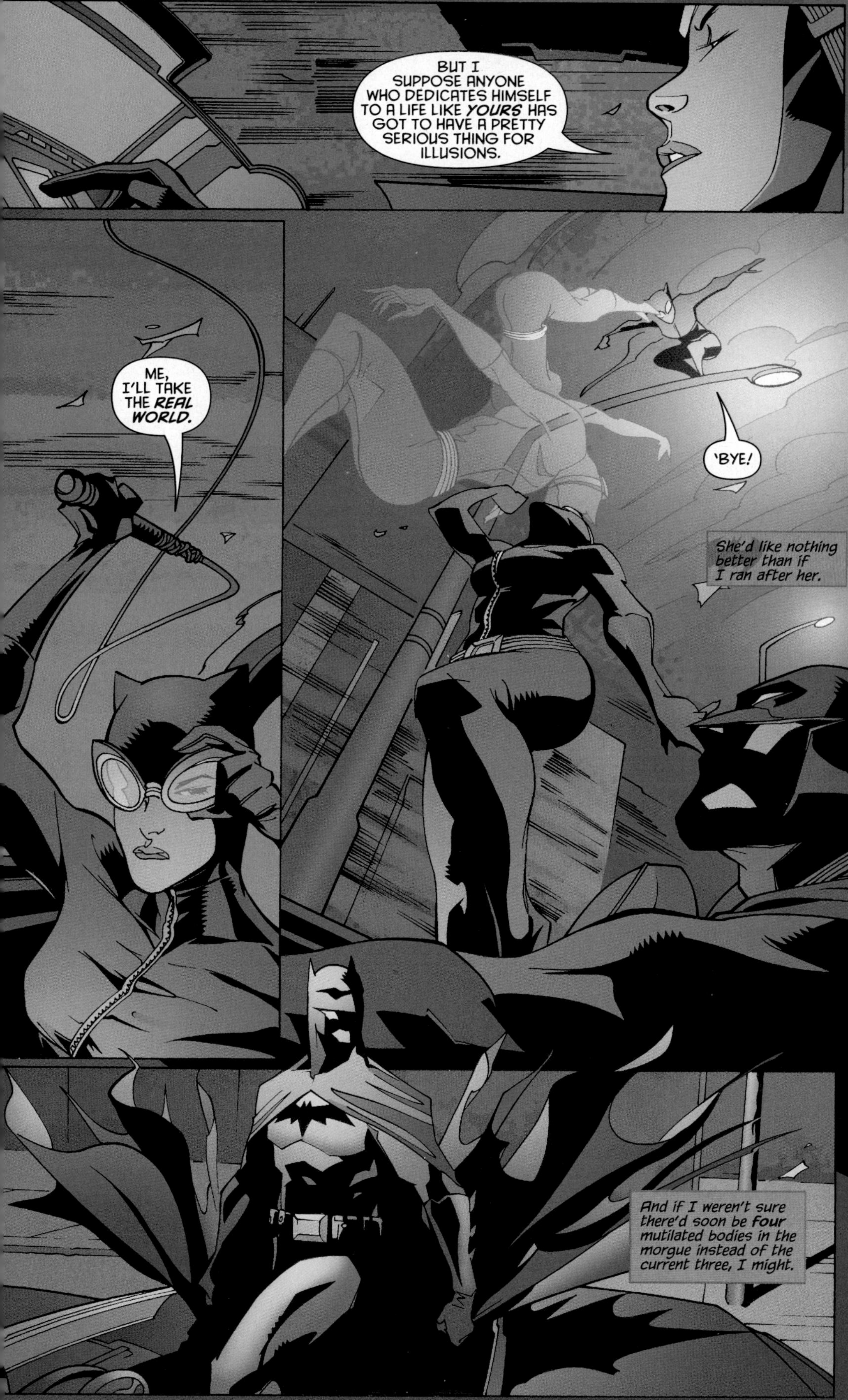
BUT I SUPPOSE ANYONE WHO DEDICATES HIMSELF TO A LIFE LIKE YOURS HAS GOT TO HAVE A PRETTY SERIOUS THING FOR ILLUSIONS.
ME, I'LL TAKE THE REAL WORLD.
'BYE!
She'd like nothing better than if I ran after her.
And if I weren't sure there'd soon be four mutilated bodies in the morgue instead of the current three, I might.

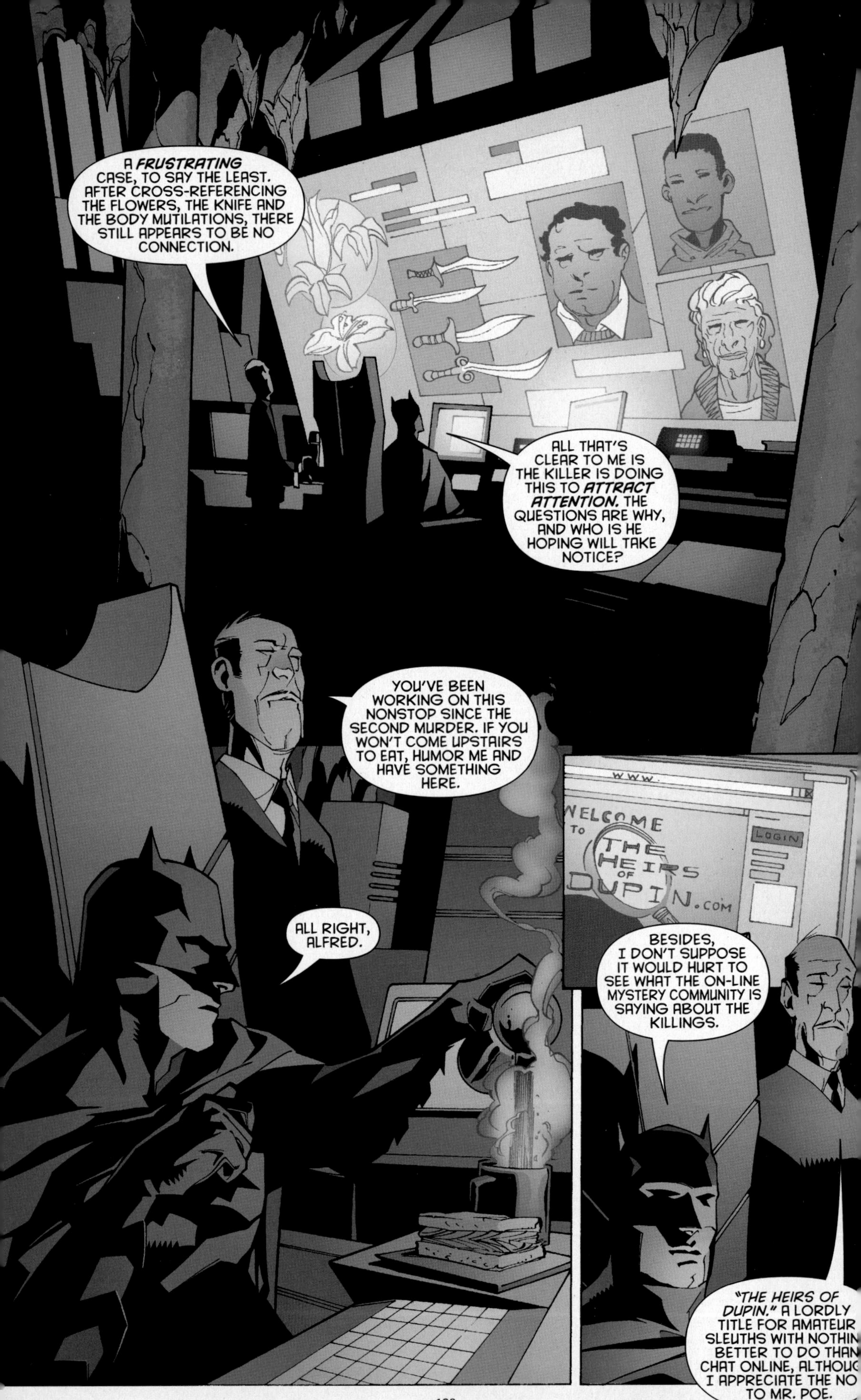
A *FRUSTRATING* CASE, TO SAY THE LEAST. AFTER CROSS-REFERENCING THE FLOWERS, THE KNIFE AND THE BODY MUTILATIONS, THERE STILL APPEARS TO BE NO CONNECTION.
ALL THAT'S CLEAR TO ME IS THE KILLER IS DOING THIS TO *ATTRACT ATTENTION.* THE QUESTIONS ARE WHY, AND WHO IS HE HOPING WILL TAKE NOTICE?
YOU'VE BEEN WORKING ON THIS NONSTOP SINCE THE SECOND MURDER. IF YOU WON'T COME UPSTAIRS TO EAT, HUMOR ME AND HAVE SOMETHING HERE.
ALL RIGHT, ALFRED.
WWW.
WELCOME TO THE HEIRS OF DUPIN.COM
LOGIN
BESIDES, I DON'T SUPPOSE IT WOULD HURT TO SEE WHAT THE ON-LINE MYSTERY COMMUNITY IS SAYING ABOUT THE KILLINGS.
"THE HEIRS OF DUPIN." A LORDLY TITLE FOR AMATEUR SLEUTHS WITH NOTHIN BETTER TO DO THAN CHAT ONLINE, ALTHOUG I APPRECIATE THE NO TO MR. POE.

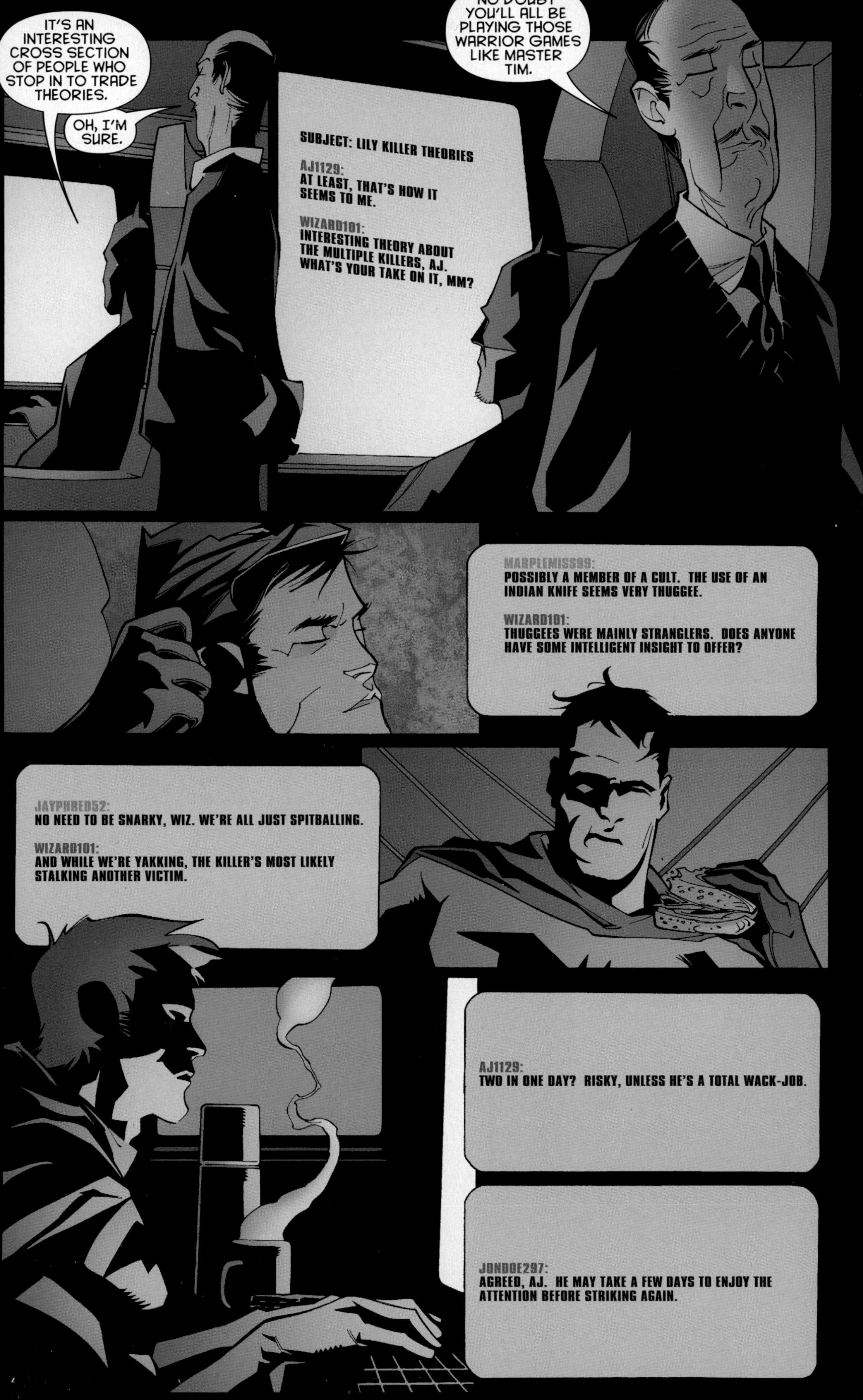
IT'S AN INTERESTING CROSS SECTION OF PEOPLE WHO STOP IN TO TRADE THEORIES.
OH, I'M SURE.
SUBJECT: LILY KILLER THEORIES
AJ1129:
AT LEAST, THAT'S HOW IT SEEMS TO ME.
WIZARD101:
INTERESTING THEORY ABOUT THE MULTIPLE KILLERS, AJ. WHAT'S YOUR TAKE ON IT, MM?
NO DOUBT YOU'LL ALL BE PLAYING THOSE WARRIOR GAMES LIKE MASTER TIM.
MARPLEMISS99:
POSSIBLY A MEMBER OF A CULT. THE USE OF AN INDIAN KNIFE SEEMS VERY THUGGEE.
WIZARD101:
THUGGEES WERE MAINLY STRANGLERS. DOES ANYONE HAVE SOME INTELLIGENT INSIGHT TO OFFER?
JAYPHRED52:
NO NEED TO BE SNARKY, WIZ. WE'RE ALL JUST SPITBALLING.
WIZARD101:
AND WHILE WE'RE YAKKING, THE KILLER'S MOST LIKELY STALKING ANOTHER VICTIM.
AJ1129:
TWO IN ONE DAY? RISKY, UNLESS HE'S A TOTAL WACK-JOB.
JONDOE297:
AGREED, AJ. HE MAY TAKE A FEW DAYS TO ENJOY THE ATTENTION BEFORE STRIKING AGAIN.

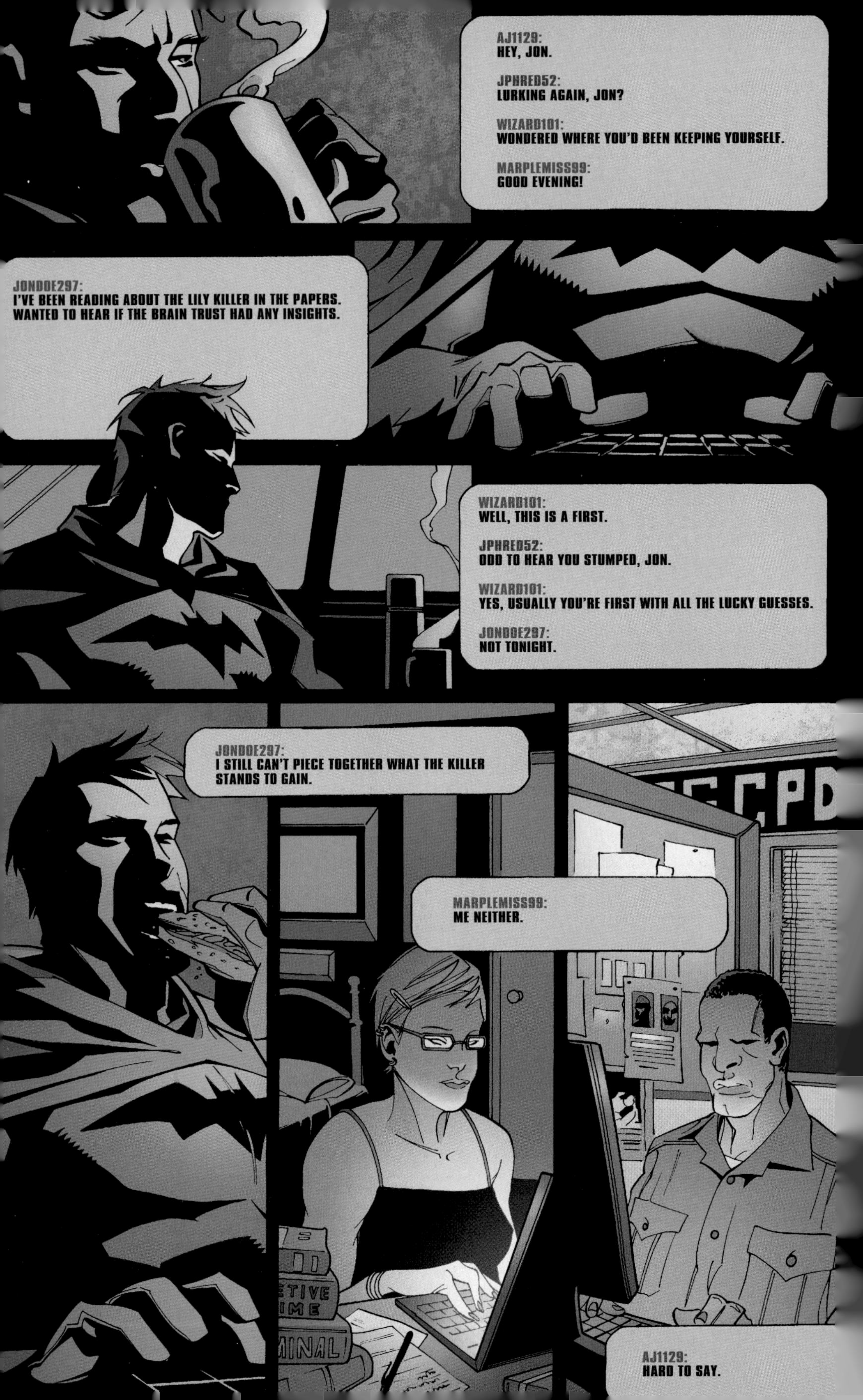
AJ1129:
HEY, JON.
JPHRED52:
LURKING AGAIN, JON?
WIZARD101:
WONDERED WHERE YOU'D BEEN KEEPING YOURSELF.
MARPLEMISS99:
GOOD EVENING!
JONDOE297:
I'VE BEEN READING ABOUT THE LILY KILLER IN THE PAPERS. WANTED TO HEAR IF THE BRAIN TRUST HAD ANY INSIGHTS.
WIZARD101:
WELL, THIS IS A FIRST.
JPHRED52:
ODD TO HEAR YOU STUMPED, JON.
WIZARD101:
YES, USUALLY YOU'RE FIRST WITH ALL THE LUCKY GUESSES.
JONDOE297:
NOT TONIGHT.
JONDOE297:
I STILL CAN'T PIECE TOGETHER WHAT THE KILLER STANDS TO GAIN.
GCPD
MARPLEMISS99:
ME NEITHER.
AJ1129:
HARD TO SAY.

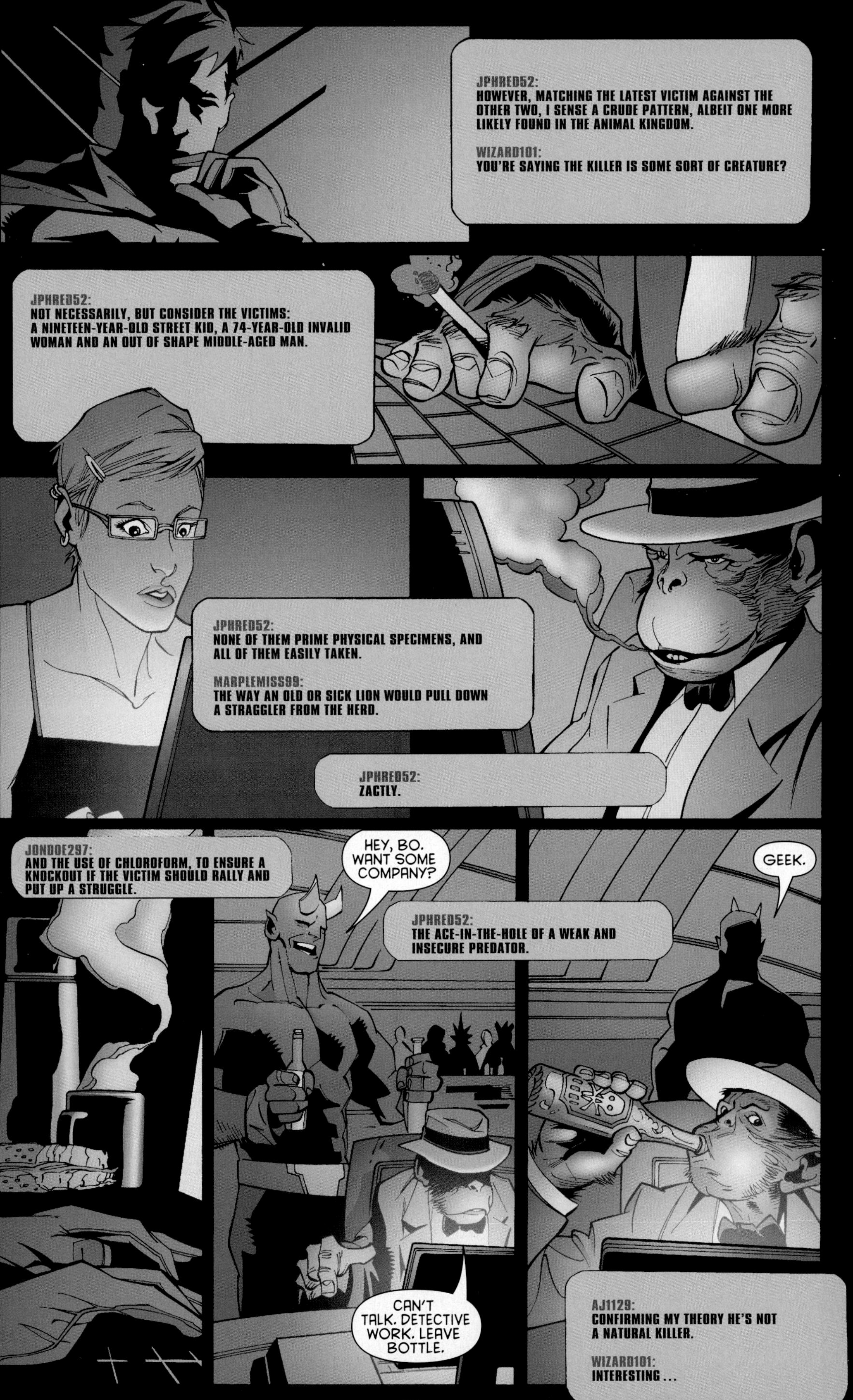

JPHRED52:
HOWEVER, MATCHING THE LATEST VICTIM AGAINST THE OTHER TWO, I SENSE A CRUDE PATTERN, ALBEIT ONE MORE LIKELY FOUND IN THE ANIMAL KINGDOM.
WIZARD101:
YOU'RE SAYING THE KILLER IS SOME SORT OF CREATURE?
JPHRED52:
NOT NECESSARILY, BUT CONSIDER THE VICTIMS: A NINETEEN-YEAR-OLD STREET KID, A 74-YEAR-OLD INVALID WOMAN AND AN OUT OF SHAPE MIDDLE-AGED MAN.
JPHRED52:
NONE OF THEM PRIME PHYSICAL SPECIMENS, AND ALL OF THEM EASILY TAKEN.
MARPLEMISS99:
THE WAY AN OLD OR SICK LION WOULD PULL DOWN A STRAGGLER FROM THE HERD.
JPHRED52:
ZACTLY.
JONDOE297:
AND THE USE OF CHLOROFORM, TO ENSURE A KNOCKOUT IF THE VICTIM SHOULD RALLY AND PUT UP A STRUGGLE.
HEY, BO. WANT SOME COMPANY?
JPHRED52:
THE ACE-IN-THE-HOLE OF A WEAK AND INSECURE PREDATOR.
CAN'T TALK. DETECTIVE WORK. LEAVE BOTTLE.
GEEK.
AJ1129:
CONFIRMING MY THEORY HE'S NOT A NATURAL KILLER.
WIZARD101:
INTERESTING . . .

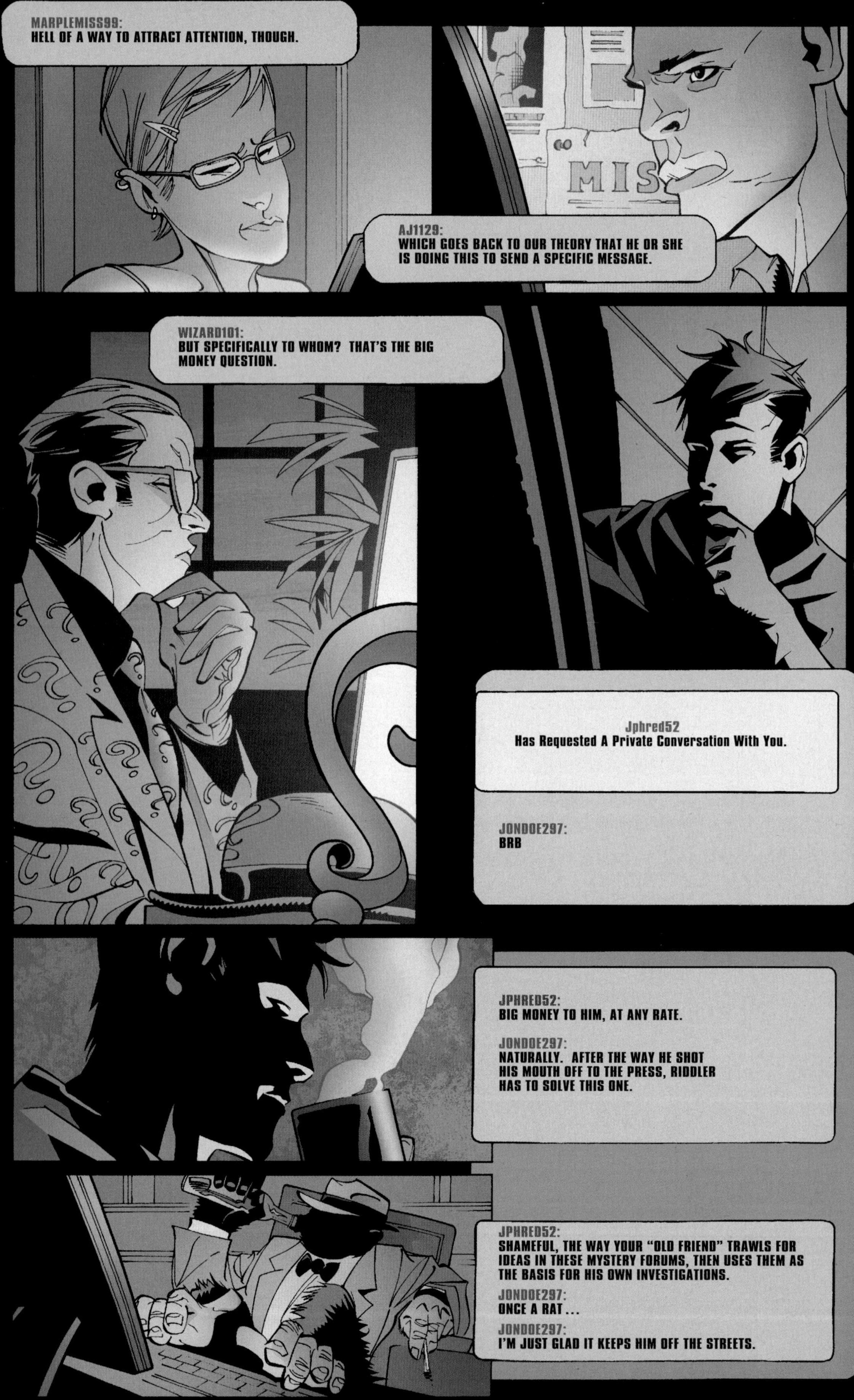
MARPLEMISS99:
HELL OF A WAY TO ATTRACT ATTENTION, THOUGH.
AJ1129:
WHICH GOES BACK TO OUR THEORY THAT HE OR SHE IS DOING THIS TO SEND A SPECIFIC MESSAGE.
MIS
WIZARD101:
BUT SPECIFICALLY TO WHOM? THAT'S THE BIG MONEY QUESTION.
Jphred52
Has Requested A Private Conversation With You.
JONDOE297:
BRB
JPHRED52:
BIG MONEY TO HIM, AT ANY RATE.
JONDOE297:
NATURALLY. AFTER THE WAY HE SHOT HIS MOUTH OFF TO THE PRESS, RIDDLER HAS TO SOLVE THIS ONE.
JPHRED52:
SHAMEFUL, THE WAY YOUR "OLD FRIEND" TRAWLS FOR IDEAS IN THESE MYSTERY FORUMS, THEN USES THEM AS THE BASIS FOR HIS OWN INVESTIGATIONS.
JONDOE297:
ONCE A RAT...
JONDOE297:
I'M JUST GLAD IT KEEPS HIM OFF THE STREETS.

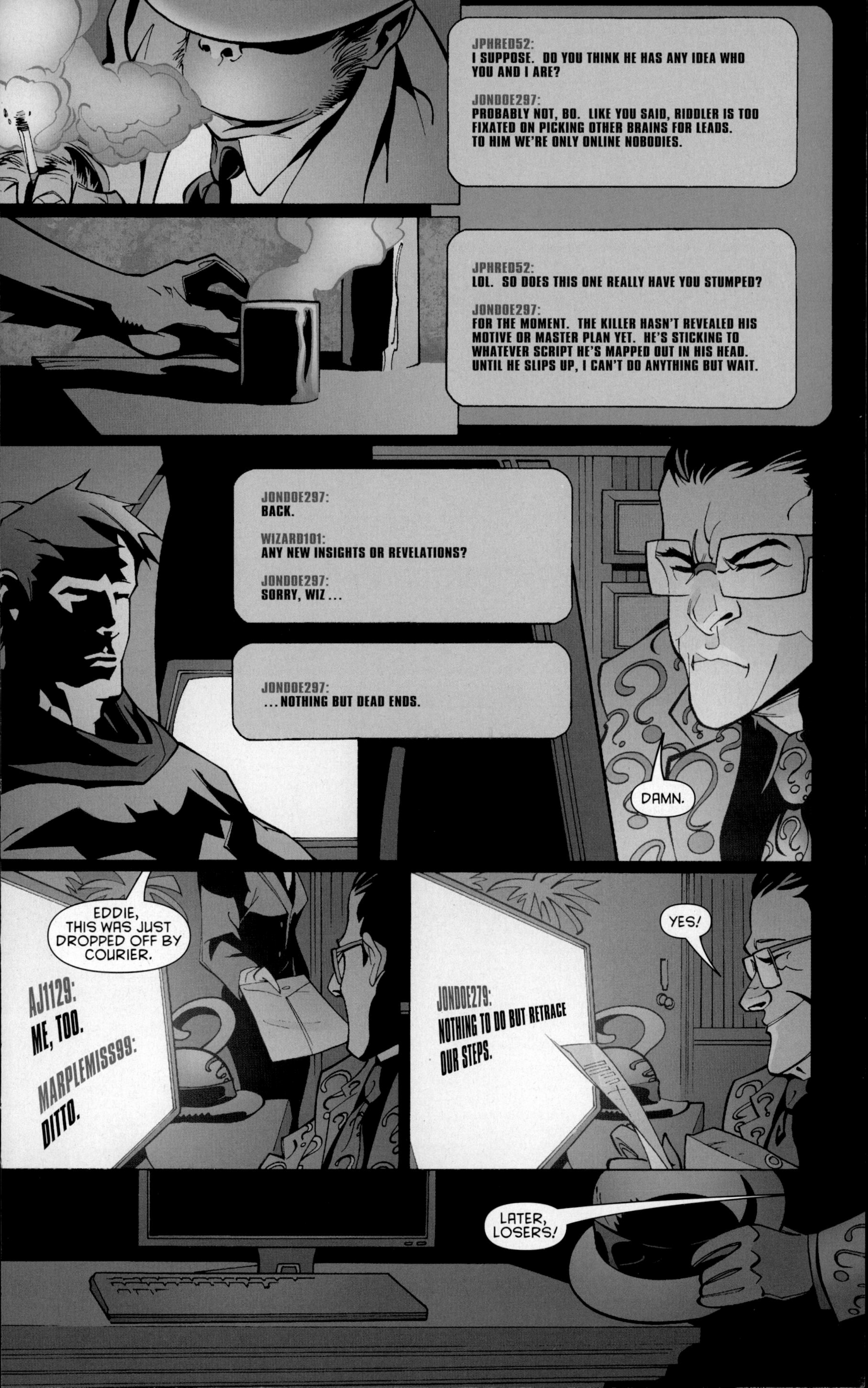
JPHRED52:
I SUPPOSE. DO YOU THINK HE HAS ANY IDEA WHO YOU AND I ARE?
JONDOE297:
PROBABLY NOT, BO. LIKE YOU SAID, RIDDLER IS TOO FIXATED ON PICKING OTHER BRAINS FOR LEADS. TO HIM WE'RE ONLY ONLINE NOBODIES.
JPHRED52:
LOL. SO DOES THIS ONE REALLY HAVE YOU STUMPED?
JONDOE297:
FOR THE MOMENT. THE KILLER HASN'T REVEALED HIS MOTIVE OR MASTER PLAN YET. HE'S STICKING TO WHATEVER SCRIPT HE'S MAPPED OUT IN HIS HEAD. UNTIL HE SLIPS UP, I CAN'T DO ANYTHING BUT WAIT.
JONDOE297:
BACK.
WIZARD101:
ANY NEW INSIGHTS OR REVELATIONS?
JONDOE297:
SORRY, WIZ . . .
JONDOE297:
. . . NOTHING BUT DEAD ENDS.
DAMN.
EDDIE, THIS WAS JUST DROPPED OFF BY COURIER.
AJ1129:
ME, TOO.
MARPLEMISS99:
DITTO.
YES!
JONDOE279:
NOTHING TO DO BUT RETRACE OUR STEPS.
LATER, LOSERS!

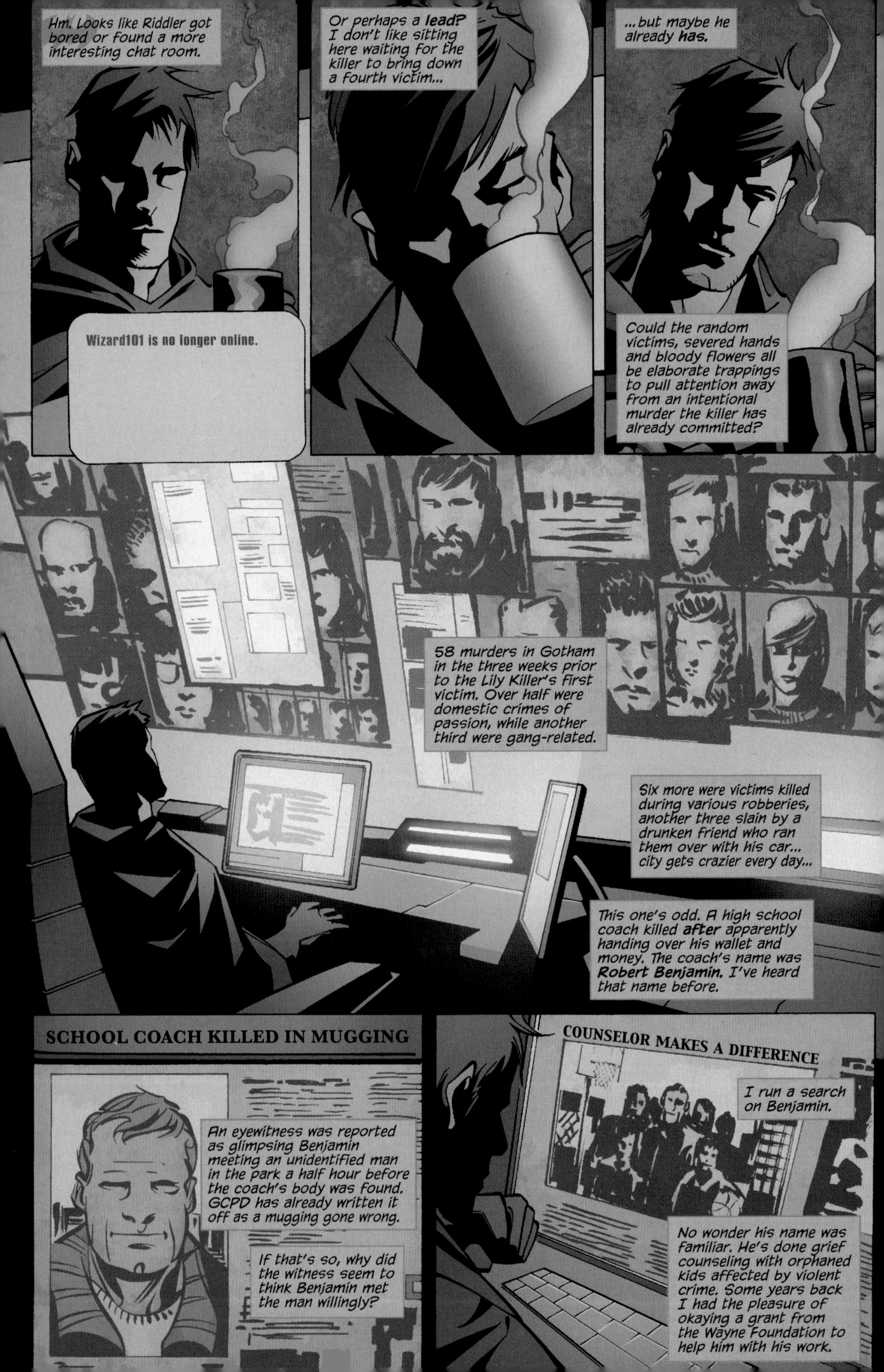
Hm. Looks like Riddler got bored or found a more interesting chat room.
Wizard101 is no longer online.
Or perhaps a lead? I don't like sitting here waiting for the killer to bring down a fourth victim...
...but maybe he already has.
Could the random victims, severed hands and bloody flowers all be elaborate trappings to pull attention away from an intentional murder the killer has already committed?
58 murders in Gotham in the three weeks prior to the Lily Killer's first victim. Over half were domestic crimes of passion, while another third were gang-related.
Six more were victims killed during various robberies, another three slain by a drunken friend who ran them over with his car... city gets crazier every day...
This one's odd. A high school coach killed after apparently handing over his wallet and money. The coach's name was Robert Benjamin. I've heard that name before.
SCHOOL COACH KILLED IN MUGGING
An eyewitness was reported as glimpsing Benjamin meeting an unidentified man in the park a half hour before the coach's body was found. GCPD has already written it off as a mugging gone wrong.
If that's so, why did the witness seem to think Benjamin met the man willingly?
COUNSELOR MAKES A DIFFERENCE
I run a search on Benjamin.
No wonder his name was familiar. He's done grief counseling with orphaned kids affected by violent crime. Some years back I had the pleasure of okaying a grant from the Wayne Foundation to help him with his work.

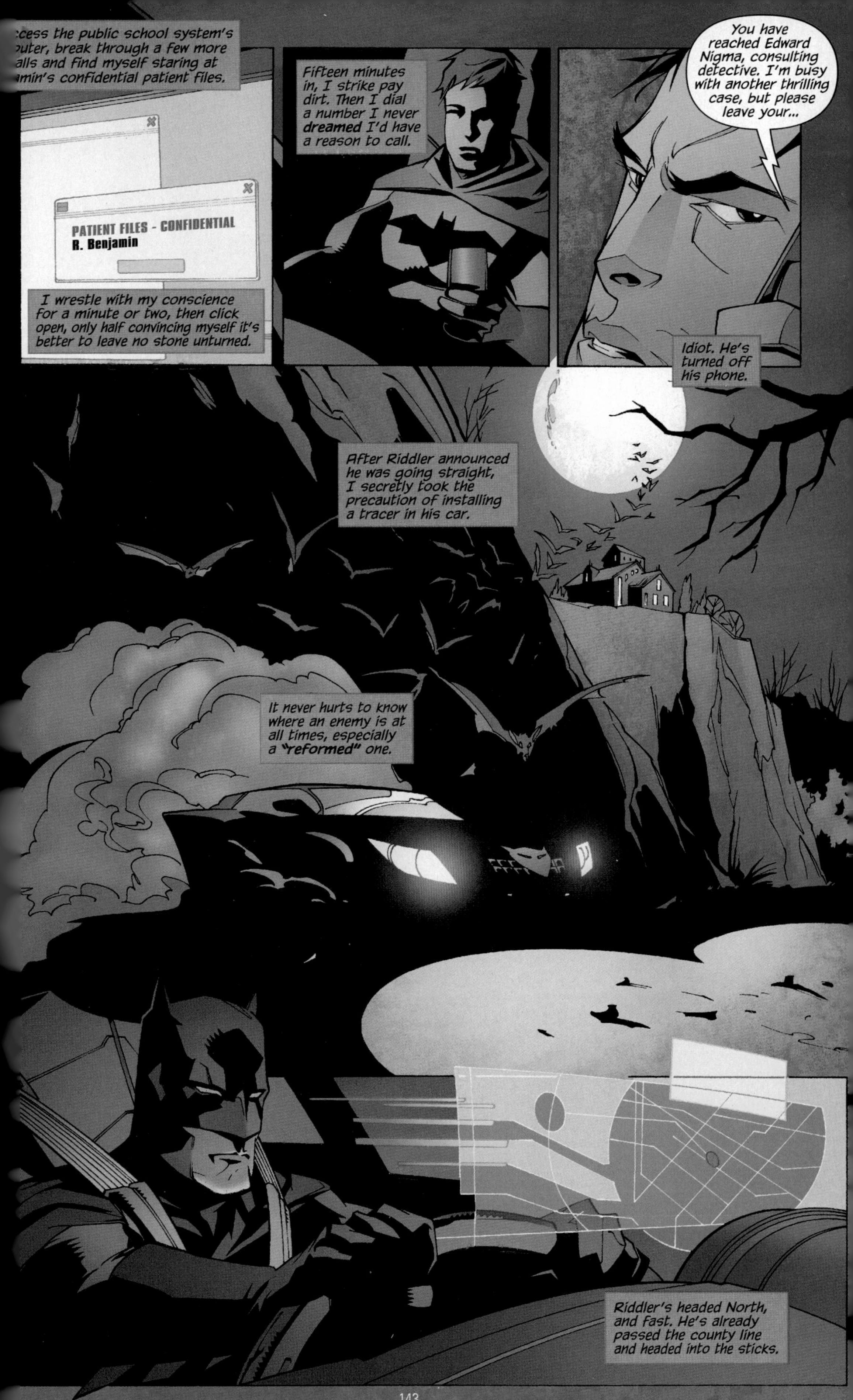

...ccess the public school system's ...puter, break through a few more ...alls and find myself staring at ...amin's confidential patient files.
PATIENT FILES - CONFIDENTIAL
R. Benjamin
I wrestle with my conscience for a minute or two, then click open, only half convincing myself it's better to leave no stone unturned.
Fifteen minutes in, I strike pay dirt. Then I dial a number I never dreamed I'd have a reason to call.
You have reached Edward Nigma, consulting detective. I'm busy with another thrilling case, but please leave your...
Idiot. He's turned off his phone.
After Riddler announced he was going straight, I secretly took the precaution of installing a tracer in his car.
It never hurts to know where an enemy is at all times, especially a "reformed" one.
Riddler's headed North, and fast. He's already passed the county line and headed into the sticks.

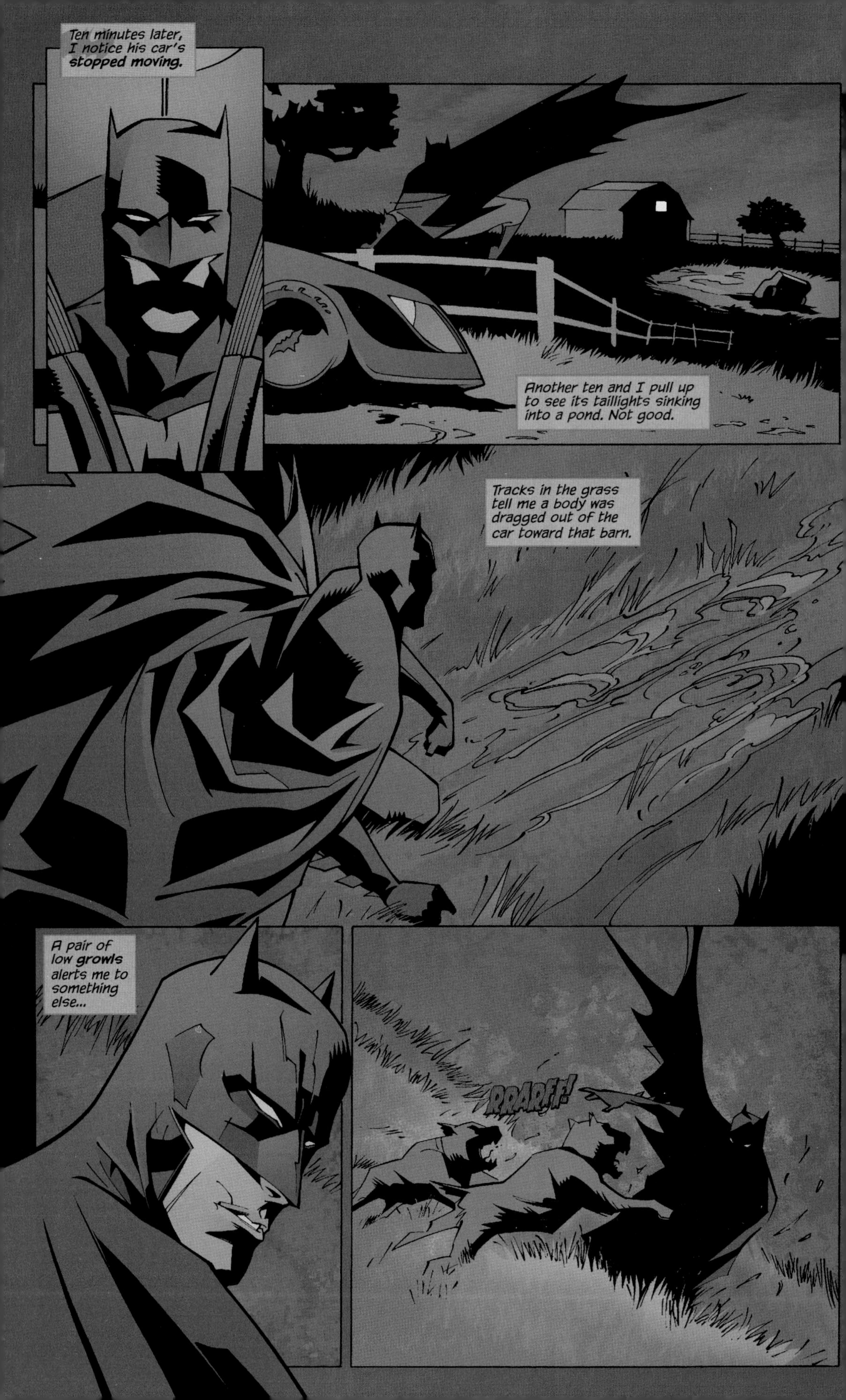

Ten minutes later, I notice his car's **stopped moving.**
Another ten and I pull up to see its taillights sinking into a pond. Not good.
Tracks in the grass tell me a body was dragged out of the car toward that barn.
A pair of low **growls** alerts me to something else...
RRARFF!

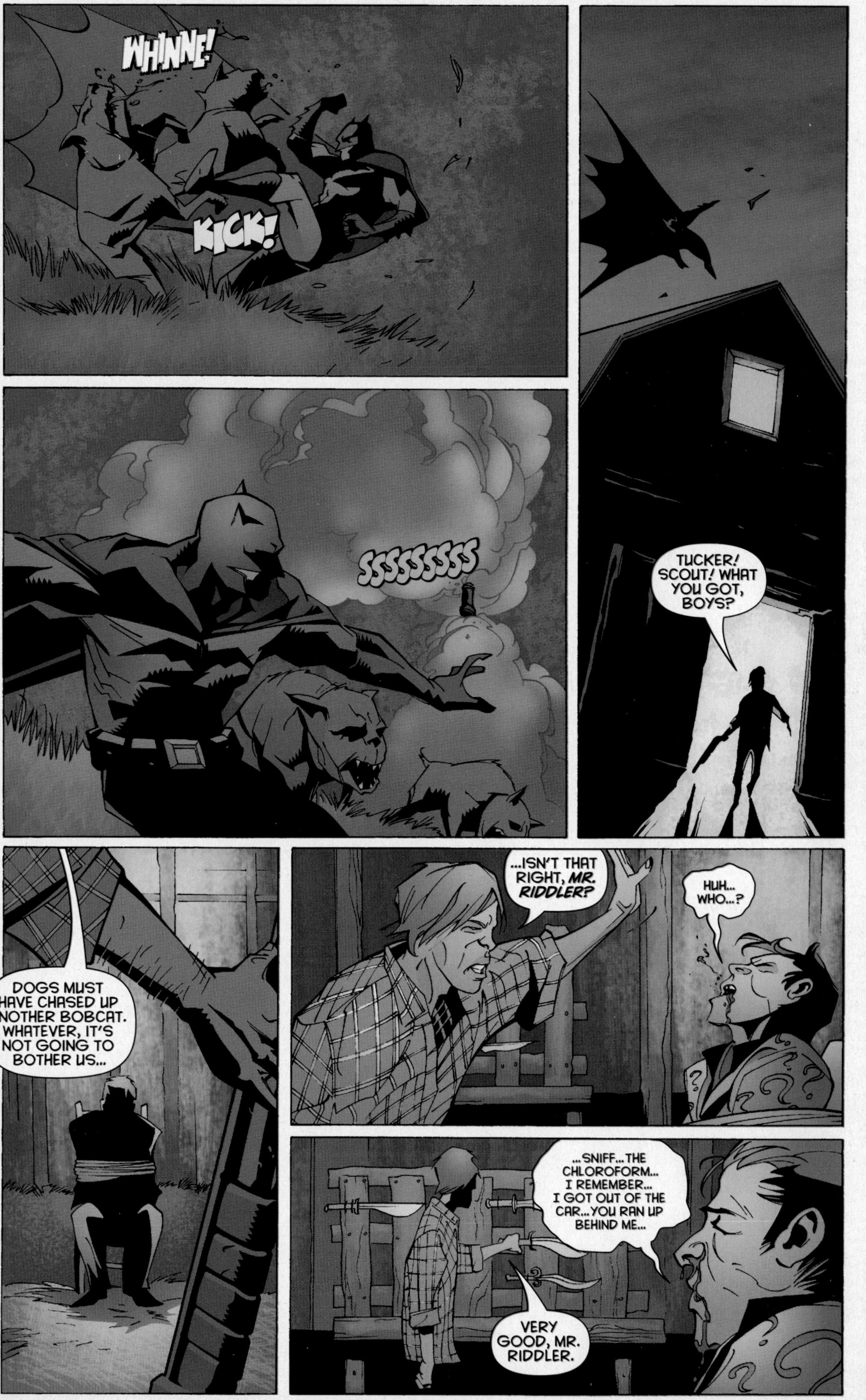

WHINNE!
KICK!
SSSSSSSS
TUCKER! SCOUT! WHAT YOU GOT, BOYS?
DOGS MUST HAVE CHASED UP NOTHER BOBCAT. WHATEVER, IT'S NOT GOING TO BOTHER US...
...ISN'T THAT RIGHT, MR. RIDDLER?
HUH... WHO...?
...SNIFF... THE CHLOROFORM... I REMEMBER... I GOT OUT OF THE CAR... YOU RAN UP BEHIND ME...
VERY GOOD, MR. RIDDLER.

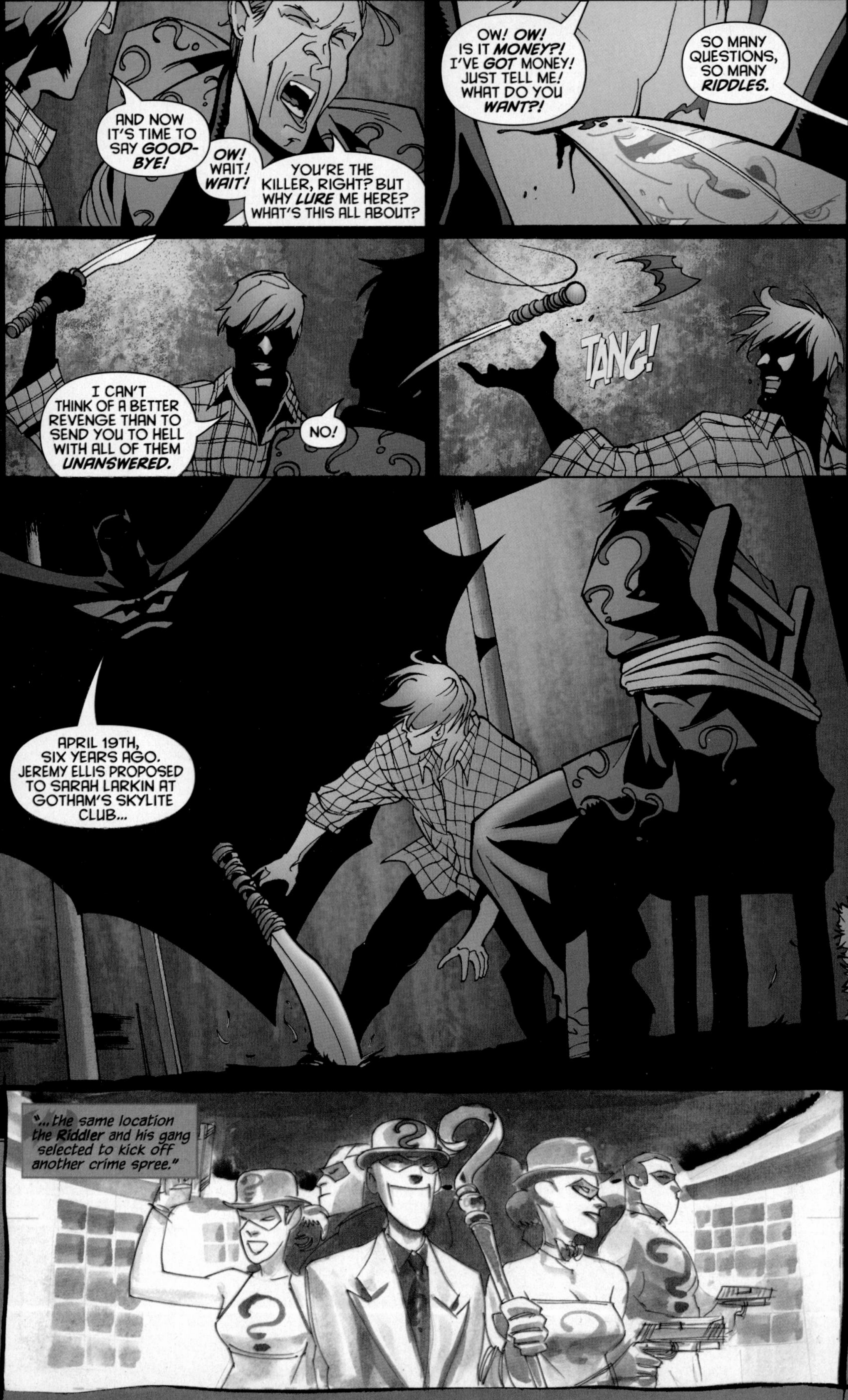
AND NOW IT'S TIME TO SAY GOOD-BYE!
OW! WAIT! WAIT!
YOU'RE THE KILLER, RIGHT? BUT WHY LURE ME HERE? WHAT'S THIS ALL ABOUT?
OW! OW! IS IT MONEY?! I'VE GOT MONEY! JUST TELL ME! WHAT DO YOU WANT?!
SO MANY QUESTIONS, SO MANY RIDDLES.
I CAN'T THINK OF A BETTER REVENGE THAN TO SEND YOU TO HELL WITH ALL OF THEM UNANSWERED.
NO!
TANG!
APRIL 19TH, SIX YEARS AGO. JEREMY ELLIS PROPOSED TO SARAH LARKIN AT GOTHAM'S SKYLITE CLUB...
"...the same location the Riddler and his gang selected to kick off another crime spree."

"Someone protested when his wife's jewelry was taken. A warning shot was fired. Security guards ran in and more *guns* went off."

"Jeremy quickly pulled Sarah to safety as the bullets flew."

"Within seconds the gang was gone, leaving behind a few riddles to goad me into another pointless confrontation..."

"...and one casualty--*Sarah.* Whether it was a ricochet or a deliberate shot didn't really matter. She was dead and all Jeremy could ask himself was '*Why?*'"

LOOKING FOR SOLACE AND HAVING NO FAMILY, JEREMY WENT BACK TO THE ORPHANAGE WHERE HE GREW UP. THERE HE POURED HIS HEART OUT TO HIS ONE-TIME COUNSELOR, *ROBERT BENJAMIN.*

FOR SIX YEARS, JEREMY STRUGGLED TO MAKE PEACE WITH WHAT HAPPENED, BUT EVENTUALLY GAVE IN TO HIS GRIEF AND RAGE.

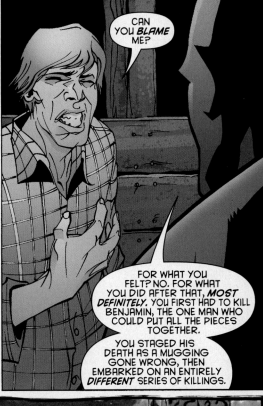

CAN YOU *BLAME* ME?

FOR WHAT YOU FELT? NO. FOR WHAT YOU DID AFTER THAT, *MOST DEFINITELY.* YOU FIRST HAD TO KILL BENJAMIN, THE ONE MAN WHO COULD PUT ALL THE PIECES TOGETHER.

YOU STAGED HIS DEATH AS A MUGGING GONE WRONG, THEN EMBARKED ON AN ENTIRELY *DIFFERENT* SERIES OF KILLINGS.

"The chloroform ensured they would be quiet while you finished them off. The exotic knives, severed hands and lilies created the illusion that a new serial killer was at large.

"Once Riddler bragged to the press that he would bring the murderer to justice, all you had to do was reel in your fish."

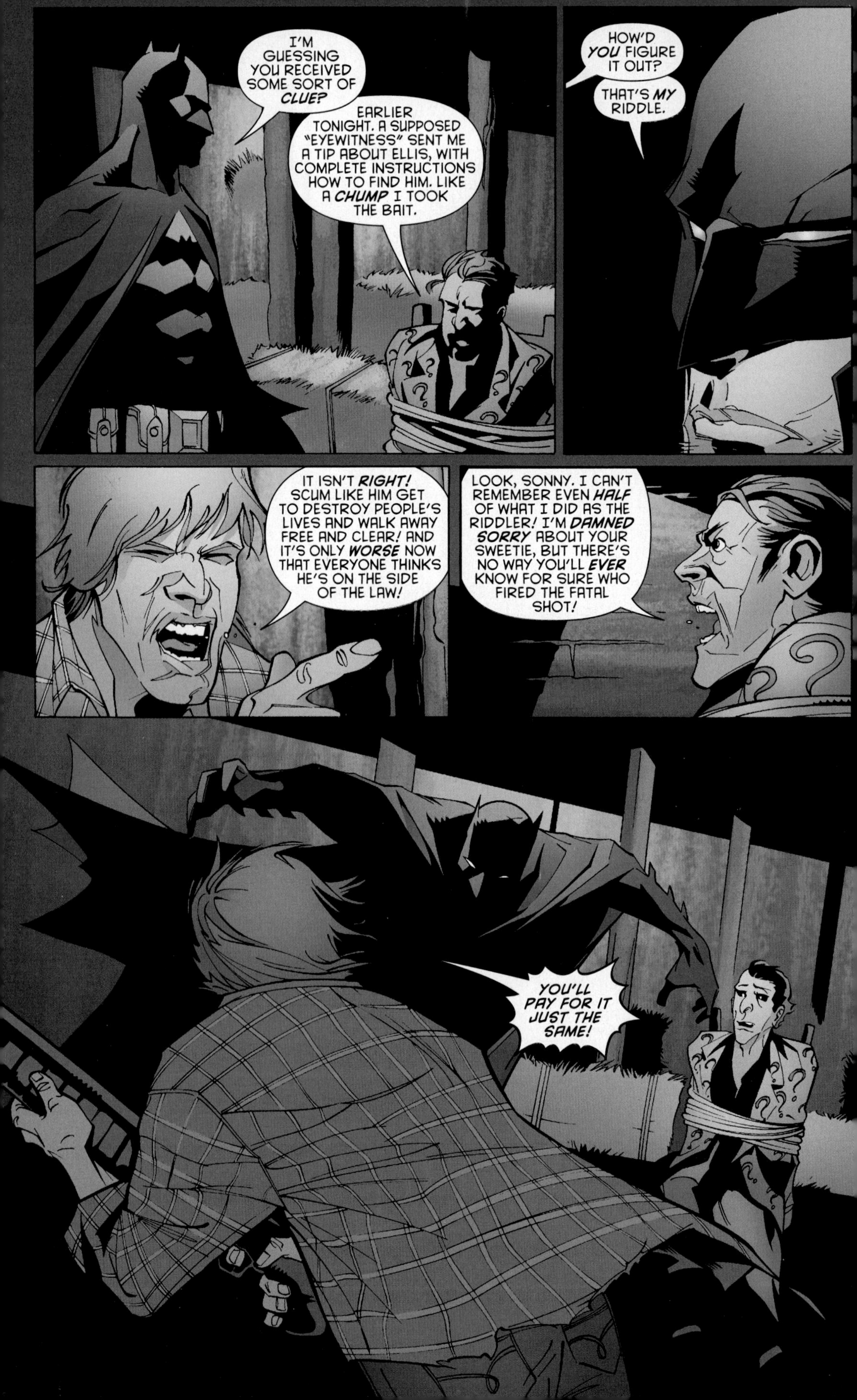
I'M GUESSING YOU RECEIVED SOME SORT OF *CLUE?*
EARLIER TONIGHT. A SUPPOSED "EYEWITNESS" SENT ME A TIP ABOUT ELLIS, WITH COMPLETE INSTRUCTIONS HOW TO FIND HIM. LIKE A *CHUMP* I TOOK THE BAIT.
HOW'D *YOU* FIGURE IT OUT?
THAT'S *MY* RIDDLE.
IT ISN'T *RIGHT!* SCUM LIKE HIM GET TO DESTROY PEOPLE'S LIVES AND WALK AWAY FREE AND CLEAR! AND IT'S ONLY *WORSE* NOW THAT EVERYONE THINKS HE'S ON THE SIDE OF THE LAW!
LOOK, SONNY. I CAN'T REMEMBER EVEN *HALF* OF WHAT I DID AS THE RIDDLER! I'M *DAMNED SORRY* ABOUT YOUR SWEETIE, BUT THERE'S NO WAY YOU'LL *EVER* KNOW FOR SURE WHO FIRED THE FATAL SHOT!
YOU'LL PAY FOR IT JUST THE SAME!

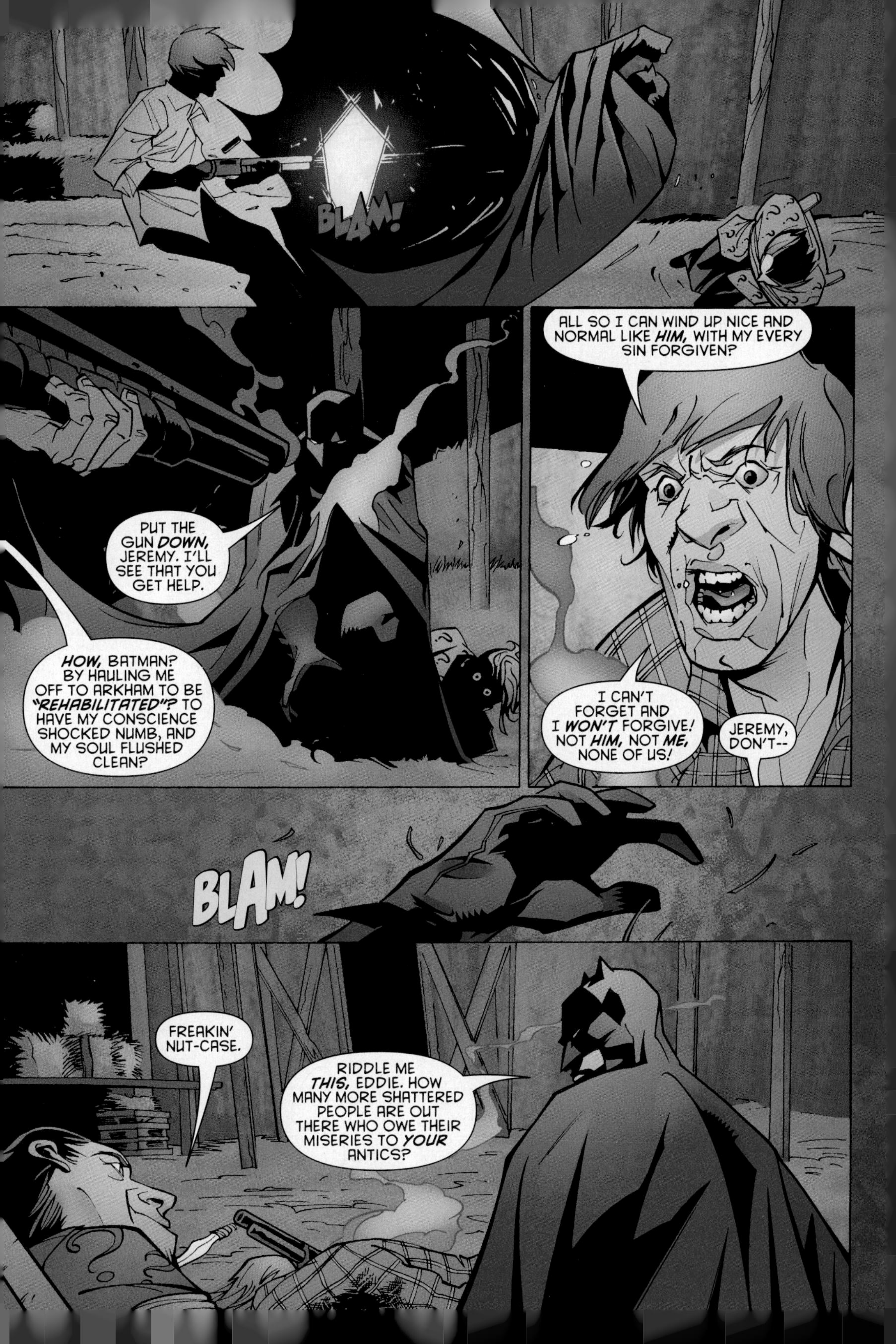
BLAM!
PUT THE GUN DOWN, JEREMY. I'LL SEE THAT YOU GET HELP.
HOW, BATMAN? BY HAULING ME OFF TO ARKHAM TO BE "REHABILITATED"? TO HAVE MY CONSCIENCE SHOCKED NUMB, AND MY SOUL FLUSHED CLEAN?
ALL SO I CAN WIND UP NICE AND NORMAL LIKE HIM, WITH MY EVERY SIN FORGIVEN?
I CAN'T FORGET AND I WON'T FORGIVE! NOT HIM, NOT ME, NONE OF US!
JEREMY, DON'T--
BLAM!
FREAKIN' NUT-CASE.
RIDDLE ME THIS, EDDIE. HOW MANY MORE SHATTERED PEOPLE ARE OUT THERE WHO OWE THEIR MISERIES TO YOUR ANTICS?

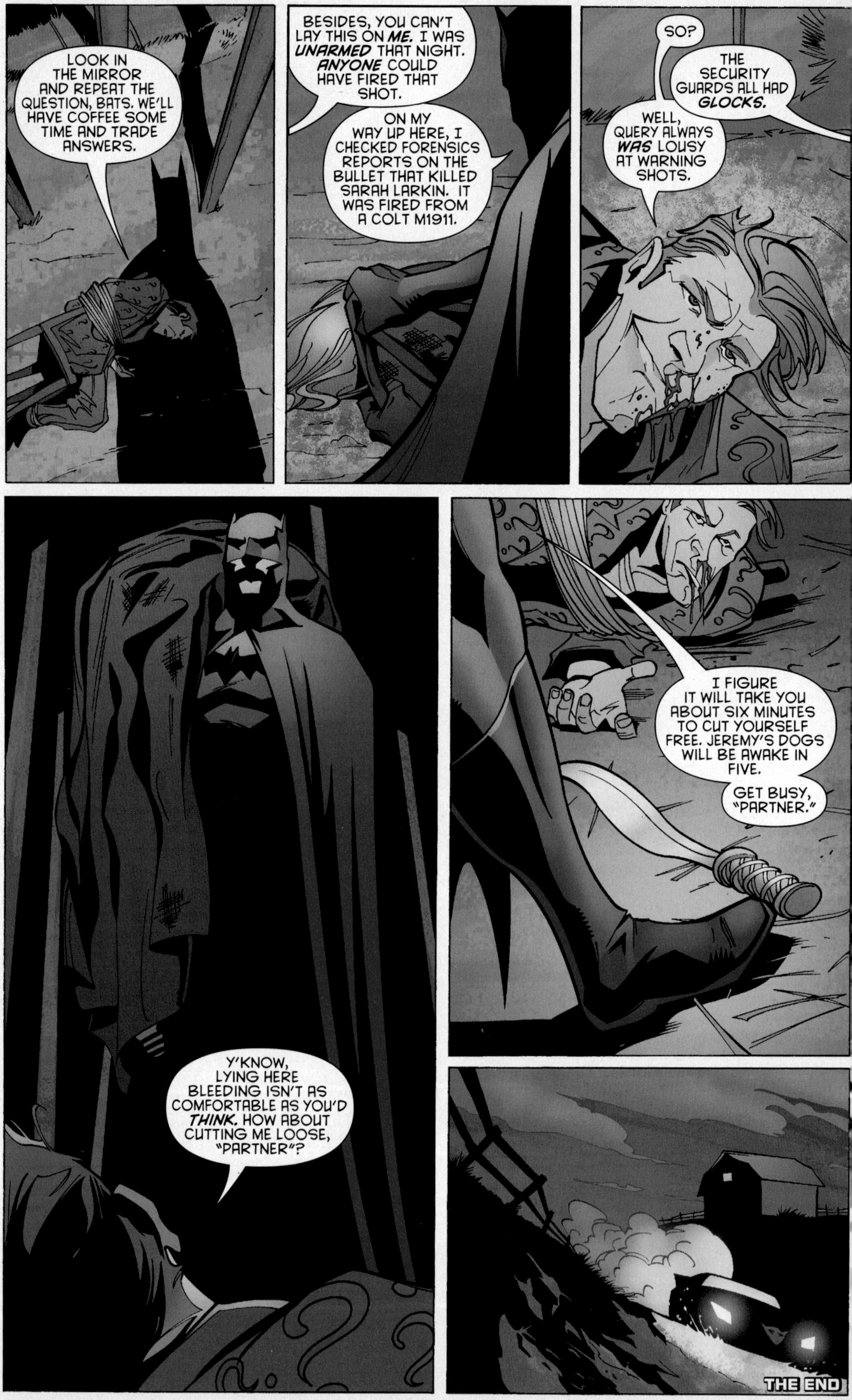
LOOK IN THE MIRROR AND REPEAT THE QUESTION, BATS. WE'LL HAVE COFFEE SOME TIME AND TRADE ANSWERS.
BESIDES, YOU CAN'T LAY THIS ON **ME.** I WAS **UNARMED** THAT NIGHT. **ANYONE** COULD HAVE FIRED THAT SHOT.
ON MY WAY UP HERE, I CHECKED FORENSICS REPORTS ON THE BULLET THAT KILLED SARAH LARKIN. IT WAS FIRED FROM A COLT M1911.
SO?
THE SECURITY GUARDS ALL HAD **GLOCKS.**
WELL, QUERY ALWAYS **WAS** LOUSY AT WARNING SHOTS.
Y'KNOW, LYING HERE BLEEDING ISN'T AS COMFORTABLE AS YOU'D **THINK.** HOW ABOUT CUTTING ME LOOSE, "PARTNER"?
I FIGURE IT WILL TAKE YOU ABOUT SIX MINUTES TO CUT YOURSELF FREE. JEREMY'S DOGS WILL BE AWAKE IN FIVE.
GET BUSY, "PARTNER."
THE END

Kcirt Ro Taert

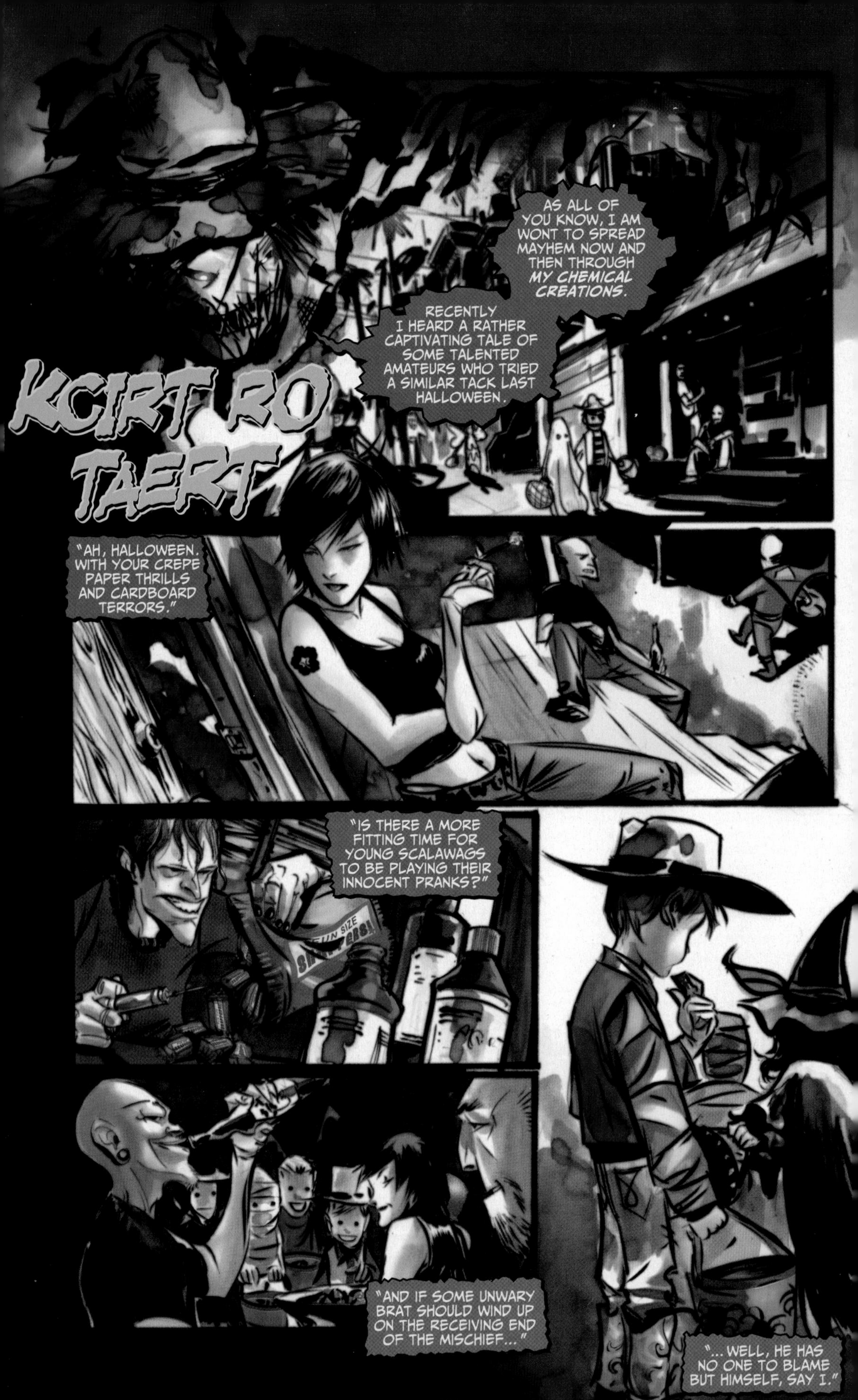
KCIRT RO TAERT
AS ALL OF YOU KNOW, I AM WONT TO SPREAD MAYHEM NOW AND THEN THROUGH MY CHEMICAL CREATIONS.
RECENTLY I HEARD A RATHER CAPTIVATING TALE OF SOME TALENTED AMATEURS WHO TRIED A SIMILAR TACK LAST HALLOWEEN.
"AH, HALLOWEEN. WITH YOUR CREPE PAPER THRILLS AND CARDBOARD TERRORS."
"IS THERE A MORE FITTING TIME FOR YOUNG SCALAWAGS TO BE PLAYING THEIR INNOCENT PRANKS?"
FUN SIZE
"AND IF SOME UNWARY BRAT SHOULD WIND UP ON THE RECEIVING END OF THE MISCHIEF..."
"...WELL, HE HAS NO ONE TO BLAME BUT HIMSELF, SAY I."

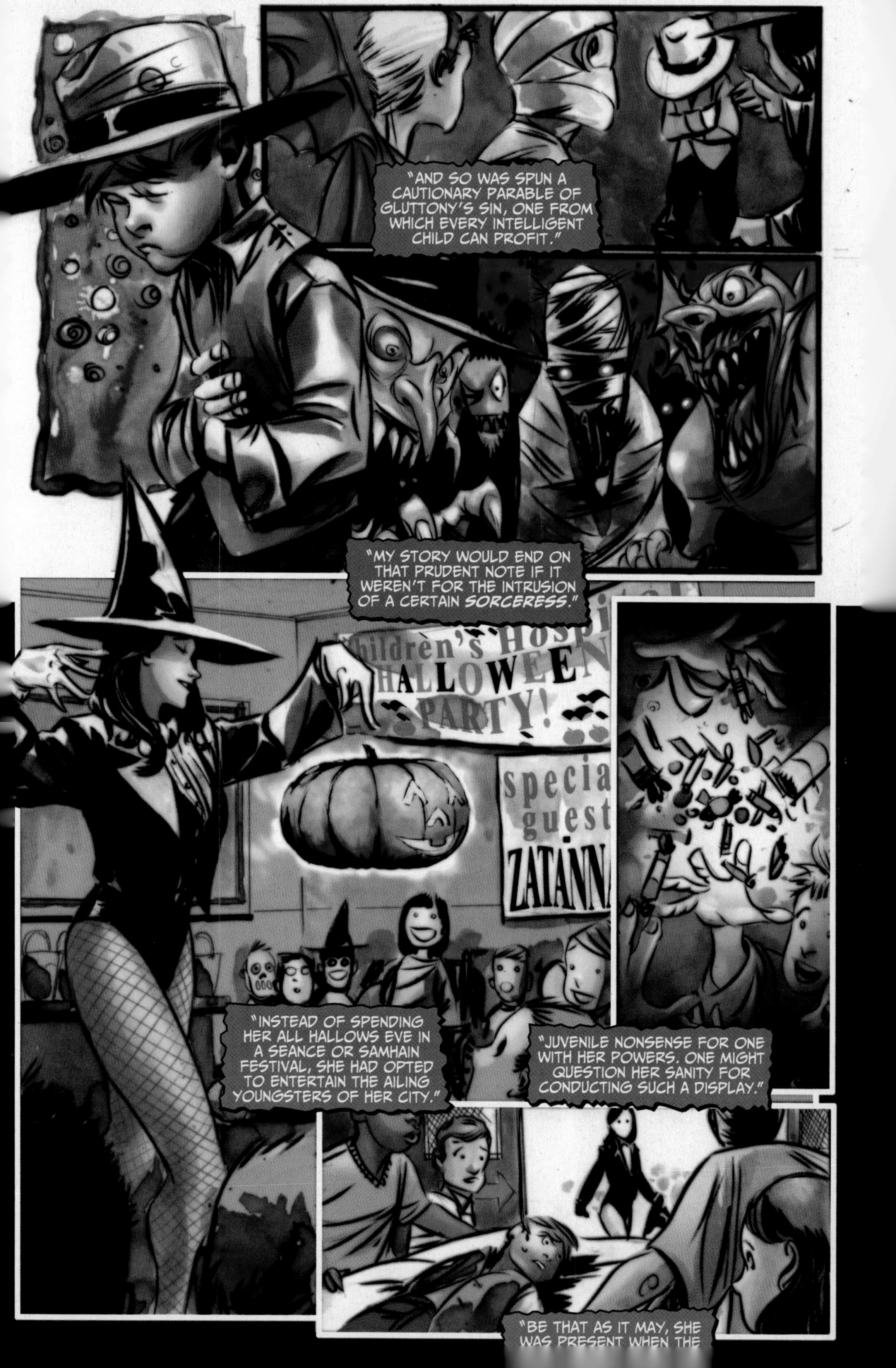
"AND SO WAS SPUN A CAUTIONARY PARABLE OF GLUTTONY'S SIN, ONE FROM WHICH EVERY INTELLIGENT CHILD CAN PROFIT."
"MY STORY WOULD END ON THAT PRUDENT NOTE IF IT WEREN'T FOR THE INTRUSION OF A CERTAIN SORCERESS."
Children's Hospital HALLOWEEN PARTY!
special guest ZATANNA
"INSTEAD OF SPENDING HER ALL HALLOWS EVE IN A SEANCE OR SAMHAIN FESTIVAL, SHE HAD OPTED TO ENTERTAIN THE AILING YOUNGSTERS OF HER CITY."
"JUVENILE NONSENSE FOR ONE WITH HER POWERS. ONE MIGHT QUESTION HER SANITY FOR CONDUCTING SUCH A DISPLAY."
"BE THAT AS IT MAY, SHE WAS PRESENT WHEN THE

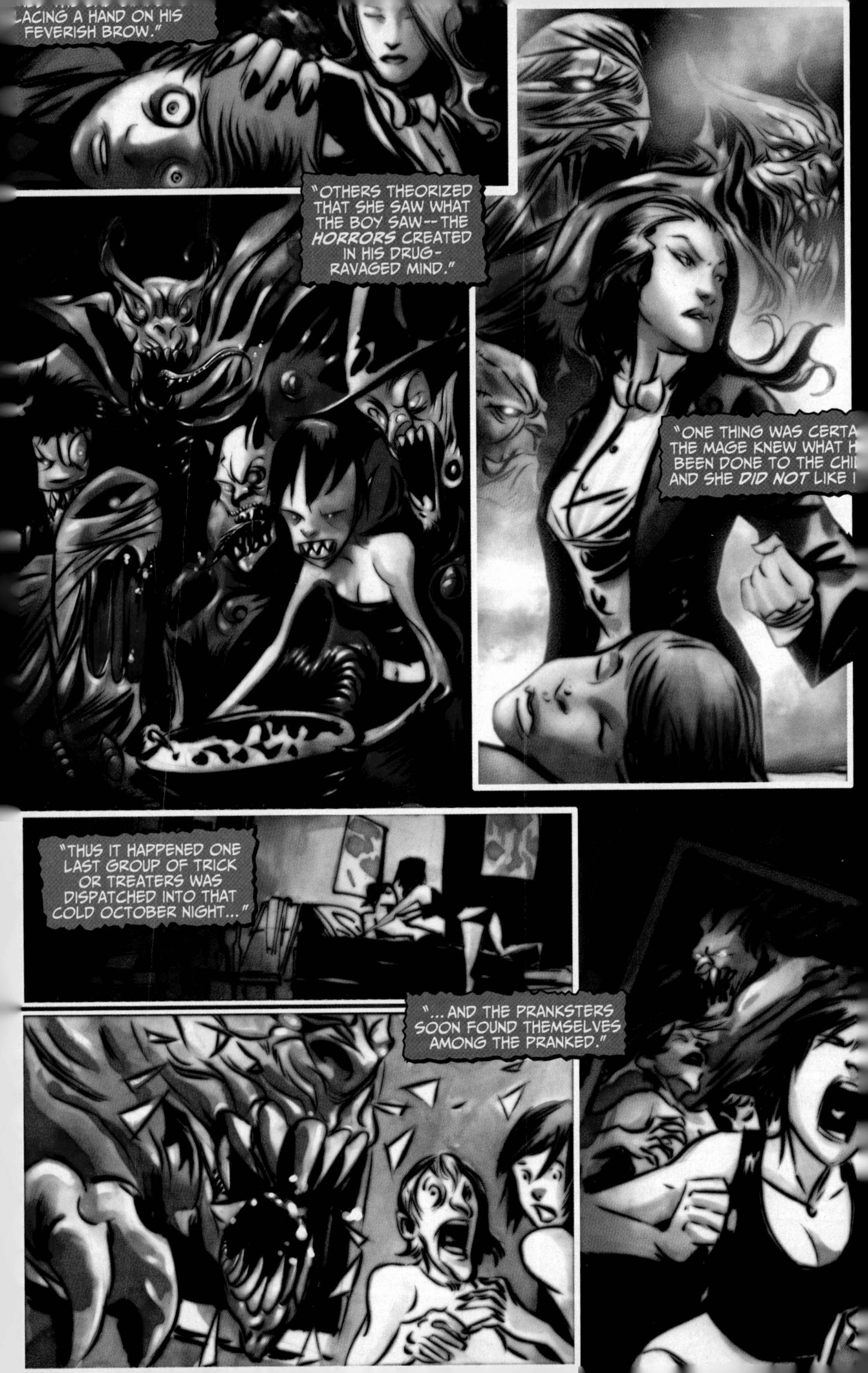

LACING A HAND ON HIS FEVERISH BROW."
"OTHERS THEORIZED THAT SHE SAW WHAT THE BOY SAW--THE HORRORS CREATED IN HIS DRUG-RAVAGED MIND."
"ONE THING WAS CERTA THE MAGE KNEW WHAT H BEEN DONE TO THE CHI AND SHE DID NOT LIKE I
"THUS IT HAPPENED ONE LAST GROUP OF TRICK OR TREATERS WAS DISPATCHED INTO THAT COLD OCTOBER NIGHT..."
"...AND THE PRANKSTERS SOON FOUND THEMSELVES AMONG THE PRANKED."

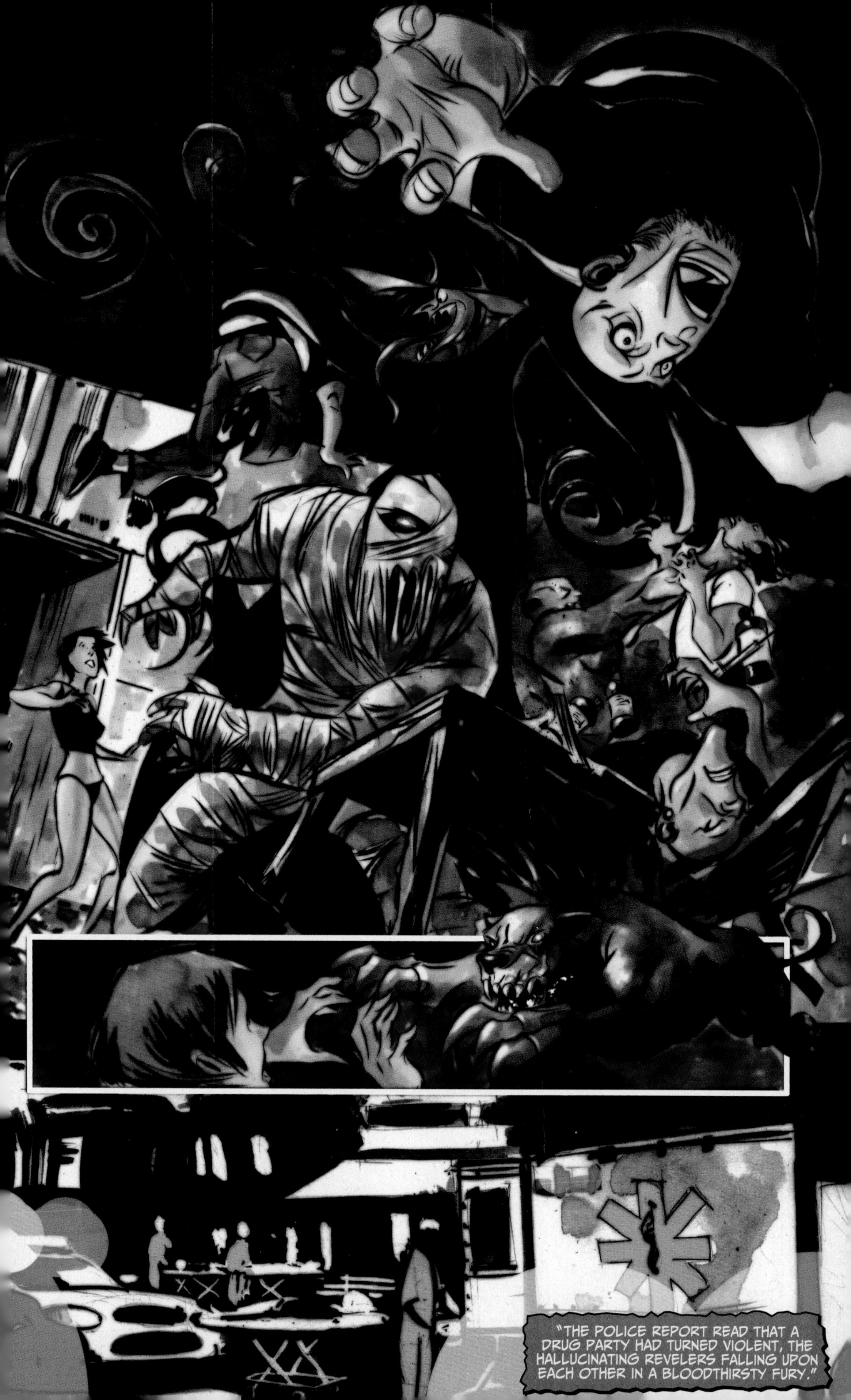
"THE POLICE REPORT READ THAT A DRUG PARTY HAD TURNED VIOLENT, THE HALLUCINATING REVELERS FALLING UPON EACH OTHER IN A BLOODTHIRSTY FURY."

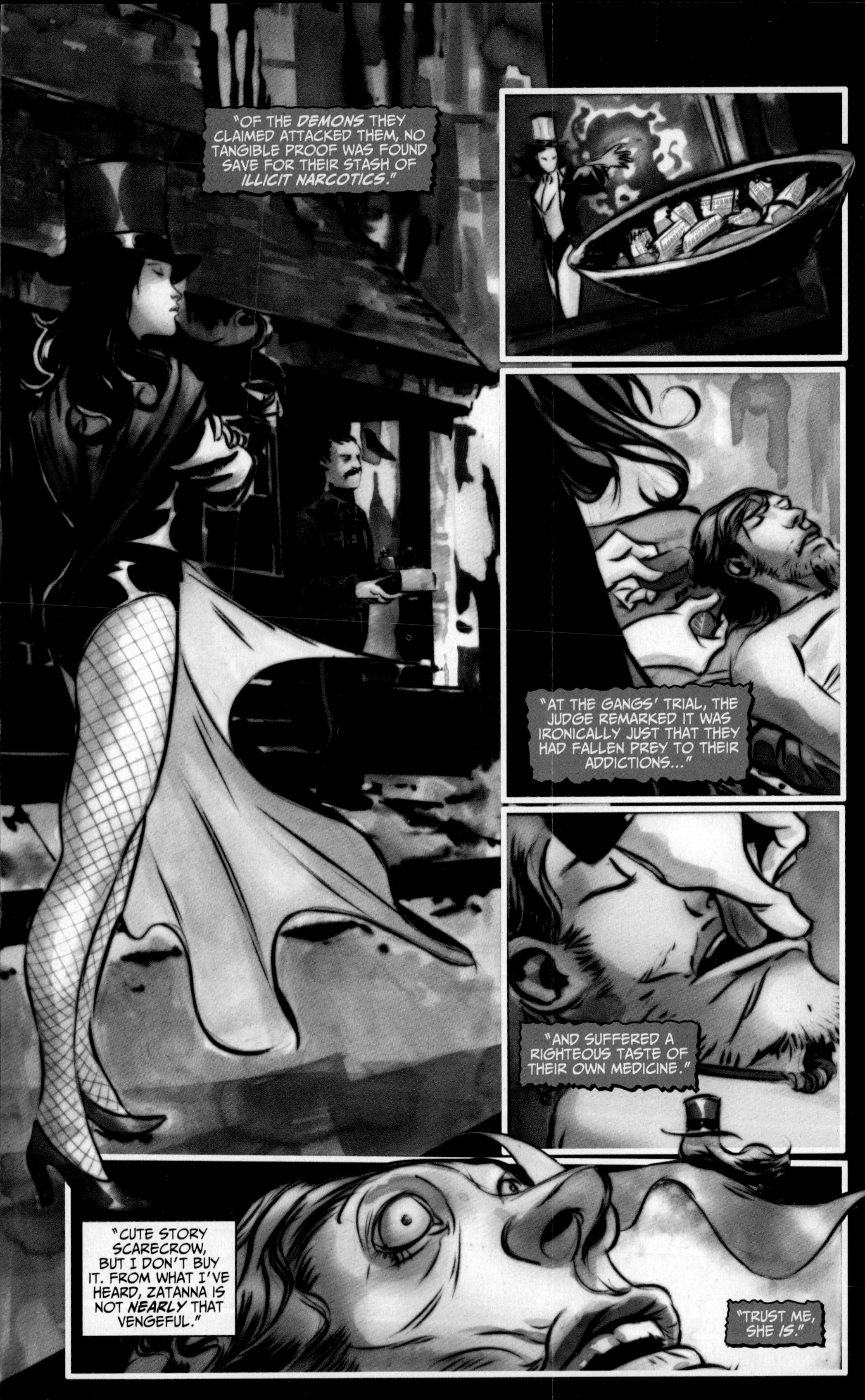
"OF THE DEMONS THEY CLAIMED ATTACKED THEM, NO TANGIBLE PROOF WAS FOUND SAVE FOR THEIR STASH OF ILLICIT NARCOTICS."
"AT THE GANGS' TRIAL, THE JUDGE REMARKED IT WAS IRONICALLY JUST THAT THEY HAD FALLEN PREY TO THEIR ADDICTIONS..."
"AND SUFFERED A RIGHTEOUS TASTE OF THEIR OWN MEDICINE."
"CUTE STORY SCARECROW, BUT I DON'T BUY IT. FROM WHAT I'VE HEARD, ZATANNA IS NOT NEARLY THAT VENGEFUL."
"TRUST ME, SHE IS."